CHINA'S CULTURAL HERITAGE
The Ch'ing Dynasty, 1644–1912

About the Book and Author

China's Cultural Heritage:
The Ch'ing Dynasty, 1644 – 1912
Richard J. Smith

The Ch'ing dynasty (1644–1912)—a crucial bridge between "traditional" and "modern" China—was a period remarkable for its expansiveness, cultural sophistication, and stability. Professor Smith shows how the Chinese of the Ch'ing dynasty viewed the world; how their outlook was expressed in their social and political institutions, material culture, and customs; and how China's preoccupation with order, unity, and harmony contributed to the remarkable cohesiveness and continuity of traditional Chinese civilization. In addition to offering a new and challenging interpretation of Chinese culture as a whole and a convenient framework for analyzing the period, he provides a fresh perspective on a variety of topics, from the family system, religion, and the Confucian classics, to cosmology, aesthetics, and symbolism. He also examines a number of important but too-often neglected aspects of traditional Chinese culture, including food, sexual life, festivals, child rearing, and games.

China's Cultural Heritage: The Ch'ing Dynasty, 1644–1912 is the clearest and fullest account to date in English of traditional Chinese culture in the late imperial period. Although confined chronologically to the last 250 years of imperial rule, it not only sheds valuable light on the distant past, but also helps us to understand China's modernizing problems of the twentieth century.

A specialist in modern Chinese history and traditional Chinese culture, Dr. Richard J. Smith is professor of history at Rice University and master of Hanszen College, adjunct professor at the Center for Asian Studies at the University of Texas, Austin, and recipient of three George R. Brown Teaching Awards. His publications on China include *Mercenaries and Mandarins: The Ever-Victorious Army in Nineteenth Century China* (1978) and *Traditional Chinese Culture: An Interpretive Introduction* (1978).

CHINA'S CULTURAL HERITAGE
The Ch'ing Dynasty, 1644–1912

Richard J. Smith

Westview Press • Boulder, Colorado
Francis Pinter (Publishers) • London

The paper used in this publication meets the requirements of the American National Standard for Permanence of Paper for Printed Library Materials Z39.48-1984.

Credits

Figure 2.1, "The Ch'ing Empire," on page 12, is from Immanuel C. Y. Hsü, *The Rise of Modern China,* 2nd ed. (Oxford University Press, 1975). Copyright © 1975 by Oxford University Press, Inc. Reprinted by permission.

Four of the poems on pages 197, 199, and 200 are taken from Wu-chi Liu and Irving Yucheng Lo, eds., *Sunflower Splendor.* Copyright © 1975 by Wu-chi Liu and Irving Lo. Reprinted by permission of Doubleday & Co. Inc.

The two lines of poetry on page 197 by Wang Wei are taken from Cao Xuequin, ed., David Hawkes, trans., *The Story of the Stone: 2* (Penguin Classics, 1977), page 459. Copyright © 1977 by David Hawkes. Reprinted by permission of Penguin Books Ltd.

Figure 10.3, "The Traditional Chinese House," on page 218, is from Lucian W. Pye, *China: An Introduction,* 3rd ed. (Little, Brown and Company, 1984). Copyright © 1984 by Lucian W. Pye. Reprinted by permission of the publisher, Little, Brown and Company.

Figure 10.5, "A Chinese Official and His Footbound Wife," page 224, is from Clark Worswick and Jonathan Spence, *Imperial China: Photographs 1850–1912* (Crown/Pennwick, 1978) and is reprinted courtesy of Pennwick Publishing.

The explanation of the Wade-Giles pronunciation that appears in Appendix A: A Note on Chinese Names, page 265, is from John Meskill, ed., *An Introduction to Chinese Civilization.* Copyright © 1973 by D. C. Heath and Co. Reprinted by permission of the publisher.

Copyright © 1983 by Westview Press, Inc.

Published in 1983 in the United States of America by
  Westview Press, Inc.
  5500 Central Avenue
  Boulder, Colorado 80301
  Frederick A. Praeger, President and Publisher

Published in 1983 in Great Britain by
  Frances Pinter (Publishers) Limited
  5 Dryden Street, London   WC2E 9NW

Library of Congress Catalog Card Number 83-10188
ISBN (U.S.) 0-86531-627-9
ISBN (U.S.) 0-86531-628-7 (pbk.)
ISBN (U.K.) 0-86187-348-3

Printed and bound in the United States of America

10   9   8   7   6

To my parents, Joseph and Margaret Smith,
who have given so much, in so many ways

Contents

Figures

Preface

A major theme throughout China's imperial history has been the tension between the inherently divisive tendencies of a huge, geographically fragmented, and ethnically diverse land mass and the unifying impulses of a centralized bureaucratic empire administered by highly educated scholar-officials who shared a remarkably uniform cultural outlook. This book examines the interplay between these two contending influences during the Ch'ing dynasty (1644–1912), a period remarkable for its expansiveness, cultural splendor, stability, and staying power. My thesis is that the Chinese of the Ch'ing era, as in earlier periods, were obsessed with the concept of order (*chih*) and that this preoccupation was expressed not only in their highly refined bureaucratic institutions and methods of social and economic organization but also in their philosophy, religious and secular ritual, standards of literary and artistic achievement, and comprehensive systems of classifying all natural and supernatural phenomena. This obsession was also evident in their cultural psychology—notably in their attitudes toward social conformity, consensus, collective responsibility, and their almost pathological fear of disorder (*luan*). But the effort to impose order on all aspects of the known world was at once China's greatest cultural strength and its most critical weakness, for the very factors that contributed to an unparalleled record of cultural cohesiveness and continuity also prevented a rapid and creative response to the challenges of the modern world in the nineteenth and twentieth centuries.

Although this book is interpretive rather than purely descriptive, it is not my purpose to drain the lifeblood from China's rich cultural tradition by subjecting it only to cold and detached analysis. This study is also intended as an exercise in appreciation, a sympathetic inside look at one of the world's most refined and impressive civilizations. Although it makes an intellectual argument, it also seeks an emotional response. For those with little prior knowledge of China, the book should promote greater understanding and a new respect for Chinese culture; and for fellow academic specialists, it should provide a fresh perspective on some familiar, but endlessly absorbing, cultural terrain. In all events, I hope it will encourage discussion, debate, and further analysis.

This book owes a great deal to students and colleagues, both of whom I have kept in mind and consulted at every stage of research and writing. I am especially grateful to three people: Allen Matusow, for urging me to undertake this study in the first place and for offering unfailing encouragement and valuable advice over a long span of time; John Fairbank, for his sustained scholarly interest, broad vision, and incisive criticisms; and K. C. Liu, for his inspirational example, limitless patience, and gentle guidance. Many other friends and colleagues, in a wide variety of disciplines, have read all or part of the manuscript and offered useful comments. These people are too numerous to mention individually, but their collective contribution is enormous and much appreciated. I would like to thank Rice University for its generous assistance in the form of summer research grants, the American Philosophical Society for its financial support of a related project, and the University of California, Davis, for sponsoring a productive summer spent as a visiting research scholar. Gratitude also must be expressed to the staff members of the East Asiatic libraries at Berkeley, Davis, Harvard, and Columbia for their efficiency and assistance. Finally, I would like to thank my wife and son for once again cheerfully enduring the inconvenience involved in writing a book— most particularly Tyler, who competed with the typewriter for my attention but not for my affection.

Richard J. Smith
Rice University

CHAPTER 1

Introduction

During the past several years, the study of premodern China has become highly sophisticated. The recent proliferation of specialized journals devoted to topics such as Chinese philosophy, Chinese religion, Chinese linguistics, and Chinese literature is one indication of this growing sophistication. Another is the attention lavished on selected aspects of China's historical experience not only by humanists but also by anthropologists, sociologists, political scientists, and economists. Multidisciplinary forays into documentary records and the field have vastly enhanced our knowledge of both elite and folk culture in traditional China.[1] Few efforts have been made, however, to develop any sort of scholarly synthesis out of this huge corpus of valuable, but specialized, work. Most general books on China simply chronicle or catalogue China's glittering cultural achievements, building a mosaic of undeniable brilliance but uncertain significance. Few scholars—Western or Chinese—have considered carefully the relationship of the parts of traditional Chinese culture to the whole, and fewer still have attempted a broad interpretation of that culture on the basis of its structural principles.[2]

This book offers such an interpretation. Drawing on the recent theoretical literature of history, anthropology, and sociology and an extensive investigation of primary and secondary materials in both Chinese and Western languages, I have developed a framework for analysis that I believe will shed valuable light on all major aspects of traditional Chinese culture, including those not afforded detailed treatment in this volume. Although confined chronologically to the last two and a half centuries of imperial rule, this study should say something important not only about the previous two thousand years of Chinese history but about modern China as well. Deeply ingrained patterns of thought and behavior did not, after all, disappear instantly after the fall of the Ch'ing dynasty in 1912.

My primary interest is in the traditional Chinese elite, or "gentry" (*shen-shih*), a group formally defined as holders of official degrees earned by passing the prestigious civil-service examinations. The group, which together with their families constituted less than 2 percent of the entire population of China in late imperial times, nonetheless dominated much of Chinese social life and also provided the pool of highly literate talent from which the majority of Chinese bureaucrats were drawn.[3] Despite certain significant differences in their respective social backgrounds and specific interests, these individuals had a remarkably uniform cultural outlook, as well as a common stake in the protection, promotion, and perpetuation of China's ancient and glorious cultural tradition. How did this unique class of scholars, artists, and administrators organize and explain the world around them? How did their conceptual structures and interpretations affect their behavior, and how, in turn, did these patterns of perception and behavior influence traditional Chinese society as a whole?

As indicated in the preface, my chronological focus is the Ch'ing dynasty, the last imperial regime and a crucial bridge between traditional and modern life in China. The Ch'ing was the largest consolidated empire in Chinese history and by far the most successful dynasty of conquest. On the whole, the Ch'ing period witnessed the fullest development of traditional political, economic, and social institutions, as well as the greatest degree of regional integration within China proper. No dynasty was more "Confucian" in outlook and emphasis or more self-consciously antiquarian. Furthermore, thanks largely to the systematic policy of sinicization undertaken by China's Manchu conquerors and to the phenomenal peace and prosperity enjoyed by most Chinese during the reigns of the K'ang-hsi (1662–1722), Yung-cheng (1723–1735), and Ch'ien-lung (1736–1795) emperors, the Ch'ing was a period of enrichment and "leisurely fulfillment" in material culture and the arts. Contrary to stereotype, in many ways the Ch'ing epitomized the best of China's cultural tradition, although ultimately the dynasty and the dynastic system itself fell victim to unprecedented internal pressures and erosion by Western technology and ideas in the late nineteenth and early twentieth centuries.[4]

What did members of the Chinese elite have in mind when they spoke (or, more aptly, wrote) of "culture"? The core term in classical Chinese is *wen*. *Wen* conveys a wide range of meanings, most of which derive from the basic sense of "markings" or "patterns." *Wen* refers narrowly to Chinese writing and literature, but more broadly to a whole constellation of distinctive cultural attributes—art, music, ritual, and so on—each of which, like literature, had an expressly moral component. *Wen* was the measure of a Confucian gentleman in traditional China, the mark of true "civilization." *Wen* did not, however, carry any of the primary meanings we associate with the Latin terms *civis* or *civitas*. Members of the Chinese elite did not consider themselves to be "citizens" in the classical Western sense, and although Chinese cities were often the source of gentry amusement, they were not really centers of culture in the way the elite defined it.[5]

Nor was culture simply a matter of individual preference and life-style. China itself was viewed primarily as a cultural entity. Although the frequently used term for China, *Chung-kuo* (the "Central Kingdom"), implies an awareness of the country as both a political and geographical unit, a common alternative term, *Chung-hua* (the "Central Cultural Florescence") reflects a long-standing emphasis on the cultural basis of the Chinese state. Few Ch'ing scholars would have disagreed with the following fourteenth-century definition of China:

> Central Cultural Florescence is another term for Central Kingdom. When a people subjects itself to the Kingly Teachings [i.e., Confucianism] and subordinates itself to the Central Kingdom; when in clothing it is dignified and decorous, and when its customs are marked by filial respect and brotherly submission; when conduct follows the accepted norms and the principle of righteousness, then one may call it [a part of the] Central Cultural Florescence.[6]

Barbarian conquest affirmed and reinforced this Sinocentric world view rather than shattering it.

How did the Chinese order their vast cultural world, which embraced "all under Heaven" (T'ien-hsia)? One useful, but seldom used, index is the famous Ch'ing encyclopedia *Ku-chin t'u-shu chi-ch'eng* (Complete Collection of Writings and Illustrations, Past and Present) completed in 1725 after decades of imperially commissioned collective labor. This massive and well-organized compendium, repository of "all that was best in the literature of the past, dealing with every branch of knowledge," was intended not only as a kind of moral and practical guide for the emperor and his officials but also as an expression of the unity and totality of Chinese culture. I have used the encyclopedia, together with a great many other official and unofficial compilations of the period, as a guide to the cultural concerns of the Ch'ing elite.[7] Collectively, these sources attest to the extraordinary holism of the Chinese cultural vision—the conviction that "all strains of thought, all institutions, [and] all forms of behavior should embody and express a common set of values."[8]

Three related themes serve as the interpretive foundation of this book. All of these loom large in the Chinese documentary record, but they have received inadequate attention in the West. The first is cognition, the way the Chinese viewed the world around them. Despite the complexity of this outlook, with its intersecting Confucian, Buddhist, and Taoist elements and elaborate interplay between elite and popular conceptions of reality, we can identify at least one construct, or paradigm, that transcended ideology and class. Sometimes described as "complementary bipolarity," this viewpoint was expressed by the well-known, but much abused, concepts of *yin* and *yang*. These terms and their equivalents appear everywhere in the Chinese language and literature, yet too often they are taken for granted by Chinese scholars and either misunderstood or underestimated by scholars in the West.[9]

In traditional times, *yin* and *yang* were used in three main senses, each of which may be illustrated by the following excerpts from *Hung-lou meng* (Dream of the Red Chamber), China's greatest and most influential novel. In a colorful conversation with her maidservant, Kingfisher, Shih Hsiang-yün remarks: "Everything in the universe is produced by the forces of *yin* and *yang*. . . . All the transformations that occur result from the interaction of *yin* and *yang*. . . . When *yang* is exhausted, it becomes *yin*, and when *yin* is exhausted, it becomes *yang*. . . . Yin-yang is a kind of force in things that gives them their distinctive form. For example, Heaven is *yang* and Earth is *yin*; water is *yin*, fire is *yang*; the sun is *yang*, the moon is *yin*." "Ah yes," replies Kingfisher, "that's why astrologers call the sun the *"yang* star" and the moon the *"yin* star." After a lengthy discussion of several other such associations and correlations, Kingfisher ends the conversation by observing: "You're *yang* and I'm *yin*. . . . That's what people always say: the master is *yang* and the servant is *yin*. Even I can understand that principle."[10]

Yin and *yang* were, then, (1) cosmic forces that produced and animated all natural phenomena; (2) terms used to identify recurrent, cyclical patterns of rise and decline, waxing and waning; and (3) comparative categories, describing dualistic relationships that were inherently unequal but invariably complementary. Virtually any aspect of Chinese experience could be explained in terms of these paired concepts, ranging from such mundane sensory perceptions as dark and light, wet and dry to abstractions such as real and unreal, being and nonbeing. *Yin-yang* relationships involved the notion of mutual dependence and "harmony based on hierarchical difference."[11] *Yin* qualities were generally considered inferior to *yang* qualities, but unity of opposites was always the cultural ideal.

Perhaps no other major civilization in world history has had such a pervasive, tenacious, and essentially naturalistic world view—an accommodating outlook contrasting sharply with the familiar religious dualisms of good and evil, God and the Devil, which are so prominent in the ancient Near Eastern and Western cultural traditions. Much that is most distinctive about traditional Chinese culture can be explained by reference to *yin-yang* conceptions and to the elaborate correlative thinking associated with these ideas. *Yin-yang* polarities appear explicitly or implicitly in the description or evaluation of nearly every area of traditional Chinese life, from cosmology, politics, aesthetics, and science to astrology, geomancy, ancestor worship, and sexual relations. All classes of literature employ *yin-yang* terminology and symbolism, from the exalted Confucian classics to popular proverbs. Surprisingly, however, very little scholarly attention has been given by either historians or anthropologists to the broad cultural implications of Chinese *yin-yang* concepts and correlations.[12]

The second major theme of this study is ethics, an abiding cultural concern, as a glance at any Chinese political, social, or philosophical tract will clearly indicate. Like the concepts of *yin* and *yang*, ethical terms pervade virtually every area of traditional Chinese culture, including music and the arts. The modern Chinese philosopher Chang Tung-sun tells us that the most numerous terms in the Chinese language come from the related realms of kinship and ethics, and the index to Fung Yu-lan's well-known abridged history of Chinese philosophy states apologetically, "So much of Chinese philosophy is ethical that a complete list of 'ethical' references would be almost impossible."[13]

Yet it is not only the pervasiveness of ethical concerns in China that is striking. It is also the essentially nonreligious source of basic moral values. In sharp contrast to many other cultural traditions, the Chinese moral order was essentially secular in nature. Although Chinese philosophers perceived a fundamental unity between the mind of Heaven and the mind of Man, the ethical system prevailing in China throughout the entire imperial era did not emanate from any supernatural authority. The major institutional religions of late imperial times—Buddhism and Religious Taoism—made no major contribution to the preexisting core of Confucian values, although they did play an important role in reinforcing secular norms.[14]

The relationship between secular values and traditional Chinese religion is reflected in the following inscription taken from a stele in the temple of the Consort of Heaven (*T'ien-hou*) in Fo-shan, Kwangtung:

> When administrative orders from the national and local capitals attain their objectives, and when there is the Way of Man [*jen-tao*] to provide effective principles and discipline, it is not necessary that spirits and gods play an impressive and prominent role [in government]. But when [such orders and the Way of Man] fail to effect justice, spirits and gods will be brought to light. . . . As the ancients put it, in the age of perfect government, spirits became inefficacious. It is not that the spirits are inefficacious; . . . it is that when rewards and punishments are just and clear, the *yang* [human elements] function effectively, and the *yin* [spiritual elements] retreat into the background . . . so there is no need for the efficaciousness [of spirits and gods].[15]

Supernatural authority might always be invoked in China, but in the ideal Confucian world it was considered unnecessary.

At the core of the orthodox Chinese ethical system in the Ch'ing period were the so-called Three Bonds (*san-kang*), explicitly identified throughout most of the imperial era with the *yin-yang* notion of complementary inequality. The three bonds were those between ruler and subject, father and son, husband and wife. The nonreciprocal obligations owed by inferiors to superiors within this framework set the authoritarian tone of much of life in traditional China and gave concrete expression to two of the most powerful organizational symbols or metaphors in the Chinese sociopolitical vocabulary—the bureaucracy and the family.[16] Undergirding both these symbols and these relations was an expansive, cosmologically based structure of ritual (*li*).

Ritual provides the third major theme of this book, in a sense uniting the other two themes with itself. Like art, ritual may be viewed as a kind of "language" that celebrates man-made meaning. It indicates the way a culture group represents its situation to itself, how (in the words of Clifford Geertz) it links "the world as lived and the world as imagined." As a cultural performance, ritual articulates in symbolic action the concerns of the illiterate masses as well as those of the literate elite. Of course, there are many different kinds and definitions of ritual, but in its broadest sense the term may be said to include all forms of artificially structured social behavior, from the etiquette of daily greetings to solemn state ceremonies and religious sacrifices.[17]

Such a broad definition accords well with traditional Chinese usage. Although the term *li* never completely lost either its original religious and mystical connotations or its close association with music as a source of moral cultivation, by late imperial times *li* had come to embrace all forms of sacred and secular ritual, as well as the entire body of social institutions, rules, regulations, conventions, and norms that governed human relations in China. *Li* has been variously translated as standards of social usage, mores, politeness, propriety, and etiquette, but no single term does justice to the wide range of its meanings and manifestations.[18]

Testimony to the enduring value of *li* in traditional China may be found in the venerated classic texts *I-li* (Etiquette and Ritual), *Chou-li* (Rites of Chou), and *Li-chi* (Record of Ritual), which together exerted a profound influence on the Chinese elite from the Han period through the Ch'ing. These three works alone provided hundreds of general principles and guidelines, as well as literally thousands of specific prescriptions, for proper conduct in Chinese society. For hundreds of years the Chinese commonly referred to China as "the land of ritual and right behavior" (*li-i chih pang*), equating the values of *li* and *i* with civilization itself.

One measure of esteem for ritual in the Ch'ing dynasty may be found in the *T'u-shu chi-ch'eng* (*TSCC*), which devotes nearly 350 of its 10,000 *chüan* (volumes) to *li*. This figure does not include the 320 *chüan* devoted to the subcategory on religion (which overlaps ritual in subject material to a significant degree), nor does it take into account the prominent place occupied by the teachings of ritual (*li-chiao*) and ritual institutions (*li-chih*) in subcategories such as music, Confucian conduct, classical and noncanonical writings, human affairs, social intercourse, family relations, official careers, examinations, government service, and political divisions. Indeed, there are very few of the *TSCC*'s thirty-two subcategories that are devoid of references to *li*.[19]

The observations of longtime Western residents in China provide yet another index of the importance of ritual in the Ch'ing period. Even during the nineteenth century, when Chinese society seemed to be disintegrating in many areas, informed Westerners repeatedly remarked on the scrupulous attention still given to all forms of ritual by the Chinese. S. W. Williams spoke for many in asserting that "no nation has paid so much attention to . . . [ceremonies] in the ordering of its government as the Chinese. . . . The importance attached to them has elevated etiquette and ritualism into a kind of crystalizing force which has molded [the] Chinese character in many ways." Arthur H. Smith maintained that "ceremony is the very life of the Chinese," echoing John Nevius: "Politeness [in China] is a science, and gracefulness of manners a study and a discipline."[20]

No major aspect of Chinese life was devoid of ritual significance, and ritual specialists were ubiquitous at all levels of society. Everyone from emperor to peasant recognized the importance of ritual in preserving status distinctions, promoting social cohesion, sanctifying ethical norms, and transmitting tradition. Closely linked to both cosmology and law, ritual in China performed the function Geertz assigns to "sacred symbols" in synthesizing moral values, aesthetics, and world view.[21] Perhaps no other single focus allows us to see so clearly the preoccupations of the Chinese people in late imperial times.

Although this book is organized topically for clarity and convenience, it emphasizes the interrelationship of the parts of traditional Chinese culture to the whole. Therefore, in addition to weaving a web of significance around the distinctive unifying themes of cognition, ethics and ritual, I have tried to build an integrated structure of meaning through the sequential presentation of the topical material. The first chapter, for example, indicates some of the ways in which China's physical endowment and historical experience shaped both the outlook and institutions of the Chinese in imperial times. The next two chapters analyze Ch'ing institutions in some detail, illustrating the various ways in which traditional political, social, and economic organizations simultaneously reflected and reinforced the Chinese sense of order and cultural unity. The discussions of language, thought, and formal philosophy help us to understand certain distinctive patterns of perception and expression in China, and the chapter on religion underscores the complex interaction between Chinese ideas, values, and institutions. The following chapters on art, literature, and social customs are designed to show how shared symbols, organizing principles, aesthetics, and ethical values were manifest in various important areas of Chinese artistic and social life. By the end of these discussions, the reader should have a clearer understanding not only of the internal "logic" of the Chinese cultural system but also an appreciation for why it lasted so long and held together so well.[22]

I do not, of course, deny the diversity of traditional Chinese culture, nor do I subscribe to the absurd notion of an "unchanging China." China's long history, huge size, regional variety, and ethnic cleavages present a picture of staggering political and social complexity. A vast cultural gulf separated commoners and the elite: They wore different clothes, ate different foods, lived in different dwellings, and occupied different positions in the eyes of both society at large and the state. Traditional China was full of tensions, contradictions, and conflicts. The Ch'ing government waged a perpetual war against bandits, rebels, feuding ethnic groups, warring clans, and other divisive elements.[23]

Yet on balance it seems evident that the various social classes and culture groups in Ch'ing China had more in common than often has been assumed, that their cultural similarities outweighed by far their cultural differences. I am persuaded, for example, that fundamental elite concepts, values, and attitudes penetrated and interacted with traditional folk culture to a much greater extent than is generally recognized. Commoners shared with the elite a penchant for organizing phenomena in terms of *yin-yang* relationships, as well as a political, social, and religious outlook based solidly upon bureaucratic lines of authority and Confucian values. Ritual observances were extremely important to the religious life of commoners and predicated on many of the same basic symbols and assumptions as elite ritual. Thus, what may appear on the surface to be significant differences in organization and outlook on the part of various groups in Chinese society may in fact be reflections or expressions of basic uniformities—important cultural common denominators. The evidence for this hypothesis may be found in many areas of traditional Chinese life, including not only ethics, religion, and ritual but also language, art, literature, amusements, orthodox institutions, and even secret societies.[24]

The fate of traditional Chinese culture in modern times remains to be more fully explored. Unprecedented internal pressures and the devastating impact of Western imperialism during the latter half of the nineteenth century led in the twentieth to a fundamental reevaluation of China's inherited culture. Cultural iconoclasts assailed the Confucian political and social tradition and gravitated toward Western forms of art, literature, music, and recreation. Yet throughout the first half of the twentieth century, traditional Chinese patterns of perception, thought, belief, and behavior continued to have remarkable staying power, and even today we can see the obvious presence of tradition on both sides of the Taiwan straits.

CHAPTER 2

The Ch'ing Inheritance

The most powerful influence on the character of the Ch'ing dynasty was the dual inheritance of a vast and variegated land area (extended considerably by the Manchus after their military conquest of China in 1644) and a long, unbroken cultural tradition. From the standpoint of geography, the diversity of China posed a formidable obstacle to national integration: Feelings of local affinity (*hsiang-t'u ch'ing-i*) ran deep, and regional peculiarities were vividly expressed in the common saying "Customs differ every ten *li* [i.e., several miles]." On the other hand, since unification of the empire in 221 B.C., the Chinese elite had made a conscious and concerted effort to standardize customs (*t'ung feng-su*) and to unify the country by means of a centralized bureaucracy and well-organized systems of propaganda, penal law, ritual, and formal education. Over time, the progressive sophistication of Chinese techniques of political, social, and intellectual control produced a powerful sense of China's cultural unity (*t'ung-i*), but regional differences in natural resources, climate, productivity, communications, population, ethnic groups, dialects, and life-styles continued to challenge this ordered outlook.[1]

THE LEGACY OF THE LAND

It is clear that no single factor, geographical or otherwise, can explain the special character (*t'e-chih*) of Chinese civilization. But Chinese and Western scholars alike long have recognized the close relationship existing between the land and the people in China. The following quotation is representative:

> More people have lived in China than anywhere else. Upwards of 10 billion human beings have moved across her good earth; nowhere else have so many people lived so intimately with nature. A thousand generations have left their indelible impression on soil and topography, so that scarcely a square foot of earth remains unmodified by man. . . . Few landscapes are more human.[2]

Since earliest times, the land has remained a paramount Chinese value, exalted in the classical literature, celebrated in popular mythology, and enshrined in the naturalism of *yin-yang* cosmology.

Throughout the imperial era, geography was a highly respected sphere of scholarly activity in China. As a result, Chinese geographical writings were probably unparalleled in premodern times for their extent and systematic comprehensiveness. Of the four major types of monographs (*chih*) in the traditional dynastic histories under the general category of governmental institutions (civil and military administration, geography, economy, and law), geography usually ranks first in percentage of space. In the massive Ch'ing encyclopedia *Ku-chin t'u-shu chi-ch'eng*, geography is one of six main divisions, and its four subsections on the earth, political divisions, topography, and foreign countries together account for 2,144 out of the encyclopedia's 10,000 *chüan*—second only to the division on human relations with 2,604. This obsessive concern with geography did not stem only from its intrinsic attractions and the obvious relationship between geography and the practical concerns of political control, military defense, and even dynastic legitimacy; it also derived from the fact that many Chinese scholars found in the study of geography the key to a fuller understanding of both history and the classics.[3]

Geographical writing flourished in China during the Ch'ing period. Three of the most distinguished geographers of the day were Ku Tsu-yü (1631–1692), Liu Hsien-t'ing (1648–1695), and Li Chao-lo (1769–1841). Ku's famous *Tu-shih fang-yü chi-yao* (Essentials of Historical Geography) is considered a masterpiece of careful and comprehensive scholarship. Not only did he utilize more than a hundred Chinese geographical works and all of the traditional dynastic histories (see Chapter 6), but he also traveled extensively, gathering valuable information firsthand. Liu Hsien-t'ing did the same. We are told,

> He . . . studied the topography of mountains and rivers, visited famous retired men, made heroes his friends, observed local customs, [and] assembled anecdotes widely. . . . He discussed the changes in the ways of the universe and of the *yin* and *yang*, the grand strategies of the hegemons and kings, military arts, literature, institutions and regulations, and important points in various localities.[4]

Li Chao-lo, who dutifully studied the geographical writings of Ku Tsu-yü, is best known for his dictionary of Chinese place-names, arranged by rhymes and subdivided by dynastic periods. It was first printed in 1837. Later editions of this work included a supplement of Ch'ing dynasty place-names, also arranged according to rhymes and broken down into standard administrative subdivisions. Like Ku and Liu, Li became deeply involved in the compilation of local gazetteers (*fang-chih*). These historical and geographical compilations, often patronized by the government and always highly regarded, might center on a single administrative area or embrace the entire empire. The most noteworthy single achievement of this sort in the Ch'ing period was the huge, imperially commissioned *Ta-Ch'ing i-t'ung chih* (Comprehensive Gazetteer of the Great Ch'ing Dynasty), patterned after a similar, but rather unsatisfactory, Ming publication.

Compiled under the general direction of Hsü Ch'ien-hsüeh (1631–1694), with the able assistance of Ku, Liu, and many other competent scholars, the *Ta-Ch'ing i-t'ung chih* was first printed in the mid eighteenth century. A later edition (1790) included additional information concerning new territories incorporated into the Ch'ing empire as a result of the famous Ten Great Campaigns of the Ch'ien-lung emperor. Organized by provinces (*sheng*), the gazetteer discusses each in terms of conventional categories such as boundaries, topography, official personnel, population, taxation, and famous statesmen. Under lower-level administrative divisions, it focuses on cities, educational institutions, topography, historical sites, passes, bridges, defenses, tombs, temples, noteworthy residents, famous travelers, local products, and so forth. At the end, the gazetteer devotes a large amount of space to China's colonial dependencies and to the countries and culture groups within the expansive sphere of China's tributary system of foreign relations. Such comprehensive gazetteers and their local counterparts were, and continue to be, invaluable sources of information on nearly every facet of traditional Chinese life.[5]

During much of the Ch'ing period, the Chinese empire encompassed a vast area, estimated at 4,278,352 square miles (see Figure 2.1). This included the eighteen regular provinces of China Proper (totaling 1,532,800 square miles), the Ch'ing homeland of Manchuria (363,700 square miles), and the colonized dependencies of Mongolia (1,367,953 square miles), Chinese Turkestan (550,579 square miles), and Tibet (463,320 square miles). At its height, the Ch'ing empire stretched from the northern tip of Sakhalin Island to Hainan Island in the south and from the Pacific Ocean to the Aral Sea. About half of this gigantic empire was quite mountainous, however, and only about 10 percent of it was regularly under cultivation. About 90 percent of the Chinese people lived on roughly 12 percent of the land.[6]

Throughout most of the imperial era, China's population hovered between 50 and 100 million. At the beginning of the Ch'ing period, it probably stood at a little over 100 million. But during the extraordinary time of domestic peace and prosperity from the late K'ang-hsi reign to the end of the Ch'ien-lung emperor's reign, the Chinese population skyrocketed until it reached an estimated 450 million people by 1850. This exponential increase in people created an increasingly unfavorable population-to-land ratio, monumental economic and administrative problems, and severe social strains. The implications of this situation for China's modern development were profound and sustained.[7]

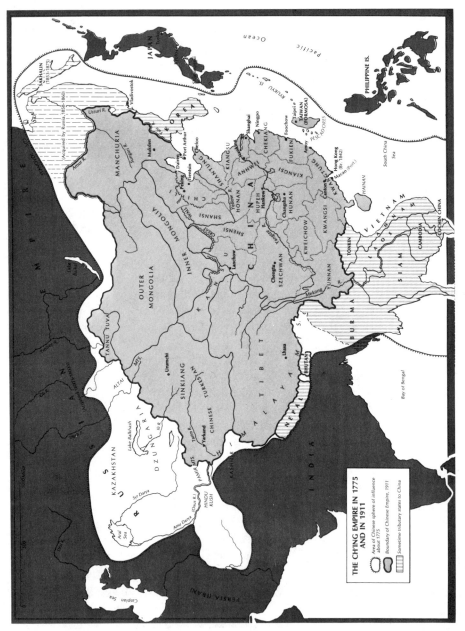

FIGURE 2.1 The Ch'ing Empire.

Throughout its long history, China has been surrounded by formidable geographic barriers, which have impeded direct contact with other advanced civilizations. This geographic isolation unquestionably contributed to the unity and continuity of Chinese civilization while it fostered a profound sense of cultural distinctiveness and superiority. China's eastern border was the awesome Pacific Ocean; to the south lay steaming and nearly impenetrable tropical jungles; to the southwest loomed the lofty plateau of Tibet and the towering Himalayas; and to the west and north were vast expanses of desert or grassland suited only for a harsh, essentially nomadic style of life. Significantly, China's closest neighbors were either sedentary peoples who openly sought to emulate Chinese culture—notably the Koreans, Annamese (Vietnamese), and Japanese— or pastoral peoples who periodically offered a military challenge to China but never presented a cultural threat. Until the traumatic nineteenth century, foreign visitors to China, including Europeans, regularly submitted to the humbling ritual of the Chinese tributary system (see Chapters 3 and 6), and often they adopted Chinese clothes and customs. Small wonder the Chinese perennially thought of themselves as the Middle Kingdom, the Central Cultural Florescence.

At the same time, however, China's massive size, huge population, and regional diversity posed formidable problems of administrative and cultural integration for the Ch'ing government, creating a constant tension between centrifugal and centripetal forces. Two great geographical contrasts existed in traditional China. One was between the highly developed agricultural area of China Proper south of the Great Wall and the less productive but strategically important outlying regions of the empire known collectively as Inner Asia. The other was between North and South in China Proper.

The Inner Asian regions on China's periphery had negligible economic value, but they provided a crucial buffer zone between China and border barbarians on horseback. The great expansive empires of Han and T'ang (see the next section on the historical background) spent huge sums of money on military operations designed to pacify external invaders and stabilize China's frontiers. Similarly, security considerations rather than economic motives dictated the Ch'ing conquests of Inner Asia in the seventeenth and eighteenth centuries.

For most of the Ch'ing period, China's rulers did not even attempt to integrate their Inner Asian dependencies with China Proper. In fact, they made a conscious effort to maintain Manchuria as an exclusively Manchu tribal preserve and allowed considerable cultural and administrative leeway to the deliberately isolated colonized areas of Mongolia, Chinese Turkestan, and Tibet. Although each of these three regions was garrisoned by Ch'ing troops, overseen by a military governor (*chiang-chün*), and supervised by the Court of Colonial Affairs (Li-fan yüan) in Peking, the Ch'ing government granted local tribal elites a large measure of political authority and allowed much of the indigenous governmental apparatus in these areas to remain intact. In

Mongolia and Tibet, for example, Peking supported the Lamaist hierarchy common to both regions, granted imperial titles to the hereditary ruling elites, and encouraged the preservation of their original tribal organizations and customs. Chinese Turkestan was by far the most ethnically diverse territory in Inner Asia; although governed like a huge garrison under the military governor in Ili, it too had native rulers and officials who enjoyed considerable cultural and administrative autonomy.[8]

Yet the Ch'ing government's deliberate policy of segregating Inner Asia from China Proper was only partially successful. By the beginning of the nineteenth century, the expansion of native (Han) Chinese into Inner Asia had begun in earnest, precipitated in part by severe population pressures. Sometimes illegally and sometimes abetted by the Ch'ing authorities, Chinese farmers penetrated the Manchurian frontier and the grasslands of Inner Mongolia and began eking a living out of the stubborn soil of Tsinghai (northeastern Tibet) and parts of Chinese Turkestan. In 1884, Sinkiang was actually made a Chinese province, and by the first decade of the twentieth century the regular Chinese system of field administration had been extended to the "three Eastern Provinces" of Manchuria. Nonetheless, the political and cultural integration of these areas was never complete, and in the waning years of the Ch'ing dynasty, each one became a serious trouble spot.[9]

The other major geographic contrast in China was between North and South, below the Great Wall. This contrast has been obvious to anyone who has ever traveled in China, past or present. The boundary between North and South is, of course, transitional; many geographical characteristics overlap or merge gradually from one area to the other. Still, striking and significant differences separate the regions north and south of the thirty-third parallel— a dividing line roughly marked by the Huai River in the east and the Ch'in-ling Mountains in the west. These differences can best be represented in simple chart form:[10]

North China	*South China*
Limited, uncertain rainfall	Abundant rainfall
Frequent floods and droughts	Adequate water year round
Unleached, calcareous soils	Leached, noncalcareous soils
4–6 month growing season	9–12 month growing season
1–2 crops per year; relatively low yields; frequent famines	2–3 crops per year; relatively high yields; prosperity
Major crops: kaoliang, millet, wheat, and beans	Major crop: rice
Work animals: donkeys and mules	Work animal: water buffalo
Mud-walled houses with heated brick beds (*k'ang*)	Woven-bamboo-walled and thatch-roofed houses
Wide city streets	Narrow city streets

North China	South China
Smooth coastline with poor harbors; little fishing	Rough coastline with many good harbors; much fishing
Foreign intercourse by land	Foreign intercourse by sea
Longtime residence; the nuclear area of Chinese culture	Populated mainly by southward migrations since T'ang times
Comparatively uniform ethnic makeup	Numerous ethnic groups
Mandarin dialect (*kuo-yü*)	Many different dialects

Such differences help account, in turn, for other contrasts between North and South. The greater strength of the clan system in South China, for example, may be explained at least in part by the requirements of a productive, labor-intensive southern rice economy based on extensive, cooperative waterworks. Similarly, the greater political instability of the South can be attributed not only to the simple fact of distance from the political power center of Peking but also to the specific ethnic and other tensions arising out of the unique South China economic and social milieu.[11]

In addition to the basic North-South division in China Proper, we can also identify several other regional divisions, based either on administrative (and often artificial) boundaries or on natural geographic factors such as soil and climate, mountain ranges, river and urban systems, linguistic and ethnic groups, and strategic defense areas. Traditionally, the Chinese have divided the realm below the Great Wall either into provinces and their administrative subunits or into a half-dozen or so major geographic sectors that transcend provincial boundaries. One common division has been into the Northwest, Northern China, Southern China, the Southeast, and the Southwest. By and large, these designations correspond to major economic areas defined primarily by prominent river drainage systems.[12]

In traditional usage, the Northwest referred to the upper basin of the Yellow River, a relatively thinly populated area extending from the eastern border of Russian Turkestan to the T'ai-hang Mountains—in other words, present-day Sinkiang, Kansu, Tsinghai, Shensi (north of the Ch'in-ling Mountains), and Shansi. Outside the riverine plains near the base of the loop of the Yellow River, agricultural activity in the Northwest has suffered from a chronic lack of adequate rainfall; but in those areas where rainfall has been sufficient, the rich, self-fertilizing soil known as loess has been extremely productive. Elsewhere in the Northwest livestock raising has prevailed, often undertaken by non-Chinese minority groups.

Northern China, also known as the Central Plain (*chung-yüan*), included the lower basin of the Yellow River and the drainage areas of the Wei, Huai, and other rivers. It embraced the heavily populated provinces of Chihli (modern-day Hopei), Honan, Shantung, northern Anhwei, and northern Kiangsu. Like the Northwest, Northern China was blessed with loess soil but cursed with light and unpredictable rainfall. Furthermore, Northern China had to contend with the peculiarities of the Yellow River floodplain. In most rivers of the world, a silt content of 5 percent is considered high, but the Yellow River has been known to carry as much as 46 percent, and one of its upriver tributaries, an astonishing 63 percent. In the absence of any tributaries for the last five hundred miles of its course, the Yellow River has continually built up its channel with sediment, so that now, as in Ch'ing times, the bed of the heavily dyked river actually lies above the surrounding countryside in some places. Historically, and especially in times of dynastic decline when maintenance efforts slackened, the Yellow River repeatedly broke its dykes, flooding hundreds of square miles and affecting the livelihood of millions. In 1852, the eastward course of the river shifted from the south of the Shantung promontory to the north, a distance of several hundred miles! "China's Sorrow" demanded continual attention from the Ch'ing government, but did not always receive it.

Southern China, including the basins of the four major tributaries of the mighty Yangtze River (the Han, Kan, Hsiang, and Yüan rivers), consisted of the provinces of Hupei, Hunan, Kiangsi, Shensi (south of the Ch'in-ling Mountains), southern Anhwei, southern Kiangsu, and northern Chekiang. Although much of this region is hilly, it has been favored by adequate rainfall and an abundance of lakes, rivers, streams, and other waterways. Agriculture and inland fishing have always been extremely productive in these areas. The Yangtze plain, at the base of a 750,000-square-mile drainage area, is laced with canals and other navigable waterways. Floods in this area are relatively infrequent, but often devastating when they occur. The famous flood of 1931, for example, was the most disastrous in world history, inundating some 34,000 square miles of land and affecting over 25 million peasants.

The Southeast, like Southern China, has long been known for its economic productivity. Traditionally the Southeast included the areas of southern Chekiang, Fukien, Kwangtung, Kwangsi, Taiwan (made a province in 1885), and the island of Hainan. These ethnically and linguistically diverse regions—hilly, heavily terraced, and well irrigated—are fed by numerous rivers, among which the Hsi (West) River is the most prominent. The people of the Southeast are renowned as the seafarers and adventurers of China. In Ch'ing times, and more recently, thousands of sailors from coastal areas braved the open sea in small junks as well as oceangoing merchant vessels, while their less intrepid but no less enterprising fellow provincials worked the near-shore waters for oysters, shrimp, and prawns.

The Southwest embraced three rather remote provinces: Yunnan, Kweichow, and Szechwan. In both Yunnan and Kweichow, large tracts of rugged mountains and high plateaus, deep gorges, and swift rivers have hindered transportation and agriculture. Szechwan, on the other hand, supported a wide variety of profitable crops and other products despite its comparatively rough terrain;

it was favored by a moist, temperate climate and endowed with a long-standing, ingenious, and highly effective irrigation system serving the fertile Chengtu plain. The "four streams" that give Szechwan its name (the Min, Lu, Sui-ning, and Chia-ling rivers) are all south-flowing tributaries of the Yangtze.

Within China Proper there were several dozen ethnic minorities, distinct from the Han Chinese, or black-haired people (*li-min*), who constituted about 94 percent of the total population of the realm. Among these minorities, the most statistically (and therefore politically) significant were the Chuang (in Kwangsi and Yunnan), the Hui or Muslims (Kansu and Shensi), the Uighurs (Sinkiang), Yi (Szechwan and Yunnan), and Miao (Kweichow, Yunnan, and Hunan). Some of these groups, such as the Uighurs and Hui, were supervised by officials appointed by the Court of Colonial Affairs; others—especially the smaller and in general more "primitive" indigenous minorities of the Southwest—were administered directly by their own hereditary local chieftains (*t'u-ssu*).[13]

At times these tribal leaders oversaw standard units of jurisdiction and received regular official titles, preceded by the character *t'u* (native or local). However, as with Ch'ing policy toward ethnic minorities in the dependencies of Inner Asia, the government's concern was more with control and stability than with cultural integration, and assimilation was not normally a conscious administrative goal. As a result, the ethnic minorities under local chieftains in China Proper, like their Inner Asian counterparts, enjoyed a considerable degree of autonomy in their language, religious beliefs, customs, and government. Occasionally, however, minority peoples did suffer discrimination by both local Han Chinese and the state, and when they did, social conflict or outright rebellion sometimes ensued. Under these circumstances, Chinese officials might more readily advocate "sinicization of the barbarians" through education and other means in order to encourage social stability.[14]

The cultural assimilation of Han Chinese was always assumed, but often difficult to achieve in practice. Regional differences in dialect, resources, population, and settlement patterns naturally contributed to different regional identifications and life-styles. Although these differences were seldom as striking as those between Han Chinese and aborigines, Tibetans, Mongols, or Turkic peoples, in many respects the Cantonese, Hakkas, and Hokkienese of South China were as distinct from one another as, say, Spaniards are from the French and Italians.[15]

In geographic terms, then, China was far less united than the base area of traditional Western civilization or even the subcontinent of India. Moreover, it lacked the convenient coastal communications of the Mediterranean. Divided into a complex patchwork of mountain and river systems, premodern China did not possess anything like a single communications network. Rather, it consisted of a series of more or less closed transportation systems within discrete physiographic regions. Until the introduction of railroads and steamships in the late nineteenth century, long-range travel—and even intraprovincial transport—was extremely difficult and often hazardous. Although the Ch'ing government helped maintain some major roads connected with the government relay system for transmitting official documents (*i-chan*), land transportation was at best costly and uncomfortable—especially in the outlying regions of the empire. Even in the North China plain the roads were deeply rutted and usually either dusty, muddy, or flooded. Springless two-wheeled carts, wheelbarrows, and sedan chairs provided the principal means of transport, cheap by day but expensive by the mile. The cost of transporting freight by land in many areas of China might be anywhere from twenty to forty times the usual standard for easily navigable rivers.[16]

Most Chinese preferred to travel by inland water routes if they had to travel at all. Unfortunately, there were few readily accessible and easily navigable north-south inland waterways in all of China. Most major Chinese rivers ran west to east, and only the famous Grand Canal, extending about seven hundred miles from Hangchow to Peking, provided long-distance water transport north to south. Like the Yellow River into which it flowed, the Grand Canal required, but did not always receive, regular upkeep from the Ch'ing government.

The best communications in China could be found in the south, particularly in the lower Yangtze valley. More navigable waterways existed in this region than in any comparable area of the world—including literally tens of thousands of miles of canals. These canals, varying in width from 10 to 100 feet, often widened into small lakes. Narrow roads usually followed alongside the principal waterways, serving as footpaths and towing paths for boats. Walled cities could often be found at the confluence of two or more canals, their size dictated by the economic and strategic importance of the intersecting waterways.[17]

Yet even in areas where communication routes and urban systems were relatively well developed, regional identifications remained extremely strong. One obvious reason was the centrifugal pull of Chinese localism (*hsiang-t'u se-ts'ai*). In the words of G. W. Skinner,

> Native place was an essential component of a person's identity in traditional Chinese society. Strangers thrown into contact would in their initial conversational exchange invariably ascertain one another's native place as well as surname. A person's native county [i.e., district] commonly appeared on doorplates (and invariably appeared on tombstones) and was used in correspondence and belles lettres as a surrogate given name for prominent figures. The normative pattern was clear: a young man who left to seek his fortune elsewhere was expected to return home for marriage, to spend there an extended period of mourning on the death of either parent, and eventually to retire in the locality where his ancestors were buried. Even when these expectations were not realized, the son born to a sojourner inherited his father's native place along with his surname.[18]

Regional differences and local identifications naturally encouraged regional stereotypes. These stereotypes, which were often included in the official dynastic histories and in local gazetteers, were derived from a wide variety of sources. Some reflected concrete geographical circumstances. The richly productive agricultural areas and well-developed commercial activities of South China, for example, encouraged the regional stereotype of southerners as greedy, shrewd, and sometimes unscrupulous. Northerners, by contrast, were viewed as upright and honest. Some regional stereotypes were based on historical and literary associations. Thus, the people of Hunan province were assumed to possess the sentimentality and emotionalism of their poetic countryman Ch'ü Yüan (third century B.C.); the people of Szechwan, the love of music and adventure of their countryman Ssu-ma Hsiang-ju (179–117 B.C.); and the people of Shantung, the frugality, simplicity, honesty, and sincerity of Confucius himself.[19]

Still other stereotypes were based on cosmological or pseudoscientific principles. According to the pervasive Chinese theory of the five elements, or activities (see Chapter 6), the element metal (*chin*) was associated with the direction west. People in West China were therefore believed to enjoy using weapons and to favor "cutting" (i.e., spicy) food. Since the South was associated with fire (*huo*), southern Chinese were naturally supposed to be fiery in temperament. Northerners, by contrast, were like water (*shui*)—cold, stern, slow, and straight. The east belonged to the element wood (*mu*), giving Easterners the characteristics of growing, flourishing, and constantly changing. The center corresponded to the element earth (*t'u*), considered by the Chinese to be stable, well balanced, and harmonious. Thus the people of Central China (variously defined) were solid and down to earth, without eccentricities.

Multiple regional stereotypes were common, and occasionally they conflicted; the striking feature of such stereotypes, however, was their tenacity and widespread acceptance over time. A recent study of contemporary Chinese regional stereotypes on Taiwan, for instance, indicates a remarkable affinity with Ch'ing dynasty stereotypes.[20] According to this study the following major traits can be identified for each of the eighteen provinces of China Proper:

Province	Physical Trait(s)	Nonphysical Traits
Hopei	Tall, strong	Frank, honest, good-mannered, simple
Shantung	Tall, heavyset	Frank, honest, straight, simple, upright
Shansi	Tall	Business-minded, simple, honest, resolute
Shensi	Strong, medium to tall	Honest, sincere, resolute, enduring
Kansu	Tall to medium strong	Enduring, honest, simple

Province	Physical Trait(s)	Nonphysical Traits
Honan	Tall, strong	Honest, straight, mannered, violent temper
Kiangsu	Medium to small, delicate	Cunning, crafty, versatile, refined, luxury-loving, good in business
Anhwei	Medium size	Good in business, simple, frugal, clever
Chekiang	Medium to small	Cunning, clever, obstinate, good in business
Kiangsi	Medium to small	Profit-hungry, scheming, not good as friends
Hupei	Medium to small	Scheming, crafty, unreliable
Hunan	Medium to small	Emotional, heroic, military, upright
Szechwan	Medium to small	Violent temper, too much talk
Fukien	Small to medium	Petty-minded, cunning, risk-taking, clannish
Kwangtung	Small	Innovative, risk-taking, clannish
Kwangsi	Small	Enduring, hard, culturally backward
Kweichow	Medium	Frugal, straight, poor, underdeveloped
Yunnan	Medium to small	Barbaric, enduring, frugal

By way of comparison, we might consider the K'ang-hsi emperor's observations concerning the personality traits of his subjects:

> Sometimes I have stated that the people of a certain province have certain bad characteristics: thus the men of Fukien are turbulent and love acts of daring . . . while the people of Shensi are tough and cruel. . . . Shantung men are stubborn in a bad way; they always have to be first, they nurse their hatreds, they seem to value life lightly, and a lot of them become robbers. . . . The people of Shansi are so stingy that they won't even care for the aged in their own families; . . . and since the Kiangsu people are both prosperous and immoral—there's no need to blow their feathers to look for faults.

At another point he remarked, "The people of the North are strong; they must not copy the fancy diets of the Southerners, who are physically frail, live in a different environment, and have different stomachs and bowels."[21]

The prevalence of such regional stereotypes unquestionably affected the outlook and policies not only of the throne, but also (and perhaps especially) of Ch'ing officials, who were prohibited by law from serving in their home provinces. It also probably affected the conduct of Chinese personal and commercial relations and encouraged local identifications and affiliations. It may even have influenced the subconscious self-image of individuals in China. Obviously, it posed an obstacle to nationwide social and political integration.

Given China's regional diversity and rampant provincialism, we may well wonder how China managed to thrive as a single political and cultural entity for so many millennia. Part of the answer may be found by examining the general patterns of China's historical evolution.

THE HISTORICAL BACKGROUND

China's cultural development from Neolithic times through the Ch'ing period may be viewed as a process, not always gradual, of expansion, incorporation, and progressive integration. Some recent scholars, notably Ho Ping-ti, have emphasized the pristine origins and independent early development of Chinese civilization, but for most of Chinese history, foreign conquest and "barbarian" influences have contributed significantly to the character and quality of Chinese culture.[22]

China's direct cultural roots may be traced to the Yellow River Valley some seven thousand years ago. There, sustained by the rich and uniquely self-fertilizing loess soil, a Neolithic culture eventually developed that exhibited many of the traits that have come to be identified with Chinese civilization in its mature form: the cultivation of millet, rice, and other staple crops; the domestication of animals such as pigs and dogs; the use of silk and hemp for clothing; distinctive housing, food preparation, and artistic styles; divination; ancestor worship; and ideographic writing. Over a period of time, this northern Chinese culture base interacted with other Neolithic cultures scattered throughout various parts of East Asia, receiving enrichment without losing cultural predominance.[23] The result was the emergence around 1800 B.C. of China's first fully historic dynasty, the Shang (traditional dates: 1766–1122 B.C.).

Many aspects of Shang life show unmistakable Neolithic origins, but the Shang dynasty marks a dramatic new stage in China's cultural development. Building mainly on indigenous foundations, the Shang peoples in northern China developed a sophisticated sociopolitical system based on ancestor-related theocratic rule over city-states, as well as an advanced bronze technology, a highly refined writing system, and well-defined forms of social, economic, and military organization. Shang archaeological sites have been found in at least ten modern provinces, indicating the wide spread of Chinese culture by means of both trade and military expansion.

The long-term cultural legacy of the Shang was primarily one of attitudes: an obsessive concern with ritual (*li*), a strongly bureaucratic outlook (especially evident in an abiding love of hierarchy, order, and classification), a consuming interest in the family and in ancestor worship, a fully articulated script, and the beginnings of *yin-yang*–style art motifs and metaphysics. Significantly, we find in Shang culture "a congruence of function and expression between religious practice, political organization, kinship descent, artistic expression, and divination forms," suggesting the remarkable integrative capacity of traditional Chinese civilization as early as Shang times.[24] We also find in the Shang period the emergence of a strongly authoritarian pattern in government and society, well before the establishment of large-scale, state-coordinated water-control projects in North China that enhanced "despotic" rule.

The Chou dynasty (traditional dates: 1122–256 B.C.) replaced the Shang in what became a familiar conquest pattern. In traditional Chinese historiography, the early Chou is considered to be the Golden Age of Chinese history, a time of peace and prosperity under sage rulers such as the legendary King Wen (the Cultured King), King Wu (the Martial King), and the Duke of Chou. Idealized accounts of the period in the *Chou-li, I-li,* and other works describe an elaborate system of kingship, investiture, noble rank, lord-vassal relationships, fiefs, manors, knights, and serfs—similar in many ways to the feudalism of medieval Europe. Significantly, however, China's knights (*shih*) seem to have been more literate and cultivated than their Western counterparts of a later period, and feudal ties in the Chou were apparently based more on blood and pseudokinship ties than on contract and Western-style feudal principles. Furthermore, Chou feudalism seems to have been more highly centralized, at least in principle, than Western feudalism and governed more by the dictates of ritual and ceremony (*li*) day to day. Most important, as a stage of historical development, feudalism in China never developed into capitalism.[25]

By the seventh century B.C., the political and social structure of the early Chou had begun to break down. Barbarian invasions precipitated the erosion of Chou authority. Widespread fighting among contending Chinese states (*kuo*) proved disruptive and demoralizing. "Chivalry" died a painful death as the interstate struggles grew ever more intense. Some principalities even went so far as to break the dykes of the Yellow River deliberately in order to flood the territories of their enemies. On the more positive side, new technological developments contributed to important economic and social changes. The use of iron revolutionized warfare and also facilitated important changes in agriculture, hydraulic engineering, and communications. Commercial activity and urbanization followed, transforming the old social order. New professions arose, and social mobility ensued. Land, once the sole possession of the king, became purchasable and transferable. Money circulated freely. Traditional values fell by the wayside or at least came under direct assault. In the midst of the chaos and uncertainty, the search began for a means of restoring order and unity to China.[26] This quest led to a flowering of Chinese philosophy as impressive as the roughly contemporary great age of Classical thought in the West.

Between the sixth and the third centuries B.C., a succession of brilliant and articulate Chinese thinkers offered a wide variety of solutions to China's pressing social problems. Confucius (c. 551–479 B.C.) and his followers, notably Mencius (c. 372–289 B.C.) and Hsün-tzu (c. 300–235 B.C.), advocated a return to the lost virtues of the early Chou, to family-centered ethics, ritual, and social responsibility. The followers of Mo-tzu (c. 470–391 B.C.) criticized the excessive ritual, lack of religious spirit, and particularism of Confucianism, but shared many of the same general social goals and ethical concerns. By contrast, the Taoist philosophers Lao-tzu (sixth century B.C.), Chuang-tzu (c. 369–286 B.C.), and their disciples sought release from social burdens; they were at heart individualists and escapists, concerned less with changing the world in an active way than with finding their special niche in the natural order. Related to the Taoists, at least in their interest in nature and natural process, were the followers of Tsou Yen (c. 305–240 B.C.), who developed an elaborate cosmology based on *yin-yang* principles and the five agents, or activities, associated with the elements of wood, metal, fire, water, and earth. Other schools of thought, such as the School of Names (*ming-chia*), contributed to the development of epistemology and ontology, but left little long-term philosophical legacy in China.[27]

Ironically, it was the school of thought known as Legalism, which can barely be called a philosophy, that exerted the most immediate and profound influence on Chinese society. Legalism was little more than an administrative approach emphasizing pragmatic government, universal and codified law rather than morality (contrary to the Confucian ideal), and state power as an end in itself. But guided by these basic principles and blessed with capable leadership, the Ch'in state—one of several major contenders for political supremacy during the late Chou period—embarked on a systematic campaign of conquest that resulted in the fall of the Chou ruling house in 256 B.C. and culminated in the subordination of all of China by 221 B.C.

The Ch'in dynasty lasted only fifteen years, but it left an enduring imprint on Chinese culture for the next two millennia. Its sovereign, King Cheng, who adopted the title of emperor (*huang-ti*) for the first time in Chinese history, brought unprecedented cultural unity to China. Dismantling the vestiges of Chou feudalism, including the practice of primogeniture, he instituted a nationwide system of freehold farming and imposed centralized, bureaucratic rule over the entire realm. At the same time, he initiated massive public-work projects (including waterways and the Great Wall) and standardized weights, measures, coinage, axle lengths, and even the Chinese script. Less laudably, the first Ch'in emperor imposed rigid thought control on Chinese intellectuals and tried to suppress all nonutilitarian works. This policy, commonly known as the Burning of the Books and the Burying of the Scholars (*fen-shu k'eng-ju*), although not entirely successful, resulted in the destruction of great amounts of priceless literature and created countless later controversies over the authenticity of reconstituted texts.[28]

Joseph Needham and others have argued persuasively that the crucial requirements of water control and management in North China, together with the need to provide widespread famine relief and to defend China against barbarian incursions, all encouraged the unification and bureaucratization of the realm.[29] But the harsh policies and rapid changes introduced by the first Ch'in emperor proved to be too disruptive for the regime. Not only did they help stifle emerging capitalism and stigmatize the idea of codified law, but they also generated empire-wide dissatisfaction, which quickly erupted into rebellion. Within four years of the first emperor's death, the Ch'in dynasty was overthrown.

The Han dynasty that followed (206 B.C.–A.D. 222) was one of the most glorious periods in all of Chinese history. Indeed, later generations of Chinese proudly called themselves "the people of Han" (Han-jen). The key to Han administrative success was the creation of an effective blend or balance of diverse cultural elements under the powerful and energetic emperor Wu-ti (reigned 141–87 B.C.). Wu-ti's government, for example, was Legalist in structure but Confucian in spirit; the economy involved both state monopolies and private enterprise; Han foreign relations were marked by both aggressive expansion and strategic appeasement. This type of balance was also evident in the Confucianism of Tung Chung-shu (179–104 B.C.), which drew freely upon other ideas, including Taoism and especially *yin-yang*/five agents cosmology. Han art and literature reflected a similar balance of cultural influences— not only Confucian and Taoist, but also courtly and popular, foreign and native.[30]

The legacy of Han culture was enduring. Under the growing influence of state-sponsored Confucianism, ritual and ceremony once again assumed their early Chou importance as a means of maintaining social order, transmitting tradition, and regulating state affairs, including the highly sophisticated Han tributary system that now embraced both diplomacy and foreign trade. Moreover, in its government institutions, ideology, scholarship, artistic and literary accomplishments, economic policies, and even its system of foreign relations, the Han set the style and pattern for most later dynasties. Important changes took place over the next two thousand years, to be sure, but a Han scholar would have had very little difficulty adjusting to life in any subsequent dynasty up to the late Ch'ing. One could hardly make the same claim for a Roman patrician in nineteenth-century Italy.[31]

The fall of the Han in A.D. 222 ushered in an extended period of political disunity known as the Six Dynasties (A.D. 222–589). For much of this time, China was divided into two distinct areas, North and South, with the dividing line about the Huai River. The North suffered repeated barbarian invasions and chronic political instability, while the South remained immune from barbarian conquest and comparatively stable. But these were not China's Dark Ages, especially in the South. In fact, traditional Chinese culture flourished, receiving enrichment from Indian Buddhism, which spread rapidly in China during the centuries following its introduction from India during the later Han period. Buddhism brought to tormented and disillusioned Chinese individuals the hope of escape from worldly suffering and sorrow. It introduced new ideas of reincarnation, karmic retribution, and the release of Nirvana and exerted a lasting influence on many aspects of Chinese philosophy, religion, art, literature, music, and architecture. At the same time, Buddhist monasteries began to exert their influence on Chinese economic, social, and even political life, in both North and South. On the other hand, Buddhism became transformed by Chinese culture. Early attempts to translate Buddhist sutras invariably involved linguistic and social compromises. Familiar, but not necessarily equivalent, Chinese terms were initially used to translate Buddhist notions, and various attempts were made to match concepts (*ko-i*) in order to establish parallels between Buddhist and indigenous Chinese sets of ideas. Even transliterations of Sanskrit words tended to carry the original meanings of the Chinese characters used to render them. Further, in order to minimize conflict between original Buddhist ideas and entrenched Chinese social values, passages in Buddhist sutras were sometimes altered or simply omitted. Over time, Buddhism became heavily sinicized.[32]

The nearly universal acceptance of Buddhism by all levels of society by the sixth century, together with the strong memory of Han unity and glory, undoubtedly contributed to the political and cultural reunification of China in A.D. 589 by the Sui dynasty (A.D. 589–618). During the Sui-T'ang period (A.D. 589–907), Buddhism received official patronage, becoming an integral part of state ritual and Chinese high culture generally. But a series of politically inspired persecutions directed against the Buddhist religious establishment in the mid ninth century effectively undercut Buddhism's institutional power in China. Meanwhile Confucianism, which had been used selectively by the Sui-T'ang rulers as a convenient source of political theory and ritual precedent for the conduct of imperial affairs, witnessed an intellectual revival. Thereafter, Buddhism continued to inspire, but never to dominate, Chinese intellectual life. Controlled by the state from above, it became appropriated by Chinese popular religion from below.

The intellectual vitality of the T'ang was but one indication of the general growth and refinement of Chinese culture during the period. Like the Han, the T'ang was expansive, cosmopolitan, creative, and self-confident. In the words of Michael Sullivan, "T'ang culture was to the culture of the Six Dynasties as was Han to the Warring States, or, to stretch the parallel a little, Rome to ancient Greece. It was a time of consolidation, of practical achievement, of immense assurance."[33]

In government, the Sui-T'ang examination system represented a major advance over the Han recruitment apparatus in opening channels of bureaucratic mobility. During the T'ang period there were several regular examinations, which tested classical scholarship, law, calligraphy, mathematics, and literary skills. Of these, the literary examination became the most prestigious and the chief route to high government office. Although social origins, family connections, and proper "breeding" still gave distinct advantages to well-born candidates for official position, the T'ang marks the beginning of a trend toward the replacement of aristocratic rule by "meritocratic" rule in Chinese government.[34] By Ming-Ch'ing times (A.D. 1368–1912) this leveling, unifying, and stabilizing process was largely complete.

Another T'ang contribution to the character of Chinese government in late imperial times was its highly refined law code, which provided the general format of the law codes of subsequent dynasties down to the Ch'ing, as well as many specific statutes. T'ang law was overwhelmingly penal in emphasis and designed primarily to preserve the entire Chinese social order against acts of moral or ritual impropriety. It was only secondarily interested in defending the rights of an individual or group against another individual or group and not at all concerned with defending such rights against the state. As a result, law in the T'ang and later periods "always operated in a vertical direction from the state upon the individual, rather than on a horizontal plane directly between two individuals."[35] It was an instrument of state power and control, not a source of individual autonomy in any sense.

After a brief period of disunity following the downfall of the T'ang, the Sung dynasty (A.D. 960–1279) reestablished centralized rule over all of China. Building on early T'ang political institutions as well as late T'ang economic foundations, the Sung carried Chinese material culture to new heights, combining remarkable administrative stability with unprecedented economic growth.

Sung China was the most populous and most urbanized country in the world, with over 100 million inhabitants and over fifty cities with populations in excess of 500,000. Sung agriculture was probably the most sophisticated anywhere at the time; foreign and domestic commerce flourished; and great industrial enterprises, employing hundreds and sometimes thousands of workers, produced massive amounts of iron, steel, textiles, and other valuable commodities. In most respects, the Sung level of economic development was not achieved by any European country until the eighteenth century.

The spectacular growth of the Sung may be attributed to several related factors. One was certainly the stability of Sung government and the state's unprecedentedly positive attitudes toward trade and economic development. Another was the loosening of traditional controls on merchants and the growth of new marketing centers. Yet another was the rapid expansion of credit facilities and the development of a sophisticated money economy. Population growth, urbanization, agricultural and industrial productivity, and commerce reinforced one another, and Chinese society as a whole benefited from a spate of inventions in virtually every area of science and technology, from biology, mathematics, chemistry, and medicine to hydraulic engineering, bridge building, shipbuilding, and architecture. Improvements in transport and communications, coupled with the expansion of education and the invention of printing (a T'ang development), helped disseminate the new knowledge of the period.[36]

Although the Sung was an age of great scientific and technological advancement, literature and the arts did not take a back seat to practical pursuits. Prose and poetry prospered, as did art and calligraphy. The Sung is also noteworthy for a second great flowering of Chinese philosophy—an outgrowth of social and economic changes, the Confucian revival begun in the T'ang, and technological factors such as the invention of printing. During the Sung, neo-Confucianism—as expounded by such brilliant and diverse thinkers as Chou Tun-i (1017–1073), Shao Yung (1011–1077), Chang Tsai (1020–1077), the great synthesizer Chu Hsi (1130–1200), and his intellectual rival Lu Hsiang-shan (1139–1193)—not only reasserted (and in many cases redefined) the ancient principles of Confucius and his more immediate successors but also buttressed these principles with cosmological and metaphysical speculations inspired by Buddhism and Taoism.[37]

What is striking about the burst of intellectual energy and inventiveness in the Sung is that together with dramatic economic growth, population growth, and urbanization, it did not produce far-reaching revolutionary change in China. We know, after all, that three simple Chinese inventions of the T'ang-Sung period—gunpowder, the magnetic compass, and printing—profoundly altered the contours of European history: Gunpowder weapons spelled the doom of European armored knights and feudal castles; the magnetic compass (and the axial rudder) enabled Europeans to discover the New World; and printing helped launch the Renaissance, the Reformation, and the Commercial Revolution in the West. Other Chinese inventions, coming in clusters to Europe, produced further important changes.[38] Why did these inventions fail to transform China in a similar manner?

The reason, in brief, is that by Sung times, China's highly evolved political, social, and economic institutions could accommodate internally generated change without fundamental disruption. Feudalism had broken down over a thousand years before, giving rise not to capitalism but to an increasingly centralized, bureaucratic managerial state. Chinese government became all powerful, capable of controlling, dominating, or at least channeling change of almost any kind, if it had the will. The state had the ability to establish monopolies, supervise trade, control guilds, coopt inventions, and mobilize vast human and material resources in support of its own interests. Cities in China were not centers of political or personal freedom with distinctive legal institutions as in the postfeudal West, but rather microcosms of the state. Commerce depended on an alliance between bureaucrats and merchants in the absence of a well-developed tradition of protective commercial law. Furthermore, the state determined the content of the civil-service examinations and in so doing, either directly or indirectly, shaped the curriculum of the empire's schools. What is more, by opening the examinations to merchants in post-Sung times, the Chinese government gave them every incentive to invest in education rather than commerce as a means of achieving upward social mobility.[39]

The invasion of the Mongols and the founding of the Yüan dynasty (1279–1368) followed a pattern of barbarian conquest that had antecedents in the Six Dynasties period and that would later be repeated by the Manchus in the seventeenth century. This pattern involved the seizure of power in North China at a time of political disorder, the enlistment of Chinese as well as foreign advice and assistance, the conscious copying of Chinese administrative techniques and institutions, the use of both terror and appeasement in consolidating power, and the maintenance of an external base beyond the Great Wall in addition to military predominance in China Proper.[40]

Mongol military rule stifled much of Sung economic growth, tarnished the bright cultural image of Sung, stigmatized its policies, and brought both rising despotism and racial discrimination against Han Chinese. Yet the harshness and oppressiveness of Yüan administration could not stay the advance of traditional Chinese culture, which flourished in areas such as art, vernacular literature, and especially operatic drama. Loyalist Confucian eremitism, as it developed, paid handsome cultural dividends. Moreover, in time the Mongols became increasingly sinicized, as a comparison of the administrative attitudes and personal life-styles of Chinggis Khan (1155–1227) and his grandson Qubilai Khan (reigned 1260–1294) clearly indicates. In testimony to the Yüan dynasty's patronage of Confucian scholarship in its later years, the civil-service examinations, which had fallen into abeyance, were reestablished in the early fourteenth century. Characteristically, however, the Mongols imposed a rigid orthodoxy on the content of the examinations, incorporating the commentaries of Chu Hsi into the official examination syllabus, where they remained until 1904.[41]

The Ming dynasty (1368–1644) expelled the Mongols, but continued the trend toward despotic rule by means of the early abolition of certain important institutional checks on imperial power, including the office of prime minister. In the Ming, more than ever before, China's pyramidlike structure of civil, military, and censorial government, dating from Ch'in-Han times, completely dominated the Chinese world. In the words of a leading authority, "There was no group or force in society that served as a countervailing influence against the government, so that [Chinese] society was a single-centered rather than a multi-centered one."[42] Overall, however, Ming despotism neither stifled artistic and literary activity nor hindered economic growth. Indeed, by Ming times, the Chinese economy had once again become highly commercialized, with complex farm technology and sophisticated production methods. As late as the sixteenth century, and perhaps later, the Chinese economy was still the most sophisticated and productive in the world, and the Chinese probably enjoyed a higher standard of living than any other people on earth.[43]

What is more, contrary to stereotype, the Ming was a time of considerable vitality and diversity in Chinese intellectual life. The great scholar and Confucian activist Wang Yang-ming (1472–1529) was a towering figure in Chinese philosophy during the Ming era, but he did not stand alone. Early Western contact with the Ming brought some new Western scientific, technological, and religious knowledge to China, but it did little to alter the character of Ming intellectual life, much less Chinese political, social, and economic institutions. The Jesuits, who succeeded in accommodating themselves in a deliberate way to the Chinese cultural and social milieu, were able to win a number of high-level converts and even to achieve some positions of responsibility within the Ming bureaucracy. But they depended completely on imperial support to maintain themselves and never came close to achieving any significant political power or intellectual influence. Later, their somewhat idealized accounts of China came to exert a small but significant impact on Enlightenment thinkers such as Voltaire, who is said to have written (in 1764) that the Chinese empire was the best the world had ever seen.[44]

But for all the grandeur of the Ming, with its impressive public-works projects, economic growth, and cultural refinement, dynastic decline came inexorably, as it had come to all previous ruling houses. The pattern was a familiar one: reign by weak and self-indulgent emperors, official corruption and bureaucratic factionalism, eunuch abuses (a particularly acute problem in the Ming), fiscal irresponsibility, neglect of public works, natural disasters, and the rise of rebellion. Meanwhile, outside the Great Wall in southern Manchuria, a tribal confederation of Tungusic peoples under an able leader named Nurhachi (1559–1626) waited in the wings. In the early seventeenth century Nurhachi had succeeded in building a formidable conquest force consisting of a large number of 300-man companies (*niru* or *tso-ling*) under various colored banners (*gusa* or *ch'i*). His Manchu successors refined this Banner fighting machine, built up a Chinese-style administration in Mukden (Shen-yang), and in 1636 adopted the dynastic name Ch'ing (pure).

Less than a decade later, after the rebel marauder Li Tzu-ch'eng had taken Peking in 1644, the Manchus joined forces with Ming troops under Wu San-kuei (1612–1678) to expel the insurgents and declared that they had come to save China from rebel depredations. But while the Manchus sought to legitimize themselves as the protectors of China's cultural tradition, they also crystallized their image as "barbarian" conquerors by forcing the Chinese to shave the front of their heads and grow the Manchu-style queue as a sign of submission. Consolidation of the empire took several decades in the face of Ming loyalism and resistance to "barbarian rule"; but by the 1690s the

Ch'ing had eliminated or driven underground the last pockets of anti-Manchu resistance and had established a strong, stable regime.[45]

The K'ang-hsi, Yung-cheng, and Ch'ien-lung reigns of the seventeenth and eighteenth centuries marked the high-water point of Manchu rule in China. Under these three great imperial patrons, nearly every aspect of traditional Chinese culture flourished, from literature, art, and scholarship to music and drama. Contemporary accounts of the period suggest a prosperous society with abundant natural resources, a huge but basically contented population, and a royal house of great prestige, both at home and abroad. Small wonder Ch'ing chroniclers of the eighteenth century referred to their time as being "unparalleled in history."[46]

Viewed from a nineteenth-century perspective (see Chapter 11), such claims sound like pathetic pride before the inevitable fall. In fact, however, they had substance, and there can be little doubt that for most of the imperial era, one reason for the astonishing staying power of traditional Chinese civilization was simply its ability to satisfy the needs of its vast population in ways that no other society on earth could match. A recent study of modernization in China suggests:

> If a line is drawn in history at the seventeenth century or at practically any time during the previous millennium, the case could be argued, some believe convincingly, that no peoples can lay claim to higher incomes per capita or to a more equal distribution of opportunities to win a large share of such income, to higher levels of literacy, to more sophisticated arts and crafts, to more highly developed commerce, or to markedly more elaborate adornment of such marks of "civilization" as the fine arts of sculpture, painting, calligraphy, and music, the intellectual arts of philosophy and knowledge in its various forms (save that we know today as "science"), and the minor arts of cooking, gracious living in general, and humor, or the arts of governance and even war.[47]

This, in brief, was the Ch'ing inheritance.

CHAPTER 3

The Ch'ing
Political Order

The primary focus in this chapter and the next is on those political, social, and economic institutions that together played a particularly important role in the ordering of Ch'ing society. Later chapters will discuss in detail the philosophical and religious underpinnings of these institutions. Although the following analysis is largely ahistorical, significant changes did take place in nearly every area of Chinese institutional life in the two and a half centuries from the founding of the Ch'ing to its fall in 1912. Nonetheless, the striking feature of the traditional Chinese state in Ch'ing times, as in earlier periods, was its capacity to accommodate change without fundamental disruption, to restore homeostatic balance. One crucial reason for this success was a highly evolved governmental structure that maintained central authority and at least the illusion of comprehensive rule, despite its superficiality and surprising administrative flexibility.

IMPERIAL RULE AND METROPOLITAN OFFICES

In its broad outlines, and in most specific respects, the government of the Manchus was patterned consciously on the Ming model. At the top stood the emperor, the Son of Heaven (T'ien-tzu) and supreme executive of the Chinese state. He was the mediator between Heaven and Earth—less than a god, but more than a mere mortal—the arbiter of all human affairs. He served, in the well-chosen words of John Fairbank, as "conqueror and patriarch, theocratic ritualist, ethical exemplar, lawgiver and judge, commander-in-chief and patron of arts and letters, and all the time administrator of the empire."[1] To play these roles effectively required a ruler of heroic talent and energy, and in the first two centuries of Ch'ing rule there were several such individuals.

China's nineteenth-century emperors tended to be weaker, or at least less effective, but the challenges they faced were staggeringly complex. And even in decline, imperial power remained formidable in the eyes of both bureaucrats and commoners.

Most Ch'ing emperors labored long hours, from dawn to dusk. Memorials from provincial and metropolitan officials, sometimes over a hundred a day, had to be read and acted upon. Emperors met every morning with officials and advisers to formulate domestic and foreign policies. During the rebellion of Wu San-kuei in the 1670s, the K'ang-hsi emperor handled as many as five hundred items of business a day and could not retire to bed until midnight. Both publicly and privately, the Ch'ing rulers spoke often of the heavy burdens of their office and the enormous responsibilities involved in "giving life to people and killing people."[2]

Huge amounts of time were consumed by ceremonial activities, from mundane life-cycle rituals to solemn sacrifices of truly cosmic significance. The ritual role of the emperor was of special importance to the conduct of state affairs, for it was through his ritual responsibilities that the emperor legitimized his position, promoted confidence among his family members and within the bureaucracy, and inspired awe among the common people. He personally held countless inspections, audiences, and banquets; conferred titles on officials and gods; ratified agreements with foreign dignitaries; received tributary envoys from foreign states; sanctioned the Dalai Lama and other religious figures within the realm; conducted state sacrifices to Heaven, Earth, and a host of lesser "deities"; prayed for relief from natural disasters; participated in the worship of his own and other imperial ancestors; oversaw the final stages of the civil and military examinations; and acted as the symbolic head of the imperial clan organization. These and other such ritual activities demanded painstaking and unwavering adherence to long-standing and carefully prescribed ceremonial requirements.[3]

Everything about the imperial institution was designed to foster a sense of awesome power and unapproachable remoteness. "Heaven is high and the emperor is far away" (T'ien kao huang-ti yüan) went a common saying. Ensconced in the walled, moated, and heavily guarded Forbidden City (Tzu-chin ch'eng) within the so-called Imperial City (Huang-ch'eng) of Peking, the emperor carried out his daily tasks beyond the sight and sound of commoners. No buildings in the Inner (Manchu) or Outer (Chinese) cities of Peking proper were permitted to rival the imperial palaces of the Forbidden City in size or splendor (see Figure 3.1), just as no other individual in the entire empire was allowed to wear the special designs that graced the emperor's clothing and other items of personal use. The Forbidden City was itself a symbol of the emperor's unique position at the center of the universe and the apex of the world (see Figure 3.2).[4]

FIGURE 3.1. Partial View of Peking from the Air. The large rectangle is the walled Forbidden City. Prospect Hill lies to the north (toward the top in this photo) of the Forbidden City. The lakes to the west were part of the Imperial City complex, which surrounded the Forbidden City and included Prospect Hill. To the north of the Forbidden City and Imperial City was the Inner (Manchu) City; to the south, the Outer (Chinese) City. Taken from Michael Sullivan (1977).

The emperor wrote in red, whereas his officials wrote in black. In audience, he alone faced south, while they faced north. Only the emperor could use the special term *chen*, meaning *I*. The characters of his personal name were taboo throughout the land, and any reference to the emperor or the imperial will was always separated from, and elevated above (*t'ai-t'ou*), the rest of the lines of any document in which it appeared. Imperial edicts were received with incense and ritual prostrations, and temples were built for the worship of His Majesty. All subjects performed the traditional kowtow (*k'o-t'ou*) in

North

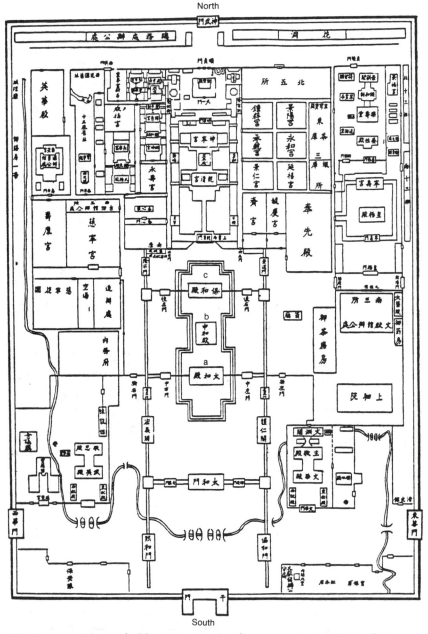

FIGURE 3.2. The Forbidden City. In the diagram, *a* is the Hall of Supreme Harmony, *b* is the Hall of Central Harmony, and *c* is the Hall of Preserving Harmony. To the north of these Three Great Halls were three corresponding palaces (*kung*) that formed part of the Inner Court, where the Ch'ing emperors lived and worked day to day. Taken from Herman Koester, "The Palace Museum of Peking," *Monumenta Serica* 2 (1936–1937).

FIGURE 3.3. Imperial Halls. *Right*, the Forbidden City's Hall of Central Harmony; *left* and *center*, the Hall of Preserving Harmony. The former was primarily a staging ground for the rituals undertaken by the emperor in the Hall of Supreme Harmony; the latter, the site of the palace examinations (*tien-shih*) after 1789. Photo by author.

the emperor's presence, but by design, few individuals saw him face to face. Contemporary accounts of the emperor's processions outside the Imperial City (i.e., through the Inner and Outer cities of Peking) and his tours of the provinces attest to the careful cultivation of an imperial aura of sacred splendor and dignified isolation. In fact, the term *sheng* (lit., sacred) was conventionally and rather indiscriminately applied to nearly everything about the emperor, from his appearance and activities to his desires and personal attributes.[5]

In theory, imperial power was absolute, as long as the emperor ruled by virtue (*te*). In practice, however, his power was often limited by his work load and abilities; by tradition, precedent, and bureaucratic inertia; and by familial obligations. Of these, the last exerted an especially profound influence. Few emperors were inclined to alter the policies of their ancestors without careful consideration, and filial piety (*hsiao*) often proved to be a formidable factor in imperial politics.[6]

The dedication of imperial sons to their mothers might simply take the form of extravagant and costly displays of indulgence, such as those of the Ch'ien-lung emperor, but filial devotion might also allow empresses dowager

36

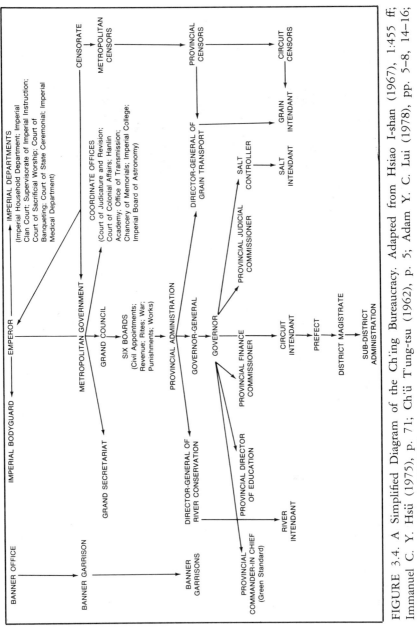

FIGURE 3.4. A Simplified Diagram of the Ch'ing Bureaucracy. Adapted from Hsiao I-shan (1967), 1:455 ff; Immanuel C. Y. Hsü (1975), p. 71; Ch'ü T'ung-tsu (1962), p. 5; Adam Y. C. Lui (1978), pp. 5–8, 14–16; R. J. Smith (1974), pp. 126–135.

to wield considerable influence in affairs of state. The most dramatic illustration of this phenomenon in the Ch'ing period was the rise to power of Yehonala, a low-ranking concubine of the Hsien-feng emperor (reigned 1851–1861) and mother of the young boy who eventually became the T'ung-chih emperor (reigned 1862–1874). As the Empress Dowager Tz'u-hsi, Yehonala executed a coup d'etat in 1861 and assumed the reins of government directly, serving as coregent for the youthful emperor and by some accounts encouraging his premature demise. She then placed her infant nephew on the throne as the Kuang-hsü emperor (reigned 1875–1908), flouting the laws of dynastic succession, but retaining power. To legitimize the act, she adopted him as her son. Even after the Kuang-hsü emperor had attained majority, Tz'u-hsi continued to play an active role in imperial politics and dominated her adopted son through fear and the manipulation of traditional values. On those rare occasions when the emperor attempted to challenge Tz'u-hsi's authority, he paid a heavy price.[7]

Although the Ch'ing emperors (and empresses) fully accepted the ritual symbolism and traditional values undergirding the Chinese imperial institution, they never completely abandoned their ethnic identity as Manchus. Indeed, they anxiously sought to preserve at least a measure of their cultural distinctiveness by prohibiting the Chinese practice of footbinding among Manchu women, by outlawing intermarriage between Manchus and Chinese, by maintaining a homeland base in Manchuria, and by keeping intact the native Manchu military system known as the Eight Banners. In addition, the Manchus promoted certain tribal customs (such as shamanism), encouraged Manchu-style education among members of the imperial clan, and often gave Manchus preferential treatment in official appointments, under the law, in the examinations, and in many other areas. The effectiveness and rigor with which these policies were pursued varied over time, but they served as a constant reminder to the Manchus of their precarious position as alien conquerors.[8] This awareness tended to encourage them to ally with the most culturally conservative elements in Chinese society, since the Manchus had originally justified their rule by proclaiming themselves to be the protectors of China's cultural heritage. The alien origins of the Manchus and their cultural conservatism created insurmountable problems for the dynasty in the last decades of Ch'ing rule (see Chapter 11).

The day-to-day personal and administrative needs of the Ch'ing emperors were met by the Imperial Household Department (Nei-wu-fu)—a kind of private, minigovernment within the Forbidden City staffed primarily by imperial bond servants (*pao-i*). Among the most important of its numerous subdepartments were the Office of Ceremonial (Chang-i ssu) and the Office of the Privy Purse (Kuang-ch'u ssu).[9] (Figure 3.4 points out the relationship of the imperial, metropolitan, and provincial departments to be discussed.)

The Office of Ceremonial, as its name suggests, regulated the sacrificial and other ritual observances of the inner court. In addition, it managed the affairs of the imperial harem and controlled the eunuchs who served in menial positions within the harem and elsewhere in the Forbidden City. Unlike the Ming emperors, who employed tens of thousands of eunuchs in various administrative capacities and who often surrendered substantial power to them, the Ch'ing emperors retained only a few hundred and kept them under close supervision. As the K'ang-hsi emperor once remarked: "Eunuchs are basically *yin* in nature. They are quite different from ordinary people. . . . In my court I never let them get involved with government—even the few eunuchs-of-the-presence with whom I might chatter or exchange family jokes . . . [are] never allowed to discuss politics." Still, by virtue of their closeness to the emperor and to imperial concubines, eunuchs in the Ch'ing period, such as the notorious Li Lien-ying (d. 1911), might exert considerable political influence.[10]

The Office of the Privy Purse handled the Imperial Household Department's financial affairs. It derived revenue directly from the management of imperial estates in Manchuria and around Peking, from the ginseng trade and other commercial operations, from the collection of customs revenue and foreign tribute, from loans to merchants, and from the expropriation of private property. These resources not only sustained the emperor, his family, and his entourage in proper imperial fashion but also provided occasional funds for charitable purposes, such as disaster relief, and for rewards to meritorious officials. In addition, the Office of the Privy Purse supplied money for military campaigns and for public-works projects. Its primary purpose, however, remained the maintenance of the imperial establishment and all its opulence.[11]

In addition to the Imperial Household Department, several other agencies attended to the emperor's personal, familial, and administrative needs. These included the Imperial Clan Court (Tsung-jen fu), the Department of the Imperial Bodyguard (Shih-wei ch'u), and the Banner Office (Chih-nien ch'i). As a general rule, administrative responsibility for the affairs of the Manchu ruling house and the multiethnic banner military organization lay outside of the regular bureaucratic apparatus, creating an extra echelon of imperial government. At this level, the Manchu language gave the Ch'ing rulers a special channel of privileged information regarding secret or sensitive matters of state. As had been the case during previous conquest dynasties, alien rule necessitated special mechanisms of security and control.

The single most important and influential regular organ of government during most of the Ch'ing period was the Grand Council (Chün-chi ch'u). Established about 1730 to assist the Yung-cheng emperor in conducting military operations, the Grand Council soon replaced the Grand Secretariat (Nei-ko) as the closest advisory body to the emperor on civil, as well as military, matters. The prestigious grand councillors, usually about a half dozen in number, met at least once a day with the emperor to discuss all aspects of imperial administration. As the emperor's most trusted bureaucratic assistants, the grand councillors read secret palace memorials (*tsou-che*) after they had been seen by the emperor, recommended policies, and carried out the imperial will by issuing orders to other governmental agencies within the regular bureaucracy. The Grand Council did not, however, enjoy independent executive power, which resided in the hands of the emperor alone. As a result, the effectiveness of the Grand Council was related directly to the energy and ability of the throne. In the absence of imperial initiative, the Grand Council became unresponsive.

Below the Grand Council stood the Six Boards: Civil Appointments (Li-pu), Revenue (Hu-pu), Rites (Li-pu), War (Ping-pu), Punishments (Hsing-pu), and Works (Kung-pu). These overlapping organs were responsible for the routine administration of the empire at the central governmental level, and each organization had its equivalent at lower bureaucratic echelons down to the district (*hsien*). Even the Ch'ing law code was divided into these six categories.

First among the Six Boards was the Board of Civil Appointments. This board was responsible for most matters relating to the appointment, evaluation, promotion, demotion, transfer, and dismissal of officials in the 20,000-man metropolitan and provincial civil bureaucracy. Although Ch'ing personnel administration was highly complex and not always bureaucratically "rational," on the whole the Board of Civil Appointments proved remarkably successful in establishing uniform standards for the appointment, evaluation, and discipline of both metropolitan and provincial officials. Particularly noteworthy as a control mechanism was the sophisticated Ch'ing system of administrative sanctions embodied in the dynasty's *Ch'u-fen tse-li* (Regulations on Administrative Punishment).[12]

The Board of Revenue, second in rank among the Six Boards, held responsibility for empire-wide population and land registration; regulation of coinage; collection of duties, taxes, and grain tribute from the provinces; payment of salaries and stipends to officials and nobles; audits of central government and provincial treasuries and granaries; supervision of commerce, industry, state monopolies, and communications; and management of certain special administrative tasks relating to personnel and judicial affairs. Despite its wide-ranging bureaucratic scope and access to detailed economic information, the Board of Revenue—like the Ch'ing government as a whole—preferred to confine its activities primarily to raising revenue, promoting economic stability, and maintaining political power and control. (The Board of Revenue's sources of revenue and its categories of expenditures are shown in Figure 3.5.)[13]

The Board of Rites, although ranked only third among the Six Boards, had extremely weighty responsibilities. Of its four major departments, the

FIGURE 3.5. Central Government Income and Expenditures, 1899

	Millions of taels
REVENUE	
Land-poll tax	24.0
Wastage allowance (*huo-hao*)	2.5
Tribute grain commutation and allowance	2.5
Salt taxes	13.5
Likin tax (instituted in 1853 on goods in transit)	16.5
Customs	26.6
Native opium tax	1.8
Others	1.0
Total	88.4
EXPENDITURES	
Provincial administration	9.1
Foreign loans	24.0
Army	31.0
Navy	5.0
Customs administration and services	3.6
River conservancy	2.5
Frontier defense	2.0
Imperial household	1.0
Legations	1.0
Railways	0.8
Miscellaneous expenses	21.0
Total	101.0

Source: Adapted from Immanuel Hsü (1975), p. 528. Compare Hsü's data for earlier periods, pp. 81 and 83–84 of the same work.

Note: This breakdown obviously includes sources of revenue and expenses that were not always as important. Prior to the nineteenth century, for example, the central government received a far smaller share of its revenue from foreign customs and none at all from the likin transit tax. On the other hand, the central government did not have to pay for railways, customs services (such as lighthouses), foreign legations, or foreign loans. Throughout the Ch'ing period, military expenses consumed a large share of the central government budget, even when the dynasty had no appreciation of the need to acquire modern Western technology.

Department of Ceremonies handled regular court ritual, the examination system, regulations regarding official dress and other marks of status, forms of etiquette between various ranks, and forms of written communication. The Department of Sacrifices oversaw state sacrifices, funerals, the dispensing of posthumous rewards, and the editing of the Imperial Calendar (*Shih-hsien shu*). The Reception Department managed the highly ritualized tributary system of China's foreign relations, as well as the giving of gifts to officials and other miscellaneous activities; the Banqueting Department, as its name implies, was responsible for the preparation of food for banquets and sacrifices. Breaches of etiquette in these realms were often punished by law.[14]

Closely associated with the Board of Rites, and at times during the Ch'ing period directly attached to it, were three so-called courts: the Court of Sacrificial Worship (T'ai-ch'ang ssu), in charge of all state sacrifices performed directly by the emperor or his appointed deputies; the Court of Banqueting (Kuang-lu ssu), responsible for providing food and drink for special ritual occasions, including tributary feasts; and the Court of State Ceremonial (Hung-lu ssu), charged with the task of instructing guests at banquets in proper ceremonial observances. A Board of Music (Yüeh-pu) also fell under the general direction of the Board of Rites, indicating the central importance of music to nearly all forms of Chinese ritual activity.[15]

The Board of War supervised various military rituals, but its major responsibilities were the instruction and maintenance of the Chinese constabulary known as the Army of the Green Standard (see Chapter 4). It handled the majority of regular military appointments, dismissals and transfers, undertook the registration and periodic review of imperial troops, administered the military examinations, dispensed rewards and punishments, played a role in the making of military policy, and managed the dynasty's relay system of official communications. Although most matters relating directly to the Banner armies of the empire were beyond its purview, the Board of War remained responsible for the allocation of about two-thirds of the central government's total expenditures and for the deployment of Green Standard forces to suppress rebellion and maintain local control.[16]

The Board of Punishments provided a symbolic counterpoint to the Board of Rites, since law in traditional China was invoked only after ritual had failed. The penal emphasis of Chinese law was reflected not only in the title of the Board of Punishments itself but also in the contents of the legal code known as the *Ta-Ch'ing lü-li* (Fundamental Laws and Supplementary Cases of the Great Ch'ing Dynasty). The Ch'ing code, in turn, was incorporated into the massive *Ta-Ch'ing hui-tien* (Collected Statutes of the Great Ch'ing Dynasty) and its supplements.

The Board of Punishments often undertook its responsibilities in consultation with representatives from the Court of Revision (Ta-li ssu) and the Censorate (Tu-ch'a yüan). Together, these three offices were known as the Three Courts of High Adjudicature (San-fa ssu). Routine legal matters flowed through one of the eighteen major departments of the Board of Punishments. These, like the departments in the Board of Revenue, were organized along geographical lines but had responsibilities and jurisdictions that extended beyond provincial boundaries. Various other offices within the Board of Punishments dealt with matters such as judicial review, revision of the legal code, and management of prisons. Although the Chinese legal system had no "due process" in the Western sense, no trial by jury, and no formal representation by counsel, it did at least provide convicted persons with recourse to appeal. On the other hand, it functioned primarily as an instrument of social and political control, to be used by the state with a vengeance—and often quite arbitrarily—when it perceived a threat to its interests.[17]

The Board of Works was the lowliest of the Six Boards, yet its functions were vital. In general, the Board of Works maintained all public shrines and temples, imperial tombs, official buildings, military and naval installations, city walls, granaries, treasuries, public timberlands, official communication routes, and government-sponsored dykes, dams, and irrigation systems. In addition it provided military stores and other essential supplies (including copper coins) to appropriate governmental agencies. Contrary to stereotype, the Board of Works often operated quite efficiently. A recent study of food and famine in Chinese history concludes, for example, that the traditional state, particularly in Ch'ing times, "played a significant role in the feeding of the population" and that the power of the government to affect the movements of the population, to distribute resources among regions, to regulate the use of land and water, and to control the circulation of grain was a critical factor in the presence or absence of food crises and famines. In the eighteenth century the Ch'ing government carried out these functions admirably, but in the nineteenth century population pressure "rendered ineffective the power of the state to perform the same functions of regulation, or at least intervention, that it had apparently done so well in the previous era."[18]

The Six Boards, like all other regular bureaucratic organs (with the noteworthy exception of the Grand Council), fell under the close and continual scrutiny of the Censorate. This long-standing Chinese institution served as the "eyes and ears" of the emperor, providing him with secret information on the activities of civil and military officials at all levels. Although theoretically bound to guide and admonish even the emperor himself, in practice many censors became little more than imperial agents, tools of the autocracy. The dynastic record abounds with examples of noble and upright censors who sacrificed their careers and lives for their principles, but it also indicates that many censors became corrupted by power and ambition and embroiled in destructive factional politics.[19]

One last metropolitan institution merits brief discussion: the Court of Colonial Affairs, mentioned briefly in Chapter 2. Unlike most Ch'ing institutions, the Court of Colonial Affairs had no direct historical antecedent. Designed initially to oversee Ch'ing relations with the Mongols, with the expansion of the Chinese empire the court's responsibilities grew to embrace not only the areas of Tibet, Mongolia, and Chinese Turkestan but also the management of ethnic minorities within China Proper. In addition, the Court of Colonial Affairs handled China's "special relationship" with Russia, which had the status of neither a colonial dependency nor a tributary state. After 1860, under duress, the Ch'ing government established an office of foreign affairs (known as the Tsungli Yamen) for the regular conduct of China's relations with Western nations, including Russia. But this body was only an ad hoc graft on the existing administrative structure; it had no regular institutional status and was viewed by the Ch'ing government as merely a subcommittee of the Grand Council.[20]

ADMINISTRATIVE INTEGRATION

The relationship between the governmental organs at the capital and in the provinces was extremely complex and maintained by the unceasing flow of documents to and from the throne. Information from provincial officials arrived at Peking via the imperial postal service in the form of rigidly formalized memorials and petitions. Routine memorials (*t'i-pen*) were received by the metropolitan Office of Transmission (T'ung-cheng ssu), which opened, checked, copied, and forwarded them to the agencies concerned and to the Grand Secretariat. The Grand Secretariat, in turn, drafted replies to these memorials for imperial approval. Special palace memorials, first used during the K'ang-hsi reign, were transmitted directly to the emperor through the Chancery of Memorials (Tsou-shih ch'u) and were supposed to be initially for his eyes alone. Although the palace-memorial system greatly increased the emperor's personal workload, it also provided him with direct information that could be used as a check on the bureaucracy.[21]

The emperor also received valuable information from his frequent "business" audiences (*yü-men*, *pi-chien*, etc.) with metropolitan and provincial officials. These highly ritualized face-to-face encounters not only resulted in the mutual exchange of information but also enhanced the aura of the throne and reinforced bonds of loyalty. Imperial tours of the provinces performed much the same function. The large-scale ceremonial audiences known as *ta-ch'ao* and *ch'ang-ch'ao*, which took place at the Hall of Supreme Harmony (T'ai-ho tien) of the Forbidden City, lacked the intimacy of business audiences held in the inner court, but they performed the vital function of confirming symbolically a world view based upon "notions of order, coherence, hierarchy, and the focal sacrality of the Chinese emperor."[22]

Aside from the very general proclamations (*chao*) issued at large-scale audiences to announce joyous events, the imperial will was conveyed to the bureaucracy chiefly by means of edicts (*shang-yü*), court despatches (*t'ing-chi*), court letters (*tzu-chi*), oral instructions (*ch'eng-chih*), rescripts (*chih*), vermillion comments written by the emperor on memorials (*chu-p'i*), and various general circulars (*t'ung-hsing*). In analogous fashion, provincial officials sent down orders (*cha, cha-fu, kuan-wen*, etc.) to their subordinates, commented upon (*p'i*) petitions and reports, and circulated rules and regulations. At the local level, imperial yellow posters (*t'eng-huang*) and other public announcements informed gentry and literate commoners of official policy. Government business at all levels had to be validated by official seals, which varied according to the department that handled their manufacture, the material used to make them, their design and style of script, their size, designated name, and of course the office to which they were assigned. The *Ta-Ch'ing hui-tien* lists twenty-five different official seals for the emperor alone.[23]

The so-called Peking Gazettes (*Ching-pao*) and their provincial counterparts provided a valuable source of information on public policy. Although issued by various publishers under different names, the Peking Gazettes were alike in that they were supervised by the Communications Department of the Board of War and contained official documents released by the Grand Secretariat or the Grand Council. In the words of a well-informed foreign observer in nineteenth-century China, the Peking Gazettes were "very generally read and talked about by the gentry and educated people in the cities." In the provinces, thousands of individuals found employment copying and abridging the gazettes for readers who could not afford to purchase complete editions. Circulated both officially and privately, the Peking Gazettes provided a valuable means of horizontal communication in an empire where vertical communications were generally emphasized.[24]

The most exalted figure in the regular provincial adminstrative hierarchy was the governor-general (*tsung-tu*, sometimes translated viceroy). His jurisdiction encompassed at least one, usually two, and sometimes three provinces. Within this wide sphere he supervised and evaluated the work of civil and military officials, reported on provincial finances, and reviewed judicial cases. Below him stood the governor (*hsün-fu*), charged with the civil and military affairs of a single province. His responsibilities were similar to those of the governor-general, but he also held specific responsibility for overseeing the collection of customs duties (*kuan-shui*), managing the salt administration, superintending the local examination system, and administering the grain tribute system. The provincial finance commissioner (*pu-cheng shih*, sometimes translated treasurer), served as a lieutenant governor, with primary responsibility for fiscal administration, the provincial census (taken every ten years), the promulgation of imperial commands, and a wide range of other administrative and judicial tasks. Most routine judicial responsibilities fell to the provincial judicial commissioner (*an-ch'a shih*), who also helped manage the provincial postal system, evaluated officials, and helped supervise the local civil-service examinations. Most of the educational affairs of a province were supervised by a specially appointed officer from Peking known as the director of education (*hsüeh-cheng*).[25]

The lower echelons of provincial administration were divided into a complex hierarchy of geographically based circuits (*tao*), prefectures (*fu*), independent departments (*chih-li chou*) or subprefectures (*chih-li t'ing*), and districts (*hsien*). At the bottom of the bureaucratic ladder stood the district magistrate (*hsien-chih*), who had direct responsibility for from 100,000 to well over 250,000 people. Horribly overburdened, the magistrate functioned as a kind of mini-emperor, playing the role of a "father-mother official" (*fu-mu kuan*) to his constituents, undertaking religious and other ritual responsibilities, dispensing justice, maintaining order, sponsoring public works, patronizing local scholarship, and all the while collecting taxes for the state.

The yamen (office) of the magistrate, which was always located within a walled city (*ch'eng*), served as both his residence and work place. Within this large compound, hundreds of regular administrative personnel and other functionaries might work: the assistant magistrate (*hsien-ch'eng*), the district registrar (*chu-pu*), educational officials, jail wardens, clerks, and runners, as well as private secretaries, personal servants, and family retainers. None, however, came close to matching the magistrate in prestige or power. Private secretaries usually enjoyed high status, since most were degree holders like the magistrate, but they did not hold formal positions and had to be content to act in an advisory capacity. Clerks were usually commoners who had little hope of obtaining degrees or official rank; they handled routine documentation in each of the district yamen's six major departments corresponding to the Six Boards at Peking. Yamen runners were the lowest functionaries, socially disesteemed and officially classified as *chien-min* ("mean" people). They served as court attendants, prison guards, policemen, and tax collectors. Although lacking in formal authority, they often enjoyed considerable local power. And since they relied upon informal fees for their livelihood, they often found themselves in a position to gouge the local populace.[26]

Subdistrict administration rested with a variety of institutions that had no formal legal status. Each basic rural division (*hsiang*), town (*chen*), and village (*ts'un*), for instance, had its own locally "elected" headman or headmen. In order to exert more effective bureaucratic control over these units, however, and to cut across clan lines and other natural divisions in Chinese society, the Ch'ing government also attempted to impose its own artificial administrative order on subdistrict urban and rural areas. These efforts included the tax-collection and registration system known as *li-chia* and the similar local security system called *pao-chia*—both based on decimal groupings of mutually responsible families. The heads of these organizations, usually commoners with some degree of local influence, reported to the magistrate periodically and could be punished by him for inattention to duty.

The effectiveness of such tax-collection and local control systems varied widely from place to place and from time to time during the Ch'ing period. As a rule, however, from the eighteenth century on, district magistrates increasingly assigned local commoners known as constables (*ti-pao* or *ti-fang*) to urban wards (*fang*) and rural subdivisions (*t'u* or *li*) within the formalized *li-chia* and *pao-chia* networks to assist or supplant the local heads of these organizations. These unsalaried agents of the magistrate often combined the roles not only of *li-chia* and *pao-chia* headmen, but also of yamen runners. They reported crimes, property disputes, fires, magical practices, and other suspicious activities; provided witnesses for inquests; assisted in public-works projects; helped collect taxes; and played a role in the registration of individual households. Like yamen runners, local constables made their living by levying informal fees and sometimes by outright extortion.[27] During and after the Taiping Rebellion (1850–1864), gentry-led militia organizations known as *t'uan-lien* (lit., grouping and drilling) began functioning as quasi-official subdistrict administrative organs, assuming not only *pao-chia* and *li-chia* functions but also judicial functions. This development only enchanced the already considerable power of the rural-based gentry class.[28]

For all the state's effort to dominate Chinese society from the district capital and above, successful administration—especially in the countryside—depended on an informal alliance between officialdom and the rural-based gentry (see Chapter 4). Since a district magistrate's bureaucratic reach could not possibly extend directly to the hundreds of villages under his immediate jurisdiction even with the assistance of agents such as constables and runners, he had to rely upon the prestige and authority of the local elite to maintain order and stability. A symbiotic relationship thus developed. Gentry members in rural areas helped assure public security and acted as buffers between the peasantry and officialdom, while urban-based bureaucrats helped to further gentry interests through direct patronage, favorable treatment in taxation and other matters, and provision of official access to higher provincial authority. Just as a balance existed within the district yamen between the state interests represented by the centrally appointed magistrate and his personal secretaries on the one hand, and the local interests represented by clerks, runners, and constables on the other, so a balance existed between the district magistrate and the local gentry class.[29]

The cultural common denominator of both officials and the gentry, and the primary source of their social prestige, was preparation for, and success in, the civil-service examinations. These examinations tested moral knowledge, which in the traditional Chinese view was considered essential to good government. Although lower degrees and even substantive offices might be purchased on occasion, especially in periods of administrative decline, on the whole the examination system provided the major means of bureaucratic mobility in Ch'ing times.

FIGURE 3.6. Examination Halls. Candidates for the civil-service examinations were confined in these "cells" for the duration of the long testing process. Yet the social and bureaucratic rewards that came with success in the examinations amply compensated for the temporary discomfort of self-imposed imprisonment. Photo courtesy China Trade Museum, Milton, Mass.

The system imposed rigid requirements on candidates for degrees. Success in the examinations demanded diligent application on the part of males from the age of five on. Beginning with primers such as the *Ch'ien-tzu wen* (Essay of a Thousand Characters), students went on to memorize the so-called Four Books and Five Classics—a total of some 430,000 characters—by the age of eleven or twelve. Training in calligraphy, poetry composition, and the difficult "eight-legged essay" (*pa-ku wen-chang*) style followed. In addition, aspirants for degrees had to familiarize themselves completely with a huge body of classical commentaries, histories, and other essential literary works. Enterprising private publishers produced collections of examination essays designed as a shortcut to study, but few candidates could normally afford to place sole reliance on such aids for their future well-being.[30]

The Chinese examination system consisted of an elaborate battery of tests at various levels (see Figure 3.7). Success in the initial series of tests at the district level, held twice every three years, brought the *sheng-yüan* (government student) degree and eligibility for the triennial examinations at the provincial level. Successful candidates at this level won the *chü-jen* ("recommended

FIGURE 3.7. The Examination System

LEVELS OF EXAMINATION

PRELIMINARY EXAMINATIONS
 District-level (*hsien-k'ao*)
 Prefectural-level (*fu-k'ao*)
 Examination for *sheng-yüan* degree (*yüan-k'ao*)—district quotas

PROVINCIAL EXAMINATIONS
 Examination for *chü-jen* degree (*hsiang-shih*) after preliminary
 test known as *k'o-k'ao*—district quotas

METROPOLITAN EXAMINATIONS
 Major examination known as *hui-shih* for *chin-shih* degree—provincial
 quotas
 Palace examination (*tien-shih*)
 Further examination for specific official appointment (*ch'ao-k'ao*)

SUCCESSFUL *CHIN-SHIH* CANDIDATES, 1890 (BY PROVINCE)

PEKING
Manchu Bannermen	9
Mongol Bannermen	4
Chinese Bannermen	7

PROVINCES
Kiangsu	26
Chihli	24
Shantung	22
Kiangsi	22
Fukien	20
Honan	17
Anhwei	17
Kwangtung	17
Hupei	15
Szechwan	14
Hunan	14
Shensi	14
Kwangsi	13
Yunnan	12
Kweichow	10
Shansi	10
Kansu	9
Taiwan	2
Total	328

Source: NCH, June 13, 1890; cf. Ho Ping-ti (1962), pp. 189, 228–229. In 1702 a sliding scale of provincial *chin-shih* quotas was instituted based on the total of participants from each province in the three preceding examinations. This system became virtually frozen, with only minor adjustments during the latter half of the nineteenth century.

man") degree and a chance at the coveted metropolitan *chin-shih* ("advanced scholar") degree. The triennial examination for this degree, like the provincial examination, consisted of three main sessions (*san-ch'ang ti-ko*). The first focused on the Four Books, the second on the Five Classics, and the third on questions of policy formulation (*ts'e-lun*). Successful candidates were ranked in order of excellence and invited to a special congratulatory banquet (*ch'iung-lin yen*) provided by the Board of Rites.

The last stage in the process was the more or less *pro forma* palace examination (*tien-shih*), held for the top three classes of metropolitan graduates in the Hall of Preserving Harmony (Pao-ho tien) in the Forbidden City. The emperor generally presided over this affair with the assistance of various high-ranking civil officials who acted as readers (*tu-chüan ta-ch'en*). In contrast to the brevity of the questions at lower examination levels, the emperor's questions were elaborate and florid in style. The responses of the candidates, in turn, were couched in the self-deprecating language and rigid form of a memorial to the throne. Following the announcement of the results of this examination, a series of banquets and ceremonies ensued, all of which enhanced the prestige of the *chin-shih* graduates and served as reminders of status distinctions and obligations. The top *chin-shih* were immediately appointed to the Hanlin Academy, where they performed various important editorial, pedagogical, and ritual functions for the emperor. Service in the Hanlin Academy virtually guaranteed metropolitan graduates of rapid promotion in the regular bureaucracy.[31]

Competition for degrees at all levels was ferocious. Tight government quotas limited the number of successful candidates in each examination. At the metropolitan level, for example, only about three hundred individuals could pass at any given time. Most provinces were allowed a quota of from fifteen to twenty *chin-shih* per examination, although some received fewer than ten slots and others as many as twenty-five (see Figure 3.7). A certain quota also was set aside for Manchu, Mongol, and Chinese bannerman—generally in descending numbers for each group. At the lower levels of examination the quotas were less restrictive. About fifteen hundred *chü-jen* degrees could be granted at one time, and as many as thirty thousand *sheng-yüan* degrees. Nonetheless, an aspirant for the lowest degree had only about one chance in sixty of success and only one chance in six thousand of ultimately attaining the *chin-shih* degree. Candidates often took the examinations many times. One could not normally hope to acquire the *sheng-yüan* degree before the age of twenty-four, the *chü-jen* degree before the age of thirty, or the *chin-shih* degree before the age of thirty-five.[32]

Furthermore, the best minds of the empire were not always successful, as many frustrated Ch'ing scholars were quick to point out. Although the examination system did create a highly literate, culturally homogeneous elite, it placed a heavy premium on tradition, rote memorization, calligraphic skill, and literary style at the expense of creative thought and independent judgment. In addition, the examiners were often capricious and occasionally corrupt. Cheating scandals plagued the system.[33]

As if this were not enough, Chinese scholars also faced the problem of limited bureaucratic opportunities once they had earned a degree. By design, only a small fraction of the empire's total number of degree holders (over a million, in the Ch'ing period) could expect to gain one of the twenty thousand or so official civil-government positions. *Chin-shih* status almost automatically placed an individual in the middle stratum of the nine-rank bureaucracy, which ranged from metropolitan posts such as deputy commissioner in the Transmission Office (rank 4A) or reader in the Grand Secretariat (rank 4B), to local offices such as circuit intendant (rank 4A), prefect (rank 4B), and district magistrate (rank 7A). But *chü-jen* degree holders could be assured of only the most minor posts, and *sheng-yüan* had very few opportunities for regular bureaucratic employment. The vast majority of *sheng-yüan* languished as "lower-gentry," enjoying certain gentry privileges to be sure, but forced to "plow with the writing brush" by teaching in local schools or serving as family tutors. Many of these individuals became small tradesmen or entered other "demeaning" occupations in order to sustain themselves.[34]

Yet for all the frustrations of examination life, with its fierce competition and tightly controlled degree quotas, the lure of gentry status and the ultimate possibility of bureaucratic service—with its rich social and financial rewards—kept the vast majority of Ch'ing scholars loyal to the system and the state. Officials, of course, had every reason to support the status quo. But the paranoid Manchus—outnumbered perhaps 100 to 1 by the Chinese—made an unrelenting effort to ensure administrative control through an elaborate system of checks and balances inherited from the Ming and refined for their own purposes.

One important check on the bureaucracy was the despotic power of the emperor, which reached new heights in the Ch'ing period. Another was the appointment of more or less equal numbers of Manchus and Chinese to head most top-level organs of government and the practice of appointing a careful mixture of Manchus and Chinese to oversee provincial administration. Typically, a Chinese would serve as a governor, while a Manchu would occupy the position of governor-general. A third check was the use of "ideologically uncommitted" Manchu Banner forces to maintain military control at the capital and in the provinces. Although outnumbered at least two to one by the 500,000-man Chinese Army of the Green Standard, the multiethnic but predominantly Manchu Banner Army forces were carefully concentrated and positioned to assure them strategic superiority over Chinese forces in China Proper as well as in Inner Asia. Their principal task was, of course, the protection of Peking and Manchuria, but the Banners also served as a check on the Army of the Green Standard, greater in absolute numbers, but more fragmented in deployment.[35]

Furthermore, military authority was carefully diffused. Although the governor-general and governor exercised administrative jurisdiction over regular provincial military forces, they had no authority over Banner garrisons in the provinces, which were commanded by so-called Tartar generals (*chiang-chün*). Furthermore, governors-general and governors shared responsibility for the Green Standard troops in the areas of their jurisdiction with a military officer entitled the provincial commander-in-chief (*t'i-tu*). As with the civil bureaucracy, the system of shared responsibilities and overlapping jurisdictions contributed to administrative stability, but often stifled initiative.

Other Ch'ing checks and balances included the effort to balance regular and irregular (i.e., purchased) bureaucratic appointments, the frequent transfer of officials (usually every three years or less), and rules prohibiting bureaucratic service in one's home province. Ironically, this "law of avoidance" had somewhat opposite the intended effect, since officials in unfamiliar areas often found it necessary to rely on clerks, runners, constables, and others who had precisely the kinds of local ties and loyalties that the avoidance rule was designed to overcome.[36]

The problem of local ties and conflicting loyalties was evident at all levels of traditional Chinese government (see also Chapters 4, 6, and 10). As Tom Metzger has noted,

> For all its stress on loyalty and hierarchy, Chinese society has been characterized by a remarkably fluid pattern of betrayal and intrigue. Individuals frequently oscillated between cooperation with the centralized state bureaucracy and support for smaller, often more ascriptive groupings, such as lineages, clubs, cliques, or secret societies, inhibiting political centralization.

Even at the metropolitan level of government, particularistic personal relationships (*kuan-hsi*) based on local affinity, educational background, and other common denominators affected the style and tone of bureaucratic politics. These relationships, as Lucian Pye and others have shown, extended well beyond what might be called the "old boy network" of acquaintances in the West and implied a much stronger sense of responsibility, obligations, and indebtedness. No Ch'ing official could afford to overlook *kuan-hsi* in political calculations, regardless of the issue at stake.[37]

The particularism of traditional Chinese society also helps explain the system of "organized corruption" within the Ch'ing bureaucracy. To be sure, in part the extraction of revenue in the form of "gifts" from subordinates can be attributed to unrealistically low official salaries and high administrative costs (see Figure 3.8 and Appendix B, which includes a note on prices). The tenure of most bureaucrats was short, and there were many expenses involved in

FIGURE 3.8. Official Salaries

Post	Annual Salary (taels)	Rice Stipend (shih)
Prince of the Blood	10,000	5,000
Duke (First Grade)	700	350
Earl (First Grade)	610	305
Count (First Grade)	510	255
Viscount	410	205
Baron	310	155
Civil official, Grade 1A-B	180	90
Civil official, Grade 2A-B	155	77.5
Civil official, Grade 3A-B	130	65
Civil official, Grade 4A-B	105	52.5
Civil official, Grade 5A-B	80	40
Civil official, Grade 6A-B	60	30
Civil official, Grade 7A-B	45	22.5
Civil official, Grade 8A-B	40	20
Civil official, Grade 9A	33.1	16.5
Civil official, Grade 9B	31.5	15.7

Source: Chart taken from Immanuel C. Y. Hsü (1975), pp. 82–83.

Note: From the early eighteenth century on, Ch'ing officials received a supplementary salary known as *yang-lien* (lit., to nourish integrity). Thus, a governor-general (grade 2A), whose salary was 155 taels, received in addition between 13,000 and 20,000 taels to encourage integrity. Similarly, at the lower ends of the bureaucratic scale, a district magistrate (grade 7A), whose salary was about 45 taels, would receive a supplement of from 400 to over 2,000 taels, depending on the locality in which he served. Even so, unbudgeted administrative costs at all levels perpetuated the system of "customary fees" (*lou-kuei*), a system that was regulated by local custom, but often led to abuses. See Ch'ü T'ung-tsu (1962), pp. 22 ff.

preparing for an official career. But another factor was assuredly the institutionalized gift giving characteristic of individuals related by some form of *kuan-hsi* or of those hoping to expand their network of useful acquaintances. Gift giving was essential to bureaucratic advancement, but the line between voluntary gifts and extortion was not always easy to draw. Even apparently honest officials derived much of their income from presents. According to the records of one late Ch'ing metropolitan official, over 30 percent of the 16,836 taels he received from 1871 to 1889 was in the form of gifts. We can assume a much higher percentage in the case of the infamous imperial bodyguard Ho-shen, favorite of the Ch'ien-lung emperor, who is said to have amassed a private fortune of some 800 million taels in the late eighteenth century.[38]

Corruption within the bureaucracy was also encouraged by the central government's chaotic fiscal system—as confused as "tangled silk" in the words of a late Ch'ing encyclopedia. Although the central government knew whether or not its prescribed tax and tribute quotas had been received from the provinces, it had no precise way of determining what sums beyond the quota had been collected and retained by provincial officials. This, together with the pressing fiscal needs and inadequate budgets of locally minded officials, fostered the widespread practice of tax farming, which often led to abuse. At the same time, the comparatively small amount of revenue received regularly by Peking made the Ch'ing government, in the words of Dwight Perkins, "an almost unbelievably weak [financial] instrument," especially in periods of dynastic decline.[39]

Another problem, common to all bureaucracies but especially acute in traditional China, was the double curse of massive paperwork and multifarious regulations. Officials could either drown in a sea of documents or be strangled by red tape. A bewildering variety of documents circulated within the Ch'ing bureaucracy, each a reflection of the relative rank of the correspondents and the type of office involved.[40] The requirements of bureaucratic protocol, and the system of shared responsibilities and overlapping jurisdictions at all levels of government, increased the volume of documents without facilitating the flow. Meanwhile, literal and tedious adherence to a vast number of minutely prescribed administrative rules and regulations imposed a crushing burden on Chinese bureaucrats.

Yet despite the elaborate checks and balances, particularism, corruption, paperwork, and overlegality of Ch'ing administration, it would be wrong to dismiss the traditional Chinese state as nothing more than a ponderous, inflexible, and inefficient monolith. Notwithstanding the Manchu preoccupation with administrative control, it is clear that in practice Peking allowed considerable leeway to local officials in the handling of affairs within their jurisdictions. Moreover, as a matter of principle many Ch'ing officials demonstrated what has been aptly characterized by Tom Metzger as a "pervasive moral commitment to flexibility."[41]

Administrative adaptations were often conceived in terms of, and legitimized by, the classical notion of "making adjustments to meet changing conditions" (*pien-t'ung*). Respected writers in late imperial China repeatedly emphasized that the essence of statecraft was in making allowances for "human situations." In the words of Wang Hui-tsu (1731–1807), the well-known author of several extremely influential works on Chinese local government, "Law must distinguish between right and wrong, but the situation may allow moderation of the strict standard of right and wrong."[42] This meant that it was always possible for an official to "bend" regulations in the interest of justice and in the best interests of the state.

Confucian morality remained the paramount consideration in traditional Chinese government—more important than either abstract law or technical specialization in the eyes of scholar-officials. But Ch'ing administration was not merely a matter of mouthing moral platitudes. Administrative handbooks, encyclopedias, and compilations on statecraft provided much concrete, practical, and valuable guidance for Chinese officials. What is more, in the evaluation of bureaucrats—whether through the annual process known as *k'ao-ch'eng* or in the triennial reckonings known as *ta-chi* (for provincial officials) and *ching-ch'a* (for metropolitan officials)—the criteria for achievement were also concrete and practical. Personal integrity (*shou*) was important, to be certain, but so were an official's ability (*ts'ai*) and administrative skill (*cheng*). And for all the Chinese government's stress on moral suasion, it also placed a premium on impartiality (*hsü*), attention to detail (*hsiang*), and carefulness (*shen*).[43]

Even emperors were evaluated posthumously in terms of specific administrative categories. One index is the organization of each major division of the *Shih-ch'ao sheng-hsün* (Imperial Injunctions of Ten Reigns), which collected various important edicts and decrees of the Ch'ing rulers up through the T'ung-chih reign and categorized them according to about forty areas of imperial concern. Taking the imperial injunctions for the Tao-kuang reign (1821–1850) as illustration, we can see that while considerable space is given to categories such as imperial virtue (*sheng-te*), imperial filial piety (*sheng-hsiao*), and improvement of moral customs (*hou feng-su*), far more attention is devoted to such categories as military exploits (*wu-kung*), fiscal administration (*li-ts'ai*), strictness of law and discipline (*yen fa-chi*), and frontier administration (*chi pien-chiang*).[44]

In all, then, Ch'ing government represented a remarkably effective balance between the emperor and the bureaucracy, civil and military rule, central control and local leeway, formal and informal authority, morality and law, idealism and realism, rigidity and flexibility, personalism and impersonality.[45] This balance gave Chinese government great strength and staying power, just as a similar set of balanced elements gave cohesiveness and continuity to Chinese social and economic life.

CHAPTER 4

Social and Economic Institutions

Ch'ing social and economic life reflected many of the attitudes and assumptions underlying Chinese political behavior—notably a concern with hierarchical order, unity and social harmony, moral suasion, bureaucratic supervision, collective responsibility, and group consensus. It also reflected the same persistent tension between the universalistic demands imposed by the state through its laws, rules, and regulations and the particularism of local customs, organizations, and personal relations. At the core of all traditional Chinese social relations was the concept of *jen-ch'ing* (lit., human feelings). As a social principle, *jen-ch'ing* implied an acute sensitivity to status obligations and an effort to bring nonfamilial relationships within the general framework of family or friendship obligations. To achieve this necessitated the use of intermediaries, or middlemen, in all aspects of political and social life—not only to preserve face but also to prevent confusion and disorder (*luan*).[1]

SOCIAL CLASSES

Traditional Chinese society was highly stratified, with status distinctions that were carefully preserved and protected by both *li* and law. At the top of the Ch'ing social hierarchy stood three main groups of hereditary nobles: (1) imperial clansmen, (2) bannermen, and (3) civil or military officials granted titles for conspicuous achievement. Each of these status groups received special allowances of property, food, and money, in addition to certain other social and economic privileges, depending on rank. In the case of bannermen, however, grants of land, rice, cloth, and money were allocated in a downward sliding scale not only for different ranks but also for Manchu, Mongol, and Chinese bannermen of the same rank.

FIGURE 4.1. Manchu Bannerman. Photo courtesy China Trade Museum, Milton, Mass.

Civil bureaucrats enjoyed enormous prestige, whether or not they possessed titular nobility. As indicated in Chapter 3, the nine-rank bureaucracy was divided into three strata—an upper level (ranks one through three), a middle level (ranks four through seven), and a lower level (ranks eight and nine). Each of these ranks (*p'in*) had two classes (*chi*), conventionally designated "A" and "B," and each rank had its own official dress, colored hat button, and other marks of status. Officials of the first rank, for example, wore a ruby button (*hung-pao shih*), a white crane (*hsien-hao*) embroidered on the breast and back of their official robes, and a jade girdle clasp set with rubies.

At the other end of the bureaucratic scale, rank nine, officials wore a silver button (*lou-yin ting*), a white-tailed jay (*lien-ch'üeh*) embroidery square, and a clasp of buffalo horn. In addition to official titles and ranks, which usually graced formal papers, family records, ancestral tablets, and tombstones, the state also granted a variety of distinctions of merit (*shang-kung*), including the right to ride horseback within the Forbidden City and the right to wear a decorative peacock feather.[2]

Government statutes distinguished between ceremonial regulations appropriate for officials (*p'in-kuan*), for scholar-gentry (*shu-shih*), and for commoners (*shu-jen*). Although officials ranked above scholar-gentry on the Chinese social ladder, in fact the two groups overlapped significantly. In marriage and mourning ceremonies, for example, the ritual stipulations for the first group applied only to officials of the seventh rank and above; lower-ranking officials performed rituals appropriate to the second group, the gentry. Moreover, in public ceremonies at the local level, holders of the *chin-shih* and *chü-jen* degrees (the upper gentry) were generally considered equivalent in status to officials of the seventh rank and therefore included in the first group.[3]

As is apparent, upper-degree holders had a social status at least as exalted as that of lower officials. Even lowly *sheng-yüan* and holders of various purchased titles such as *chien-sheng* (student of the Imperial College, the Kuo-tzu chien) enjoyed social prestige and substantial privilege. As a class, both upper and lower gentry members were entitled to special terms of address, special clothing, and other badges of rank. Degree holders wore gold or silver hat buttons, black gowns with blue borders, and luxury items such as furs, brocades, and fancy embroidery. By statute no commoners were permitted to wear these items. Gentry members also received favorable legal treatment (including immunity from corporal punishment and exemption from being called as witnesses by commoners), official exemption from labor service or the labor service tax, and, above all, easy access to officialdom, which brought additional advantages and preferential treatment. Frederic Wakeman has vividly shown how elite cultural common denominators, and not simply wealth, gave access to officials and provided the key to power holding and power wielding in traditional China.[4]

The social life of the gentry class will be treated in detail later in this book. For now it is sufficient to note the substantial outlays of money required by the extravagant gentry life-style, which often included lavish parties, large numbers of servants, and expensive hobbies such as the collecting of books and art. Fortunately for most of the Chinese elite, adequate financial resources were within easy reach. Chang Chung-li estimates that at times the gentry class enjoyed a per capita income about sixteen times that of commoners, and other scholars have written about the "huge disparity of income" between degree holders and the masses.[5]

Contrary to stereotype, the gentry class was not simply a landed elite. Although a majority of degree holders did live in rural areas and many were indeed landlords comfortably ensconced in country villas, by the early eighteenth century income derived from local managerial services (such as the mediation of legal disputes, supervision of schools and academies, management of public works and welfare projects, militia organization, and proxy remittance of peasant land and labor taxes to the district yamen clerks) began to replace landed wealth as the key economic underpinning of the gentry class—especially at the lower levels. And for those gentry who were primarily landlords, collusion with officialdom usually enabled them to pay taxes at much lower rates than the rates applied to middle or poor peasants.[6]

Below the scholar-gentry class were three broad classes of commoners. According to long-standing Chinese usage, they were ranked under scholars (*shih*) in the following order: (1) peasants (*nung*), (2) artisans (*kung*), and (3) merchants (*shang*). In reality, individuals or families in each status group could be further subdivided according to specific occupation, income, lifestyle, and local prestige. Sometimes, for example, large property holders might be accorded polite terms of address and special privileges regardless of their education; and on occasion philanthropic commoners (*i-min*) came to be considered philanthropic officials (*i-kuan*) because the government had accorded them certain privileges in acknowledgement of their generosity to the state. Similarly, upright elderly people might be officially recognized and socially honored as longevous commoners (*shou-min*) and eventually as longevous officials (*shou-kuan*). Thus, in some local ceremonies, wealthy or aged commoners could hold positions of honor and respect right along with the educated elite.[7]

Although rated second on the traditional Chinese social scale, peasants—constituting at least 80 percent of the population in late imperial times—were often exploited and were generally illiterate. Working long hours on the land, at the mercy of the elements, their chances for meaningful social mobility were slim, and many lived on the barest margin of subsistence. Tenancy was common, especially in South China. Rents were high, and rural interest rates could approach 40 percent or more per year. For lack of an alternative, peasants often found it necessary to practice infanticide, and many were forced in hard times to sell themselves or members of their families into prostitution or slavery.

Numerous local histories, official memoirs, and other accounts of the Ch'ing period attest to the harshness and brutality of the Chinese rural life. Listen to the residents of T'an-ch'eng, Shantung, describe conditions in their district during the early Ch'ing: "T'an-ch'eng is only a tiny area, and it has long been destitute and ravaged. For thirty years now fields have lain under flood water or weeds; we still cannot bear to speak of all the devastation. On top of this came the famine of 1665; and after the earthquake of 1668 not a single ear of grain was harvested, over half the people were dying of starvation, their homes were all destroyed and ten thousand men and women were crushed to death in the ruins." The district magistrate of the area later remarked, "When I was serving in T'an-ch'eng, many people held their lives to be of no value, for the area was so wasted and barren, the common people so poor and had suffered so much, that essentially they knew none of the joys of being alive."[8]

It is true, of course, that the times were not always so bad. Moreover, the term *peasant* covered a wide spectrum of rural inhabitants, from impoverished tenant farmers and itinerant farm laborers to comparatively well-to-do private landowners and petty landlords. Local economic conditions and individual resources obviously affected the outlook of the peasantry and determined in large measure the extent to which they participated in the ritualized activities and everyday indulgences of the elite. Peasants could not always afford the luxury of close adherence to gentry values, much less a gentry style of life. Nonetheless, it is evident that many characteristic features of the gentry outlook were in fact closely mirrored in Chinese peasant life. One striking indication is the general willingness of peasants to go deeply in debt in order to fulfill the ritual responsibilities of marriage and mourning (see Chapter 10).

Artisans—or, more generally, workers—ranked third on the traditional Chinese social scale. Although lower in theoretical status than peasants, artisans often earned as much, or more, income per capita. In the words of a late Ming scholar (quoted by Ku Yen-wu), "Agriculture gives a one-fold return on capital and needs the most labor of all, therefore fools do it. Manufacture provides a two-fold profit and requires a great deal of labor; clever fingers do it." During most of the Ch'ing period, artisans and laborers probably averaged between 70 and 150 cash per day, when a pound of pork cost between 30 and 50 cash, and a pound of rice cost perhaps 10 to 20 cash.[9]

A wide variety of occupational groups fell under the general designation *kung*: craftsmen such as metalworkers, carpenters, potters, masons, coffin makers, tailors, and jewelers; manufacturers of commodities such as silk, tea, paper, cooking oil, and candles; and service persons such as barbers, doctors, fortune-tellers, geomancers, tool-sharpeners, cooks, maids, and marriage brokers. Transport laborers were also considered *kung*, since even peasants avoided, if possible, this "degrading" form of manual activity. Artisans and laborers were either independent operatives or regular employees of gentry families, merchant families, or the state. Most independent artisans and laborers were members of occupational groupings known as guilds, but these organizations had little in common with their namesakes in the West.[10]

Merchants occupied the lowest position in the formal four-class structure of traditional China, at least in theory. Ch'ing writers generally identified three main types of merchants: simple traders (*tso-ku*), brokers (*ya-seng*), and wealthy consignment merchants (*k'o-shang*). Lowly street peddlers at one extreme of the commercial spectrum might barely make ends meet, but at the other end the great families of silk, tea, and salt merchants in the late imperial period often amassed huge fortunes and wielded substantial influence.

Stigmatized in the official literature as unscrupulous and parasitic, most Chinese merchants were chronically insecure. Institutionally, they lacked the power to command bureaucratic obedience: They had little protective commercial law, no political or organizational autonomy in urban areas, and no hope of operating large-scale business without official sponsorship. Yet official support could often be bought by outright bribes or through profit sharing. In many areas of China during the Ch'ing period, official and gentry families readily engaged in warehousing, usury, pawnbroking, and various lucrative wholesale and retail enterprises. Mark Elvin indicates that by the early nineteenth century, if not well before, "the more important merchants and gentry of Shanghai had become, to a substantial extent, members of the same class"; and Ho Ping-ti asserts that "in Ch'ing times the social distinction between officials and rich merchants was more blurred than at any time in Chinese history except for the Mongol Yüan period."[11] As one indication, Ho notes that the so-called Co-hong merchants engaged in foreign trade at Canton in the eighteenth and nineteenth centuries were commonly addressed by Chinese and Westerners alike as *qua*, a Cantonese corruption of the term *kuan*, or official.

Furthermore, rich merchants could generally use their wealth to acquire exalted academic-bureaucratic status. In Ming-Ch'ing times, merchants and their sons were allowed to take the civil-service examinations and to acquire official gentry rank and bureaucratic position. In the absence of effective barriers to elite status, they thus had no incentive to challenge the existing Confucian social order.

Certainly no bourgeois urban culture developed in China comparable to that of, say, late medieval Europe or Tokugawa Japan. As Frederic Wakeman points out, Chinese merchants had no distinct class manner, or life-style, of their own.

> Emulating the gentry's status manner on a colossal scale, they consumed their capital conspicuously, dissipating the possibility of more productive investments and reaffirming the hegemony of the literati's high culture. There was a uniquely mad and millionarish quality to the "salt fools" (*yen tai-tzu*) who lavished fortunes on mechanized toys, Lake T'ai rock decorations, and exotic pets, but this was just a magnified perversion of gentry fashion. And for all the squander, families like the Ma clan of salt merchants not only presided over one of the most famous literary salons of the eighteenth century and patronized many of the noted artists of the day, they also amassed private libraries of rare editions which were the envy of the Ch'ien-lung Emperor.[12]

Through association and especially education, social mobility remained a distinct possibility in Ch'ing China—certainly more so than in Tokugawa

Japan. In the Ming-Ch'ing period as a whole, we know that over 40 percent of the upper-degree holders (*chin-shih* and *chü-jen*) came from families that had not produced an office holder or upper-degree holder in the preceding three generations. It is true that orthodox channels for social mobility were not as open in the Ch'ing as in the Ming, but all classes in China continued to be attracted by the lure of the examinations until their abolition in 1905.[13]

Even peasants and artisans hungered after the carrot of social mobility offered by the examination system. The vast majority, of course, had no real possibility of attaining the necessary formal education, which was overwhelmingly private in traditional China and beyond the financial reach of most of the population. Individual tutors, private schools (*ssu-shu*), local academies (*shu-yüan*), and Confucian school-temples (*hsüeh-kung*) were all closely associated with elite education and normally sustained either by private tuition, private subscriptions, or official subsidies. The families of scholar-officials and rich merchants were naturally the principal beneficiaries of these major educational institutions.[14]

At the same time, however, some educational opportunities did exist for the poor and disadvantaged in Ch'ing China—notably charitable schools (*i-hsüeh*) and community schools (*she-hsüeh*) established by philanthropic individuals or groups. Although designed in part as a rudimentary device for the ideological indoctrination of the lower classes, such schools also provided the chance for latent academic talent to blossom. Furthermore, there were just enough Chinese-style Horatio Alger success stories to perpetuate a compelling social myth. In the words of Frederick Mote, "The belief in the active possibility of social mobility—perhaps even more than the actual statistical incidence of it—kept the different levels of cultural life coherent and congruent, if not truly identical in quality and character, for each level of life was an active model to be imitated by the one below it."[15] The examinations thus served as a powerful vehicle for the preservation and transmission of China's Confucian cultural heritage.

In addition to the four major classes discussed above, several other Chinese social groups warrant mention. One was the regular Buddhist and Taoist clergy, reported to number in the hundreds of thousands. By late imperial times, Buddhism and Religious Taoism had lost virtually all of the economic and institutional power they had once possessed. Only a few prominent monasteries, most of them Buddhist, still had substantial landholdings and large numbers of monks (four to five hundred). The great majority of the religious establishments in Ch'ing China were small, poor, and weak.

Lacking adequate financial resources, these institutions provided few social services, aside from sponsoring occasional religious fairs and feasts and putting up pilgrims for the night. Although a number of monasteries and temples boasted libraries and even printing facilities, they played no role at all in the Chinese educational system. In fact, Buddhist books were not even used in the regular curriculum of Chinese schools. The primary function of Buddhist priests and nuns in Chinese society was to undertake various ceremonies and sacrifices connected with ancestor worship and to attend to certain other religious and personal needs of males and females, respectively. Fees for these services, together with solicited and unsolicited donations from pilgrims and lay people, sustained the Buddhist and Taoist establishment. The larger monasteries and temples also derived food and rent from private landholdings.[16]

In China Proper, priests and nuns had little social standing and even less formal political influence. Aside from comparatively well educated abbots (*fang-chang*), most seem to have been illiterate and ignorant. The majority came from base origins. Many were individuals with few prospects in normal society—beggars, drifters, criminals, and so forth. Not a few had originally been sold or given to monasteries as children. Although monastic rules were often strict and detailed, apparently they were seldom followed. And if monastic discipline became intolerable, priests and nuns found it very easy to return to lay life. Given the social composition and protective environment of monasteries and temples, it is not surprising that they occasionally became havens for gamblers, thieves, and vagabonds, as well as rallying points for disaffected members of Chinese society.

Although ideologically willing to tolerate Buddhism and Religious Taoism as doctrines that "encourage what is good and reprove what is evil" (in the words of the Chia-ch'ing emperor), the Ch'ing government greatly feared the potential political power of organized religion. As a result, it imposed a number of restrictions on Chinese monastic life. Limitations were placed on the size of the clergy, the number of officially sanctioned monasteries and temples, and the scope of their religious activities. Abbots, priests, and nuns were licensed by the Board of Rites and subject to indirect state supervision. The Ch'ing government's administrative statutes contained a complete scheme of ecclesiastical gradations of rank and authority that conferred a kind of legitimacy on the religious establishment but at the same time subordinated the church to the state and officialdom. The principal supervisory officials of the church, chosen by the local Ch'ing authorities from among the leading abbots of each district and prefecture, were known as religious superiors (*seng lu-ssu* for Buddhists and *tao lu-ssu* for Taoists). These individuals provided the major link between China's secular authorities and the formal priesthood.[17]

Another prominent but disesteemed social group in Ch'ing China was the hereditary Army of the Green Standard. Unlike the Banner Army, which the Manchus originally intended solely as a fighting machine, the Army of the Green Standard by design undertook a variety of diverse and often nonmilitary responsibilities. In addition to meeting the needs of national defense and internal security, soldiers from the Army of the Green Standard provided an escort service for state funds, provisions, and prisoners; guarded granaries, tombs, and city gates; carried out government postal functions; and stood ready to undertake other designated tasks, such as providing labor for public-works projects. Unfortunately, for common soldiers the levels of pay, training, and general morale were low. Although officers of the middle grade and above were transferred regularly in the fashion of civil bureaucrats, the rank and file lived in a designated garrison area with their families for life. This arrangement had the advantage of placing soldiers in an environment where social restraints might operate to keep the men under control and where sons could learn military skills from their fathers. But it was precisely such a situation that bred vested interests and made it possible for underpaid and exploited soldiers to seek nonmilitary occupations in order to support their families.[18]

Officers for the Army of the Green Standard were supposed to be chosen from successful candidates for the military-examination system, which paralleled the civil-service examinations in both levels and degrees. But the military examinations tested physical prowess and required almost no literary ability. Although military degrees brought official gentry status, they were disesteemed by scholars and not necessary for promotion within the army itself. In fact, most officers in the Ch'ing military were not products of the military-examination system, but rather, men who had come up through the ranks. They, like their more esteemed counterparts in the civil bureaucracy, were divided into nine ranks, each distinguished by colored hat buttons, embroidered "mandarin squares," and other official regalia.[19]

With the decline of both the Banner and the Green Standard armies by the end of the eighteenth century, mercenary armies known as *yung* (lit., braves) or *yung-ying* ("brave battalions") began to shoulder the dynasty's principal military burdens. These armies were organized along highly personalistic lines and usually commanded at the top by Ch'ing civil officials. Comparatively well trained and well paid, *yung* and *yung-ying* recruits were heavily indoctrinated with Confucian morality. In the management and financing of such mercenary forces, local officials and their gentry advisers enjoyed considerable administrative leeway, but they were never beyond Peking's reach. The throne's undiminished power of appointment and manipulation of empire-wide finances prevented the emergence of "warlordism" during the Ch'ing period.[20]

At the very bottom of the Ch'ing social ladder were several groups of declassed, or "mean," people (*chien-min*). Included in this category were various slaves and indentured servants, entertainers, prostitutes, criminals, government runners, and certain regionally defined groups such as the beggars of Kiangsu and Anhwei (*kai-hu*), the lazy people (*to-min*) of Chekiang, and the boat people (*tan-hu*) of Kwangtung. Members of these and related social groups suffered various forms of discrimination, from simple prejudice to unfavorable legal treatment. For much of the Ch'ing period, mean people and their descendants could not take the civil-service examinations or intermarry freely with ordinary commoners.[21]

As a rule, the Ch'ing legal code considered mean people to be subordinate as a class to ordinary commoners, just as commoners were subordinate to officials. It followed, then, that crimes committed by mean people against commoners had to be punished more severely than crimes by commoners against mean people, just as crimes by commoners against officials brought more severe punishment than crimes by officials against commoners. In accordance with the spirit of *li*, the relative class status of offender and victim was always a central factor in determining penalties.[22]

Yet despite the depressed legal status of *chien-min* during the Ch'ing period, a few opportunities for personal advancement did exist. Like lowly eunuchs at court, certain kinds of slaves and indentured servants came to acquire substantial power. This was certainly the case with imperial bond servants such as the rich and famous Ts'ao Yin (1658–1712), reading companion and trusted informant of the K'ang-hsi emperor. But it was also true of some indentured servants (*chia-jen*) and permanent attendants (*ch'ang-sui*) attached to Chinese officials, who, like yamen runners, used their close association with government authority to protect personal investments or peddle influence. Some such servants acquired so much illicit power that they became known as officials (*t'ang-kuan*) themselves.[23]

Women also might occasionally break the shackles of traditional Chinese society, despite their low position and general lack of either legal rights or formal education. To be certain, the vast majority of Chinese women accepted the inequality of marriage or concubinage (see Chapter 10), the depressed status of prostitution, or employment in one of the humble "six service positions" (*liu-p'o*—brokers, matchmakers, sorceresses, "smooth-talkers," doctors, and midwives). A considerable number, however, became accomplished writers and painters in the Ch'ing period, including the poets Ts'ai Wan (1695–1755) and Wang Tuan (1793–1839) and the famous landscape artist Ch'en Shu (d. 1736). Some women, such as Ch'in Liang-yü (d. 1648), led Chinese troops against bandits, rebels, and foreign invaders and received official titles, and at least a few—notably Lin P'u-ch'ing (1821–1877)—played active administrative roles.[24]

FORMS OF CHINESE SOCIOECONOMIC ORGANIZATION

The social groups described in the preceding section operated day to day in a complex network of interrelationships. The context of these relationships ranged from the formal structure of the state and the informal structure of various nonadministrative urban and rural systems down to the clan and nuclear family. The Ch'ing government's attitude toward these informal institutions was characteristically ambivalent—at once supportive and suspicious—and always oriented strongly toward the concept of collective responsibility.[25]

Theoretically, the state had nothing to fear from the family, which it touted as the model for Chinese society at large. After all, the emperor acted as the father (*fu*) of his subjects (*tzu*, lit., children); district magistrates were designated "father-mother officials"; and the Chinese people as a whole were known as one large family (*ta-chia*). The problem with the family system from the Ch'ing government's point of view was that it tended to compete for the loyalties of its members with the state and that it affected in fundamental ways the conduct of political as well as social and economic relationships.[26]

The philosophical and religious assumptions that lay behind the Chinese family system will be discussed more fully in subsequent chapters. For now, it should suffice to outline the fundamental features of the system. The organization of the Chinese family was hierarchical, authoritarian, and patrilinear. The head of the household was the father, who generally passed on leadership of the family to his eldest son. The theme of Chinese family life (and social life generally) was subordination: the individual to the group, the old to the young, and females to males. Kinship terminology, which reflected specific status rights and nonreciprocal status obligations, was highly refined, with nearly eighty major kinship terms in general usage. The five basic degrees of mourning relationships (*wu-fu*), which extended outward in ever-widening circles, dictated ritual responsibilities within the family and also affected the legal decisions of the state (see Figure 4.2). In the absence of a well-developed system of protective civil or commercial law, kinship bonds were the closest and most reliable ties in traditional Chinese society, even when the relationships were far removed from the nuclear family.[27]

The Chinese nuclear family, which averaged a little over five persons in the Ch'ing period, was a self-contained and ideally self-sufficient social and economic unit. Extended families of three or more generations under one roof were comparatively rare in traditional China and confined almost exclusively to the well-to-do gentry class and rich merchants, who could afford to support a number of nonproductive family members and a large retinue of servants. In both the nuclear family and the extended family, family members were expected to live together in harmony. Responsibility for the care of the aged and infirm fell primarily on the family unit, which also disciplined and controlled its members. Social values were transmitted and reinforced by informal family instructions (*chia-hsün*), family ritual (*chia-li*), family religious practice, and the deliberate policies of the state. The enormous strength of the Chinese family system lay precisely in its multifaceted relationship to both religious and secular life.[28]

One illustration of the complexity of this relationship may be found in the practice of ancestor worship (see also Chapters 7 and 10). By late imperial times, family ancestor worship had become virtually a cultural universal in China. Even kinship-renouncing Buddhist monks were required by law to observe mourning rites for their parents. Enriched by Confucian, Buddhist,

FIGURE 4.2. The Five Degrees of Mourning (*Wu-fu*): A Simplified Picture

Degree	Appropriate apparel	Duration of mourning	Representative relationships requiring specified degree of mourning
1. *Chan-ts'ui*	unhemmed sackcloth	3 years	Mourning by a man for his parents By a wife for her husband and husband's parents By a concubine for her "husband" (master)
2. *Tzu-ts'ui*	hemmed sackcloth	1 year (or less)	By a man for his grandparents, uncle, uncle's wife, spinster aunt, brother, spinster sister, wife, son, daughter-in-law (wife of first-born), nephew, spinster niece, grandson (first-born son of first-born) By a wife for her husband's nephew and husband's spinster niece By a married woman for her parents and grandparents By a concubine for her "husband's" principal wife, his parents, his sons (by the principal wife or other concubines), and her own sons Lesser period of mourning for great-great grandparents within the second degree

3. *Ta-kung*	coarse cotton	9 months	By a man for his married aunt, married sister, brother's wife, first cousin, daughter-in-law (wife of a younger son or son of a concubine), nephew's wife, married niece, and grandson By a wife for her husband's grandparents, husband's uncle, husband's daughter-in-law, husband's nephew's wife, husband's married niece, and grandson By a married woman for her uncle, uncle's wife, spinster aunt, brother, sister, nephew, spinster niece By a concubine for her grandson
4. *Hsiao-kung*[a]	less coarse cotton than for *ta-kung*	5 months	Includes mourning by a man for his grand-uncle, grand-uncle's wife, spinster grand-aunt, father's first cousin, etc. Many more relationships
5. *Ssu-ma*[a]	plain hempen cloth	3 months	Includes mourning by a man for his great grand-uncle, great grand-uncle's wife, spinster great grand-aunt, married grand aunt, grandfather's first cousin, grandfather's first cousin's wife, spinster first cousin of grandfather, etc.

Source: Adapted from Chai and Chai (1967), 2:202–208 and tables.

[a]These last two degrees are especially complex.

Note: In all the above categories, the linkage is through the male line, so that "cousin" means only a father's brother's son, not a father's sister's son or daughter. Also, in practice the actual wearing of mourning clothes was generally considered a duty juniors owed seniors, rather than the reverse.

and Religious Taoist ideas, ancestor worship buttressed the Chinese family system not only by cementing social relationships and reinforcing status obligations but also by fostering a profoundly conservative precedent-mindedness at all levels of society. Important decisions within the family, whether made by common peasants or by the emperor himself, required the "consent" of the ancestors, and all major social events were "shared" with them.[29]

The policies of the Ch'ing government were closely linked to the practice of ancestor worship. On the one hand, the state used negative sanctions to maintain order by addressing the most compelling concerns of the ancestral cult. Rebel leaders, for example, stood the chance of having their entire families wiped out and their ancestral tombs destroyed. Punishments such as mutilation of the body (a gift from one's ancestors) and banishment (detachment from the family and natal community) were clearly designed as deterrents to the filial minded. On the other hand, the state actively supported ancestor worship as a matter of Confucian conviction. Officials were required to withdraw from duty for up to three years of mourning upon the death of a parent, and the Ch'ing legal code even stipulated that criminals convicted of capital offenses might be allowed to receive a greatly reduced penalty and remain at home in order to continue family sacrifices if they were the sole male heirs of deceased parents.[30]

Confucian family values mitigated the law in other significant ways. Punishments, for example, were meted out within the family system according to the five degrees of mourning. These relationships were based on the superiority of the senior generation over the junior generation and of the male over the female. Thus, a son who struck or beat a parent (degree 1 relationship) was liable to decapitation, irrespective of whether or not injury resulted, but no penalty applied to a parent who beat a son (degree 2b), unless the son died. Likewise, a wife who struck her husband (degree 1) received a hundred blows of the heavy bamboo, but a husband who struck his wife (degree 2a) was punished only if he inflicted a significant injury—and then only if the wife personally lodged a complaint with the authorities. Perhaps the most astonishing feature of the Ch'ing code was its stipulation that accusations— even if true—by subordinate members of a family against their superiors would entail legal punishment for the reporter. The false accusation of a father by his son was punished by strangulation, but a true report (except in the case of treason or rebellion) still brought a penalty of three years penal servitude plus one hundred blows of the heavy bamboo.[31]

The five mourning relationships extended into the lineage (or, more generally, clan, *tsu*), which reflected the same social assumptions and organizational principles as the Chinese nuclear family. Such patrilinear descent groups varied widely in size and influence, but the largest might number as many as ten thousand members and possess enormous corporate wealth. Chinese clan organizations tended to be largest and most highly developed in the southeast, well organized and widely distributed in the lower and central Yangtze provinces, but rather underdeveloped and thinly distributed in the northern provinces. Naturally enough, the social role of the clan differed substantially from place to place, but in both single-clan and multiclan villages, kinship organization invariably affected the leadership and general tenor of village life.[32]

Chinese clans, dominated in the main by prestigious gentry families but composed of all social classes, undertook social responsibilities that lay beyond the capacity of the nuclear or simple extended family. These responsibilities included providing welfare services, maintaining local order, encouraging economic cooperation, and securing educational opportunities for clan members. The educational role of the clan was particularly important, both in perpetuating the notion of social mobility and in encouraging orthodox social values.

Clan charitable schools, sustained by revenue derived from clan property, gave poor, but promising, members the chance to acquire formal education. Part of the motive may have been Confucian altruism and the desire to give meaning to the Confucian dictum that "in education there are no class distinctions." More often than not, however, the motive was probably corporate self-interest. Success in the civil-service examinations did, after all, bring prestige and usually wealth to the clan as a whole, making the investment in worthy candidates from any social class a wise one. Significantly, a number of clans expressly stipulated that educational priority be given to orphans and other poor clan members. In all, charitable schools provided perhaps the best opportunity in traditional Chinese society for disadvantaged individuals to acquire a formal education.[33]

Clans did more than simply provide formal educational opportunities. They were also an important means of transmitting elite values to all classes of society within the clan. The principal device was clan rules (*tsung-kuei*) compiled by the elite for the edification of all clan members. In the main they were Confucian in content, emphasizing family values, community harmony, ritual, respect, and self-control. Most clan rules included quotations from the classics, neo-Confucian writings, imperial injunctions (*sheng-yü*), the so-called local covenant (*hsiang-yüeh*), and other inspirational sources. Although the Ch'ing government officially charged bureaucrats, gentry, and "virtuous and reliable" community elders with the task of periodically lecturing to the Chinese populace on the Confucian moral maxims and social imperatives contained in imperial injunctions and the local covenant, it is clear that such exercises were formalistic, infrequent, and largely ineffective. Undoubtedly, regular lectures on the clan rules in clan meetings provided a much more effective channel for the communication of orthodox values to commoners, at least within the clan itself.[34]

Hui-chen Wang Liu has shown that orthodox Confucian values were often adjusted in clan rules to conform more closely to the realities of Chinese everyday life, especially the outlook of commoners. She finds, for example, that many clan rules represented a creative blend of Confucianism, Buddhism, Taoism, and folk religion. Some rules advised members to read Buddhist or Taoist religious tracts, others cited Buddhist authority for sanction, and still others went so far as to allow Buddhist images to be placed next to ancestral tablets in the clan shrine. Through such forms of accommodation, the clan rules—like vernacular literature—provided a convenient meeting point between elite and popular culture.[35]

Clan solidarity and adherence to clan rules were based in part on the clan's ability to impose on its members punishments ranging from reprimands, fines, and suspension of privileges to corporal punishment, expulsion, and even death (although only the state could legally execute individuals). Clan heads (*tsu-chang*) used the public format of clan meetings to exert enormous social pressure on members, censuring deviant behavior and rewarding adherence to group norms. Meritorious deeds might be publicly announced, recorded in special "books of virtuous clansmen," or commemorated by clan petitions to the government for honorary plaques or arches. Such plaques and other honors were displayed conspicuously in the ancestral temple, where clan meetings generally took place.

Collective ancestor worship unquestionably provided a strong sense of tradition, group cohesiveness, and conformity within the clan. The ancestral temple, which was usually the largest and most impressive clan building, was more than a mere meeting place; it also served as a constant and powerful reminder of the link between the dead and the living, the past and the present. Tiered rows of spirit tablets, sometimes numbering over a thousand, were organized by generations on the clan ancestral altar. Around them were the honorific plaques and moral exhortations left by clan forefathers that inspired moral behavior and promoted positive ambition among their posterity.[36]

In this environment many collective clan sacrifices and ceremonies took place on important occasions, such as the birth or marriage of clan sons, and on major festival days (see Chapter 10). These rites, and the clan feasts that followed, helped, in the words of C. K. Yang, "to perpetuate the memory of the traditions and historical sentiments of the group, sustain its moral beliefs, and revivify group consciousness. Through these rites and the presence of the group in its full numerical strength, the clan periodically renewed its sentiments of pride, loyalty, and unity."[37]

The state recognized the positive role of the clan in promoting orthodox values, providing social services, and maintaining local control. At the same time, however, it feared well-organized but nonofficial corporate entities. Thus, on the one hand, the Ch'ing government willingly rewarded meritorious clansmen and exhorted clans to compile genealogies and to establish ancestral shrines, clan schools, and charitable lands (*i-t'ien*). On the other hand, it sought whenever possible to make the clan system an adjunct of the official *pao-chia* local control apparatus by requiring officially sanctioned clan officers known as *tsu-cheng* (not to be confused with clan heads) to report on the affairs of their respective clans to the district authorities.[38]

Ultimately, the Ch'ing government was as unsuccessful in imposing direct control over Chinese clans as it was in exerting control over Chinese villages. This is not surprising, since clans and villages were closely related and held together with ties and loyalties that were not totally susceptible to bureaucratic manipulation. Nonetheless, the throne and local bureaucrats never abandoned their effort to limit the political and economic power of clans and to supervise closely their social activities. For all the advantages of clan organization as a self-regulating control mechanism, the particularism of Chinese blood relationships could cause formidable political problems to the state. The massive Taiping Rebellion in the mid nineteenth century, for example, which resulted in the loss of perhaps 20 million lives, had its origins precisely in the endemic clan conflict of South China.[39]

Many disputes between clans, and social tensions generally, stemmed from economic causes. Often at issue were questions of land ownership, water rights, and related agricultural concerns. Arable land remained a scarce and precious commodity in traditional China, and competition for it was fierce. Ch'ing official land records distinguished several kinds of land, including private land (*min-t'ien*), banner land (*ch'i-t'ien*), military colony land (*t'un-t'ien*), imperial estates (*chuang-t'ien*), ritual land (*chi-t'ien*), and so forth. In practice, most of the land in China was privately owned and graded for tax purposes into over twenty separate classes. Individual Chinese landholdings were generally fragmented into small plots averaging perhaps twenty to thirty *mou* (three to five acres) per family in the North and perhaps twelve to fifteen *mou* (two to three acres) per family in the South. Holdings of this size, which might be located in several different areas near a village, would barely sustain a family of five, thus forcing many peasant families to engage in household industries such as cotton spinning and weaving in order to supplement their income. In the South especially, peasant women often played a major role in both home industry and field labor, thus enhancing their economic importance and also presumably their family status.[40]

The Ch'ing system of land tenure, based on a general freedom to buy and sell land, varied from place to place, depending primarily on productivity. In China as a whole, about 30 percent of farm families were tenants (see Figure 4.3), and a further 20 percent or so were petty landowners who also worked rented land. Landlordism was much more prevalent in South China than in the North, not only because the land was more productive but also because so much property was corporately owned by wealthy clans. In the absence of primogeniture in China, private landownings were often quickly broken up; but wealth derived from corporately owned property permitted many clans to acquire and maintain economic power.[41]

FIGURE 4.3. Some Estimates of Tenancy in Traditional China

PROVINCE	LATE 1880s[a]		ca. 1920s AND 1930s[b]
	Owners (%)	Tenants (%)	Tenant Households as a Percentage of Peasant Households
Chihli (Hopei)	70	30	11
Honan			20
Shantung	60-90	10-40	10
Shansi	70	30	16
Shensi			18
Kansu	70	30	18
Kiangsu	30-90	10-70	30
Anhwei			43
Chekiang	50	50	41
Hunan			41
Hupeh	10-30	70-90	37
Kiangsi			39
Fukien	50	50	42
Kwangtung			49
Kwangsi			26
Szechwan			53
Kweichow	70	30	44
Yunnan			35
China as a whole			32.1

[a]Chang Chung-li (1962), p. 145, citing George Jamieson, "Tenure of Land in China and the Condition of the Rural Population," *Journal of the Royal Asiatic Society,* North China Branch, n.s. 23 (1888).

[b]Esherick (1981), pp. 394 ff., calculating on the basis of seven different estimates and surveys made between 1918 and 1937.

For some estimates of the purchase price of land in Chihli and land rents in Honan during the 1810s, consult Naquin (1976), appendix 3.

Clan economic resources sustained clan services, but they also generated intense rivalries. Thus, the Ch'ien-lung emperor remarked in 1766:

The ritual land attached to the ancestral halls in the eastern part of Kwangtung has frequently caused armed feuds [between clans]. . . . Ancestral halls are built and ritual land instituted normally for the purpose of financing the sacrificial rites and supplying the needs of the clansmen. If the land is used lawfully to consolidate and harmonize [kinship relations] . . . it is not a bad practice at all. But if [it induces people] to rely on the numerical strength or financial power of their clans, to oppress their fellow villagers, or even worse, to assemble mobs and fight with weapons, . . . [such a practice] surely should not be allowed to spread.[42]

The Ch'ing government's response to such abuses of power was to tighten bureaucratic supervision of clans, to punish clan leaders, and even to redistribute clan land.

Chinese landlords, whether individuals or clans and other corporate entities, extracted rents in money or in kind. These rents might amount to well over 50 percent of the yield, while official land taxes averaged only about 6 percent of the yield. In South China, fixed rents and generally longer leases encouraged farm improvements by tenants, but even in the North, increased inputs of labor allowed agricultural productivity to keep pace with population growth over the long run. Landlord exploitation varied according to place and time, but as a rule it was most acute in periods of dynastic decline and in areas where competition for land was most severe. Throughout most of the Ch'ing period, absentee landlords were a distinct minority, and the physical proximity of peasants and elites, tenants and landlords, encouraged a certain rapport (*kan-ch'ing*) between them.[43]

Although direct social contact between elites and commoners was minimal, both groups operated day to day within the shared context of a flourishing rural market system centered on one of forty thousand or more market towns distributed throughout China Proper. These market towns were linked, in turn, to higher-level markets and finally to major commercial cities. Each basic market town served as the nucleus of a marketing "cell" that typically included between fifteen and twenty-five villages, averaging perhaps one hundred households (about five hundred persons) each. This *standard marketing community*, comprising an area of perhaps twenty square miles, allowed all villagers within two or three miles of the town easy access to its periodic markets, held every three days or so. In contrast to officially registered, licensed, and taxed markets at higher levels, lower-level markets generally supported only unlicensed petty brokers, who were self-regulated and self-taxed. Although most sellers (including peasants) at any standard market were likely to be itinerants, the standard market town normally possessed certain permanent facilities, including eating places, teahouses, wineshops, and at least a few shops selling basic items such as oil, incense and candles, looms, needles and thread, and brooms. Normally the town also supported a number of craftsmen and perhaps a few crude workshops for processing local raw materials.[44]

Standard marketing communities were, in the words of G. William Skinner, "the chief tradition-creating and culture-bearing units of rural China." Every few days, "the periodically convened local market drew to the center of social action representatives of households from villages throughout the system, and in so doing facilitated the homogenization of culture within the intervillage community." The standard market town was the major rural focus of extradomestic religious life, recreation, social interaction, and conflict resolution. The marketing community contributed to the integration of local social groups, the standardization of local weights and measures, and linguistic unity. In some respects this only reinforced China's inveterate localism, but in others it promoted the spread of elite culture throughout Chinese society.

One important reason was the cultural predominance of the gentry in nearly every market town. Landlords (or their agents) regularly dealt with tenant farmers in market towns, and on market days various gentry leaders and aspirants to local leadership "held court" in their favorite teahouses, publicly dispensing wisdom and solving local problems, such as disputes among peasants from different villages. In Skinner's words, the gentry class provided "*de facto* leadership within the marketing community *qua* political system" to which virtually every peasant, petty craftsman, and petty trader in traditional Chinese society belonged. Local villages might well be administratively self-sufficient, as James Hayes has ably shown; but to the extent that villagers participated in the traditional standard market system, they could scarcely avoid exposure to gentry cultural influences.[45]

In higher-level commercial centers, and especially walled cities (*ch'eng*), the urban ecology seems to have been characterized by two principal spheres of activity—one for merchants and the other for officials and gentry. Gentry and officials tended to reside and work in or near government yamens, Confucian school temples, and other educational centers, whereas merchants tended to be situated on or near major communication routes—locations determined more by transport costs than by convenience for consumers. Sharpening the distinction between merchant and scholar-official spheres of activity in Chinese cities was the general government prohibition that merchant shops should not be located too near to the local yamen lest they "spoil its dignity."[46]

In fact, however, the mutual commercial and cultural interests of well-to-do merchants and scholar-officials lessened the gap between the two spheres of activity in China's urban centers. Furthermore, although the style of life and range of diversions in Chinese cities could not possibly be matched in standard market towns, a striking feature of Chinese culture in late imperial times was the lack of a sharp urban-rural dichotomy.

Chinese cities in the Ch'ing period were very much unlike their counterparts in medieval and early modern Europe. One difference was the direct role of the state in the supervision of urban affairs. Another was the cosmological significance of the walled city and the persistent *yin-yang*/five elements symbolism associated with it. Yet another was the absence in China of religious structures comparable in size and importance to those in Western cities. Also significant is the fact that no Chinese building was obviously datable by a particular period style. "Time did not challenge time in the eyes of a wanderer in a city street in traditional China. . . . No traditional Chinese city ever had a Romanesque or a Gothic past to be overlaid in a burst of classical renascence, or a Victorian nightmare to be scorned in an age of aggressive functionalism."[47]

But the most outstanding feature of Chinese cultural life in late imperial times was its perceptible unity along an urban-rural continuum. In the Ch'ing period, only about 25 percent of the Chinese elite had permanent urban residences. Although in their capacity as officials members of the elite necessarily resided in urban areas, the majority came from the countryside and returned to the countryside upon retirement. No significant differences existed between urban and rural elites regarding basic family structure, housing, dress, eating and drinking habits, transport, and general cultural style. Many famous centers of learning were located in rural areas, as were great libraries and art collections. Just as there was no major gulf between the capital and the provinces in the cultural life of the Chinese elite, so there was no glaring cultural distance between the city and the countryside. Differences that did exist were differences in degree or intensity rather than kind.[48]

We do see, however, a distinct set of contrasting elite attitudes toward urban-rural relations. In office, Chinese scholars tended to emphasize the civilizing functions of the city; out of office, they esteemed the purity of the rural sector. Institutionally, the elite served predominantly public interests in one capacity and primarily private interests in another. Thus a gentry member might become an upright and incorruptible district magistrate outside his native place, but then return home to the countryside to use his bureaucratic influence and social status to obtain preferential treatment in taxation and to protect kinship interests. As Frederic Wakeman remarks,

> Local social organization . . . embodied contrary principles: integration into the imperial system and autonomy from it. The dynamic oscillation between these poles created the unity of Chinese society, not by eliminating the contradictions but by balancing them in such a way as to favor overall order. The balance was expressed in ideal terms as a Confucian compromise between Legalist intervention and complete laissez-faire.[49]

We can observe a similar balance in the Ch'ing government's approach toward corporate organization in urban areas. Clan ties in Chinese cities were comparatively weak, since many, if not most, of the most influential urban residents were sojourners. There were, however, other social entities that embodied similar organizational principles, performed similar services, and posed similar problems to the state. Quite naturally the Ch'ing government tried to control them, but predictably with less than complete success.

The most important of these organizations were guilds and religious temple associations. Guilds went by a bewildering variety of names: *hang* (lit., lane), *hui-kuan* (local lodges or *Landsmannshaften*), *kung-so* (public associations), *pang* (clique or subguild), and so on. Some were simply units of professional affiliation (trade, crafts, or services); others were business organizations based on geographical affinity (*t'ung-hsiang*); still others were primarily hostels for sojourning scholars and officials from the same areas. Yoshinobu Shira's illuminating case study of Ningpo in late imperial times admirably illustrates the central importance of particularistic ties of kinship and local affinity in the economic life of Ch'ing China.[50]

Guilds operated as self-governing corporate organizations, analogous in many respects to clans. Commercial guilds, for example, disciplined their members (individuals or businesses) through normative sanctions, fines, and the threat of expulsion; they sponsored business activity and regulated business practices; they mediated disputes among members; and they attempted, when possible, to resist excessive official pressure. Significantly, guild rules were often designed to preserve a stable economic environment by keeping outsiders out and limiting competition through control of prices and even regulation of quality. Guild revenues might be derived from contributions from corporately owned land and houses, rental income, interest from bank deposits, fines, dues, and levies.

Guilds performed a variety of important social functions. Some services were extended only to members. These included financial support to individuals and families that had fallen on hard times, family-style burial services and cemeteries for those who died away from home, and sponsorship of feasts and other special celebrations. In addition, guilds and associations—sometimes in combination—often provided services for the wider urban community, such as local policing, fire fighting, disaster relief, welfare (for orphans, the aged, and the poor), health care, education, and local defense. These efforts paralleled and complemented clan-supported and independent, gentry-supported social services in both rural and urban areas—services that were more extensive than generally supposed.[51]

The Ch'ing government naturally applauded and encouraged the self-regulation and social service of guild organizations. At the same time, however, it made every effort to limit the scope of their activity and the extent of their power. One means was by supervising and directly controlling certain spheres of Chinese economic activity. The principal device was a pervasive system of formal and informal licensing, which allowed Ch'ing bureaucrats to extend monopoly rights to individual entrepreneurs or to guilds for a fee. Sometimes these monopolies were official and national in scope, such as the salt monopoly and the Co-hong monopoly on foreign trade at Canton; other arrangements were local and contingent on personal ties and informal agreements. The monopoly mentality was widespread in Chinese economic life. In John

Fairbank's memorable words, "The incentive for innovative enterprise, to win a market for new products, has been less than the incentive . . . to control a market by paying for an official license to do so. The tradition in China has not been to build a better mousetrap but to get the official mouse monopoly."[52]

The Ch'ing government relied on guild cooperation for the collection of commercial taxes, but guilds depended on official support for commercial success. Although the detailed regulation of much of Chinese trade and industry, as well as the adjustment of disputes within these spheres, fell to organizations of merchants and craftsmen, the guilds were licensed by the state, subject to bureaucratic supervision, and always susceptible to official exploitation. Even in the absence of official pressures, guilds frequently called upon the local Ch'ing authorities to validate their guild rules and occasionally to assist in enforcing them. Undoubtedly urban gentry members involved in trade acted periodically as intermediaries between merchants and officials, helping to bridge the gap between commercial and bureaucratic points of view.

Religious temples (*miao, ssu, tz'u*) in cities and towns were often closely linked with guilds and other common-interest organizations such as *hui* (associations) and *t'ang* (lodges). These societies—whether bound by ties of kinship, surname, home area, profession, scholarly interest, religious outlook, or simply mutual aid—patronized a particular deity, or deities, that protected their own special interests but that also promoted the general welfare of people living and working in the sphere of the deity's specific "jurisdiction." One common focus for such religious patronage was the local Lord of the Earth (T'u-ti kung). Devotion to this deity involved a degree of community participation as well as special interest: Neighborhood guilds, associations, and lodges often shared responsibility not only for local sacrifices and general upkeep of his temple or shrine but also for local security, neighborhood cleanup and ritual purity, and occasional entertainment such as dramatic presentations and feasts. Religious activity in these urban organizations transcended the particularism of Chinese society more effectively than did ancestor worship in clan organizations, but it was not free from risks.[53]

The state paid close attention to the religious activities of *hui* and *t'ang*. From the Ch'ing government's standpoint (and often in fact), a thin line separated "legitimate" associations and lodges from the subversive secret societies that often went by the same generic names. To the degree that *hui* and *t'ang* were secular in character and charitable in purpose they were tolerated and even encouraged by the state; but as they became more religious and political in orientation, they became more threatening.

In Ch'ing times there was no accepted Chinese equivalent for the Western term secret society. Traditionally, the expressions *chiao-men* ("sects") and *hui-t'ang* ("association lodges") were used to refer to potentially threatening politico-religious cults. In such usage, sects were identified primarily with peasant-based religious organizations in North China, while association lodges were linked more closely with politically oriented organizations in the South based on declassed elements from both urban areas and the countryside.

In general, Chinese secret societies may be defined as associations whose policies were characterized by some form of religious, political, or social dissent from the established order. When dissent became disloyalty, members of such organizations were condemned as heretical (*hsieh*) and branded bandits (*fei*). The Ch'ing code specified that leaders of "heretical organizations" were to be strangled and their accomplices to receive 100 blows of the heavy bamboo and banishment to a distance of 3,000 *li* (about 1,000 miles). Although some groups, such as the millenarian, anti-Manchu White Lotus sect, seemed especially threatening, heresy was a relative concept—in practice defined by the Ch'ing government more in political and ritual terms than in ideological or theological terms. As a result, even the Lung-hua sect, which placed great emphasis on Confucian ethics, did not always escape harsh persecution by the state.[54]

To be sure, it would be a mistake to underestimate the subversive character of certain sectarian associations, notably those of the Triad and White Lotus type. Yet in traditional China, even the most heterodox organizations were susceptible to domestication. Philip Kuhn warns against distinguishing "too sharply between . . . [orthodox and heterodox organizations] on grounds of supposed ideological differences"; and as if to underscore Kuhn's point, Frederic Wakeman suggests that the transformation of Chu Yüan-chang from sectarian leader into founder and first emperor of the Ming dynasty may well have been "eased by certain ideological similarities between rebel heterodoxy and Confucian orthodoxy."[55] Perhaps such ideological affinities, including shared ritual symbols and assumptions, may help explain the endurance of the dynastic system in the face of frequent sectarian uprisings (see also Chapter 7).

In any case, during the heyday of the dynasty, Ch'ing social institutions operated for the most part in mutual interaction and harmonious balance. There was considerable geographic and social mobility as well as a substantial amount of elite-commoner rapport within the traditional land system and market structure. The markets and fairs that brought merchants from dispersed places to a common center "fostered cultural exchange among local systems within the trading area in question," while the travels of successful scholars to far-flung places "increased their social and cultural versatility and enlarged the cultural repertoire from which they could draw upon their return home." Within their wider local market community, peasants were exposed to customs, values, and exogenous norms originating not only in other villages like their own but also in cities—cultural elements "drawn not only from other little traditions but also from the great tradition of the imperial elite."[56] In contrast to many other traditional "peasant communities," local systems in rural China were wide open when the dynasty was at its peak. Social and cultural integration in both the rural and urban sectors was substantial.

But in periods of dynastic decline, local communities in China began to close up. Resistance to exogenous cultural influences arose, and economic closure ensued. Local society became increasingly militarized, and tensions increased between elites and commoners. A *sauve qui peut* mentality prevailed. Urban-rural and gentry-peasant friction increased as gentry power grew, and landlords began to flee the countryside for the relative security of the cities, leaving rent collection in the hands of impersonal bursaries (*tsu-chan*). The rapport that had existed between landlords and tenants in better times could not possibly be maintained under such circumstances. Social services probably declined in quality and number. The state used its coercive power more ruthlessly and perhaps more arbitrarily. This was the unhappy situation Westerners encountered and described in nineteenth- and twentieth-century China. It was not invariably so.[57]

CHAPTER 5

Language and Symbolic Reference

Like Ch'ing political and social institutions, the Chinese language exemplifies both the diversity and the unity of traditional Chinese culture. On the one hand, the spoken language was fragmented into about a dozen major regional dialects, most of which were mutually unintelligible. On the other hand, the written language could be understood by anyone who had mastered it, regardless of the dialect he or she spoke. On balance, the unifying features of the language outweighed the divisive features. This chapter is concerned primarily with the classical Chinese written script, the related system of "symbolic reference" embodied in the *I-ching* (Book of Changes), and the role played by both of these media in contributing to the cohesiveness, continuity, and special character of traditional Chinese culture.

DISTINCTIVE FEATURES OF THE LANGUAGE

A discussion of spoken Chinese need not detain us long. Of the various major dialects in Ch'ing China, the most widespread and significant was mandarin (*kuan-hua*, lit., the speech of officials). Native speakers of mandarin predominated in most of north, west, and southwest China; and even in non-mandarin-speaking areas (primarily the provinces of Chekiang, Fukien, Kwangtung, and Kwangsi) scholars had every incentive to learn the mandarin dialect because it served as the lingua franca of Chinese administrators. During the K'ang-hsi period, the emperor ordered the governors of Kwangtung and Fukien to establish schools for instruction in mandarin so that officials coming from these areas would be able to communicate more effectively in audience, but neither this measure nor any other eliminated the problem of verbal communication at the local level. Since the rule of avoidance prohibited officials from serving in their home provinces, they often did not speak the dialect of the area in which they served. Legal proceedings were thus conducted empire wide in mandarin, with the awkward result that the remarks of Ch'ing magistrates often had to be rendered by "translators" into the local dialect and local testimony in turn into mandarin.[1]

Despite some regional peculiarities, the grammatical principles of spoken Chinese were (and are) the same, regardless of dialect. The basic semantic units (morphemes) of spoken Chinese are monosyllabic sounds, some which have meaning by themselves and others which have meaning only in combination with other monosyllables. For each syllable (with only a few exceptions), a written character exists, but a knowledge of the character is not, of course, necessary for comprehension of everyday speech. In mandarin, there are only a little more than four hundred individual sounds, resulting in a great number of homophones. Even with the use of four separate tones (*sheng-tiao*) as a means of differentiation, there are still many words with precisely the same pronunciation and tone. Through the use of various linguistic devices, including the joining of related morphemes, Chinese—like any mature spoken language— can express virtually any idea with full clarity. Nonetheless, the Chinese have long prized the ambiguity of their language, its musical rhythm and tone, and its marvelous capacity for rhymes and puns.[2]

Not surprisingly, Chinese scholars have traditionally devoted much attention to phonology. During the Ch'ing period, phonological scholarship flourished, beginning with the study of rhymes in classics such as the *Shu-ching* (Book of Poetry) and *I-ching*, but progressing to the study of phonetic changes in the Chinese language over time and in different regions and eventually extending to an analysis of the human voice itself. Most of the great phonological achievements of the Ch'ing period were made by exponents of the school of learning associated with Tai Chen (1724–1777) and Tuan Yü-ts'ai (1735–1815); but the critical questioning and careful scholarship of this school had its Ch'ing intellectual antecedents in the scholarship of Ku Yen-wu (1613–1682), whose valuable writings include an extremely influential collection entitled *Yin-hsüeh wu-shu* (Five Books on Phonology). Ku's approach to empirical research (*k'ao-cheng*), which emphasized originality, evidence, and utility, led to much creative and iconoclastic work in Ch'ing times.[3]

The study of phonology was only part of a broader scholarly interest in linguistics during the Ch'ing. Although some noteworthy studies, such as Tai Chen's *Fang-yü shu-cheng* (Commentary on the *Dialects*), were concerned primarily with speech and sounds, the major focus of Ch'ing linguistic scholarship was on the written language. The reasons are not hard to find. From Shang times to the Ch'ing, the classical script had been the primary vehicle for the transmission of China's entire cultural tradition. In late imperial times, familiarity with the literary language in effect defined the Chinese elite. No attribute was more highly prized, none brought greater prestige or social rewards, and none was more closely linked with moral cultivation and personal refinement.[4]

In the Ch'ing, as in earlier periods, Chinese characters had a magical, mystical quality, presumably deriving from their ancient use as inscriptions on oracle bones or on bronze sacrificial vessels. Many Ch'ing scholars traced Chinese writing to the revered *I-ching*. So venerated was the written word that anything with writing on it could not simply be thrown away but had to be ritually burned. One well-informed foreign observer during the late Ch'ing wrote:

> They [the Chinese] literally worship their letters [i.e., characters]. When letters were invented, they say, heaven rejoiced and hell trembled. Not for any consideration will they tread on a piece of lettered paper; and to foster this reverence, literary associations employ agents to go about the street, collect waste paper, and burn it on an altar with the solemnity of a sacrifice.[5]

These altars, known as Hsi-tzu t'a (Pagodas for Cherishing the Written Word), could be found in virtually every city, town, and village in traditional China.

The special reverence attached to Chinese writing may be illustrated in a variety of other ways. During the Ch'ing period an official could be degraded for miswriting a single character in a memorial to the throne, and stories of the political and personal consequences of using taboo or even vaguely suggestive characters are legion. During the Yung-cheng reign, for example, an official named Cha Ssu-t'ing (1664–1727) was imprisoned for selecting a classical phrase for the provincial examinations in Kiangsi that contained two characters similar in appearance to those of the emperor's reign title if the top portions had been cut off. This was interpreted as expressing the wish that the emperor would be decapitated. Cha died in prison, and orders were given for his body to be dismembered.[6] On a more upbeat note, inscriptions of various kinds, such as spring couplets (*ch'un-lien*), were believed to bring good luck to Chinese households and businesses, and the dissection of characters (*ts'e-tzu*) was a popular form of divination. Calligraphic scrolls adorned every gentry home, and word games, including the rapid creation of classical verse, were a favorite social diversion of the gentry class.[7]

From a scholarly standpoint, Ch'ing intellectuals looked upon the study of language as "a gateway to the classics," and they were profoundly devoted to it. In addition to works on phonology, the Ch'ing period witnessed a proliferation of linguistic studies on ancient lexicons such as the *Shuo-wen* (Explanation of Script), as well as the creation of new dictionaries and other etymological and philological research aids. One outstanding achievement was the imperially commissioned *K'ang-hsi tzu-tien* (K'ang-hsi Dictionary), ordered in 1710 and completed about five years later. This work, which became the standard Chinese dictionary for the next two and a half centuries, begins with a quotation from the *I-ching*: "The Great Commentary says, 'In ancient times people knotted cords in order to govern. The sages of a later age used written documents instead to govern officials and supervise the people.' "[8] This quote testifies to the political importance attached to the written word in China from time immemorial.

Chinese scholars have generally distinguished six major types of Chinese characters: (1) representations of objects (*hsiang-hsing*); (2) indicative characters (*chih-shih*), whose forms indicate meaning; (3) grouped elements (*hui-i*) that suggest meaning through the relationship of concepts; (4) semantic and phonetic combinations (*hsing-sheng*); (5) "borrowed" words (*chia-chieh*); and (6) "turned" or "transformed" characters (*chuan-chu*).[9] H. G. Creel points out that many of the characters designated *chia-chieh* or *chuan-chu* may also belong to one or more other word classes and that these two groups are themselves "so obscure that nearly two thousand years of discussion have not produced an agreement, among Chinese scholars, even as to the fundamentals of their application." Cheng Chung-ying contends, however, that the principles of phonetic borrowing and semantic extension expressed in these two categories reflect the inherent capacity of the Chinese written language for expressing deep, multidimensional philosophical meaning.[10]

By far the largest class of Chinese characters is that of semantic and phonetic combinations, sometimes called phonograms. Perhaps 90 percent of the lexical items in the *K'ang-hsi tzu-tien* are characters of this type. Each has a semantic indicator (radical) and a phonetic element, which can usually stand alone as an individual character. The phonetic element indicates the way a written word is probably pronounced, while the radical suggests the category of phenomena to which the word belongs. These categories include animals (humans and other mammals, reptiles, birds, fish, and mythical beasts such as dragons); parts of animals; minerals; natural phenomena and physical formations; structures; utensils; descriptives (colors, shapes, smells, and so on); and actions.[11]

Not all 214 radicals are equally helpful in indicating the meaning of Chinese characters, but most provide fairly reliable and sometimes very illuminating clues. We find, for example, that the "sun" radical (*jih* 日) together with the phonetic element *fang* (lit., square 方) represents the idea of "dawning" or "appearing" and is pronounced *fang* 昉. The same phonetic joined with the "speech" radical (*yen* 言) means "to ask" (also pronounced *fang* 訪). With the "silk" radical (*ssu* 糸) it means "to spin" (again, pronounced *fang* 紡); and with the "grass" radical (*ts'ao* 艹), "fragrant" (*fang* 芳). The limited number of sounds in Chinese, and the visual similarity between many characters, makes the written language an especially congenial medium for both aural and visual plays on words, without diminishing its capacity to create new terms and concepts.[12]

Although the written Chinese language boasts about fifty thousand characters, only a tenth or so had to be mastered for substantial literacy in Ch'ing times. As Henry Rosemont has pointed out, the major paradigmatic writings of the Chou period are based on a core vocabulary of only about twenty-five hundred separate characters. Although the Four Books and Five Classics total well over four hundred thousand characters, the *Lun-yü* (Analects) of Confucius, one of the Four Books, has only twenty-two hundred different lexical items and the classic known as the *Ch'un-ch'iu* (Spring and Autumn Annals), only about a thousand.[13]

Facility in classical Chinese has never been simply a matter of recognizing large numbers of characters; rather it has been a matter of understanding fully the wealth of accumulated meanings and associations a given term has acquired over time. Some of the most common words in the classical language have the widest range of meanings. *Ching* 經 , for example, can mean (among other things) "warp" (as opposed to "woof"); "longitude"; "vessels in a body"; "to manage, plan, arrange, regulate or rule"; "to pass through, experience or suffer"; "constant or standard"; "classical canon"; and even "suicide by hanging." *Shang* 尚 can mean "still or yet"; "in addition to or to add"; "to honor"; "to surpass"; "to proceed"; "to be in charge of"; and so on. Philosophical terms often had literally dozens of meanings or shades of meaning.[14]

Complicating matters was the absence of a formal grammar in classical Chinese. The written script did, of course, follow certain basic structural rules, but most characters did not belong to a single word class, and there were no conjugations, declensions, or other inflections. Since many individual characters could serve as nouns, verbs, or other parts of speech in different situations, word order was absolutely crucial to understanding. The expression *shang-ma* 上馬, for instance, might mean "to get up on a horse" or "a superior horse (or horses)"; whereas the reverse expression, *ma-shang* 馬上, could mean "on top of a horse" or, by extension, "immediately." Similarly, but less ambiguously, *shou-pei* 手背 denotes the back of the hand, while *pei-shou* 背手 indicates putting the hands behind the back. In the classical phrase *ming ming-te* 明明德, "to illustrate (or exemplify) illustrious virtue," the character *ming* (lit., bright) is employed in two different usages, first as a verb and then as an adjective. Thus, we find that instead of universal statements about Chinese grammar, we get statistical correlations of the following form: "in context A, character X [serves as a means] Y $n\%$ of the time." And even in the same general linguistic environment a given character may occur, say, 40 percent of the time as a noun, 30 percent as a modifier, and 30 percent in other grammatical functions.[15]

Furthermore, classical Chinese texts were normally not punctuated. Certain characters could be employed to indicate partial or full stops, questions, exclamations, and so on, but even they were sometimes ambiguous and not always used consistently and systematically. In the absence of clear-cut punctuation, the inherent ambiguity of written Chinese was amplified, with the result that classical texts were often subject to a wide variety of possible readings. This necessitated heavy reliance on commentaries and lexicons. Such works were also useful in identifying and explaining the wealth of recondite historical and literary allusions in Chinese writing, as well as the huge number of specialized meanings acquired by certain characters in different philosophical or other contexts.

In all, there was no real alternative to rote memorization and intensive tutorial assistance as a means of mastering the classical language. Beginning with specially designed primers full of Confucian moral maxims, students recited passages aloud in rhythmic fashion with no initial appreciation of meaning. By stages, these texts were carefully explained, and students then advanced to more complicated materials. By memorizing vast amounts of diverse classical literature in this way, students internalized specific patterns of characters contained in a wide variety of paradigmatic sources—patterns that became indelibly etched in their consciousness. The same painstaking approach applied to the writing of Chinese characters. Over a long period of time, and with Herculean effort, the student eventually attained the necessary skills to chart his own scholarly path.[16]

The memorization of Chinese texts was facilitated by the rhythm and balance of the classical script. Although the written language had been from early times a visual rather than a verbal medium, each character, when pronounced, was monosyllabic, and each occupied the same amount of space in a text, regardless of the number of strokes it contained. Thus each character became a convenient rhythmic unit. This naturally encouraged the Chinese, perhaps more than any other culture group, to think and write in terms of polarities. In the words of the world-famous linguist Y. R. Chao, "I venture to think that if the Chinese language had words of such incommensurable rhythm as *male* and *female, heaven* and *earth, rational* and [*ab*]*surd,* there would never be such far-reaching conceptions as *yin-yang,* [and] *ch'ien-k'un.*"[17]

But *yin-yang* and *ch'ien-k'un* (the symbolic equivalents of *yang* and *yin* in the hexagrams of the *I-ching*) were only two of a huge number of such polarities. Many, if not most, of these polarities can be correlated directly with *yin* and *yang*—an expression of the central Chinese notion that ideas are complemented and completed by their opposites. Thus we find that the *Shuo-wen* defines *ch'u* (going out) in terms of *chin* (coming in) and *luan* (disorder) in terms of *chih* (order). Distance is *yüan-chin* (far-near); quantity, *to-shao* (much-little); weight, *ch'ing-chung* (light-heavy); length, *ch'ang-tuan* (long-short); and so forth. Possession (or existence) is expressed by the terms *yu-wu* (lit., have-not have, presence-absence); and in Chinese discourse of all kinds it is common to find juxtapositions such as ancient and modern (*ku-chin*), beginning and end (*pen-mo*), difference and similarity (*i-t'ung*), loss and gain (*shih-te*), continuity and change (*yen-ko*). In these and other dualistic expressions we find a characteristic concern with the "relation of opposites" rather than with separate qualities and the "law of identity."[18]

Two things seem significant. The first is that for most Chinese polarities, descriptions such as antithesis, contradiction, and dichotomy are misleading, since the Chinese terms involved usually imply either complementary opposition or cyclical alternation. The second is that the widespread use of such polarities in both everyday discourse and formal philosophy suggests a distinctive attitude toward abstraction—one in which abstract ideas tend to be expressed in concrete terms without "dialectical" resolution into a new abstract term as in the Indo-European linguistic tradition.[19]

One index of the prevalence of polarities in Chinese writing is their frequent use in the classical literature. In the first eighty characters of the Great Commentary of the *I-ching*, for instance, there are nearly a dozen prominent *yin-yang*–style juxtapositions, ranging from man and woman (*nan-nü*), sun and moon (*jih-yüeh*), and Heaven and Earth (*t'ien-ti*) to honorable and lowly (*tsun-pei*), activity and quiescence (*tung-ching*), and good and bad luck (*chi-hsiung*). A great many other such polarities are scattered throughout the classic, and indeed throughout all major works in the Chinese literary tradition. In imperial times, lists of polarities were compiled for ease of reference, and Ch'ing documents sometimes contain as many as six sets of polarities strung together for effect.[20]

Another indication of the importance of polarities is their frequent use as subject headings in encyclopedias such as the *Ku-chin t'u-shu chi-ch'eng*. In the subcategories on human affairs and social intercourse, for example, we find many headings such as love and hate (*hao-o*), guest and host (*pin-chu*), teacher and pupil (*shih-ti*), fortune and misfortune (*kuo-fu*), and high and humble (*kuei-chien*). In the subcategory on Confucian conduct there are literally dozens of common polarities, including righteousness and profit (*i-li*), good and bad (*shan-o*), influence and response (*kan-ying*), substance and function (*t'i-yung*), knowledge and action (*chih-hsing*), names and realities (*ming-shih*), and hard and soft (*kang-jou*).[21]

Such polarities were not only semantically significant, they were also aesthetically attractive. Good prose demanded them. Consider the following examples taken from the enormously influential compilation entitled *Chin-ssu lu* (Reflections on Things at Hand):

> In the changes and transformations of *yin* and *yang*, the growth and maturity of things, the interaction of sincerity and insincerity, and the beginning and ending of events, one is the influence and the other, the response, succeeding each other in a cycle.
>
> By calmness of nature we mean that one's nature is calm whether it is in a state of activity or a state of tranquility. One does not lean forward or

backward to accommodate things, nor does he make any distinction between the internal and the external.

The difference between righteousness and profit is only that between impartiality and selfishness. As soon as we depart from righteousness, we will be talking about profit. Merely to calculate is to be concerned with advantage and disadvantage.[22]

Significantly, in the last example cited, the term *righteousness* (*i*) was substituted for the original term *humaneness* (*jen*) in order to employ a more satisfactory juxtaposition of ideas, namely, *i-li*. In translation, formulations such as those cited above often appear unsubstantial and unsatisfying, but to the Chinese reader, completely conversant with the full range of meanings and associations of a given word, term, or phrase, they were not only beautiful but also compelling.

The same emphasis on rhythm and balance in the use of polarities may be found in the use of whole phrases in classical Chinese. In the *Wen-hsin tiao-lung* (The Literary Mind and the Carving of Dragons), considered by the Ch'ing scholar Juan Yüan (1764–1849) to be the very foundation of China's "literary laws," we find the following passage in the section on parallelism:

The "Wen-yen" and "Hsi-tz'u" [Commentaries of the Book of Changes] embody the profound thought of the Sage. In the narration of the four virtues of the hexagram *ch'ien* [i.e., *yang*], the sentences are matched in couplets, and in the description of the kinds of responses evoked by the dragon and the tiger, the words are all paralleled in pairs. When describing the hexagrams of *ch'ien* and *k'un* [i.e., *yin*] as easy and simple respectively, the passage winds and turns, with lines smoothly woven into one another; and in depicting the going and coming of the sun and the moon, the alternate lines form couplets. Occasionally there may be some variation in the structure of a sentence, or some change in word order, but parallelism is always the aim.

This parallelism, in the view of the author, Liu Hsieh (c. A.D. 465–562), was as natural as the endowment of living things with paired limbs.[23]

Of the four main types of parallelism distinguished by Liu Hsieh, the most esteemed was the couplet of contrast. Liu provides an example: "Chung I, the humble, played the music of Ch'u; Chuang Hsi, the prominent, groaned in the manner of Yüeh." Both parts of the contrasted couplet refer to spontaneous expressions of homesickness, and each requires familiarity with a historical background naturally assumed by the author.[24]

Virtually all of the most influential forms of Chinese writing, from simple primers to the most sophisticated poetry and prose, employed some type of linguistic parallelism, and a good "eight-legged essay" for the civil service examinations could not, of course, be written without it. Four-character phrases were especially common. The great majority of Chinese fixed expressions, or aphorisms (*ch'eng-yü*), whether derived from the classics, poetry, or popular literature, consisted of four characters. Four-character expressions are particularly prevalent in classics such as the *Shih-ching* and *I-ching*, but they also are employed in many Chinese folk sayings. Indeed, the succinctness, balance, and rhythm of the classical Chinese language made it eminently well suited for popular proverbs, which helped bridge the gap between the mental world of the Confucian elite and the Chinese masses.[25]

The use of balanced phrases in prose often required considerable stylistic manipulation in the form of either expansion through the addition of superfluous, or empty (*hsü*), characters, or ruthless contraction. Succinctness was always esteemed. As Victor Purcell has observed,

> The rule is, if you can possibly omit, do so. The result may be that the meaning is quite hidden, but the reader is supposed not only to have an encyclopaedic knowledge to assist him in his guesswork, but to have unlimited time for filling in ellipses. This does not mean that the language has no words to fill in the ellipses, or that there are no words to convey tense, number or mood. It merely means that the spirit of the language is against their use.

Many other authorities, Western and Chinese, have made the same basic point.[26]

The brevity and grammatical flexibility of classical Chinese have been compared to modern telegrams and newspaper headlines, but the parallel can be taken no further. Rhythm, poetic suggestiveness, and economy of expression were not simply convenient means in China but rather literary ends. Chinese authors regularly and happily sacrificed precision for style, encouraging an intuitive as well as an intellectual approach to their work.[27]

Although Ch'ing scholars distinguished between learning (*hsüeh*) and thinking (*ssu*) and between erudition (*po*) and grasping the essence (*yüeh*), neo-Confucian "rationalism" did not on the whole involve a conscious exaltation of reason over intuition. Indeed, Chinese thinkers often showed a marked preference for the latter—perhaps in part because the brevity, subtlety, and suggestiveness of the classical language encouraged an intuitive approach to the most profound understanding. A. C. Graham rightly observes that the Chinese have generally been most impressed by "the aphoristic genius which guides thought of the maximum complexity with the minimum of words, of which the *Tao-te ching* [The Way and Its Power] presents one of the world's supreme examples."[28]

LANGUAGE AND CULTURE

What else does the classical language tell us about traditional Chinese patterns of perception and thought? Certainly it provides important clues regarding elite social attitudes. We see, for example, that the classical language is extraordinarily rich in kinship terminology, indicating an intense and pervasive concern with family relationships. The early Chinese lexicon known as the *Erh-ya*, which dates from the pre-Christian era, contains over one hundred specialized kinship terms, most of which have no counterpart in English. Later works of a similar nature, including those by Ch'ien Ta-hsin (1727–1804), Liang Chang-chü (1775–1849), and Cheng Chen (1806–1864) in the Ch'ing period, continued to place special emphasis on the highly refined nomenclature of family relationships. Even the works on local dialects by scholars such as Hang Shih-chün (1696–1773) and Ch'ien Tien (1744–1806) devote inordinate attention to kinship terms and their variants. The great Ch'ing encyclopedia *T'u-shu chi-ch'eng* includes two large subcategories—one on clan and family names and one on family relationships—that together account for 756 of the encyclopedia's total of 10,000 *chüan*. Although not all of this material is related directly to kinship nomenclature, it does indicate the central significance of the family in traditional Chinese society.[29]

Chinese kinship terminology underscores the importance of social distinctions based on age and sex. A Chinese writer in traditional times (and in fact more recently) could never, for example, simply refer to another person as "cousin." He (or she) would have to employ a much more specific term that distinguished between male and female gender, between paternal and maternal affinity, and between relative age. Thus, a male cousin on the father's side older than oneself would be referred to as *t'ang-hsiung*, a male cousin on the father's side younger than oneself as *t'ang-ti*, a male cousin on the mother's side older than oneself as *piao-hsiung*, and so on for five other types of cousins.

Similar distinctions were obligatory for other members of both the male line, or *nei-ch'in* (lit., inner relationship), and the female line, or *wai-ch'in* (lit., outer relationship). This latter category was further divided into the subcategories of mother's kin (*mu-tang*), wife's kin (*ch'i-tang*), and daughter's kin (*nü-tang*). These and other status distinctions were carefully preserved and expressed in the ritual vocabulary of the five mourning relationships discussed briefly in Chapter 4. In practice, of course, the ritual requirements of mourning might be modified or ignored, especially if they involved distant relatives or mourning for junior family members by their seniors. But while the rituals might not always be strictly observed, the relationships were seldom forgotten.[30]

Other linguistic evidence may be adduced for the special importance of kinship identifications in Chinese society, as well as for the principle of the subordination of the individual to the larger social group. Derk Bodde writes, for example, that "the Westerner asserts his ego by placing his personal name first, then his family name" (John Jones rather than Jones John), whereas the Chinese does just the reverse (Sun Yat-sen rather than Yat-sen Sun). Further, Bodde notes, "The Westerner unthinkingly speaks and writes in terms of 'I' and 'you.'" The Chinese (in the past, much less now) tended to avoid such direct address by using instead indirect locutions in the third person, such as "humble person" (referring to self) and "sir" or "gentleman" (referring to the other person).[31] Among the major honorific terms in traditional China—used both within and outside the family—were *ling* ("excellent" or "illustrious"), *tsun* ("honorable"), *hsien* ("virtuous"), *kuei* ("exalted"), and *ta* ("great"). *Yü* ("simple" or "stupid") and *hsiao* ("small" or "inferior") were commonly used in self-deprecation. Naturally enough, usage varied according to the relationship. Thus, while a man might speak of his wife as "the mean one of the inner apartments" (*chien-nei*), a guest of the household would refer to her as "the honorable one of the inner apartments" (*tsun-nei*) or "your honorable wife" (*tsun-k'un fu-jen*).[32]

The question of the place of women in traditional Chinese society is an intriguing one. On first glance, the large amount of space devoted to women (*kuei-yüan*, lit., beauties of the female living quarters) in the *T'u-shu chi-ch'eng* (376 *chüan*) would indicate a more exalted status than is generally supposed; and, as we have seen, a number of women during the Ch'ing period, as in earlier times, achieved considerable distinction. But in the main, the individuals discussed in the encyclopedia are distinguished less by their personal accomplishments than by their exemplary Confucian virtues—notably female chastity. Of all the various subsections on women, by far the largest is "Widows Who Would Not Remarry" (*kuei-chieh*, 210 *chüan*), followed by "Women Who Preferred Death to Dishonor" (*kuei-lieh*, 74 *chüan*). By contrast, 7 *chüan* are devoted to women writers (*kuei-tsao*), 4 to wise women (*kuei-chih*), and only 1 each to artistic women (*kuei-ch'iao*) and witty women (*kuei-hui*).[33] It is also interesting to note the relatively large number of Chinese characters with the "female" radical (*nü* 女) that have decidedly pejorative connotations, including *chien* [奸] (villainous), *fang* [妨] (to hinder), *tu* [妒] (to be jealous), *nu* [奴] (slave), *mei* [媚] (to flatter), and *chien* [姦] (licentious). It is true, of course, that a number of very positive terms also contain the *nü* radical, but most of these have to do with feminine beauty or traditional female roles and relationships. In any case, such associations, both positive and negative, were undoubtedly more obvious to the visually oriented, language-conscious Chinese than are the few vaguely comparable expressions in modern English such as *sissy*.

There are other significant ways in which the Chinese language reflects basic cultural attitudes. Chang Tung-sun has pointed out, for example, that the language is extraordinarily rich in ethical terms and concepts, indicating

China's long-standing preoccupation with moral values. Fung Yu-lan, for his part, suggests that the traditional use of expressions for the world such as *T'ien-hsia* ("all under Heaven") and *ssu-hai chih nei* ("all within the four seas") reflects a decidedly continental orientation very much unlike the outlook of the ancient maritime Greeks. And Chang Kwang-chih has employed a sophisticated analysis of early Chinese texts and terminology to support his contention that the Chinese are "probably among the peoples of the world most preoccupied with eating." Overall, however, the study of the Chinese language and its cultural implications is still in its infancy, especially in the West.[34]

On the other hand, the relationship between the Chinese language and formal philosophy has been much discussed by both Western and Chinese scholars. Clearly Chinese language and thought enjoyed a mutually supporting, mutually enriching relationship. Yet it may be argued that classical Chinese had an especially significant impact on the development of Chinese philosophy, not only because it endured so long as a living language (a point we shall take up later), but also because of the striking visual properties of the characters themselves.[35]

While the ambiguity of the Chinese language may have encouraged an intuitive approach to understanding, it is also evident that the ideographic features of the script led to thinking along concrete, descriptive lines. Many scholars have observed that classical Chinese is relatively poor in resources for expressing abstractions. Thus, the idea of "Truth" tended to devolve into something like "that which is true"; and "Man" into "the people" (general, but not abstract). "Hope" was difficult to abstract from the notion of "a series of expectations directed toward specific objects."[36] Yet it certainly cannot be said that the Chinese lacked the capacity to think abstractly. What can be said is that the Chinese tended to view the abstract and general in terms of the concrete and the particular. The *I-ching*, as Cheng Chung-ying has observed, is an especially apt illustration of this particular attitude or orientation. In the highly refined symbolic system of the *I-ching*, philosophical principles are "embodied in concrete instances of things and their relations." Viewing the matter from a somewhat different perspective, we might say that universal or abstract principles have been significant to the Chinese only when realized or revealed in concrete things and particular contexts.[37] This may help account for the practical orientation of so much of Chinese philosophy and for the general lack of speculation for speculation's sake in China.

Another prominent feature of Chinese philosophy, already alluded to, may also be explained by reference to the classical language: the strong emphasis on what has been variously called relational, associational, or correlative thinking. Traditionally the Chinese have been less concerned with ontology or epistemology than with an analysis of relations among and between things, events, concepts, and qualities. Chu Yu-kuang believes that the emphasis on word relations in Chinese is "probably correlated with relational thinking in many areas of Chinese life and culture." We have already noted Cheng Chung-ying's use of the *I-ching* as an illustration of Chinese relational thinking; other Chinese and Western scholars, such as Chang Tung-sun and Joseph Needham, also have used the ancient classic to make the same important point.[38]

China's *yin-yang*–oriented "logic of correlative duality" (to borrow Chang Tung-sun's felicitous phrase) certainly differed from classical Aristotelian logic in the West. Yet it must be stressed that this does not mean that the Chinese lacked the capacity to reason "logically." Many authorities—Westerners as well as Chinese—have demonstrated with abundant documentary evidence that logical rigor was possible, and even prominent, in certain types of Chinese philosophical discourse. Overall, however, it is true that the structure of the Chinese language, the aesthetics associated with it, and the penchant for relational thinking among the Chinese made some forms of argumentation far more appealing and persuasive than others. This helps explain, for example, the powerful Chinese preference for argument by analogy and the widespread use of numerical categories and correlations in all kinds of philosophical writing.[39]

Although *yin-yang* dualism lay at the heart of Chinese relational thinking, most Chinese numerical categories involved groups of more than two. Most of these were odd (*yang*) numbers—notably threes, fives, and nines. Thus, we find in Chinese philosophical writing (and in daily discourse) repeated references to the "three sovereigns" (Fu-hsi, Shen-nung, and Huang-ti), the "three teachings" (Confucianism, Buddhism, and Taoism), the "three obe-diences" (subject to sovereign, son to father, and wife to husband—relationships more commonly referred to as the three bonds), the "three powers" (Heaven, Earth, and Man), the "three [types of womanly] dependence" (on father, husband, and son), and so forth. In all, over three hundred different numerical correlations or associations were current in Ch'ing times, ranging from groups of two or three (there were about seventy for the number three alone) to groups of one hundred or more. Such categories not only identified certain important relationships but also served as a convenient philosophical "shorthand." Like the concepts *yin* and *yang*, with which they were invariably correlated, numbers indicated hierarchy and precedence, expressed in a highly formalistic style.[40]

Correlational thinking, together with an emphasis on balance and rhythm (and the attractiveness of puns) in the Chinese language, helps explain the popularity of four-character philosophical "definitions" of the following sort: *jen-che jen-yeh* ("*jen* [humaneness] means to be human [*jen*]"); *i-chih i-yeh* ("*i* [righteousness or duty] means what is appropriate [*i*]"); and *cheng-che cheng-yeh* ("*cheng* [government] means what is correct [*cheng*]"). Henry Rosemont argues that the advantage of such formulations is that they allowed a Chinese thinker to "maintain the semantic richness of his general terms and their relational representations yet unpack them when necessary—with or without logical explicitness—to elaborate one of their specific significations."[41]

This relational, or associational, process, so prominent in the classical language, was also central to the process of the *I-ching*—described by one modern Chinese authority as "the detection of analogous precepts, concepts and ideas in interrelated symbols, and a synthesis of them into more elaborate metaphysical or ethical notions."[42] In the following chapters we will take up the place of the *I-ching* in Chinese cosmology, ethics, divination, and popular religion, but here we are concerned with the classic as a supplementary system of Chinese language, or to use Alfred North Whitehead's term, of "symbolic reference."[43]

The authority of the *I-ching* in late imperial China is seldom fully appreciated. Consider, however, the following quotation from the famous *Chin-ssu lu*, described by one scholar as "unquestionably the most important single work of philosophy produced in the Far East during the second millennium A.D.": "The *I-ching* is comprehensive, great and perfect. It is intended to bring about accord with the principle of [human] nature and destiny, to penetrate the causes of the hidden and the manifest, to reveal completely the nature of things and affairs, and to show the way to open up resources and to accomplish great undertakings."[44] In a similar vein, the great Ch'ing scholar Wang Fu-chih (1619–1692) wrote:

> It [the *I-ching*] is the manifestation of the Heavenly Way, the unexpressed form of nature, and the showcase for sagely achievement. *Yin* and *yang*, movement and stillness, darkness and brightness, withdrawing [*ch'ü*] and extending [*shen*]—all these are inherent in it. Spirit [*shen*] operates within it; the refined subtlety of ritual and music is stored in it; the transformative capacity of ghosts and spirits [*kuei-shen*] emerges from it. The great utility [*ta-yung*] of humaneness and righteousness issues forth from it; and the calculation of orderliness or chaos, good or bad luck, life or death is in accordance with it.[45]

Throughout the Ch'ing period, as Toda Toyosaburo's admirable research has shown, the *I-ching* remained a sacred work of nearly unchallenged scriptural authority, serving not only as a moral guide to action but also as a rich source of concepts and symbols.

According to Confucius (as cited in the Great Commentary of the *I-ching*), "Writing cannot express words completely. Words cannot express thoughts completely. . . . The holy sages set up images [*hsiang*] in order to express their thoughts completely; [and] they devised the hexagrams [*kua*] in order to express the true and false completely." In other words, to the Chinese the hexagrams of the *I-ching* represented symbolically the images or structure

1 kua	2	3	4a	4b	5	6	7	8	9	10	11	12	13	14	15	16
1 ☰	Ch'ien	乾	♂	father	dragon, horse	heaven	metal	S	NW	late autumn	early night	king	deep red	head	Being, strength, force, roundness, expansiveness	Donator
2 ☷	K'un	坤	♀	mother	mare, ox	earth	earth	N	SW	late summer, early autumn	afternoon	people	black	abdomen	Docility, nourishment of being, square-being, form, concretion	Receptor
3 ☳	Chen	震	♂	eldest son	galloping horse, or flying dragon	thunder	wood	NE	E	spring	morning	young men	dark yellow	foot	Movement, speed, roads, legumes and young green bamboo sprouts	Stimulation, excitation
4 ☵	K'an	坎	♂	second son	pig	moon and fresh water (lakes)	water	W	N	mid-winter	mid-night	thieves	blood-red	ear	Danger, precipitousness, curving things, wheels, mental abnormality, abyss	Flowing motion (especially of water)
5 ☶	Ken	艮	♂	youngest son	dog, rat, and large-billed birds	mountain	wood	NW	NE	early spring	early morning	gate-keepers	—	hand and finger	Passes, gates, fruits, seeds	Maintenance of stationary position
6 ☴	Sun	巽	♀	eldest daughter	hen	wind	wood	SW	SE	late spring, early summer	morning	merchants	white	thigh	Slow steady work, growth of woods, vegetative force, mercantile talent	Penetration, mildness, continuous operation
7 ☲	Li	離	♀	second daughter	pheasant, toad, crab, snail, tortoise	lightning (and sun)	fire	E	S	summer	midday	amazons	—	eye	Weapons, dry trees, drought, brightnesses, catching adherence of fire and light	Deflagration, adherence
8 ☱	Tui	兌	♀	youngest daughter (concubine)	sheep	sea and sea water	water and metal	SE	W	mid-autumn	evening	enchantresses	—	mouth and tongue	Reflections and mirror-images, passing away	Serenity, joy

Key: 1=lines; 2=romanization; 3=Chinese character; 4a="sex" of the trigram; 4b=position within the family; 5=associated animal; 6=associated object or "emblem"; 7=associated element; 8=associated compass point; 9=associated compass point (later sequence than 8); 10=associated season; 11=time of night or day; 12=type of human being; 13=color; 14=part of the body; 15=primary concept or virtue of the trigram; 16=secondary concept.

FIGURE 5.1. The Primary Trigrams and Their Associations. Taken from Needham (1956), 2:312. Cf. 2:314 ff. in the same source (on the hexagrams).

of changing situations in the universe and as such were believed to have explanatory value, if correctly interpreted. Like Chinese characters, these hexagrams were a distinctly visual medium of communication, concrete but ambiguous, with several possible levels of meaning as well as a great many accumulated allusions and associations. To a greater extent than Chinese characters, however, the hexagrams came to acquire abstract significations.[46]

The basic text of the *I-ching* consists of sixty-four hexagrams, each individually named and composed of six solid (*yang,* ———) or broken (*yin,* — —) lines in various combinations, together with written decisions (*t'uan*) and appended judgments (*hsi-tz'u* or *hsiao-tz'u*) for each. The decisions are short paragraphs that explain the overall symbolic situation represented by a given hexagram. The appended judgments characterize each of the six lines in turn and usually indicate a process leading from a beginning stage (line one, at the bottom of the hexagram), to a developmental stage (lines two through five), and on to an ending or transitional stage (line six). These lines also form a pair of individually named primary trigrams juxtaposed within each hexagram. There are eight possible primary trigram configurations (see Figure 5.1). According to the theory of the *I-ching*, the interpretation of various interrelated lines, trigrams, and hexagrams and an appreciation of the changes they undergo and represent in certain concrete circumstances will clarify the structure of human experience and, in the process of divination, illumine the future.

The so-called Ten Wings of the *I-ching*, traditionally attributed to Confucius, amplify the basic text and invest it with additional symbolism and multiple layers of meaning. Together, through the use of colorful analogies, metaphors, and other forms of imagery, these poetic commentaries elucidate the structure and significance of the hexagrams in terms of individual lines and constituent trigrams as well as other hexagrams. Further, they provide a moral dimension to the *I-ching* and a solid metaphysical foundation based on *yin-yang*/five-elements principles and an elaborate numerology. The metaphysics and numerology of the *I-ching* were communicated to all levels of society during the Ch'ing period by means of fortune-tellers, almanacs, and devices such as the *Ho-t'u* (River Chart) and *Lo-shu* (Lo Writing).[47]

Although a fundamental assumption of the *I-ching* has always been the mutual interaction or interrelationship of all of its constituent hexagrams, the two most important points of symbolic reference in the classic were clearly the hexagrams *ch'ien* ("the creative") and *k'un* ("the receptive"). At the most basic level of symbolism, *ch'ien* and *k'un* represented Heaven and Earth in microcosm, as well as the generative power and potential of *yang* and *yin*, respectively. As *yin-yang* conceptual categories, these hexagrams automatically assumed all of the attributes associated with these two sets of relations, including the numerical correlations of odd and even. In addition, *ch'ien* and *k'un* acquired the associations of their constituent trigrams. Among *ch'ien*'s various attributes were thus roundness, spirituality, straightness, the color red, and the cutting quality of metal. By contrast, *k'un* came to be associated with squareness, sagacity, levelness, the color black, and the transport capacity of a large wagon. Over time, *ch'ien* and *k'un*, and to a lesser extent the other sixty-two hexagrams derived from them, became rich repositories of diverse symbols, similar to variables in symbolic logic. As substitutes for various classes of objects, the hexagrams, individual trigrams, and even single lines had wide-ranging explanatory value. Fung Yu-lan writes, for example, "Everything that satisfies the condition of being virile [*yang*] can fit into a formula in which the symbol *ch'ien* occurs, and everything that satisfies the condition of being docile [*yin*] can fit into one in which the symbol of *k'un* appears." In the simplest terms, this means that if one seeks an understanding of the role and place of, say, a ruler or a father (a *yang* relationship), he consults the hexagram *ch'ien* and its associated commentaries; and if he seeks an understanding of the role and place of a subject or a son (a *yin* relationship), he must consult the hexagram *k'un* and its commentaries.[48]

But the process of consulting the *I-ching* for insight and guidance, whether in divination or in the course of general study, was usually far more complex. As already indicated, the very structure of the *I-ching*, with its *yin-yang* style reconciliation of opposites, its cryptic language, multiple symbols, layers of meaning, and elaborate patterns of relationship among lines, trigrams, and hexagrams, militated against facile explanations except by the simple minded. As the K'ang-hsi emperor once remarked, "I have never tired of the *Book of Changes*, and have used it in fortune-telling and as a book of moral principles; the only thing you must not do, I told my court lecturers, is to make this book appear simple, for there are meanings here that lie beyond words." Even with the aid of the major classical commentaries and some two thousand years of intensive scholarship on the *I-ching*, the interpretive possibilities of any hexagram were nearly inexhaustible—not only because it was assumed that the universe and human circumstances were in a state of perpetual flux, but also because a given hexagram never stood alone, in a vacuum. At the very least, consultation of one hexagram demanded consultation of its opposite.[49]

The symbols of the *I-ching* were deemed useful for more than elucidating the nature of human affairs, although this was their primary function. They were also employed as evaluative categories in Chinese history, literature, and art. The Ch'ing scholar Chang Hsüeh-ch'eng (1738–1801), for example, used the symbolism of *ch'ien* and *k'un* in comparing the "round and spiritual" writing of the early Han historian Ssu-ma Ch'ien (c. 145 B.C.–c. 90 B.C.) to the "square and sagacious" writing of his successor Pan Ku (A.D. 32–A.D. 92). Similarly, the author of the early Ch'ing painting manual entitled *Chieh-tzu-yüan hua-chuan* (Mustard Seed Garden Manual) employed not only the vocabulary but also the numerical symbolism of the *I-ching* in a tour de force of artistic criticism.[50]

The symbolism of the *I-ching* also reportedly inspired invention. According to the Great Commentary, many fundamental features of traditional Chinese civilization, from writing and burial customs to administrative practice and agriculture, were inspired by certain relationships inherent in a dozen or so different hexagrams. What is more, the Great Commentary suggests that the forms and symbols of the *I-ching* should continue to serve as a guide to the invention and manufacture of implements and utensils.[51]

Not surprisingly, the symbols of the *I-ching* were often used to explain natural phenomena—especially since, in the words of the influential Sung scholar Ch'eng I, the classic included all things, "from heaven, earth, the hidden [i.e., the supernatural] and the manifest [human affairs] to insects, plants, and minute things." From late Han times through the Ch'ing, Chinese scholars repeatedly cited the *I-ching* in order to support their theories regarding not only social and ethical relationships but also cosmology, science, and technology. Many considered the binary number system of the *I-ching* to be the basis for all mathematics, and most employed trigrams and hexagrams to categorize and evaluate physical properties and natural processes, as well as human affairs.[52]

As scientific symbols, the hexagram *sun* ("the gentle," "the penetrating," "the wind") was commonly identified with the phenomenon of human respiration; *i* ("the corners of the mouth," "nourishment") with nutrition; and *kuan* ("contemplation," "view") with vision. Such identifications often went beyond simply equating natural phenomena with the "name" of a hexagram. Efforts were also made to explain the identification in terms of the attributes of the hexagram's constituent trigrams. Thus, the Ming scholar Wang K'uei observed, "The upper eyelid of human beings moves, and the lower one keeps still. This is because the symbolism of the hexagram *kuan* embodies the idea of vision. Windy *sun* [a trigram] is moving above, and earthly *k'un* [also a trigram] is immobile below." His explanation of *i* as a symbol for nutrition is similar, for although the two constituent trigrams of *i* are different from those for *kuan*, the lower one (*chen*, "thunder") represented to Wang the movement of the lower jaw in eating, while the upper one (*ken*, "mountain") indicated immobility. It may be added that these explanations do not represent the conventional interpretations given to the constituent trigrams in either of the two examples cited.[53]

Whole hexagrams could be juxtaposed to indicate various "natural" relationships. As indicated earlier, *ch'ien* and *k'un* were widely used to represent all kinds of *yin-yang* relations and attributes, as well as the generative powers these two terms implied. In similar fashion, the *yin* symbol *k'an* ("the abysmal," "water") and the *yang* symbol *li* ("the clinging," "fire") quite naturally served as scientific terms in a wide variety of realms, from chemistry to biology. Further, many Chinese scholars viewed the trigrams and hexagrams of the *I-ching* not only as abstract formulations but also as "invisible operators," factors that actually caused or controlled situations. This also came to be believed of a few individual characters associated with certain specific hexagrams. Yen Yüan (1635–1704), for example, constructed an elaborate cosmology based on each of the first four characters of the "decision" on the hexagram *ch'ien*—*yüan, heng, li*, and *chen*. In his view, the operation of *yin* and *yang* produced the "four powers" of originating growth (*yüan*), prosperous development (*heng*), useful advantage (*li*), and correct perseverance (*chen*). In Yen's cosmology, these "four powers" occupied the position usually held by the five elements in conventional Chinese cosmology (see next chapter).[54]

Joseph Needham blames the *I-ching* for inhibiting the development of Chinese science:

> I fear that we shall have to say that while the five-element and two-force [*yin-yang*] theories were favourable rather than inimical to the development of scientific thought in China, the elaborated symbolic system of the *Book of Changes* was almost from the start a mischievous handicap. It tempted those who were interested in Nature to rest in explanations which were no explanations at all. The *Book of Changes* was a system for *pigeon-holing novelty* and then doing nothing about it. . . . It led to a stylisation of concepts almost analogous to the stylisations which have in some ages occurred in art forms and which finally prevented painters from looking at Nature at all.[55]

Needham's judgment is perhaps too harsh, since China made many noteworthy scientific advances well after the *I-ching* had acquired the exalted status of a classic. Nonetheless, it is true that the great authority and convenient bureaucratic classifications of the work made it relatively easy for Chinese scholars to accept its symbols as irrefutable expressions of universal truths.

Needham asserts that the negative influence of the classical Chinese language on Chinese scientific thought has been vastly exaggerated, and he argues correctly that the limits to China's scientific development must be attributed primarily to nonlinguistic factors. Yet there can be little doubt that the poetic Chinese language was not the most congenial medium for the expression of precise scientific ideas. Needham himself has remarked upon the "unfortunate" tendency of the Chinese in premodern times to employ ancient words for scientific concepts rather than to develop a new scientific terminology. Part of the problem was undoubtedly China's inability to draw upon Greek, Latin, and Arabic roots in the manner of Western (European) scientists, but it is also clear that the unique style of Chinese writing continued to be a hindrance, as did the convenient symbolism of the *I-ching*.[56]

Understandably, the classical Chinese language did not provide particularly fertile soil for the independent growth of foreign ideas. Arthur Wright has discussed in detail the many problems of translation facing proponents of foreign concepts in China, from the Buddhist missionaries in the Six Dynasties period to the Jesuits and other Christian missionaries during the Ch'ing. Time and again factors such as the semantic "weight" of Chinese characters—whether used as conceptual equivalents or merely in transliteration—tended to affect the meaning of the original foreign ideas. Thus, the classical Chinese script contributed to the cohesiveness and continuity of Chinese civilization by helping to sinicize alien and potentially disruptive doctrines.[57]

The classical language contributed to cultural continuity and cohesiveness in two other important ways. First, it established a direct linguistic link between the Chinese present and a distant, but not forgotten, Chinese past. Since the ancient classics and contemporary documents were all written in the same basic script, a Ch'ing scholar had immediate intellectual access to anything written in China during the past two thousand years. The language remained alive and well, part of a long-standing and still vital literary tradition and cultural heritage. Second, the script gave tremendous cultural unity to China across space. Because each Chinese character had the same basic set of meanings and associations, regardless of how it may have been pronounced, the literary language transcended the hundreds of local dialects scattered throughout the country, many of which were otherwise mutually unintelligible. There was thus no development in China comparable to the decline of Latin and the rise of national vernaculars in Europe. There was only the glaring fact that until well into the nineteenth century the Japanese, the Koreans, and the Annamese all continued to use classical Chinese as the principal means of written communication. This, of course, only fed China's already well-nourished sense of cultural superiority.[58]

CHAPTER 6

Thought

The most striking feature of traditional Chinese thought as a whole is its extraordinary eclecticism, its ability to tolerate diverse and sometimes seemingly incompatible notions with little sense of conflict or contradiction. In part, this remarkable integrative capacity can be explained by the powerful Chinese impulse to find unity in all realms of experience, human and supernatural. It also can be attributed to the long-standing Chinese idea of *yin-yang* reconciliation of opposites—an outlook vividly expressed in late imperial times by the neat phrase *san-chiao ho-i* ("the three teachings [of Confucianism, Taoism, and Buddhism] are united into one").[1] Thus, although the chapters on thought and religion in this book have been separated for convenience and clarity, in fact the two are inextricably related.

THE CHINESE MENTAL WORLD

It is clear that geography, history, and the Chinese language all contributed to the special character of traditional Chinese thought. Among its most distinctive features—in addition to its obvious syncretic capacity—were an obsessive concern with ethics; an interest in nature and natural processes; a deep sense of cultural distinctiveness and superiority; a profound awareness of and respect for tradition; a preference for suggestiveness over articulation in philosophical discourse; an emphasis on the concrete over the abstract; and a heavy reliance on bureaucratic classification, analogy, and the "logic of correlative duality" as a means of organizing and understanding the vast whole of human experience. With these general characteristics in mind, we may now probe somewhat deeper into the mental world of the traditional Chinese elite.

Attunement to natural processes in China encouraged an organismic view of the universe, in which the cosmic forces of *yin* and *yang* continually interacted to produce the so-called five elements, or agents—wood, fire, earth, metal, and water. These elements, in various combinations under various circumstances, became the material force (*ch'i*) of which all things, animate and inanimate, were constituted. In the words of the *Chin-ssu lu*, "By the transformation of *yang* and its union with *yin*, the five elements . . . arise. When these five material forces are distributed in harmonious order, the four seasons run their course." Like the forces of *yin* and *yang*, the five elements not only produced all matter but also dominated phases of time, succeeding each other in endless patterns of mutual interaction and cyclical alternation.[2]

Conventionally, then, the Chinese viewed the universe as a regular, self-contained, self-operating whole, spontaneously generated and perpetually in motion. Everything within the cosmos existed as part of an orderly and harmonious hierarchy of interrelated parts and forces. Synchroneity (the coincidence of events in space and time) was stressed over simple causality as an explanatory principle. But the harmonious cooperation and synchronic interaction of all things in the universe were seen as arising not from the commands of an external supreme will or authority, but rather from a unified cosmic pattern or process (the natural Way, or *tao*) in which all things followed the internal dictates of their own natures. In fact, the Chinese are unique among all peoples, ancient and modern, in having no indigenous creation myth, no supreme heavenly ordainer. Eventually, in post-Han times, the Chinese borrowed a creation story based on a creature named P'an Ku, but the P'an Ku myth is the weakest in a generally weak and quite unsystematic Chinese mythology. In any case, P'an Ku was never viewed as a Logos or demiurge, much less as the omniscient, omnipowerful creator of the Semitic, Christian, and Islamic traditions.[3]

Lacking the idea of a personalistic creator external to the cosmos, the Chinese developed an approach to religious life that led to the rejection of both monotheism and theological absolutism; the weakness of institutional religion; the strength of diffused religions (such as ancestor worship, the worship of Heaven by the state, and the worship of patron gods in associations such as guilds [*hang*]); and the failure to develop a concept of evil as an active force in the personified Western sense. The introduction of Buddhism and other alien belief systems in China, and the later development of an elaborate neo-Confucian metaphysics, did nothing to alter these basic features of Chinese religious life.[4]

Neo-Confucian metaphysics did, however, contribute the idea of a prime mover, or Supreme Ultimate (*t'ai-chi*), which generated the cosmic forces of *yin* and *yang* and also served as the source (and sum) of the ideal forms, or principles (*li*), around which material force coalesced to comprise all things. But by late imperial times, interest in the metaphysical notion of *t'ai-chi* had waned considerably. Wing-tsit Chan writes, for example, "The difference between the early Ming and Ch'ing Neo-Confucians is that the earlier philosophers turned away from the Great Ultimate [*t'ai-chi*] to internal

FIGURE 6.1. *Yin-Yang* and Five-Elements Correlations

SOME BASIC *YIN-YANG* CORRELATIONS

Yang	Yin	Yang	Yin
Light	Dark	Activity	Quiescence
Hot	Cold	Life	Death
Dry	Moist	Advance	Retreat
Fire	Water	Expand	Contract
Red	Black	Full	Empty
Day	Night	Straight	Crooked
Sun	Moon	Hard	Soft
Spring-Summer	Autumn-Winter	Round	Square
South	North	Outside	Inside
Heaven	Earth	Left	Right
Male	Female		

SOME FIVE-ELEMENTS (*WU-HSING*) CORRELATIONS

Correlation	Wood	Fire	Earth	Metal	Water
Domestic Animal	sheep	fowl	ox	dog	pig
Organ	spleen	lungs	heart	liver	kidneys
Number	8	7	5	9	6
Color	green	red	yellow	white	black
Direction	east	south	center	west	north
Emotion	anger	joy	desire	sorrow	fear
Taste	sour	bitter	sweet	acrid	salty
State of Yin-Yang	*yin* in *yang* (or lesser *yang*)	*yang* (or greater *yang*)	equal balance	*yang* in *yin* (or lesser *yin*)	*yin* (or greater *yin*)

Note: Like *yin* and *yang*, the five elements were used in Chinese thought to indicate both cosmic activities and conceptual categories. In either case, as with *yin* and *yang*, the pattern of movement was one of ceaseless alteration and cyclical change. The order of the elements and the process by which one displaced another varied according to different schemes, however.

cultivation, whereas the Ch'ing Neo-Confucianists turned away from the Great Ultimate to everyday affairs.''[5]

The use of *yin-yang* as an all-encompassing conceptual paradigm, on the other hand, remained very much alive. The notion of *yin-yang* interaction generally sufficed as an explanation of cosmic creativity and change; and the specific evaluative terms *yin* and *yang* continued to be used to accommodate nearly any set of dual coordinates, from abstruse Buddhist or neo-Confucian concepts such as "perceived reality and emptiness" (*se-k'ung*), "principle and material force" (*li-ch'i*), and "substance and function" (*t'i-yung*) to such mundane but important polarities as light and dark, hot and cold, wet and dry, soft and hard, passive and active, male and female.[6] It was a natural Chinese tendency to divide phenomena into two unequal but complementary parts (see Figure 6.1).

The important point to keep in mind is that *yin* and *yang* were always viewed as relative concepts. As creative forces they were continually in flux, each growing out of the other and each in turn "controlling" situations or activities. And even as specific evaluative categories they were never viewed as absolutes. The *Tao-te ching* (The Way and Its Power) illustrates this basic point: "Being and non-being produce each other; difficult and easy complete each other. Long and short contrast each other; high and low distinguish each other. Sound and voice harmonize with each other; front and back follow each other."[7]

In the main, then, *yin* and *yang* were not things, but classifications of relations. Any given object or phenomenon might be designated *yin* in one set of relations and *yang* in another. Thus, in the vocabulary of painting and calligraphy, the brush was considered *yang* because it was the active instrument using ink (*yin*). Yet the brush could be considered *yin* in relation to the *yang* of the artist (or, for that matter, the artist's subject material); and although the ink was dark (*yin*) on the light paper or silk, it showed a *yang* aspect when considered in relation to the passiveness of the paper or silk. Similarly, although Heaven was fundamentally *yang* and Earth *yin*, at least some Chinese thinkers maintained that during the day both were *yang*, and at night both were *yin*.[8]

One's philosophical outlook also affected the perception of *yin-yang* relationships, for what one thinker saw as positive, another might see as negative. The great Ch'ing Confucian Hui Tung (1697–1758) tells us, for example: "The way of change is that the unyielding [*kang*, i.e., *yang*] triumphs, the yielding [*jou*, i.e., *yin*] endangers. Hence, the unyielding is treasured. But Taoists hold an opposite view, arguing that unyielding strength [*kang-ch'iang*] brings death. Herein lies the difference between Confucians and Taoists."[9] To an extent, of course, Hui is correct in contrasting Confucian activism and Taoist passivity. But his stark statement obscures two important points. The first is that Confucians often placed a premium on "yielding" in social situations and promoted a view of government that was in many ways quite passive (*yin*). The second point is that circumstances were continually changing, and despite Hui's assertion that strength would always prevail, most Chinese— Confucians and Taoists alike—accepted the *I-ching*'s basic premise that change was a matter of *yin-yang* alternation. Inevitably, *kang* would surrender to *jou*, even if only temporarily.

The idea of *yin-yang* alternation was of course central to the traditional Chinese conception of time, which, following the usage of the *I-ching*, came to be seen as a kind of field or receptacle for human events. Indeed, the *yin-yang* paradigm itself developed out of an early appreciation of the rhythms and regularities of cyclical change in nature—notably the twenty-four hour cycle of light and dark and the seasonal fluctuation between the two poles of summer heat and winter cold. The Chinese word for time (*shih*) originally meant "the period of sowing," and it never totally lost its specific seasonal and cyclical connotations.

"Timeliness" was of central significance to the Chinese in all facets of daily life, at all levels. Two of the most important ritual acts of a new dynasty were to regulate the calendar (*chih-li*) and to fix the time (*shou-shih* or *shih-ling*). Imperially sponsored almanacs were ubiquitous and essential to the conduct of affairs in traditional Chinese society (see Chapter 10). In everyday affairs, the water clock divided the day and night into two-hour segments, while the lunar calendar marked the twelve months of the year (with intercalary adjustments to compensate for the 11-day difference between the lunar period of 354 days and the solar period of 365 days). Longer spans of time were conventionally measured in linear order by dynastic periods and by imperial reign names (*nien-hao*) within each dynasty.

Overall, time in traditional China was usually viewed in cyclical rather than linear terms. Cycles might be as long as four Buddhist kalpas (each with a duration of more than a billion years) or as short as the common sixty-year and sixty-day cycles of the native Chinese tradition. Even dynastic periods were seen as macrocosms of the natural life cycle of birth, growth, decline, and death—comparable to the fourfold Buddhist cycle of formative growth, organized existence, disintegration, and annihilation alluded to above. In contrast with the Christian, Islamic, and Judaic traditions, Chinese history had no fixed starting point, since the human world was but a part of the larger cosmic whole and conformed like the latter to an inherent pattern of cyclical movement.[10]

Shao Yung's widespread theory of recurrent and eternal 129,600-year cycles (*yüan*), originally inspired by Buddhism, provided a convenient means by which to reconcile a cyclical view of human experience with the pervasive idea of a golden age in China's past. According to Shao, the present cycle began at a date corresponding to 67,017 B.C., reaching its peak at about 2330 B.C.—a period corresponding to the reign of the legendary sage-ruler Yao. Human society was now in decline, however, and would continue to decline until the extinction of living creatures about A.D. 46,000. In A.D. 62,583 the world would end, and a new cycle would then begin.[11]

Since dynastic history, as part of the total cosmic process, moved in a cyclical pattern, it followed that an identifiable *yin-yang* alternation between order and disorder (*chih-luan*), prosperity and decline (*sheng-shuai*), was both natural and inevitable. Each situation contained the seeds of the other. But the Chinese also believed that historical circumstances depended on human action and that dynastic decline could thus be at least temporarily arrested by the concerted efforts of moral men. Such a phenomenon was known as a restoration (lit., rising at mid-course). Only a few such restorations had been recorded in Chinese history, but one did occur in the late Ch'ing period, during the strife-torn reign of the T'ung-chih emperor. Although most Chinese thinkers rejected the idea of historical progress in the sense of progressive improvement, they continued to be moved by a strong impulse to improve society by hearkening back to earlier historical models or times.[12]

History in China was written by officials for officials. As a moral drama it reflected predominantly Confucian value judgments. The history of any dynasty, which was always written by its successor, was more than just a narrative record; it was also a guide to proper conduct for the present and the future. The Ch'ing scholar Chao I (1727–1814) put the matter this way in the preface to his famous *Nien-erh shih cha-chi* (Notes on the Twenty-two Histories): "The [Confucian] Classics are the principles of government; the histories are the evidences [lit., traces] of government." In China, as Arthur Wright has observed, historical precedent acquired something of the power we attach to law and logic in the West.[13]

The traditional Chinese dynastic histories followed a general model provided by the great Han historian Ssu-ma Ch'ien. Although no two of the twenty-six formal histories (including the draft history of the Ch'ing) are exactly the same, most consist of four major divisions: the imperial annals (*pen-chi*), chronological tables (*piao*), monographs (*chih*), and biographies (*lieh-chuan*). Of these, the monographs and biographies are especially helpful in indicating traditional categories of historical concern. Let us examine briefly the Ming history (*Ming-shih*, compiled 1678–1739) and the Draft History of the Ch'ing (*Ch'ing-shih kao*, compiled 1914–1927)—the last two traditional dynastic histories—with these concerns in mind. Among the most significant monographs in each are those on ritual, music, the calendar, astronomy, rivers and canals, food and commodities, law and punishments, the five elements, geography, literature, officials, chariots and costumes, the civil service, and the army. Among the most important shared categories of biography are those of dutiful officials, Confucian scholars, empresses, doctors, hermits, literary persons, eminent women, filial persons, and loyal subjects. Some differences may be detected— notably the special attention given to eunuchs, imperial relatives, and traitors in the *Ming-shih* biographies and the new categories of monographs in the *Ch'ing-shih kao* relating to communications and foreign relations. These differences may be explained, of course, by the differing historical circumstances and problems of the two dynastic periods.[14]

Traditionally, China's foreign relations were not considered worthy of a special place in the dynastic histories, although discussions of "barbarians" could be found sprinkled liberally throughout the various major divisions, notably the biographies. This form of neglect bears testimony to the long-standing antiforeign prejudice of the Chinese, despite the important role aliens have played throughout much of Chinese history.

The Chinese world view, which evolved over many centuries of extensive contact with foreigners within China, on China's borders, and beyond, was based on the essentially unchallenged idea of China's cultural superiority to all other states. In general terms, the Chinese distinguished three major types of barbarian states, each defined by their geographical and cultural proximity to China. The closest group, known to modern scholars as the Sinic Zone states, consisted of nearby tributaries such as Korea, Annam (Vietnam), the Liu-ch'iu Islands, and occasionally Japan; the next closest group, in the so-called Inner Asian Zone, consisted of tributary tribes and states of nomadic or seminomadic peoples on the fringes of the Chinese culture area; and the furthest group, or Outer Zone states, consisted of "outer barbarians" (*wai-i*) far from China in both physical distance and lifestyle. The further removed from the "civilizing influence" of Chinese culture, the more likely foreigners would be described by the Chinese as animals such as dogs and sheep, who were amenable only to policies such as beating, throwing them bones or food, and keeping them under loose rein (*chi-mi*).[15]

Throughout the imperial era, Chinese foreign policy varied according to China's strategic and administrative needs, the perception of an alien threat, the attitudes and activities of the barbarians themselves, and, of course, the whim of the emperor. In theory, at least, the Chinese world view was passive: Barbarians were expected to gravitate to China solely out of admiration for Chinese culture. Force was to be used as a last resort in the conduct of foreign relations. In fact, however, Chinese foreign policy in the early Ch'ing, as in other dynamic periods such as the Han and T'ang, was openly aggressive, although characteristically cast in terms of border defense.

Central to the ritualized Chinese world order was preservation of the age-old tributary system, which the Chinese viewed an as extension of their own internal social and political order. This system rested on the assumption of a hierarchical structure of foreign relations with China at both the top and center. Relationships were based on feudal principles of investiture and loyalty, with China serving as the lord and other states as vassals. According to the tributary regulations of the Ch'ing period, non-Chinese rulers were given a patent of appointment, noble rank, and an official seal for use in correspondence; they in turn presented symbolic tribute and periodic tribute memorials, dated their communications by the Ch'ing calendar, and performed the appropriate ceremonies of the Ch'ing court, including the kowtow. Loyal tributaries received imperial gifts and protection in return and were granted certain privileges of trade at the frontier and at the capital.[16]

In times of military weakness, the Chinese were often obliged to buy off barbarians with tributary gifts and to make other compromises with the theoretical assumptions of the Chinese world order. In order to make peace with the foreign-ruled Chin dynasty in 1138, for example, the founder of the Southern Sung dynasty had to accept the humiliating status of a vassal (*ch'en*); and in 1793, the British envoy Lord George Macartney consented only to bend his knee before the Ch'ien-lung emperor—although Ch'ing official documents recorded him as performing the kowtow. Further concessions followed the Opium War of 1839–1842. Yet as John Fairbank has shown, the tributary system showed remarkable staying power even after the Treaty of Nanking (1842).[17]

Moreover, the Chinese were not overly concerned with the gap between theory and practice in foreign relations. Chao I, for one, maintained that the practice of "true principle" (*i-li*) in foreign affairs necessarily involved adjustments. "The teachings of true principle," he wrote, "cannot always be reconciled with the circumstances of the times. If one cannot entirely maintain the demands of true principle, then true principle must be adjusted to the circumstances of the time, and only then do we have the practice of true principle."[18] This convenient logic also applied to the employment of foreigners in Chinese civil and military administration, a phenomenon often described as synarchy.

As might be expected, the Chinese historical record abounds with praise for barbarians who "admired right behavior and turned toward Chinese civilization" (*mu-i hsiang-hua*). Such conduct accorded perfectly with China's self-image of cultural and moral superiority. But all of China's barbarian employees did not serve the Middle Kingdom solely out of admiration. Some individuals were drawn by the prospect of financial and material rewards. Others submitted with large bodies of troops after defeat in battle or the deterioration of prospects in their homeland. A number came to China to render temporary service, returning home after a limited tour of duty. Although the general tendency was to measure barbarian devotion by the yardstick of cultural submission, Chinese policymakers recognized that personal, bureaucratic, and economic pressures and inducements necessarily complemented cultural controls.[19]

In the end, however, ethical and ritual concerns remained paramount to the Chinese. As Benjamin Schwartz points out, "A random perusal of discussions of barbarians in the various encyclopedias and other sources reveals again and again the degree of emphasis on the five relationships, the 'three bonds' (*san-kang*) and the whole body of *li* as providing the absolute criteria dividing barbarians from the men of the Middle Kingdom."[20] Although the Chinese notion of universal kingship was pre-Confucian and taken for granted by nearly all late Chou philosophical schools, no school of thought took ethics and ritual more seriously than the Confucians, for none placed greater emphasis on moral discipline and social order.

THE CONFUCIAN MORAL ORDER

Throughout most of China's imperial history, Confucianism was the predominant intellectual influence. This was especially true during the Ch'ing. P. T. Ho writes, for example, "In no earlier period of Chinese history do we find a deeper permeation and wider acceptance of the norms, mores, and values which modern students regard as Confucian." The Ch'ing emperors patronized Confucian scholarship and paid unprecedented homage to Confucius in official ceremonies, including two kneelings and six prostrations in Peking, and the full kowtow—three kneelings and nine prostrations—in Ch'ü-fu, the birthplace of Confucius. The education of Manchu princes followed carefully constructed Confucian lines, and the examination system was, of course, based almost entirely on the Confucian classics and commentaries. Lawrence Kessler writes that by the end of the K'ang-hsi emperor's reign in the early eighteenth century "the Manchu-controlled state and the Chinese-guarded Confucian value system were harmoniously joined . . . [and the] Confucian ideal of the unity of state and knowledge, under the rule of a sage-king, seemed near realization."[21]

During the Ch'ing period there were, however, several major schools of Confucianism, each with its own special emphasis. The idealistic neo-Confucian School of Sung Learning—also known as the School of Principle (*li-hsüeh*)—placed particular emphasis on moral cultivation and the power of positive example as the keys to good government. This school of thought served as official orthodoxy during the Ch'ing period and was distilled in the highly influential examination syllabus known as the *Hsing-li ching-i* (Essential Ideas of the School of Nature and Principle), commissioned by the K'ang-hsi emperor in the early eighteenth century and widely disseminated. The so-called T'ung-ch'eng School was closely allied to the School of Sung Learning, but placed particular emphasis on literature as the vehicle of Confucian "faith." Both schools were uncompromisingly hostile to the School of Han Learning, also known as the School of Empirical Research (*k'ao-cheng*), which devoted itself primarily to philological study and textual criticism. The School of Statecraft (*ching-shih*), as its name implies, took practical administration as its central concern, avoiding the moralistic extremes of Sung Learning as well as the scholastic extremes of Han Learning. The New Text (*chin-wen*) School in the late Ch'ing challenged the textual and philological conclusions of the Han Learning and offered significantly different interpretations of both the place of Confucius in Chinese history and the role of institutional change within the Confucian tradition. A central feature of the New Text outlook was a "socio-moral pragmatism," which favored a free "ideological" interpretation of Confucianism over a literal and prosaic understanding. Advocates of radical change in Chinese institutions during the latter half of the nineteenth century used New Text interpretations of the Classics as a political tool with considerable ingenuity and success.[22]

Other schools of Confucian thought arose during the Ch'ing dynasty, some championed by highly individualistic iconoclasts and others developed by eclectic thinkers searching for an effective intellectual synthesis. The syncretic tendencies of Chinese thought made it possible for a scholar-official like Tseng Kuo-fan (1811–1872) to adhere to orthodox Sung neo-Confucian ideas and to esteem the literary and moral concerns of the T'ung-ch'eng School, and yet at the same time to recognize the merits of Han Learning, to gravitate toward the School of Statecraft in seeking solutions to the dynasty's administrative problems, and even to employ essentially Legalist methods in order to achieve idealistic Mencian aims. A distinctive feature of Tseng's thought was his emphasis on *li*—by which he meant not only rules of social usage, rituals, and ceremonies but also laws and institutions—as the common denominator of China's entire, complex, Confucian tradition.[23]

During the Ch'ing period, as in earlier times, one's intellectual posture was ordinarily a function of several major variables: (1) personality and family background, (2) educational experience, (3) personal and dynastic fortunes, and (4) career concerns. Political factors were especially important in determining the popularity of a certain school of thought at a particular time, but the attachment of any individual to a given point of view might well hinge on career concerns. Thus, for example, young students and gentry awaiting official appointment could be expected to emphasize Sung idealism, if only because a mastery of Chu Hsi's thought brought the possibility of personal advancement. Officials, on the other hand, might publicly espouse neo-Confucian moral principles only to seek administrative guidance from the School of Statecraft. And retired officials might find satisfaction in pure scholarship and the contemplative life, studying works such as the *I-ching* and perhaps also investigating the officially disparaged but still attractive ideas of Wang Yang-ming, the Taoists, and even the Buddhists.

But for all the diversity of Ch'ing intellectual life, there was still a striking uniformity of outlook. Much of this uniformity can be explained by the educational common denominator of preparation for the examinations. The vast majority of Ch'ing scholars read the same basic works, prepared for the examinations in the same basic way, and used the same set of evaluative terms and conceptual categories to express their ideas. The emphasis in private academies (*shu-yüan*) might differ somewhat from the curriculum in "official" schools, but the practical aim of education in Ch'ing times remained success in the examinations, and the early patterns of rote learning directed to this goal left a deep impression on most scholarly minds.[24]

Further, as Yü Ying-shih and others have indicated, the differences between certain schools of Confucian thought have often been overemphasized. There were, for example, important affinities between Sung Learning and Han Learning in the area of philology, between Sung Learning and the School of Statecraft in the management of practical affairs (*chih-shih*), and even between Sung Learning and the intuitive School of the Mind (*hsin-hsüeh*) in the areas of both mental discipline and scholarship. New Text scholars, for their part, shared many of the same administrative concerns as the School of Statecraft, although their proposals for governmental reform were generally more radical. In all, as W. T. de Bary has suggested, the major polarities that existed in Confucianism between scholarship and public service, academic pursuits and self-cultivation, contemplation and activity, and aesthetics (or metaphysics) and practical concerns should be seen not as conflicting imperatives, but as "dynamic unities," a source of both vitality and adaptability in Chinese intellectual life.[25]

We can identify the following general features of Ch'ing Confucianism: (1) A comparative lack of interest in metaphysics; (2) a rationalistic outlook, predicated on a belief in the intelligibility of the universe; (3) a great reverence for the past; (4) a humanistic concern with "man in society"; (5) an emphasis on morality in government and a link between personal and political values; (6) a belief in the moral perfectibility of all men; (7) the supreme authority of fundamental Confucian principles; and (8) a disesteem of law. Frederick Mote explains the significance of the last point:

> In a civilization like the Chinese where there are only human sources (or among Taoists, "natural" sources) of normative ideas, law could scarcely be expected to achieve the significance it possessed in other civilizations. For in all other civilizations it was based on the supra-rational and unchallengeable law of God, which commanded all creatures, and states as well, to enforce its literal prohibitions. Nor in China could there be any priestly enforcers of divine commandment, or even governors enforcing divine law or civil law armed with the analogy between man and God's law.

In Ch'ing China, the ideal emphasis was on *li* (ritual, or more generally, rules of social usage) rather than law. As Confucius once remarked: "If the people are led by laws, and an attempt made to give them uniformity by means of punishments, they will try to avoid the punishment, but have no sense of shame [*ch'ih*]. If [however,] they are led by virtue, and an attempt is made to give them uniformity by means of ritual [*li*], they will have a sense of shame and become good."[26]

The Confucian tradition drew upon a vast corpus of classical literature and commentaries, including the so-called Five Classics (the *Shih-ching* [Book of Poetry or Songs], the *Shu-ching* [Book of Documents or History], the *I-ching*, the *Ch'un-ch'iu* [Spring and Autumn Annals], and the *Li-chi* [Record of Ritual]); the *Tso-chuan* (Commentary of Tso); *Kung-yang chuan* (Commentary of Kung-yang); and *Ku-liang chuan* (Commentary of Ku-liang); the *Chou-li* (Rituals of Chou) and *I-li* (Etiquette and Ritual); the lexicon known as the *Erh-ya*; and the famous Four Books (the *Lun-yü* [Analects of Confucius], the *Meng-tzu* [Book of Mencius], the *Ta-hsüeh* [Great Learning], and the *Chung-yung* [Doctrine of the Mean]). By late imperial times, however, the Four Books had come to be considered the supreme embodiment of Confucian thought and the nucleus of traditional Chinese education. Fung Yu-lan considers the Four Books to be "the Bible of the Chinese people," but significantly he points out that they contain no story of creation and "no mention of a heaven or hell."[27]

The values contained in the Four Books were closely related. As Cheng Chung-ying has aptly remarked, the major Confucian virtues must all "be understood in relative definitions of each other . . . for each supposes the rest." A careful reading of the Four Books confirms the correctness of this view. Although the relationships are not always spelled out logically, they are no less important for their lack of systematic exposition.[28]

At the heart of the Confucian value system in late imperial times lay the Three Bonds (*san-kang*): between ruler and minister (or, more broadly, subject), between father and son, and between husband and wife. These were the first three of the famous Five Relationships (*wu-lun*), which also included the relationship of older (brother) to younger (brother) and friend to friend.[29]

The concept of the Three Bonds may be traced to the influential Han scholar Tung Chung-shu, who wrote: "the relationships between sovereign and subject, father and son, and husband and wife, are all derived from the principles of *yin* and *yang*. The sovereign is *yang*, the subject is *yin*; the father is *yang*, the son is *yin*; the husband is *yang*, the wife is *yin*. . . . The three cords [*kang*] of the Way of the [True] King may be sought in Heaven." Of these three relationships, the bond between husband and wife was considered most basic. "That male and female should live together is the greatest of human relations," asserted Mencius. The "Orderly Sequence of the Hexagrams" of the *I-ching* indicates that all other human relationships grow out of the relationship between man and woman.

Following the existence of Heaven and Earth came the existence of all things. Following the existence of all things came the existence of male and female. Following the existence of male and female came the relationship between husband and wife. Following the relationship between husband and wife came the relationship between father and son. Following the relationship between father and son came the relationship between ruler and subject [*chün-ch'en*]. Following the relationship between the ruler and subject came the general distinction between superior and inferior [*shang-hsia*]. Following the distinction between superior and inferior came the arrangements of ritual and right behavior [*li-i*].[30]

The entire Confucian social and moral order was thus based on the natural *yin-yang* relationship of husband and wife, with its assumptions of inequality, subordination, and service. As Mencius once stated, "to look upon compliance [*shun*] as their correct course is the rule [*tao*] for women." But a central principle of Confucian family organization was also the devotion of children toward their parents (filial piety, *hsiao*) and its corollary, fraternal submission (*ti*). Mencius tells us that the filial service of one's parents is the greatest of all services (*shih*) and the foundation of all other services. The *Ta-hsüeh*, in establishing the link between family order and good government, indicates that the ruler should be served with filial piety and elders and superiors with fraternal submission. Further, the *Ta-hsüeh* remarks, "if one is not obedient to his parents, he will not be true to his friends," and "if one is not trusted by his friends, he will not get the confidence of his sovereign." The *Hsiao-ching* (Book of Filial Piety) goes so far as to claim that China "rules the world with the principle of filial piety."[31]

The *Lun-yü* states explicitly that *hsiao* and *ti* are the root of humaneness (*jen*), the most exalted of the Five Constant Virtues (*wu-ch'ang*) of Confucianism: *jen*, *li* (ritual, or norms of social usage), *i* (duty, or right behavior), *chih* (humane wisdom), and *hsin* (faithfulness). Let us now examine these five cardinal virtues in greater detail, giving particular attention to the concept of *jen*.

Neo-Confucians generally considered *jen* to be a universal cosmic virtue that, in effect, generated all the other virtues. Wing-tsit Chan's careful study of the evolution of *jen* leaves no doubt that by late imperial times the term had become all encompassing. "*Jen*," he writes, "precludes all evil and underlies as well as embraces all possible virtues, so much so that 'if you set your mind on *jen*, you will be free from evil.'" Confucius tells us that *jen* means to "love men" (*ai-jen*), and Mencius equates *jen* with the innate goodness of man's nature, which he feels is manifest in the feeling of commiseration (*ts'e-yin*) in humans—the inability to bear (*pu-jen*) the suffering of others. *Jen*, in the view of most Ch'ing scholars, was the "single thread" (*i-kuan*) unifying the teachings of Confucius, the one moral principle for all human actions.[32]

Much has been made of the negative thrust of the famous Confucian dictum, "Do not do to others what you would not want others to do to you." But it is clear that virtually all Confucian scholars in all periods understood this "Golden Rule" as having both a positive and a negative aspect. The Ch'ing commentator Liu Pao-nan (1791–1855) spoke for many in maintaining that if it is true that we must not do to others what we do not want done to ourselves, then it must also be true that "we must do to others what we want them to do to us." Further, Liu concurs with Chu Hsi and most other late-imperial thinkers in equating the principles of *chung* (usually translated "loyalty") and *shu* (reciprocity) as referring, respectively, to the full development of one's mind and the extension of that mind to others, thus giving a positive cast to Confucian responsibility. As the *Lun-yü* states: "The man of *jen*, wishing to establish his own character, seeks also to establish the character of others."[33]

This did not mean, however, that all men should be treated equally. Rather, the Confucian idea of *jen* was "love with distinctions" (*ai yu ch'a-teng*), that is, love graded outward from the family and focused particularly on the virtuous. From a Confucian standpoint, it was impossible to love all people equally (*chien-ai*) as Mo-tzu had urged, for all people were not equal, either in closeness (*ch'in*) or in social station. Different values were appropriate to different relationships. Thus, Mencius informs us that "between father and son, there should be affection [*ch'in*]; between sovereign and minister, righteousness [*i*]; between husband and wife, attention to their separate functions [*pieh*]; between elder and younger, proper order [*hou*]; and between friends, fidelity [*hsin*]."[34]

Jen, in the orthodox view, was the key to good government. The *Ta-hsüeh* states: "Yao and Shun led the kingdom with benevolence [*jen*] and the people followed them"; and again, "Never has there been a case of the sovereign loving benevolence, and the people not loving righteousness. Never has there been a case where the people have loved righteousness, and the affairs of the sovereign have not been carried to completion." Confucian government was never meant to be *by* the people, but it was *for* the people, and the assumption remained that the moral cultivation of the ruler would bring peace and harmony. In the words of the *Chung-yung*,

> By honoring men of virtue and talent, the sovereign is preserved from errors of judgment. By showing affection to his relatives, there is no grumbling and resentment among his uncles and brethren. By respecting the great ministers, he is kept from errors in the practice of government. By kind and considerate treatment of the whole body of officers, they are led to make the most grateful return for his courtesies. By dealing with the mass of people as his children, they are led to exhort one another to what is good. . . . By indulgent treatment of men from a distance, they resort to him [*kuei-chih*] from all quarters.[35]

There was also, however, a more realistic wing of Confucian political theory, which sought administrative inspiration in less idealistic works, such as the writings of Hsün-tzu, and secondary classics, such as the *Chou-li*. The *Chou-li*—which often had been cited by radical reformers in China's past, including the Sung statesman Wang An-shih (1069–1074)—provided classical precedents for systems of equitable land distribution, public security, famine relief, arbitration, and even criminal justice. When it became necessary to reconcile the idealistic Mencian emphasis on *jen* with the harsh realities of Ch'ing political life, scholar-officials like Yüan Shou-ting (1705–1782) could argue that the Ch'ing penal code was based on the concepts of the *Chou-li*, but that its aim was to implement the Mencian values of humaneness and right behavior (*i*). In any case, we find many examples of Ch'ing scholars whose idealistic Confucian values were tempered by an un-Confucian emphasis on law, rewards, and punishments.[36]

Standing between rule by moral example and rule by law, closer to the former than the latter, was rule by ritual (*li*), the second of the Five Constant Virtues. The *Li-chi* states that "ceremonies [*li*] form a great instrument in the hands of the ruler. They provide the means by which to resolve what is doubtful, clarify what is abstruse, receive the spirits [*pin kuei-shen*], examine regulations, and distinguish humaneness [*jen*] from righteousness [*i*]. . . . To govern a state without ritual would be like plowing a field without a plowshare." The seventeenth-century censor, Ch'en Tz'u-chih, spoke for many Ch'ing officials in asserting that "for managing the world [*ching-shih*] and pacifying the people [*an-min*] there is nothing greater than ritual." Wei Hsiang-shu (1617–1687) advised the early Manchu rulers, "The moral transformation of the people [*chiao-hua*] is the dynasty's first task, and the regulations of ritual [*li-chih*] constitute the great item of moral transformation."[37] Through proper ritual, the emperor not only affirmed his position as Son of Heaven and ruler of all earthly domains, but he and his officials also promoted social harmony within the realm through moral example. This, at least, was the theory of Confucian government.

In Chinese ethical life, *jen* and *li* existed in a kind of creative tension, each contributing to the meaning or manifestation of the other. Tu Wei-ming considers *li* to be the "externalization" of *jen* in concrete social circumstances. Confucius once said, "If a man is not humane [*jen*], what has he to do with *li*?" But in another context, the Master remarked, "To conquer the self and return to *li* is humaneness." When asked how one could achieve this object, Confucius replied, "Do not look at what is contrary to *li*; do not listen to what is contrary to *li*; do not say what is contrary to *li*; and do not make any movement contrary to *li*." The three major Chinese classics on ritual, the *I-li*, *Chou-li*, and *Li-chi*, prescribed, often in minute detail, the behavior appropriate to a Confucian gentleman (*chün-tzu*). Ritual handbooks of the Ch'ing dynasty did the same.[38]

The massive compendium by Ch'in Hui-t'ien (1702–1764) entitled *Wu-li t'ung-k'ao* (Comprehensive Study of the Five Rituals) provides an indication of the standard categories of Chinese ceremonial practice: auspicious sacrifices (*chi-li*), ceremonies of celebration (*chia-li*), ceremonies of visitation (*pin-li*), military ritual (*chün-li*), and ceremonies of sadness (*hsiung-li*). Ch'in devotes most of his compendium (127 *chüan* and 92 *chüan*, respectively) to auspicious ritual (state sacrifices, commemoration of temples, clan and family sacrifices, and so on) and ceremonies of celebration (events such as imperial weddings and state banquets down to local festivals and the marriage of commoners). Military rituals such as imperial expeditions, hunts, and formal inspections account for only 13 *chüan*—the same amount of space allotted to ceremonies of visitation, from tributary missions and audiences to daily social intercourse. Ceremonies of sadness, notably mourning ritual, account for 17 *chüan* in the *Wu-li t'ung-k'ao*. A similar emphasis can be found in other compilations on Ch'ing ritual, including the collected statutes of the empire.[39]

As a reading of the Four Books and other sources indicates clearly, the Chinese considered ritual to be essential to the performance of filial duties and to the harmony of the household. Together with music, poetry, and other forms of refinement (*wen*), it contributed to self-cultivation and the establishment of character. Employed by the ruler and other "superior men," it encouraged respect, reverence, and right behavior at all levels of society; and followed as a standard of proper conduct, it imposed restraints on individuals and preserved social distinctions. Mencius asserts, "Without the rules of propriety and distinctions of right [*i*], the high and low will be thrown into confusion." And the *Li-chi* states expansively:

> The rules of propriety furnish the means of determining the observances toward relatives, as near and remote; of settling points which may cause suspicion or doubt; of distinguishing where there should be agreement, and where difference; and of making clear what is right and what is wrong. . . . To cultivate one's person and fulfill one's words is called good conduct. When conduct is ordered and words are in accordance with the right course [*tao*], we have the substance of the rules of propriety.[40]

Jen represented the idealistic thrust of Confucianism, with its emphasis on altruism, compassion, and reciprocity, but *li* gave structure and concrete expression to *jen*.

The third of the Five Constant Virtues—*i*, usually rendered duty or righteousness—can be understood only in light of other Confucian virtues, including the preceding two. In general terms it can be viewed as a unifying and ordering principle and a standard for moral judgment. *I* may be defined as appropriate behavior according to circumstance. Like *li*, it presupposed objective and external standards of correct behavior, but like *jen*, it had a subjective, internal component. To employ a rather mundane mechanical metaphor, *i* served as a spring controlling the tension between *jen* and *li*. It was at once a universal and particular virtue, expressing the substance of *jen* and the form of *li*. The *Lun-yü* states that the "superior man considers righteousness [*i*] to be essential. He performs it according to the rules of propriety, he brings it forth in humility [*sun*], and he completes it with faithfulness [*hsin*]." But *i* also allows for the occasional abandonment of the rules of propriety under special circumstances. In a famous illustration, Mencius remarks that although propriety demands that men and women not touch hands in public, if a man's sister-in-law were drowning, the man who would not extend his hand to save her "is a wolf."[41] In this instance, *i* mitigates *li*, but makes manifest *jen*.

The Four Books define *i* in a variety of ways. Mencius, who often discusses the term together with *jen*, contrasts *i* with *li* (profit), defines courage (*yung*) as acting according to *i*, and describes respect for elders as "the working of *i*." Where *jen* is associated in the Four Books with filial piety, *i* is associated with loyalty to the ruler or fraternal submission. Where *jen* is associated with the feeling of commiseration, *i* is associated with feelings of shame (*hsiu*) and dislike (*o*). In many respects, *i* comes close to the idea of Confucian "conscience." Simply stated, *i* is knowing what to do and what not to do. Mencius repeatedly emphasizes the importance of a sense of shame (*ch'ih*) in pursuing the proper path.[42]

Humane wisdom (*chih*), the fourth of the Five Constant Virtues, was essential to the full expression of *i*. From a Confucian standpoint, it was the only kind of knowledge worth having. In various contexts, *chih* is defined in the Four Books as the knowledge of filial piety and fraternal submission, as a feeling of approving and disapproving, and as the ability to recognize human talent. Mencius indicates that without humaneness and wisdom there can be no ritual and right behavior (*pu-jen pu-chih wu-li wu-i*), which suggests that like *jen*, *chih* is an internal virtue made manifest in other (external) virtues. And although to Mencius all these virtues were innate in man, the *Ta-hsüeh* indicates—and Sung neo-Confucian metaphysics affirm—that some men are born with moral knowledge and others have to learn it. "Only the wise of the highest class and the stupid of the lowest class cannot be changed," the Master once said.[43]

The fifth virtue of faithfulness receives prominent exposure in the Four Books, often in combination with other values such as loyalty, reciprocity, and sincerity (*ch'eng*). Of these, the last deserves special mention. Described in the *Ta-hsüeh* as "the way of Heaven," sincerity may best be defined as being true to oneself, consistent in word and deed, fully developing one's own nature, and extending that development to others. In this, *ch'eng* is closely akin to the concepts of *chung* and *shu* discussed above. The *Chung-yung* tells us that "Sincerity is [the way of] self-completion. . . . [It] is the beginning and ending of all things; without sincerity there would be nothing. For this reason, the superior man regards the attainment of sincerity as the most exalted thing." Further, it states, "The individual possessed of the most complete sincerity is like a spirit [*shen*]."[44]

How did the Confucian gentleman achieve sincerity and self-completion? The process began with the extension of knowledge and the "investigation of things." The *Ta-hsüeh* states:

> The ancients who wished to illustrate illustrious virtue throughout the world, first put their principalities in order. Wishing to put their principalities in order, they first regulated their families. Wishing to regulate their families, they first cultivated themselves [*hsiu-shen*]. Wishing to cultivate themselves, they first rectified their hearts [*cheng-hsin*]. Wishing to rectify their hearts, they first sought to be sincere in their thoughts [*ch'eng-i*]. Wishing to be sincere in their thoughts, they first extended to the utmost their knowledge [*chih-chih*]. Such extensions of knowledge lay in the investigation of things [*ko-wu*].[45]

The "investigation of things" was variously interpreted by Confucian scholars. Chu Hsi saw it as primarily "investigating principle" (*li*); Wang Yang-ming viewed it as an effort to "rectify the mind"; and Ch'ing scholars such as Yen Yüan (1635–1704) saw it as "learning from actual experience and solving practical problems." But regardless of the interpretation attached to the term *ko-wu*, the ultimate aim of any Confucian was to develop his innate potential and extend both his knowledge and his influence. Self-improvement involved self-examination and the achievement of a balance between book study (*tu-shu*), meditative quiet sitting (*ching-tso*), and indulgence in ritual and the arts—especially music, poetry, painting, and calligraphy. The blend varied, of course, from school to school and from individual to individual.[46]

An examination of the Ch'ing encyclopedia *Ku-chin t'u-shu chi-ch'eng*'s subcategory on Confucian conduct yields a wealth of information on how orthodox Ch'ing Confucians approached the problem of self-cultivation. In addition to the basic techniques outlined above, self-improvement could be achieved through means such as "investigating principle to the utmost" (*ch'iung-li*), "nourishing the mind" (*yang-hsin*), "paying attention to fundamentals" (*wu-pen*), "regulating desires" (*li-yü*), "correcting faults" (*kai-kuo*), and "abiding in reverence" (*chu-ching*). Emphasis was also placed on proper timing (*sui-shih*), the value of "personal experience" (*t'i-jen*) in the quest for truth, and the importance of unifying knowledge and action (*chih-hsing*).[47]

The Four Books provide numerous examples of the personal attributes of the cultivated Confucian man. He is described as virtuous, industrious, intelligent, learned, thoughtful, open-minded and impartial, kind, just, generous, reverent and respectful, cultured, solid and straightforward, cautious and slow in speech, dignified, modest, courageous, and anxious to teach as well as learn. He "does what is proper to his station, and does not desire to go beyond this."

In addition, we are told a great deal about the personality, tastes, and general demeanor of Confucius. We are even given a rough blueprint for the moral development of the sage. "At fifteen," the Master said, "I had my mind set on learning. At thirty I stood firm. At forty, I had no doubts. At fifty I knew the decrees of Heaven [T'ien-ming]. At sixty, my ear was an obedient organ [for the reception of truth]. At seventy, I could follow what my heart desired, without transgressing what was right."[48]

Confucius demonstrated an abiding concern with the mean (*chung-yung*)— the path of perfect harmony and equilibrium in thought, emotions, and conduct. "The superior man embodies the course of the mean," said Confucius; "the petty man [*hsiao-jen*] acts contrary to the course of the mean." The *Chung-yung* states, "The superior man cultivates a [friendly] harmony without being weak. How firm is his strength! He stands erect in the middle, without inclining to either side." And how might the superior man determine the mean? The sage-ruler Shun provided the model. Shun questioned others, studied their words, concealed what was bad in them, and displayed what was good. "He took hold of their extremes, determined the mean, and employed it in governing the people." This reminds us that in the Confucian view, personal sagehood was never enough. Just as the internal, subjective value of *jen* required objective manifestation in *li*, so self-cultivation required manifestation in public service. Since the goal of Confucianism was social harmony rather than personal salvation, self-realization could never be divorced from service to humanity. The Confucian imperative was "internal sagehood and external kingship" (*nei-sheng wai-wang*). If the superior man could achieve complete sincerity and an undisturbed mind (*pu-tung hsin*), he might, like Confucius himself, become an uncrowned king (*su-wang*) and extend his good influence far and wide.[49]

Despite a general lack of interest in metaphysics, Ch'ing Confucians could hardly avoid considering the relationship between the moral order on earth and the great scheme, or *tao*, of the cosmos. According to orthodox neo-Confucianism, the two were one. Chu Hsi's basic assumption, in other words, was that the principle (*li*) of man's nature was his original goodness (*jen*). The *li* for all men, then, was the same. What made men different in both appearance and morality was their dissimilar endowment of "material force" (*ch'i*). Chu Hsi says, "Those who receive a *ch'i* that is clear, are the sages in whom the nature is like a pearl lying in clear, cold water. But those who receive a *ch'i* that is turbid, are the foolish and degenerate in whom the nature is like a pearl lying in muddy water." Long ago, Confucius had stated that "By nature, men are nearly alike, but by practice they get to be far apart"; and somewhat later, Mencius made the penetrating observation that men's innately good minds could be "injured by hunger and thirst." Hsün-tzu, for his part, held that man's nature was basically evil.[50]

Neo-Confucianism, however, explained evil (*o*) as arising from selfish desires and other deviant impulses inherent in one's own physical endowment. Evil was thus a kind of moral imbalance in individuals. In the words of Ch'eng Hao: "All the myriad things have their opposites. When there is *yin*, there is *yang*. When there is good, there is evil. As *yang* increases, *yin* decreases, and as goodness is augmented, evil is diminished." The purpose of neo-Confucian self-cultivation was to correct moral imbalance by refining one's *ch'i*, allowing the luster of one's *li* to shine through. Neo-Confucians believed that the mind had this transforming capacity.[51]

Some thinkers, notably Wang Fu-chih, Yen Yüan, and Tai Chen of the Ch'ing, rejected the idea of a *li-ch'i* duality, arguing that there was no "principle" apart from material force and that thus there was no evil inherent in it. The metaphysical reality of nature (*tao*) and concrete things (*ch'i*) was one. Evil arose not from man's physical endowment per se, but rather from outside influences, such as selfishness and "obscuration." "Selfishness," wrote Tai Chen, "is the product of error in desire, and obscuration is the product of error in knowledge." In the mind of most Confucians, evil had to be overcome by concerted self-cultivation and the elimination of destructive desires.[52]

Although the concepts of *yin-yang*, *li-ch'i*, and *tao-ch'i* crop up continually in Chinese discussions of philosophy, they are by no means the only dualistic terms employed by Confucian thinkers. Neo-Confucians in particular were attracted by the terms *t'i* (substance) and *yung* (function) to explain their ideas—including the basic notion that "principle is one, but the manifestations are many" (*li-i fen-shu*). *T'i* signifies the "inherent, enduring and fundamental (hence 'internal') qualities of a thing or situation," while *yung* refers to "its functional, fluctuating and secondary (hence 'external') manifestations."[53]

The *t'i-yung* formula, like the *yin-yang* paradigm, could be used in a great variety of ways, and like *yin* and *yang*, the two terms generally implied mutual dependence and the superiority or precedence of *t'i* over *yung* (again, Wang Fu-chih provides a dissenting opinion). At a mundane level, the *t'i-yung* formula might be used to distinguish between the root of a problem and its manifestations. Thus, a bureaucrat would ask, "Which . . . is the proper means of ridding an area of robbery: rigorous police measures or sound economic measure so that the people 'find it unnecessary to rob for a living?' " In the realm of ethics, the *t'i* of man's humaneness (*jen*) might be distinguished from the *yung* of his righteousness (*i*), or the *t'i* of Confucian morality in general distinguished from the *yung* of government and institutions. At a higher metaphysical plane, *t'i* might be equated with principle and *yung* with material force, or Heaven with *t'i* and fate with *yung*.[54]

The place of Heaven in Chinese metaphysics is a central one. Fung Yu-lan points out that the character *t'ien* in Chinese writing has at least five different meanings: (1) a material or physical sky, opposite the earth (*ti*);

(2) an anthropomorphic deity presiding over Heaven; (3) an impersonal dispenser of fate (*ming*); (4) the equivalent of the English word *nature*; and (5) an amorphous ethical entity embracing moral principles and responding to the morality of men. In neo-Confucianism, the term Heaven is used in several senses, but it is generally devoid of any personality or anthropomorphism.[55]

To most neo-Confucians, Heaven represented "fullness of being and goodness," a concept equivalent to the way (*tao*) of the universe or to the idea of the Supreme Ultimate (*t'ai-chi*). In the orthodox view, Heaven was a self-existent moral entity that endowed all living creatures with their natures. Heaven's will was that these creatures would all act in accordance with their respective natures. Heaven had the power to express its displeasure over the actions of men by visiting upon them natural disasters and other signs and even the power to withdraw the mandate to rule (*t'ien-ming*) from the emperor if he should prove immoral and thus unworthy of the throne. "Heaven sees as the people see, and Heaven hears as the people hear," said Mencius.[56] The idea that the people had the right to rebel against oppressive rule remained at the heart of Chinese dynastic politics until the twentieth century, and echoes of it could still be heard even after the fall of the Ch'ing dynasty in 1912.

Ch'ing Confucians, like their predecessors for centuries, saw an essential unity between Heaven, Earth, and Man. The *Chung-yung* states that he who is possessed of complete sincerity (*ch'eng*) can "assist in the transforming and nourishing powers of Heaven and Earth" and thus form a triad with them. The Great Commentary of the *I-ching* remarks, "The Changes is a book vast and great, in which everything is completely contained. The *tao* of Heaven is in it, the *tao* of Earth is in it, and the *tao* of Man is in it." By using the *I-ching*, "Man comes to resemble Heaven and Earth, [and] . . . is not in conflict with them. His wisdom embraces all things, and his *tao* brings order to the whole world; therefore he does not err. . . . He rejoices in Heaven and has knowledge of fate, therefore he is free from care."[57]

The key concept here is fate (*ming*). Although the term sometimes means Heaven's mandate, nature, or man's natural endowment, Confucian "fate" is best thought of as a series, or set, of predestined situations evolving out of the natural processes of eternal cosmic change. These situations were believed to be represented by the sixty-four hexagrams of the *I-ching* and their constituent lines. By consulting the *I-ching* and establishing a spiritual link with Heaven, a scholar could not only determine the nature and direction of universal change, but also devise an appropriate Confucian strategy for coping with any situation. He could not only "know fate" (*chih-ming*) but also "establish fate" (*li-ming*). In the words of the great Ch'ing scholar T'ang Chien (1776–1861), "He who knows fate will cultivate the Way [*tao*]; he who [merely] relies on fate will do harm to the Way."[58] The Confucian belief in predestination thus did not lead to a crippling of self-reliance, although it was sometimes used to explain personal failure and adversity.

All levels of traditional Chinese society evinced a concern with predestination, but not all had the luxury of time and money for leisurely study of the *I-ching* and the metaphysical principles that lay behind it. Nor did most have the education or the inclination to appreciate all the refinements of Confucian ethics. To the degree that economics allowed, commoners in Ch'ing China tried to adhere to basic elite values in areas such as marriage, family life, and ancestor worship. It is doubtful, however, that the vast majority were much attracted to philosophical Taoism, for as Joseph Levenson has remarked, "The pleasure of a flight from civilization is open only to civilized man."[59] Chinese peasants were perhaps too close to the land, too close to nature's cruel caprice.

TAOIST FLIGHT AND FANCY

For the elite, at least, the *yang* of Confucian social responsibility was balanced by the *yin* of Taoist escape into nature. Unlike Confucianism, which for virtually all Ch'ing scholars was a way of life, if not a living faith, Taoism was essentially a state of mind. It provided an emotional and intellectual escape valve for world-weary Confucians, trammeled by social responsibility. The writings of Taoist philosophers such as Lao-tzu and Chuang-tzu were fresh and poetic, often playful, and always paradoxical. They advocated spiritual release, communication with nature, and "not striving" (*wu-wei*). The Taoist impulse was to defy authority, question conventional wisdom, admire the weak, and accept the relativity of things. The concrete symbols of the Taoist *tao* were water, the female, the child, the emptiness of the valley, and the uncarved block (*p'u*).[60]

Although Lao-tzu took periodic mental excursions into the cosmos, he remained a child of the world, concerned with government and human affairs as well as the enjoyment and preservation of life. Thus he tells us, "in the government of the sage, he keeps their hearts empty [peaceful, pure and free from worry and selfish desires], fills their bellies, weakens their ambitions, and strengthens their bones"; and again,

> The more taboos and prohibitions there are in the world, the poorer the people will be. The more sharp weapons the people have, the more troubled the state will be. The more cunning and skill man possesses, the more vicious things will appear. The more laws and orders are made prominent, the more thieves and robbers there will be. Therefore the sage says: I take no action and the people of themselves are transformed. I love tranquillity and the people themselves become correct.[61]

Chuang-tzu lacked even the muted reformism of Lao-tzu. In the words of Chu Hsi, "Lao-tzu still wanted to do something, but Chuang-tzu did not want to do anything at all. He even said that he knew what to do but just did not want to do it." Chuang-tzu's aim was complete freedom. He wanted simply to let his mind wander with the *tao* and to "travel beyond the mundane world." Chuang-tzu's ideal was the "pure man," who

> alone . . . associates with Heaven and Earth and spirit, without abandoning or despising things of the world. He does not quarrel over right or wrong and mingles with conventional society. . . . Above he roams with the Creator [*tsao-wu che*, i.e., Nature], and below he makes friends with those who transcend life and death and beginning and end. In regard to the essential, he is broad and comprehensive, profound and unrestrained. In regard to the fundamental, he may be said to have harmonized all things and penetrated the highest level.[62]

Taoism was preeminently a philosophy of individual liberation. Where Confucianism stressed others, Taoism stressed self. Where Confucians sought wisdom, Taoists sought blissful ignorance. Where Confucians esteemed ritual and self-control, Taoists valued spontaneity and naturalness (*tzu-jan*). Where Confucianism stressed hierarchy, Taoists emphasized equality, and where Confucians valued refinement (*wen*), Taoists prized primitivity. What to Confucians were cosmic virtues were to Taoists simply arbitrary labels.

Lao-tzu highlighted the essential difference between Confucianism and Taoism in asserting:

> It was when the Great Tao declined that there appeared humanity and righteousness. It was when knowledge and intelligence arose that there appeared much hyprocrisy. It was when the six relations [father, son, elder brother, younger brother, husband, and wife] lost their harmony that there was talk of filial piety and paternal affection. It was when the country fell into chaos and confusion that there was talk of loyalty and trustworthiness. Banish sageliness, discard wisdom, and the people will be benefitted a hundredfold. Banish humanity, discard righteousness, and the people will return to filial piety and paternal affection. . . . See the simple, embrace primitivity; reduce the self, lessen the desires.[63]

This, in brief, was the Taoist message.

There was just enough affinity between Confucianism and Taoism to ensure an enduring philosophical partnership. Both schools of thought sought inspiration and guidance in the *I-ching*, both employed *yin-yang* concepts to explain their ideas, and both cherished the ideal of harmony and oneness with nature (although one posited a moral universe and the other, an amoral one). Each shared a sense of the interrelatedness of all things and each, in its own way, advocated humility, passivity, simplicity, and the avoidance of desires. Furthermore, although Taoism had no prominent philosophical proponents in late imperial times, Confucians found at least some Taoist concepts congenial to their own ideas. The *Chin-ssu lu*, for example, cites approvingly Chuang-tzu's remark that "those who indulge in many desires have very little of the secret of Nature."[64]

In all, then, Confucianism and Taoism could easily coexist in harmony. The former gave Chinese life structure and purpose, while the latter encouraged freedom of expression and artistic creativity. Most Ch'ing scholars had a healthy schizophrenia. As Theodore de Bary points out, neo-Confucians recognized that man's response to Heaven and the fulfillment of his nature were not limited to social service. He writes that "in the midst of social and political engagement," there was

> a need to keep some part of . . . [oneself] not subservient to the demands of state or society. To the neo-Confucian, the aesthetic and spiritual, or . . . 'supermoral' concerns [in the words of T'ang Chün-i] represent this area of freedom. Much of it was expressed in journals, lyrical poetry, prose-poetry, travel diaries written in a contemplative frame of mind, painting and calligraphy, and the appreciation of art expressed in poetic inscriptions.[65]

The inspiration for these activities was predominantly Taoist, even if the fruits of such labors were ultimately believed to convey moral worth.

CHAPTER 7

Religion

Contrary to persistent Western opinion, few areas of traditional Chinese life were devoid of religious sentiment or religious ritual. During the Ch'ing period, elite and popular religious beliefs and practices intertwined to produce a vast, multicolored fabric of institutional and individual worship. Henri Maspero once described Chinese religion as encompassing "an unheard-of swarm of gods and spirits of every kind, an innumerable rabble"; but there was order behind the apparent chaos. Maurice Freedman maintains, for example, that "all religious argument and ritual differentiation [in China] were conducted within a common language of basic conceptions, symbols, and ritual forms."[1] This common religious base encompassed the major elements of Chinese thought described in the preceding chapter, including the predominance of Confucian values, a concern with hierarchical order and social harmony, philosophical eclecticism, and the notion of *yin-yang* duality.

OFFICIAL SACRIFICES

Arthur Wolf has written: "Assessed in terms of its long-range impact on the people, . . . [the Chinese government] appears to have been one of the most potent governments ever known, for it created a religion in its own image. Its firm grip on the popular imagination may be one reason the imperial government survived so long despite its failings."[2] There is much to commend this view. To a remarkable extent, the organization of traditional Chinese religion mirrored the fundamental assumptions of Chinese bureaucratic behavior. This was true not only of official state ceremonies and sacrifices (*ssu-tien*), as might well be expected, but also of institutional Buddhism, Religious Taoism, and even popular religion. The state, with its pervasive powers of patronage and appointment, periodically promoted and demoted various gods within its own supernatural bureaucratic establishment, called upon Buddhist and Taoist priests to say prayers and perform sacrifices as religious agents of the state, appropriated deities from the vast pantheon of popular religion into the structure of official religion, and canonized former mortals who were either exemplars of orthodox values or whose acknowledged supernatural powers (*ling*) made them potentially valuable to the state.[3]

Stephen Feuchtwang has identified a kind of dialectic operating in Chinese religious life in which

> officials adopted deities from popular religion and bureaucratized them, while the [common] people worshipped gods that were like magic officials or that were magic official deities. Gods that in popular religion were fluid, whose identities flowed into one another, whose functions were potentially universal, and who were magic in their ability to metamorphose and to fuse man and nature in themselves, were in the official religion standardized and classed, minute distinctions and the separation of rites and cults keeping them apart.[4]

Ch'ing official religion recognized three main levels of state sacrifices, aside from the exclusively Manchu shamanistic observances undertaken by the Office of Ceremonial of the Imperial Household Department: (1) great sacrifices (*ta-ssu*), (2) middle sacrifices (*chung-ssu*), and (3) common sacrifices (*ch'ün-ssu* or *hsiao-ssu*). At each of these levels, designated officials performed elaborate ceremonies in accordance with long-standing ritual prescriptions. Auspicious dates for such ceremonies were chosen well in advance after divination by the Imperial Board of Astronomy (Ch'in-t'ien chien) and deliberations involving the Board of Rites, the Court of Sacrificial Worship, and the emperor himself. About a year in advance, the imperial sacrificial calendar was fixed, printed, and distributed to civil and military officials at the capital and in the provinces, who also received ritual guidance in the form of special ceremonial handbooks.[5]

State worship at the various levels generally required ritual bathing, fasting, prostrations, prayers, and thanksgiving offerings of incense, lighted candles, precious objects, fruits, and food and wine together with music and ritual posturing or dancing. These activities were believed to purify the mind and body and to please the gods. According to the *Ta-Ch'ing hui-tien*, official religious ceremonies had several specific purposes. Some deities were worshipped for the simple purpose of expressing gratitude and veneration; others for the beneficial or protective influences the deities were supposed to exert; still others for their outstanding civil virtues and/or military services. Some spirits were worshipped for fear that they would bring calamities to the people if not suitably appeased.[6]

But behind these rather specific purposes lay more general considerations. One of these was to exemplify the cosmic order and to affirm the emperor's place within it. Another was to reinforce status distinctions and thus to protect the social order. Yet another was to undergird the prestige and political authority of the state. Official religious ceremonies were thus seen as powerful

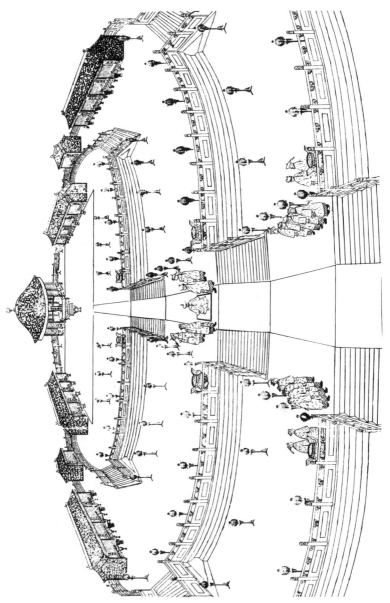

FIGURE 7.1. The Altar of Heaven (I). The Hsien-feng emperor (r. 1851–1861) worshipping at the Altar of Heaven, from a Chinese painting. The central temporary shrine is to Heaven (Shang-ti). The other temporary shrines house the tablets of the emperor's ancestors, the spirits of the Sun and Moon, and other deities. Taken from S. W. Williams (1883), vol. 1 (inside cover).

instruments of ideological control. The preface to one ceremonial handbook of the nineteenth century well illustrates the mixture of motives surrounding official religious practice. "Incense and vessels . . . [i.e., ritual sacrifices] can control the gods and spirits [*shen* and *kuei*]. Jade, silk, bells and drums can reveal the rites and music. . . . Awe of virtue and the passing on of merit [through worship] civilize the people and form customs."[7] Official religion, in other words, manipulated both the gods and the people. Some officials downplayed the spiritual aspects of the rituals they performed, but they performed them nonetheless.

The most awe-inspiring of the great sacrifices was the emperor's personal worship of Heaven, which took place during the winter solstice and on New Year's Day (from 1742 on) (see Figure 7.1). In the words of the *Li-chi*: "The sacrifice to Heaven [lit., Ti or Shang-ti] is the highest expression of reverence [*ching*]." As with most other Chinese ceremonies, great symbolic emphasis was placed on color, form, number, position, music, and sacrificial objects. The color of the jade and silk offerings to Heaven was blue-green (*ch'ing*), the altar was circular (*yang*) in shape, and the associated number was nine. Appropriately, nine music pieces were played at the sacrifice. The emperor faced north. Contemporary descriptions of the elaborate ritual and predawn procession, lighted by red lanterns and screened from public view by blue-green cloth along the specially prepared path of yellow earth leading from the Forbidden City to the enclosed Temple of Heaven complex, suggest a solemn spectacle of silent splendor, punctuated only by the periodic calls of the master of ceremonies and the clear strains of various musical instruments.[8]

The great sacrifice to Earth, also undertaken personally by the emperor and similar in most respects to the sacrifice to Heaven, took place at a square (*yin*) altar during the summer solstice. In this ceremony, the jade and silk offerings were yellow, eight musical pieces were played, and the emperor faced south. Although the sacrifices to Heaven and Earth reflect an obvious *yin-yang* symbolism, the use of the number three in the construction of the altars and in various aspects of imperial ritual, together with the importance attached to the emperor's worship of his ancestors and other notables at the Great Temple (T'ai-miao), indicates the symbolic unity of the three powers (*san-ts'ai*): Heaven, Earth, and Man. Another important great sacrifice at Peking was to the Spirits of Land and Grain (*she-chi*). In this ceremony, as in all other ritual observances, the symbolism of number and color played a significant role; the number was five, and the colors were those associated with the five elements.[9]

Middle-level sacrifices at the capital included those for local Spirits of Land and Grain; the Sun (*chao-jih*); the Moon (*hsi-yüeh*); the tablets representing Wind, Rain, Thunder, Clouds, Mountains, and Rivers; the emperors of previous dynasties; the patron deity of agriculture (Hsien-nung); and various sages, meritorious officials, wise men, and virtuous women. Confucius was worshipped

FIGURE 7.2. The Altar of Heaven (II). This marble altar, where the emperor undertook sacrifices to Heaven at the winter solstice, has three major tiers, with stairways located in the four cardinal directions. Multiplication of elements grouped in nines occurs frequently in the altar, since nine is the highest single-digit number, symbolizing *yang*, Heaven, and the emperor. Photo by author.

at this middle level until 1907, when his ceremonies were elevated to the first level of great sacrifices (see Figure 7.4). Provincial-level middle sacrifices included all of the spirits noted above with the exception of previous emperors and naturalistic deities. Sacrifices to Confucius and other virtuous and wise individuals took place in Temples of Civil Virtue (Wen-miao), also called School-Temples (Hsüeh-kung).[10]

Common sacrifices, conducted at every capital city from Peking down to the district level, included ceremonies dedicated primarily to local protective deities, the most common of which were the so-called God of War (Kuan-ti), the God of Literature (Wen-ch'ang), the Three Sovereigns (San-huang), the Fire God (Huo-shen), the Dragon God (Lung-shen) and other tutelary deities worshipped at his shrine, and the City God (Ch'eng-huang). Common sacrifices also were undertaken for the unworshipped dead (*li*), whose wandering spirits were presumed to be a potential threat to the community unless placated. Significantly, these "neglected spirits" were supposed to report any immoral or illegal activities to the City God, who would in turn relay this information to his Ch'ing bureaucratic counterpart at the appropriate level for official investigation and punishment. According to the Ch'ing statutes, the deities in official religion operated in a hierarchy that paralleled exactly the administrative structure of the empire. District-level cults were subdivisions of prefectural-level cults and so on up to the imperial capital. Tablets of local spirits such as those of land and grain were inscribed not only with their names, but also with bureaucratic designations appropriate to their

FIGURE 7.3. The Hall of Prayer for Annual Harvests. This hall, set on a triple-tiered round marble terrace modeled on the Altar of Heaven, was one of three major ritual centers in the Temple of Heaven complex (T'ien-t'an). The other two were the Imperial Heavenly Vault and the Altar of Heaven, both south of the Hall of Prayer for Annual Harvests. Photo by author.

respective administrative levels. Some received imperially bestowed titles of nobility or other marks of distinction as well.[11]

Of all the deities in the official pantheon, the City God occupied a position of particular importance at the district level. As a rule, each newly appointed magistrate, before assuming his official duties, secluded himself in the local City God temple overnight, reporting to the local deity and offering a sacrifice, which usually included an oath that he would be honest and upright. "If I govern disrespectfully," read one such sacrificial oath, "am crafty, avaricious, get my colleagues in trouble, or oppress the people, may you send down retribution upon me for three years." Other similar oaths asked for assistance in administration and for the power to fortify personal virtue.[12]

As the otherworldly equivalent of the district magistrate, the City God not only had responsibility for all the spirits of the local dead (including the unworshipped dead, or *li*), but he also was expected to cooperate with his bureaucratic counterpart in bringing peace and prosperity to his district. The following inscription on a late Ming stele expresses this charge unambiguously:

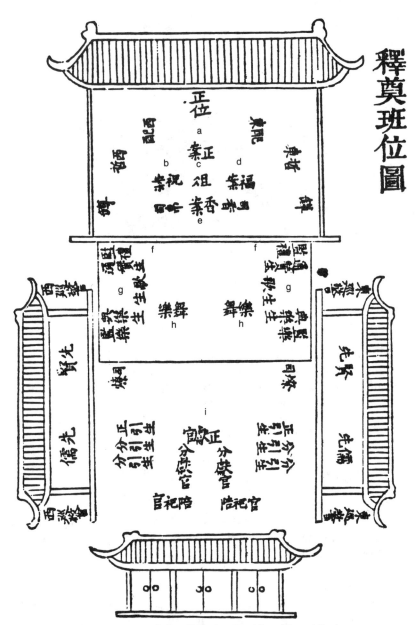

FIGURE 7.4. Arrangement of the *Shih-tien* Sacrifice. The *shih-tien* ceremony was conducted to venerate Confucius and other Confucian worthies at local Temples of Civil Virtue (*wen-miao*). The sacrificial layout indicates the symmetry of Ch'ing ritual fields, from the Forbidden City itself down to local temples and ancestral halls or shrines (see also Figures 7.6 and 7.7). Among the major elements in the *shih-tien* ritual were *a*, the primary table; *b*, prayer table; *c*, food stand; *d*, "blessings" table; *e*, incense table; *f*, supervisors of ceremony; *g*, singers and musicians; *h*, dancers; and *i*, principal sacrificial official. Source: *CCYWL, chüan* 1.

Ch'eng-huang temples are universally established, from the national capital to the prefectures and districts. While it is the magistrates who rule in the world of light [*yang*], it is the gods who govern in the world of shadows [*yin*]. There is close cooperation between the two authorities. When Emperor T'ai-tsu of the Ming dynasty [in 1370] conferred titles on the City Gods throughout the empire, there were ranks of emperors, princes, dukes, lords and marquises. . . . . The god's power is effective everywhere, rewarding the good with blessing and punishing the evil with calamity, . . . thus extending great benefit to man. Man prays to him for good harvests and for the avoidance of floods, droughts and pestilence.[13]

When trouble came, magistrates prayed to the City God for relief in the same vein, as in this impassioned appeal during the early Ch'ing:

O City God, both of us have duties to perform in this district: resisting disasters that may occur, offering protection in times of trouble, such things are part of the City God's spiritual realm and are part of the official's responsibilities. This year, while the workers were out in the fields but the grain had not matured, the eggs that had been laid by last year's locusts hatched out in the soil, causing almost half the wheat crops in the countryside to suffer this affliction. . . . The people could not repel this calamity, so they appealed to the officials for help. The officials could not repel this calamity for the people, so they [now] pray to the City God.

The prayer ends with the suggestion that the City God anticipates the needs of the people and officials and that he sympathizes with them. Could he not, then, asks the magistrate, transmit the prayers of the people and the officials to Heaven (lit., Shang-ti) in the form of a petition?[14] Like any other administrator, the City God could be appealed to by equals and inferiors, just as he could appeal to (or in fact be commanded by) a bureaucratic superior.

The bureaucratic character of the City God not only was expressed in his administrative responsibilities and his role as a transmitter of messages to higher supernatural authorities; it was also reflected in his physical image and surroundings. Although represented by a tablet at the open altars of official religious ceremonies, the City God was represented by an image when worshipped in his own temple. The temple itself was modeled precisely along the lines of a magistrate's yamen, down to the details of courtyard walls and flagstaffs, and the image of the City God was dressed in official robes and flanked by fierce-looking secretaries and yamen runners. Furthermore, the position of City God was almost invariably occupied by the spirit of a deceased former official, appointed by the emperor for a limited term, usually three years, in regular bureaucratic fashion. As a general rule, the lower the deity in the spiritual hierarchy of official religion, the more "human" it was.[15]

Spirits such as the City God were considered powerful but not omnipotent; they had specific spheres of administrative responsibility, and like their human counterparts, they were neither infallible nor incorruptable. They could be "bribed" by mortals and punished by their superiors in either the regular or the supernatural hierarchy. It was also commonly believed that spiritual officials such as the City God had their own families, including parents, wives, concubines, and children.

The City God cult represented a kind of symbolic meeting point between official religion and popular religion. Official worship of the deity involved solemn, dignified ceremonies in which only officials and degree holders could participate. These activities helped legitimize the state in the eyes of the common people and preserved local status distinctions. But popular worship of the City God had no such purpose and involved no such explicit distinctions. Individuals prayed to him for any and all kinds of favors (especially good health), and the ceremonies for the City God on his "birthday" and during his thrice-yearly tours of the city were among the largest, most impressive, and most widely observed public activities in traditional Chinese community life. On these occasions, the City God temple and its environs bustled with all kinds of activity: markets; theatrical performances; the selling of food; huge crowds; the noise of firecrackers, gongs, and drums; and the burning of incense. Most of these features were not to be found in the austere ritual of official religion.[16]

It is tempting, and I think at least partially justified, to consider certain deities associated with popular religion—notably local Lords of the Earth (T'u-ti kung)—as supernatural subdistrict administrators. Just as town or village leaders and *pao-chia* or *li-chia* headmen supervised subdistrict administrative units but were ultimately answerable to district magistrates, so in the supernatural subbureaucracy local Lords of the Earth oversaw discrete administrative areas but were ultimately responsible to City Gods. Like regular subdistrict administrators, these Lords of the Earth served localities rather than kinship groups, and although the vast majority were not based on decimal units, there is evidence to suggest that at least in some cases the subdistrict spiritual world could be organized along the same lines and designed for the same purposes as *pao-chia*. A gazetteer for the market town of Fo-shan in Kwangtung states, for example:

> Every one hundred households constitute a neighborhood [*li*]. In each neighborhood is established an altar for the gods of land and grain [*she-chi*], where annual sacrifices are offered in the spring and fall, with the head of the neighborhood officiating. . . . Before the feast that follows the sacrifice, one person reads a written oath: "All persons in this neighborhood agree to observe the rituals, and the strong refrain from oppressing the weak. . . . Those who fail to observe the common agreement, and those committing

rape, robbery, falsification, and other misdemeanors will be excluded from this organization."

This oath and the sacrifice that followed established a concrete link between the neighborhood social and moral order and the local spiritual establishment, illustrating the use of spiritual sanctions to enforce secular norms.[17]

The responsibilities of local Lords of the Earth, whether they were in charge of city wards, towns, villages, or subunits of these divisions, included "policing" the spirits of that area and reporting to the City God on human activities within the area of their jurisdiction. The Lord of the Earth's human charges, for their part, appealed to him for protection and blessings and dutifully conveyed to him information regarding recent births, marriages, deaths, and other important events. Not surprisingly, Lords of the Earth were often distinguished by status within the larger community, some being regarded as designated representatives of others.

In pursuing the idea of an analogy between Ch'ing sociopolitical institutions and the supernatural order, it may not be too farfetched to suggest that certain deities stood in relation to the local City God as the gentry class in Chinese society stood to the bureaucracy. Arthur Wolf points out, for example, that in modern Taiwan, where many traditional religious practices still persist, ritual specialists and close observers of temple affairs commonly distinguish two types of deities: officials (*shih*)—notably the City God and the Lord of the Earth—and wise persons (*fu*)—a category represented in the San-hsia area of the Taipei basin by several deities including the Holy Mother in Heaven (T'ien-shang sheng-mu, also known by her imperially bestowed title T'ien-hou [Consort of Heaven] and her popular name Ma-tsu, which means "grandmother").[18] While the comparison is not perfect, it suggests a kind of status similarity between low-ranking deities in official religion, such as the City God, and unofficial deities who performed important social roles. And just as capable gentry members might eventually find positions in the regular bureaucracy, so might wise persons in the supernatural social order become adopted into the official pantheon. The Holy Mother in Heaven was so worshipped in Ch'ing times.

In the last analysis, as Ch'ü T'ung-tsu has demonstrated, district magistrates often found it necessary to worship a wide range of official and "unofficial" deities. According to the *Ta-Ch'ing lü-li*, a magistrate could be punished with eighty strokes of the bamboo for sacrificing to a deity not included in the dynasty's book of official sacrifices; but when calamity struck, the local populace often demanded that the district magistrate offer sacrifices to any god who might be of assistance. Wang Hui-tsu informs us that during his tenure as a local Ch'ing official, concerned residents of his district once brought more than twenty images to his yamen, demanding that he pray to them for rain. He refused on grounds that the worship of these gods was unorthodox,

FIGURE 7.5. Temple of T'ien-hou. This late Ch'ing photograph shows a temple
of the Consort of Heaven (T'ien-hou), also known as the Holy Mother in Heaven
(T'ien-shang sheng-mu). The man at the entrance is a fortune-teller; the others are
idlers. The calligraphic inscriptions either identify the temple and its major deity
or serve as dedications and admonitions to good behavior on the part of the
populace. Photo courtesy China Trade Museum, Milton, Mass.

but he maintains that his refusal might have led to a disturbance had he
not already won the people's confidence. Many other local officials are known
to have succumbed to such pressure.[19]

As a general rule, we may say that a god's bureaucratic position, or at
least his relationship to officials within the natural or supernatural hierarchy,
meant more to most Chinese than any sectarian identification he possessed.
But sectarian identifications were not insignificant, especially in the realm of
nonofficial institutional religion. Before turning to the syncretism of Chinese
popular religion, let us examine briefly the major features of "orthodox"
Buddhism and Religious Taoism during the Ch'ing.

BUDDHISM AND RELIGIOUS TAOISM

Of the two liturgical teachings, Buddhism had by far the greater intellectual
appeal, as well as a greater institutional visibility and a larger number of

priests, nuns, and identifiable lay adherents (see Chapter 4). Although Religious Taoism enjoyed substantial imperial patronage in the late Ming period, it suffered some discrimination at the hands of the Ch'ing emperors. Buddhism, meanwhile, proved itself remarkably adaptable to the Chinese social and intellectual environment. Lay Buddhism in particular flourished during Ch'ing times precisely because, in Kristin Yü Greenblatt's words, it "did not demand a radical break from the social system in which it existed." It was, she maintains, "more activist than contemplative, more moralistic than theological, more world affirming than world rejecting."[20]

Institutional Buddhism also made compromises. No more vivid illustration of Buddhism's successful adaptation to the Chinese environment in Ch'ing times could be found than the common use of names such as Pao-chung ssu (Monastery for Honoring Loyalty [to the State]) or Hu-kuo ssu (Monastery for the Protection of the State). Particularly striking in light of the kinship-renouncing doctrine of Buddhism was the common designation Kuang-hsiao ssu (Monastery for the Glorification of Filial Piety).[21]

But despite these forms of cultural accommodation, the Ch'ing government displayed a profound (and predictable) ambivalence toward Buddhism. On the one hand, as alien conquerors, the Manchus made an early decision that "their most visible religio-political image was to be Chinese and Confucian." As a result, they made a concerted effort to maintain the ideological supremacy of orthodox Confucianism, with its strongly anti-Buddhist prejudices, and made no effort to impose their native shamanistic beliefs and practices on the Chinese population at large. On the other hand, the Ch'ing rulers recognized that institutional religion, if tightly controlled, could be used to substantial political advantage. Thus they found it periodically expedient to patronize Buddhism—especially in far-flung areas of the empire where the Buddhist (Lamaist) hierarchy was closely tied to local elite administration. In these regions, the Ch'ing emperors generally supported Lamaism and encouraged the image of themselves in these peripheral areas as Buddhist deities. And even in China Proper, in the nineteenth century, large amounts of imperial funds were devoted to the publication of Buddhist books and to the construction and restoration of Buddhist monasteries and temples.[22]

There was another factor that influenced the attitude of the Ch'ing government toward Buddhism: the personal beliefs of a number of Ch'ing emperors and their consorts. The Shun-chih emperor was friendly with several Buddhist monks, some of whom resided in the palace. The Yung-cheng emperor established a Buddhist publishing house and edited an anthology of quintessential Buddhist writings entitled *Yü-hsüan yü-lü* (Imperially Selected [Buddhist] Sayings); and his father and son (the K'ang-hsi and Ch'ien-lung emperors) both wrote prefaces for Buddhist books as well as dedicatory inscriptions for temples and monasteries. The ultrafilial Ch'ien-lung emperor even gave his mother more than nine thousand images of Buddhist deities on her seventieth birthday. Among nineteenth-century empresses and empresses dowager, the notorious Tz'u-hsi is well known for her Buddhist beliefs and pious devotions.[23]

Although the Ch'ing government continually worried about the seditious potential of Buddhist and other religious sects (see last section of this chapter), it was relatively unconcerned about the intellectual attractiveness of Buddhist philosophy and theology. To be sure, officially endorsed Confucian works such as the *Chin-ssu lu* emphasized that "a student should forthwith get as far away from Buddhist doctrines as from licentious songs and beautiful women. Otherwise they will infiltrate him." But most Ch'ing scholars did not reject Confucianism in favor of Buddhism, especially in their active years. Only in old age, or in times of severe social unrest and uncertainty, were significant numbers of scholars inclined to give serious attention to Buddhist doctrines. The Buddhist revival of the late Ch'ing period must be explained at least in part by the dual crises of dynastic decline and foreign invasion in the latter half of the nineteenth century.[24]

There were, of course, Confucian scholars such as P'eng Shao-sheng (1740–1796), who abandoned a promising career at the age of thirty—in the heyday of the Ch'ing empire—to become a lay monk. But even P'eng, the foremost Ch'ing scholar in popularizing Buddhism among the laity, was interested not in establishing Buddhism at the expense of Confucianism but rather in reconciling the two.[25]

Other Confucian scholars found it possible to accommodate Buddhist ideas by viewing them in a Confucian light. Chang Hsüeh-ch'eng, for example, advanced the rather common (and psychologically satisfying) argument that the origins of Buddhism could be found in the teachings of the *I-ching*. Further, he maintained that Buddhist mythology should not be taken lightly simply because it failed to make literal sense. "The Buddhists' description of Buddha as sixteen feet high with richly adorned, golden colored body, and their strange imaginings that no one has ever seen—the splendors of heaven, the torments of hell, the heavenly goddess scattering flowers, yakshas covered with hair—these things the Confucians criticize as absurd." But Chang insisted that the Buddhists were simply presenting their teachings symbolically, just as the *I-ching* did in discussing things such as "dragons with dark and yellow blood." In the end, Chang asserted, the best Buddhist writing came close to being "superior to that of the philosophers."[26]

A more down-to-earth illustration of the effort to interpret Buddhist concepts in Confucian fashion may be found in the following excerpt from a set of late Ch'ing clan rules (*tsung-kuei*):

> The Buddhists say that if you want to know about previous lives, look at the sufferings of this life. If you want to know about the next life, look at what is being done in this life. This is an excellent statement. However, what the Buddhists refer to as previous lives and the lives to come stems

from their theory of rebirth and transmigration of souls. I think what has happened before yesterday—the father and the ancestors—are really the previous lives, and that what will happen after today—the sons and the grandsons—are really the lives to come.[27]

In this view, at least, Buddhism and Confucianism were but two sides of the same coin of ethical conduct.

What, then, were the basic ideas of Buddhism? Buddhist teachings began with the Four Noble Truths: (1) life is painful, and endless cycle of births and deaths in a transient, sorrowful world; (2) the origin of pain and sorrow is selfish desire; (3) the elimination of pain and sorrow comes with the elimination of selfish desire; and (4) the elimination of selfish desire comes with following the Eightfold Noble Path. Buddhism thus shared with both Confucianism and philosophical Taoism an abiding concern with the reduction of desires.

The Eightfold Noble Path led from correct views to correct attitudes, correct speech, correct conduct, correct occupation, correct effort, correct perception and consciousness (alertness or self-examination), and correct concentration (meditation). By following Buddhist teachings as set forth in the huge corpus known as the *Tripitaka* (Chinese: *San-tsang* [Three Receptacles]) and derivative works, adherents could acquire the moral and mental discipline required to achieve Enlightenment. For the most part, Buddhist morality was based on concrete social values such as love, charity, courage, forbearance, and self-control, as well as respect for all living things; but Buddhist mental discipline was designed to demonstrate that in the end, all conceptions and distinctions were meaningless.

Buddhist Enlightenment implied a kind of transcendent understanding that permitted the perception of Ultimate Reality behind the "veil of illusion" (i.e., the false idea that ego exists). When this perception occurs, "the ties of false sensory discrimination and of the passions (greed, envy, etc.) are broken, so that we are no longer carried along in the stream of phenomenal existence." This stream of existence and continual flux, known popularly as the wheel of life and death, was based on the idea of karmic retribution (Chinese: *yeh-yin*). *Karma* literally means "act," but the concept includes both thoughts and deeds and implies causality. According to Buddhist doctrine, the accumulated karma of each sentient being in successive past existences determines the future existence of that being. Rebirths were believed to take place on several different planes (divine, human, animal, insect, etc.) depending on the net balance of "good" and "bad" karma (i.e., good or bad thoughts and deeds).[28]

Enlightenment, then, brought a state of oneness with Ultimate Reality, a break in the painful and sorrowful chain of causation. In Sanskrit this state was termed *Nirvana*, which literally means "extinction." Likened to the blowing out of a flame or the merging of a drop of water in an endless sea, the state (or one might say nonstate) of Nirvana was originally considered to be "incomprehensible, indescribable, inconceivable, unutterable." In the popular mind, however, it became equated with the idea of a heavenly repose. This was particularly the point of view encouraged by Mahayana Buddhism, a school of Indian Buddhism that developed in reaction to the austere and rather exclusive school known as Theravada, the Way of the Elders.

Although the Mahayana school considered itself to be the Great Vehicle (Chinese: Ta-ch'eng) of Buddhist truth, it could tolerate other belief systems, including Theravada, as "lesser truths," valid in some sense but ultimately inferior. This relativistic emphasis, a matter of expedience, made allowance for different levels of understanding both within Mahayana Buddhism and outside of its wide doctrinal sphere. Emphasizing salvation by faith and good works, Mahayana was more compassionate and other-oriented than Theravada. It involved more ritual and had a more elaborate metaphysics. Mahayana posited a universe consisting of an infinite number of spheres or realms going through an infinite number of cosmic periods. Within these realms were a myriad of heavens, hells, and assorted deities (all manifestations of the Buddha spirit or nature) that could be more easily comprehended by the common people. Nirvana was beyond all this. Given Mahayana Buddhism's eclectic spirit, ritualism, and polytheism, it is hardly surprising that it took firm root in China and peripheral areas such as Tibet, Mongolia, Korea, and Japan.

There were four main Mahayanist schools in late imperial China: the T'ien-t'ai, or Lotus (Fa-hua), School; the Hua-yen (lit., Flowery Splendor) School; the Pure Land School (Ching-t'u); and the Ch'an, or Meditation, School, known commonly as Zen, the Japanese pronunciation of Ch'an. Indicative of both the syncretic capacity of traditional Chinese thought and the accommodating outlook of Mahayana Buddhism, the Chinese had a common saying: "The T'ien-t'ai and Hua-yen Schools for [metaphysical] doctrine and the Ching-t'u and Ch'an Schools for practice." The scriptural common denominator of these and most other Chinese Buddhist schools was the so-called Lotus Sutra (*Miao-fa lien-hua ching*), a fascinating dramatic work blending elements of philosophy, theology, pageantry, and popular fable. In the fashion of the *I-ching*, the ideas of the Lotus Sutra were presented not in abstract terms but in concrete images and living symbols.[29]

The T'ien-t'ai School, which called the Lotus Sutra its own but could claim no real monopoly on it, distinguished three levels of "truth," each of which centered on the idea of *dharmas* (Chinese: *fa*), or psychosomatic "elements of existence." One level was the Truth of Emptiness—the idea that all *dharmas* are empty because they have no independent nature of their own. Another level was that of Temporary Truth, or "relative reality," in which *dharmas* had a temporary and dependent existence. In this realm, there were ten types of manifest existence, ranging from deities such as Buddhas ("enlightened ones") and bodhisattvas ("enlightened ones" who have postponed Nirvana to help others achieve Enlightenment) down to humans, beasts, and insects. The third level of truth was the Truth of the Mean—that *dharmas* are both empty and temporary, that the only reality was the Mind of Pure Nature, of which all phenomena were merely transient manifestations.[30]

The Hua-yen School represented the highest development of Buddhist metaphysics in China. Its central cosmological notion was that all things are "coexistent, interwoven, interrelated, interpenetrating, [and] mutually inclusive." This view was basically in accordance with the outlook of T'ien-t'ai Buddhism and was also congenial with the organic character of Chinese philosophy as a whole. In fact, the Hua-yen School contributed substantially to the development of neo-Confucian metaphysics in the Sung period. According to Hua-yen theory, each *dharma* possesses six characteristics in three complementary pairs: (1) universality and speciality, (2) similarity and difference, and (3) integration and disintegration. In *yin-yang* fashion, each opposing characteristic implied the other. As explained in the famous Chinese Buddhist analogy of the Golden Lion,

> The lion represents the character of universality. The five sense organs, being various and different, represent the character of speciality. The fact that they all arise from one single cause represents the character of similarity. The fact that its eyes, ears, and so forth do not exceed their bounds represents the character of difference. Since the combination of the various organs becomes the lion, this is the character of integration. And as each of the several organs remains in its own position, this is the character of disintegration.

Yet finally, when feelings have been eliminated and "true substance" revealed, everything becomes an undifferentiated mass. To quote again from the *Chin-shih-tzu chang* (Essay on the Golden Lion),

> When we look [clearly] at the lion and the gold, the two characters both perish and afflictions resulting from passions will no longer be produced. Although beauty and ugliness are displayed before the eye, the mind is as calm as the sea. Erroneous thoughts all cease, and there are no compulsions. One gets out of bondage and is free from hindrances, and forever cuts off the source of suffering. This is called entry into Nirvana.[31]

Ch'an Buddhism had much interest in Enlightenment, but little concern with metaphysical speculation. Ch'an was a uniquely Chinese brand of Buddhism, which had great appeal to artists and intellectuals—in part, no doubt, because of its strong affinities with philosophical Taoism. Ch'an Buddhism stressed the "Buddha-nature" within one's own mind and regarded the regular Buddhist apparatus of scriptures, offerings, recitation of the Buddha's name, and so forth as unnecessary. Rather, it favored an intuitive approach to Enlightenment. This emphasis on a direct apprehension of Ultimate Reality through meditation can be found in Confucian terms in the thought of the great Ming scholar Wang Yang-ming, whose intellectual enemies called him "a Buddhist in disguise."

Meditation appealed to virtually all members of the Chinese leisured class—Confucians, Taoists, and Buddhists alike. But orthodox Ch'an Buddhism required the discipline of a Ch'an master. The role of the master was not primarily to instruct in academic fashion, but rather to prepare the mind of the disciple to intuit Ultimate Reality. Various means were employed, notably physical shock—such as shouting or beatings—and the use of puzzling sayings, stories, or conversations known as *kung-an* (lit., "public cases"). These techniques were designed to jar the mind loose from its conventional moorings, to bring a recognition that Ultimate Reality could not be conceptualized or articulated. Such activities set the stage for fruitful meditation.[32]

Although the basic goal of Ch'an was direct intuition of the Buddha-mind, meditation could also involve deliberations of intellect. Enlightenment might come instantly or gradually. Paradoxically, in late imperial times, the "wordless doctrine" of Ch'an gave rise to an extensive literature, with commentaries and subcommentaries explaining the cryptic sayings of past Ch'an masters in even more cryptic terms. During the Ch'ing, this rather academic and somewhat fossilized form of Ch'an still enjoyed some influence, but in many cases, as E. Zürcher has remarked, it functioned more as an intellectual game of the Chinese elite than as a serious quest for Enlightenment.[33]

The most popular school of Chinese Buddhism in Ch'ing times was the Pure Land School. On the whole, this eclectic teaching avoided both the intense mental discipline of Ch'an and the scriptural and doctrinal emphasis of T'ien-t'ai and Hua-yen. The central focus of the Pure Land School was on salvation through faith and good works. The reward was rebirth in the Western Paradise (Hsi-t'ien) or Land of Eternal Life, presided over by Amitabha (Chinese: O-mi-t'o Fo), the "Buddha of Immeasurable Radiance." Chinese descriptions of this beautiful, enchanting, and serene land are as enticing as the descriptions of the bureaucratic purgatory known as the Ten Courts of Judgment (or Ten Courts of Hell) are terrifying.[34]

In the view of Pure Land adherents, faith might be expressed by the mere repetition of Amitabha's name, while good works included conventional Buddhist virtues and the avoidance of the so-called ten evils—murder, stealing, adultery, lying, duplicity, slander, foul language, lust, anger, and false views. In the popular conception, faith in Amitabha not only offered the hope of salvation but also protection from evil spirits, wild beasts, fire, bandits, and other threats on earth. Amitabha's principal agent, the female bodhisattva Kuan-yin (originally a male deity, Avalokilesvara, the "Lord Who Looks Down"), proved especially popular in China as a source of protection and blessings and as the Goddess of Fertility. Other major deities in the vast Chinese Buddhist pantheon included Yao-shih Fo (the God of Medicine, identified with Bhaisajyaguru), Mi-lo Fu (Sanskrit: Maitreya, the Buddha of the Future), Wen-shu (Sanskrit: Manjusri, a bodhisattva), P'u-hsien (Sanskrit: Samantabhadra, also a bodhisattva), and Yen-lo Wang (Sanskrit: Yama, Judge and King of Hell). These, however, represented only a fraction of the Buddhas, bodhisattvas, arhats (Chinese: *lo-hans*, disciples of Buddha), and other deities who operated in the limitless Mahayana universe.[35]

It is worthy of note that in Ch'ing times, a number of monasteries carried on the joint practice of Ch'an and Pure Land Buddhism (*Ch'an-Ching shuang-hsiu*). This usually meant that these establishments had both a meditation hall and a hall for reciting the Buddha's name (*nien-Fo*). But monasteries might also permit a special form of joint practice in one hall. Holmes Welch explains: "In both sects the goal was to reduce attachment to ego. The Pure Land method of 'no stirrings in the whole mind' (*i-hsin pu-luan*) did not differ essentially from the Ch'an method of 'meditating to the point of perfect concentration' (*ch'an-ting*)." The eminent Ch'an abbot Hsü-yün (1840–1959) is said to have remarked, "All the Buddhas in every universe, past, present, and future, preach the same *dharma* [here meaning "doctrine"]. There is no real difference between the methods advocated by Sakyamuni [the historic Buddha] and Amitabha." For this reason, Hsü-yün advised some of his disciples who would have found Ch'an meditation too difficult that they should recite the Buddha's name instead.[36]

As is well known, Religious Taoism owed much to institutional Buddhism. Wing-tsit Chan goes so far as to describe it as "a wholesale imitation of Buddhism, notably in its clergy, temples, images, ceremonies and canon."[37] But despite Religious Taoism's profound cultural debt to Buddhism, it was not simply a pale reflection of the sinicized Indian import. Not only did formal Taoist ritual and symbolism differ significantly from that of institutional Buddhism, but the major thrust of Taoist religion ran counter to the conventional Buddhist emphasis on reincarnation. For all the diversity of Taoist religious beliefs and practices, the aim of Religious Taoism was not primarily to break the chain of causation through the elimination of consciousness, but rather to achieve a special kind of transcendence, manifest in the ability to know and manipulate the supernatural environment. And although Religious Taoism shared with philosophical Taoism an organic view of man and the universe, the goal of Religious Taoist ritual and personal regimen (meditative, dietary, pharmacological, gymnastic, and sexual) was not merely to find one's niche in the cosmic order, but to acquire a form of cosmic power. Religious Taoism offered more than psychic release; it held the promise of longevity, invulnerability, and perhaps immortality.

Two main schools of liturgical Taoism flourished in late imperial times: the so-called Northern School, or Ch'üan-chen (Complete Perfection) Sect, and the Southern School, or Cheng-i (True Unity) Sect. The Ch'üan-chen Sect arose during the Sung dynasty in response to Ch'an Buddhism. Like devotees of Ch'an, Ch'üan-chen Taoists preferred the rigors of monastic discipline. Theirs was a life of celibacy, vegetarianism, and abstention from alcoholic drinks. The spiritual headquarters of this sect were located in Peking, at the White Cloud Monastery. The Cheng-i Sect, which traced its spiritual origins to the late Han period, had its headquarters in Lung-hu Mountain, Kiangsi province. The hereditary Heavenly Master (T'ien-shih) of this sect, sometimes erroneously termed the Taoist Pope, had considerable religious authority in late Ming and early Ch'ing times, but his power was considerably curtailed thereafter. Nonetheless, the Cheng-i Sect enjoyed what amounted to "liturgical hegemony" among the various schools of Religious Taoism in late imperial times and continued to receive a measure of support from the Ch'ing court.[38]

Cheng-i adherents lived a very different life from that of their spiritual brethren in the Ch'üan-chen Sect. Cheng-i priests were married, they lived at home among the people, they were not subject to monastic discipline (except by choice), and they were allowed to eat meat and drink alcoholic beverages, except during special fasts. They relied primarily on charms and magic rather than diet for self-preservation, and their principal function in traditional Chinese society was to sell charms, tell fortunes, and perform various religious ceremonies for the popular masses (see next section).

Religious Taoism, like Buddhism, had a wide variety of subsects that were at least tangentially related to one or another of the major schools. Despite some sectarian differences, most Religious Taoists embraced the same basic ideas. These were distilled from the huge Taoist canon known as the *Tao-tsang* (Receptacle of Taoism), the Taoist counterpart to the Buddhist *Tripitaka*. Among the most commonly recited official scriptures in this vast and varied corpus were the *Yü-huang ching* (Jade Emperor's Classic) and the *San-kuan ching* (Three Officials' Classic), both of which were used in Ch'üan-chen and Cheng-i devotions. Although most of the scriptural, scholastic, and historical writings in the *Tao-tsang* dealt with matters such as religious doctrine, liturgy, charms, magic, hymns, and lore, the collection also included the works of the great classical Taoist philosophers.[39]

The world view of the Religious Taoists as expressed in the *Tao-tsang* was based in a much more explicit way than that of the Buddhists on notions of *yin-yang*/five-elements cosmogony and cosmology. According to one well-known formulation, derived from the *Tao-te ching* and clearly related to orthodox neo-Confucian cosmological ideas, the nameless, unmoved Prime Mover (Tao) gives birth to the One (*t'ai-chi*, the Supreme Ultimate; or *hun-tun*, Primordial Chaos). The One gives birth to the Two (the *yang* force or principle), and the Two gives birth to the Three (the *yin* force). These three forces are personified in Religious Taoism by the Three Pure Ones (San-ch'ing): (1) the Primordial Heavenly Worthy (Yüan-shih T'ien-tsun), symbol of life-giving primordial breath (*ch'i*); (2) the Ling-pao Heavenly Worthy (Ling-pao T'ien-tsun), symbol of the spirit (*shen*) in man; and (3) the Tao-te Heavenly Worthy (Tao-te T'ien-tsun), symbol of man's vital essence (*ching*). The Three Pure Ones, in turn, generate the five elements, personified in the Five Rulers (Wu-ti) of traditional Chinese mythology. From these five elements come the myriad things of nature.[40]

A knowledge of *yin-yang* and five-elements symbolism is essential for an understanding not only of traditional Chinese cosmology and ritual but also of Taoist alchemy, for man in the Religious Taoist view was seen as a microcosm of the universe. Both the regimen of meditative "internal alchemy" (*nei-tan*)—including breathing exercises, sexual activity, and other forms of physical self-cultivation—and "external alchemy" (*wai-tan*)—including the use of chemicals, drugs, and herbal medicines—were based on *yin-yang* and five-elements correlations. So, in fact, was all of traditional Chinese medicine. Each was concerned primarily with the physical benefits to be derived from achieving a harmonious balance of *yin-yang* and five-elements influences within the body, and each assumed an integral relationship between the parts of the body and the whole. The basic principles and purposes of alchemy and acupuncture were thus essentially the same.[41]

As was the case with Mahayana Buddhism, the value system of Religious Taoism reflected heavy Confucian influence. Although orthodox Buddhists and Taoists seldom spoke of *jen* or *li* in the Confucian sense, they admired the virtues of loyalty, faithfulness, integrity, duty, and even filial piety. Significantly, the curriculum in Buddhist and Taoist monasteries often included works from the classical Confucian canon, and Confucian values found their way to the popular masses in vernacular religious tracts such as *shan-shu* ("morality books") and *pao-chüan* ("precious scrolls").[42]

In keeping with its obsessive interest in longevity, but inspired by the Buddhist idea of karmic retribution, Religious Taoism developed an accounting system of merits and demerits that rewarded good behavior with extended life and subtracted years for evil deeds. This system, which esteemed Confucian virtues but also took into account Buddhist concern for all living creatures, found its way into Buddhist thought by Ming-Ch'ing times. Like the Buddhists, the Religious Taoists worshipped a vast number of protective deities, including not only the Three Pure Ones and the Five Rulers but also such popular gods and genies as the Jade Emperor (Yü-huang), the God of Literature (Wen-ch'ang), the Royal Mother of the West (Hsi-wang mu), the Eight Immortals (Pa-hsien), and a host of spirits associated with stars and other natural objects, historical figures, and even parts of the body.[43]

POPULAR RELIGION

These Taoist gods—like those of Buddhism and the official state cult—were the common property of the Chinese masses. Although some deities were clearly identified in the popular mind with either Buddhism or Taoism (or both) and others were patronized heavily by the elitist system of official religion, they all remained part of a gigantic, fluid network of national, regional, and local gods—each of whom could be supplicated by lay worshippers with no sense of disloyalty to the others.

Popular Chinese divinities were known by the generic term *shen*, or "spirit." These spirits were often deified individuals or deified forces of nature. They were usually represented by images or tablets placed in temples or shrines. Some deities were honored by their own private shrines, while others were worshipped together in temples. The significant feature of this expansive religious world, in addition to its obvious eclecticism, was its organization along functional lines. In the words of C. K. Yang,

> In popular religious life it was the moral and magical functions of the cults, and not the delineation of the boundary of religious faiths, that dominated people's consciousness. Even priests in some country temples were unable to reveal the identity of the religion to which they belonged. Centuries of mixing gods from different faiths into a common pantheon had produced a functionally oriented religious view that relegated the question of religious identity to a secondary place.[44]

Religious Taoists claimed that the City God was their own creation, whereas frescoes depicting the Ten Courts of Judgment in the City God's temple testified to Buddhist influence; but the important point to both officials and the common people was that the City God was a local administrator, with vitally important bureaucratic responsibilities.

Professor Yang has documented in detail the functional character of popular temple cults in traditional China. His survey of nearly eighteen hundred major temples in eight representative localities, although reflecting data drawn from sources published in the 1920s and 1930s, suggests patterns of distribution that probably prevailed in Ch'ing times. Dividing these temples into five functional categories, Yang's survey yields the following information: 33.7 percent of the temples were devoted to deities associated with the well-being of the social and political order (kinship groups, local communities, and the state); 22.7 percent were devoted to the general moral order (heavenly deities and underworld authorities); 8.1 percent were devoted to economic functions (patron deities of occupational groups, etc.); 1.1 percent were devoted to the preservation of health; and 3.8 percent were devoted to general and personal welfare (including "devil dispellers," "blessing deities," and unspecified gods).

The remainder of the temples (30.6 percent) were monasteries and nunneries, the overwhelming majority of which (nearly 90 percent) were Buddhist.[45]

Yang emphasizes that this functional breakdown is somewhat misleading, since Chinese gods undertook a wide range of responsibilities and could be appealed to for many diverse purposes. Thus, the low percentage of temples specifically devoted to health-giving deities does not reflect lack of concern with good health. Quite the reverse was true. But the fact that most Chinese deities were believed to have the power to bestow or restore good health made functional specificity less important in this particular instance.

On the other hand, specific functions might be very important in individual localities. The Sea God (Hai-shen) and Holy Mother in Heaven, for example, had special significance in coastal areas. The community of Fo-shan, near Canton, which was well known for its firecracker industry, had nearly a dozen temples devoted to the Fire God. Overall, however, the most popular deities nationwide tended to be those identified with institutional religion, as discussed in previous sections. This phenomenon, it may be added, reflects the power of popular cults as well as the strength of institutional religion.

But whether patronized institutionally or not, all deities were viewed in bureaucratic terms, for no one in Chinese society could conceive of power that was not bureaucratic. The more bureaucratic the god, the more powerful—although lines of authority and responsibility were not drawn as clearly in the huge popular pantheon as they were in the more orderly hierarchy of official religion.[46]

In the popular conception, as in the elite view, all gods were subordinate to, and servants of, Heaven. Characteristically, however, Heaven was personalized in the popular religious vocabulary by terms such as the Heavenly Emperor (T'ien-ti), the Heavenly Noble (T'ien-kung), and the Jade Emperor. Although popular religion was permeated with concepts and terms derived from elite culture, it was only a version of that culture, not a direct replica. Not only were abstractions such as Heaven generally personalized, but other concepts were also manipulated to conform more closely to the social outlook of commoners. Thus, where the elite version of nature and the cosmos emphasized harmony and order, the popular emphasis was on conflict and chaos. Where elite cosmology focused on the interaction and alternation of *yin* and *yang*, popular religion saw a constant struggle between *yang* spirits (i.e., *shen*) and malevolent *yin* spirits known as *kuei* ("ghosts" or "demons").[47]

This struggle was viewed as natural and inevitable. According to a popular proverb, "Just as all things consist of *yin* and *yang*, and *yin* and *yang* are everywhere, so *shen* and *kuei* are omnipresent."[48] The struggle between *shen* and *kuei* did not, however, represent a titanic battle between cosmic forces of good and evil. Rather, the relationship between *shen* and *kuei* was viewed as analogous to that existing between the Ch'ing government and disruptive elements in society such as bandits and beggars. In a very real sense, it was the administrative task of *shen* to control *kuei*.

Kuei were held responsible for all kinds of misfortune and afflictions, from accidents, illness, and death to barrenness, crop failures, and birth defects. They were believed to possess or kidnap people, to steal things, and to play tricks on people. They could remain invisible or assume a human or animal form. Although *kuei* existed in seemingly endless profusion, they were associated primarily with the realm of *yin*: darkness, the ground, water, and lonely places. Many were believed to be unplaced spirits of the dead; others were considered to be inimical forces of nature. None were friendly. The supernatural world of the Chinese peasant, like the real one, could be a frightening place.[49]

The purpose of most popular religious practices was to enlist *shen* in controlling or neutralizing *kuei* and at the same time to appease the latter. In the popular mind, this was also the aim of official religion and much of the public religious activity of Buddhist and Taoist priests. The complex Religious Taoist rite of cosmic renewal (*chiao*), for example, was explicitly designed to "restore *yang*, that is, life, light and blessing, to its pristine state of growth, and to expel the forces of *yin*, darkness, evil and death."[50]

Kuei could be appeased by offerings of incense, food, money, or goods. They could also be repelled by various means, including the written names or images of "demon-dispelling" deities such as Chung K'uei and Chiang T'ai-kung; amulets made of peach wood or other potent materials; paper strips with the eight trigrams or the characters Heaven and Earth and *yin* and *yang* written on them; weapons such as swords, daggers, clubs, and spears; and various *yang* symbols—loud noises, fire, blood, mirrors, and so on. Significantly, many protective objects were closely identified with the scholarly life of the Chinese elite: copies or pages from the Confucian classics, written characters, calligraphy brushes, official seals, and such.

Rituals of exorcism (*chieh-chu*) employed numerous objects such as those mentioned above, as well as spells (*chieh* or *chu*) and written charms (*fu*). Some of these rituals could be undertaken individually or collectively by laymen, but most involved "professional" religious agents—Buddhist and Taoist priests, spirit mediums (*t'ung-chi*), sorcerers (*wu*), magicians (*fa-shih*), and soothsayers (*hsiang-ming shih*)—sometimes in combination. These individuals were believed to possess the special skills required to identify the source of *kuei*-related problems and to devise successful strategies for their eradication.[51]

Astrology and divination often came into play, but the primary means for expelling *kuei* were charms written in the form of commands from superiors (*shen*) to inferiors (*kuei*). Henri Doré describes charms in the following terms:

> A charm is an official document, a mandate, an injunction, emanating from the god and setting to work superhuman powers who carry out the orders

of the divinity. . . . The charm being an official document, . . . terminates in much the same manner as Chinese imperial edicts: "let the law be obeyed, let this order be respected and executed forthwith." . . . The effect of the charm, as well as that of any other decree or command, depends principally on the power of him who has issued it.

Although charms were generally associated with Taoist religious activity, Buddhist priests also employed them and sold them for profit. Charms could be used not only to drive away *kuei* in every conceivable circumstance but also to right wrongs (such as unjust lawsuits) and to provide for the needs and interests of the deceased.[52]

There are many colorful accounts of the activation and utilization of charms by priests, mediums, sorcerers, and magicians, but not all religious agents in traditional China operated with the same degree of drama and pageantry. Public divination, for example—based on the *I-ching*, physiognomy, the dissection of characters, the casting of lots, the reading of omens, and various other techniques—tended to be a rather somber and subdued ritual. The same was true of the popular form of geomantic divination known as *feng-shui* (lit., "wind and water"). The most commonly held theory of *feng-shui* was predicated on the belief that *yin-yang* currents of cosmic breath (*ch'i*), which flowed in every geographic area, influenced human fortunes. These currents, which were affected by astrological influences and by the five elements, were manifest in local topography. The task of a geomancer (*feng-shui hsien-sheng*) was to calculate, on the basis of an enormous number of topographical and astrological variables, the most favorable position to locate residences for both the living (homes, temples, businesses, official buildings, etc.) and the dead (graves).[53]

The best spot was, of course, at the proper junction of *yin* and *yang* currents. In the words of a nineteenth-century Western student of *feng-shui*,

The azure dragon [*yang*] must always be to the left [looking southward], and the white tiger [*yin*] to the right of any place supposed to contain a luck-bringing site. . . . In the angle formed by dragon and tiger . . . the luck-bringing site, the place for a tomb or dwelling, may be found. I say it *may* be found there, because, besides the conjunction of dragon and tiger, there must be there also a tranquil harmony of all the heavenly and terrestrial elements which influence that particular spot, and which is to be determined by observing the compass and its indication of the numerical proportions, and by examining the direction of the water courses.[54]

The "compass" in question was the *lo-p'an*, an elaborate instrument about the size of a small dish, with a magnetic needle pointing south and a series of concentric circles arranged in symbolic sets. Jeffrey Meyer describes the prototype:

Schematically the circles of the compass begin with an inner set which deals with the center, then a group dealing with earth, then the Prior Heavens, and finally the Posterior Heavens. Represented among the circles are nearly all the Chinese symbols which are used in dealing with space and time: the trigrams and hexagrams [of the *I-ching*] in both the Prior and Posterior Heavens sequences, the ten stems and twelve branches, the sexagenary characters, the five elements, *yin* and *yang*, the twenty-four directions, the nine moving stars, the six constellations, the twenty-eight asterisms (*hsiu*), the four seasons and directions, the animals, colors, the twenty-four fifteen-day periods of the solar year, and the seventy-two five-day divisions of the year. All these are interrelated in various combinations and thus repeated frequently in the thirty-eight circles.[55]

Geomantic compasses were not always so complex, but all assumed an integral relationship between topography (*ti-li*) and astrological configurations (*t'ien-li*).

The *lo-p'an* was often used in conjunction with the Imperial Almanac (see Chapter 10), since the fundamental assumption of both was that certain stars and groupings of stars, in phase with *yin-yang* and five-elements influences, played a role in earthly affairs. This assumption was shared by all levels of Chinese society and expressed in a variety of rituals, from the worship of Heaven in official sacrifices to the ceremonies of Religious Taoism and *feng-shui* divination. Thus, in practice, popular astrology—not to mention Buddhist notions of karmic retribution, Religious Taoist ideas of merits and demerits, and concepts such as the mysterious, slow-moving cosmic force known as *ch'i-yün*—complicated the essentially naturalistic interpretation of fate offered by orthodox Confucians.

In *feng-shui* calculations, the almanac was consulted to reveal the line on the geomantic compass that would be auspicious in a given year for the construction of a building or a grave. Modifications could often be made in an environment by the addition of artificial elements, but if the timing was wrong, there might be no alternative but to postpone construction until a lucky year. In the meantime, of course, other buildings erected in the area might alter the *feng-shui*. This led to much social conflict in traditional China as individuals competed for favorable geomantic influences.

Feng-shui specialists had comparatively high status in traditional Chinese society—despite persistent criticism from officials and other members of the orthodox elite. These criticisms were not, however, directed primarily against the general theory of *feng-shui*, for all levels of society accepted its basic assumptions. Rather, the literati objected to the *practice* of geomancy, which generated social tensions, often led to delayed burials (a serious breach of mourning ritual), and involved the manipulation of the Chinese masses by religious agents who were not part of the orthodox elite. This fear seems to have motivated much elite criticism of popular religious practice in China.[56]

Traditional Chinese homes reflected in microcosm the complex religious world outlined above. They were served by religious agents such as priests and geomancers and protected by a host of deities and guardian figures. The vast majority had an altar to the household Lord of the Earth on the floor near the door and a place for the God of the Hearth (Ts'ao-shen) near the cooking stove. Wealth gods might be located in the hall or main room of the house, along with Kuan-yin or another patron deity. But the focal point of religious life in virtually every Chinese home was the ancestral altar, located by definition in the principal room. For in Chinese society, ancestor worship was primary; individual or communal worship, only secondary. No ritual or institution did more to reinforce the solidarity of the family system than ancestor worship, and none was taken more seriously by both society and the state.[57]

The basic premise in ancestor worship was that the soul of a departed family member consisted of two main elements, a *yin* component known as *p'o* (associated with the grave), and a *yang* component known as *hun* (associated with the ancestral tablet). According to one popular conception, these basic components became three separate "souls," each demanding ritual attention: one that went to the grave with the body, one that went to the Ten Courts of Judgment and was eventually reincarnated, and one that remained near the ancestral tablet on the family altar. *P'o* had the potential of becoming *kuei* if unplacated by sacrifices, but the spirits of one's own ancestors were not generally considered to be *kuei*. One's own naturally became *shen*.[58]

There were two universal aspects of ancestor worship in traditional China, mortuary rites (*sang-li*) and sacrificial rites (*chi-li*). Mortuary rites involved elaborate mourning practices that differed in particulars from region to region but shared certain major features. Among these were reporting the death to agents of the supernatural bureaucracy, dressing the corpse in special burial clothes and placing it in a coffin with various symbolic items, and mourning ritually within the family, ideally according to the five degrees of relationship (*wu-fu*) stipulated in the *Li-chi*. Priests were called upon to say prayers for the departed, in hopes of building up merit for them in the next life and speeding their way through the Ten Courts of Judgment. A funeral procession for the body and spirit tablet and a mourning feast for the family marked the formal conclusion of the process. In all these highly ritualized activities, the size and duration of the mourning display varied according to social class and income, but all families strained their financial resources to the limit in order to exhibit the proper measure of filial devotion (and community status). Deceased children were not usually honored, however, for their premature death was itself considered an unfilial act.[59]

Sacrificial rites were of two main sorts: daily or bimonthly devotions and anniversary services. Incense was burned regularly on the ancestral altar, which housed the family spirit tablets in hierarchical order (see Figures 7.6 and

四品至七品官家廟圖

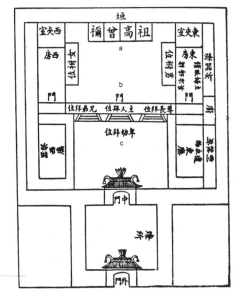

For officials of ranks four to seven

一品至三品官家廟圖

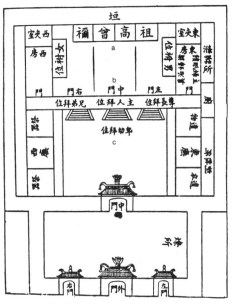

For officials of ranks one to three

八九品官家廟圖

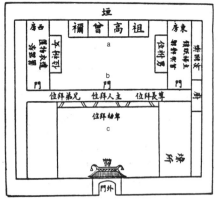

For officials of ranks eight and nine

FIGURE 7.6. Family Ancestral Temples for Officials. In the diagrams, *a* indicates ancestral tablets; *b,* gate, through which passes the principal worshipper; and *c,* junior worshippers. Source: *WHL, chüan* 14.

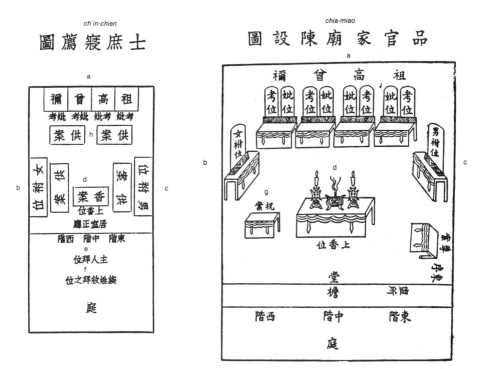

FIGURE 7.7. Ancestor Worship. Ancestor worship bound China together by reinforcing the entire kinship structure and encouraging a profound precedent-mindedness at all levels of society; it also provided a shared sense of cultural concern, manifest in common symbolism and religious practice. Note the similar layout of (*right*) the family ancestral temple (*chia-miao*) of the official class and (*left*) the more modest sacrificial shrine (*ch'in-chien*) of the gentry class and commoners. The ancestral tablets (*a*), male and female, stand in front of the incense table (*d*), flanked by tablets representing recently deceased females (*b*) and males (*c*) situated on the right (*yin*) and left (*yang*) side of the main altar (as viewed by the ancestors). The *chia-miao* shows a prayer table (*g*), while the *ch'in-chien* indicates offering tables (*h*), the primary worshipper (*e*), and the positioning of relatives in rank order (*hsü-pai*, *f*). Source: *WHL, chüan* 14.

FIGURE 7.8. Ancestral Tablets. These traditional-style ancestral tablets, arranged in hierarchical order, are from a small clan temple in contemporary Taiwan. Photo by author.

7.7). In front of these tablets often glowed an eternal flame, symbol of the ancestor's abiding presence within the household. Anniversary rites took place on the death date of each major deceased member of the family. Sacrificial food was offered, and living members of the family participated in the ceremony in ritual order based on age and generation. Sacrifices were also made to the ancestors during major festival periods and on important family occasions such as births and weddings (see Chapter 10). In general, these domestic devotions reflected a ritual apparatus characteristic of most other forms of Chinese religious practice.[60]

In the eyes of orthodox Confucians, ancestor worship was considered to be essentially a secular rite, with no religious implications. Deemed to be nothing more than the "expression of human feelings," mourning and other ritual observances expressed love and respect for the dead, at the same time cultivating the virtues of filial piety, loyalty, and faithfulness. Ancestor worship was a standard means of "honoring virtue and repaying merit" (*ch'ung-te pao-kung*), in the stock Chinese phrase. The Confucian gentleman sacrificed to his ancestors because it was the proper thing to do; lesser men did so to "serve the spirits."[61]

FIGURE 7.9. Grave. This Chinese grave in contemporary Taiwan illustrates the "horseshoe" style typical of many southern areas of China. Even today in Taiwan, such graves are usually located with *feng-shui* considerations in mind. Photo by author.

This attitude was consistent with the general neo-Confucian tendency to encourage rational and secular interpretations of otherworldly phenomena. In neo-Confucian literature, for example, the popular religious terms *kuei* and *shen* became expressly identified as the abstract forces of *yin* and *yang*. Official religion was justified at least in part as a means of motivating the masses to perform acts of Confucian piety. Sections on religion in local gazetteers often quoted the following commentary to the *I-ching*, attributed to Confucius himself: "The sages devised guidance in the name of the gods, and [the people of] the land became obedient." Even the employment of priests, geomancers, and other religious agents by elite households could be explained away as matters of habit, female indulgence, or a kind of filial insurance for ancestors in case the popular Buddhist version of the afterlife happened to be correct.[62]

But where did neo-Confucian "rationalism" end and popular "superstition" begin? Although popular religion reflected the social landscape of its adherents, it was still in many ways "a variation of the same [elite] understanding of the world." The "Heaven" of the Chinese literati may have been remote and impersonal, but it rewarded Confucian virtue and punished vice in the same spirit as the Jade Emperor and his agents. The omens and avenging ghosts of popular vernacular literature had their supernatural counterparts in the official dynastic histories. The cosmological principles of astrology and divination—not to mention many specific religious beliefs and practices—were the same for all classes of Chinese society, as was the tendency to view the spirit world in bureaucratic terms. Furthermore, the evidence suggests strongly that in the mind of the elite, *shen* and *kuei* were not always identifed simply as the abstract forces of *yin* and *yang*. It may even be suggested that the ceremonies and symbolism of official sacrifices, community religion, and domestic worship evoked many of the same emotions in the elite that they did among the common people—although the evidence is largely impressionistic. At least such rituals gave all sectors of Chinese society a sense of shared interest and common purpose.[63]

There was, of course, a heterodox tradition of popular religion that was less compatible with the elite outlook. Sworn brotherhood associations of the Triad type in southern China, and folk religious sects of the White Lotus variety in the north, challenged certain Chinese social conventions and were marked by a strong millenarian emphasis. Monotheistic religious teachings such as Islam and Christianity also contained millenarian elements and posed a threat to the Confucian order by their devotion to a religious authority higher than the state.[64]

Confucian scholars might criticize the specific beliefs of these religious groups on any number of grounds—the Triads, for example, because of their denial of the primacy of orthodox kinship bonds; the White Lotus sects for their messianic belief in the Eternal and Venerable Mother (Wu-sheng lao-mu); the Christians for their negative attitudes toward ancestor worship and for their doctrine of original sin. But, as indicated in Chapter 4, the most threatening aspect of heterodox religious traditions was their political potential, their capacity to attract and mobilize disgruntled members of Chinese society. Triad and White Lotus religious associations were closely linked with secret-society activity and popular rebellion throughout late imperial times, and during the nineteenth century, two of the most lengthy and destructive rebellions in Chinese history were inspired, respectively, by Islam and Christianity.[65]

Yet even so iconoclastic a popular movement as the Christian-inspired Taiping Rebellion (1850–1864)—which attacked Confucianism, Buddhism, and Taoism; advocated communalism and equality between men and women; and sought to eliminate long-standing social practices such as concubinage, footbinding, and ancestor worship—made many concessions to Chinese tradition in the realms of both theory and practice. The Taipings used concepts, phrases, and allusions from Confucian, Buddhist, and Taoist sources, held traditional views on the place of *li* (ritual) in preserving status distinctions (including the subordination of wives to their husbands), held Confucian views on matters such as name taboos, and employed conventional symbols of imperial legitimacy in both their political institutions and public ceremonies. Even their private devotions to God (Shang-ti or T'ien), the Heavenly Father (T'ien-fu), bore a striking resemblance to ancestor worship, down to the burning of incense before a spirit tablet in homes and offices.[66]

Undoubtedly the use of time-honored terms and concepts, sources of authority, ceremonial forms, and political symbols diminished somewhat the revolutionary impact of heterodox movements—particularly in the popular mind. It is true, of course, that even in orthodox society a tension always existed between the "ordered" realm of elite ritual and the "disorder" of popular religion.[67] But the dialectic operating between the two favored order overall, as did shared ethical attitudes, philosophical concepts, and specific ritual practices. Similar cultural common denominators existed in the areas of Chinese art, literature, music, and drama.

CHAPTER 8

Art

In the main, Chinese art reflected the cultural concerns of the orthodox Confucian elite. It was cosmologically based, tradition-bound, invariably meaningful (as opposed to purely decorative), and carefully catalogued and evaluated according to ethical as well as stylistic criteria. Despite the great range of artistic achievement in late imperial times, certain symbols and aesthetic assumptions were widely shared by all sectors of society, and although these symbols and assumptions were not always interpreted or expressed in precisely the same way, like ritual they contributed to a sense of cultural unity and integrity that transcended time and social class. Furthermore, although the Ch'ing period has been characterized as "an antiquarian age when, as never before, men looked back into the past," in the early years of the dynasty there was considerable vitality in the arts. And even in decline, Ch'ing art continued to display a high level of technical competence and visual beauty.[1]

ATTITUDES TOWARD ART

From the elite's standpoint there were two types of worthwhile art: that which the elite enjoyed but did not create, and that which the elite created and therefore esteemed most. The former included the work of skilled craftsmen, from elegant ancient bronzes to colorful contemporary ceramics; the latter embraced the refined arts of the brush—painting and calligraphy. Popular art—from wall paintings and icons to folk crafts such as basketwork, fans, umbrellas, toys, and papercuts—remained vital and vigorous throughout the Ch'ing period, but it was seldom taken seriously by Chinese art connoisseurs.

Connoisseurship in traditional China required wealth, leisure, and education. As amateur artists, gentry scholars were expected to have a discriminating eye and to possess attractive art works, but they were not always the most famous or successful collectors. The salt merchant An Ch'i (born, c. 1683), for example, was the envy of all literati in the area of Tientsin. Having purchased a number of paintings and calligraphic scrolls from well-known Ming and early Ch'ing connoisseurs, in time An became a connoisseur himself. His annotated catalogue of paintings and calligraphy, completed in 1742, was highly prized by Ch'ing collectors for its detailed descriptions of outstanding art work. It was reprinted twice by the noted antique collector and art patron Tuan-fang (1861–1911).[2]

Chinese art has long been characterized by a remarkable feeling for natural beauty, perfection of form, grace, and refinement. It is also noteworthy for its optimism, love of nature, and organic quality. As indicated in Chapter 5, much of the formal aesthetics of the Chinese elite were shaped by a long-standing cognitive emphasis on *yin-yang* principles and relationships. As with music, ritual, and much of Chinese literature, the most exalted forms of artistic achievement in China displayed patterns of dualistic balance, periodic rhythms, and cyclical sequences.[3]

These aesthetics had more than simply a linguistic foundation; by late imperial times they also had a cosmological one. Chinese art reflected life, which in turn reflected the order of the universe. Liu Hsieh's *Wen-hsin tiao-lung* expresses this artistic relationship in the following way:

> *Wen*, or pattern, is a very great power indeed. It is born together with Heaven and Earth. Why do we say this? Because all color-patterns are mixed of black and yellow [i.e., the colors of Heaven and Earth], and all shape-patterns are differentiated by round and square [i.e., the shapes of Heaven and Earth]. The sun and moon, like two pieces of jade, manifest the pattern of Heaven; mountains and rivers in their beauty display the pattern of Earth. These are, in fact, the *wen* of the *tao* itself. . . . Man, and man alone, forms with these the "three powers" [Heaven, Earth, and Man], and he does so because he alone is endowed with spirituality [*ling*]. He is the refined essence of the five elements—indeed, the mind of the universe.

In praise of the great late-Ming painter Tung Ch'i-ch'ang (1555–1636), the *Wu-sheng shih shih* (History of Silent Poetry) states, "He [Tung] held the creative power of nature in his hand and was nourished by the mists and clouds. . . . [It] may be said that everything in his paintings, whether clouds, peaks or stones, was made as by the power of Heaven, his brushwork being quite unrestrained like the working of nature."[4]

Michael Sullivan has aptly remarked that

> Just as ritual, and its extension through music, poetry, and the shape and decoration of the objects used in it, was the gentleman's means of demonstrating that he was attuned to the Will of Heaven, so was aesthetic beauty felt to be what results when the artist gives sincere expression to his intuitive

awareness of natural order. Beauty, therefore, is what conduces to order, harmony, [and] tranquility.

In the words of the *Li-chi*: "Music is [an echo of] the harmony between Heaven and Earth; ceremonies reflect the orderly distinctions [in the operations of] Heaven and Earth. From that harmony all things receive their beings; to those orderly distinctions they owe the differences between them. Music has its origin from Heaven." The goal of all artistic, literary, musical, and ritual activity in traditional China was thus to promote and display social and cosmic harmony.[5]

Since the *tao* of art, literature, music, and ritual was inseparable from the cosmic *tao* and the *tao* of human affairs, it followed that Chinese creative endeavor was never far removed from tradition. Like the Confucian classics, ancient artistic models were believed to have universal and transcendent value. As Frederick Mote reminds us, in traditional China

neither individuals nor the state could claim any theoretical authority higher or more binding than men's rational minds and the civilizing norms that those human minds had created. That is a tenuous basis of authority, and since it could not easily be buttressed by endowing it with nonrational or suprarational qualities, it had to be buttressed by the weight granted to historical experience.

This meant that in Chinese art, as in Chinese life, "the defining criteria for value were inescapably governed by past models, not by present experience or by future states of existence."[6]

The relationship between past and present in Chinese art (and other areas of Chinese aesthetic and intellectual life) may be viewed in terms of a creative tension between the polarities of tradition and innovation, orthodoxy and individualism, structure and spontaneity, intellect and intuition, didactics and aesthetics. Different individuals responded in different ways to these competing impulses. But however such tensions were conceived, and however they were resolved, the past in Chinese imaginative endeavor remained an integral part of the Chinese present.

And how was the link established? In a general sense, the aim of creative individuals was the restoration of antiquity (*fu-ku*), a fundamental neo-Confucian concern and an obsession with many Ch'ing intellectuals. But the restoration of the past did not mean simply the slavish imitation of early literary and artistic models. Rather it involved "spiritual communication" (*shen-hui*) with the ancient masters, a state in which the past and present became one in the mind of the creative individual. The greater the aesthetic or technical achievement of a Chinese writer or artist, the more he was thought to be in touch with the past—at once under its command and in command of it. Such spiritual communication required a total commitment on the part of the individual, body and mind.[7]

Chinese tradition thus suggested pattern, but it did not impose despotic rule. The result was a remarkable continuity of cultural style without the sacrifice of creative potential. In the words of Wen Fong, "in *fu-ku* the Chinese saw history not as a long fall from grace, but as an enduring crusade to restore life and truth to art."[8] That crusade gave vitality to Chinese culture in every period, including the Ch'ing.

Naturally enough, tradition influenced not only the artist and craftsman but also the collector and connoisseur:

> When his eye falls on the miniature porcelain tripod standing on his desk, not only does . . . [the Chinese collector] savour the perfection of its form and glaze, but a whole train of associations are set moving in his mind. For him, his tripod is treasured not simply for its antiquity or rarity, but because it is a receptacle of ideas, and a visible emblem of the ideals by which he lives. Indeed, although he would be gratified to know that it was the genuine Sung dynasty piece it purports to be, it would not be robbed of all its value to him if he subsequently found that it was in fact a clever imitation of the Ch'ien-lung period—particularly if it bore an appropriate inscription cut in archaic characters.

Even a fragment from the past was sufficient to conjure up the right kind of cultural image. The Ch'ing collector Lu Shih-hua notes in his fascinating *Shu-hua shuo-ling* (Collector's Scrapbook) that members of his circle of acquaintances would be quite content with one or two lines from a Sung inscription, for "as soon as one has come to know the brush technique and the spirit of the work of the ancient artists, one can derive the rest by analogy."[9]

Books on connoisseurship, such as Ts'ao Chao's *Ko-ku yao-lun* (Essential Criteria of Antiquities), advised readers on how to determine artistic worth and detect forgeries, but they did not encourage a passion for mere authenticity. Nor did they promote an attachment to individual art objects. A characteristic feature of Chinese connoisseurship in late imperial times was the trading of cultural artifacts—a Ming scroll for a Ch'ing album, a Shang bronze for a Sung ceramic. In this way, personal collections were invigorated by aesthetic variety and at the same time enriched by the scholarly associations that attached to newly acquired objects. In traditional China, prior ownership of a work of art could be as important to the collector as the work itself.[10]

The unity of cultural style in Ch'ing China was evident not only in shared aesthetics and attitudes toward the past, but also in the vocabulary of artistic, literary, and musical criticism. Terms such as *yin* and *yang*, *ch'i* (life spirit or force), *ku* ("bone," or structure), and *shen-yün* (spirit and tone, spiritual resonance, or inspired harmony) were long-standing and indispensable in the evaluation of creative work of all kinds—although each expression might have several connotations in different contexts. These critical terms suggest the thematic importance in Chinese art of life, vitality, and natural process, as well as the structural importance of rhythm and balance.[11]

Chinese symbolism, too, reflected a certain unity of cultural style. Closely linked with literary symbolism, artistic symbols were drawn from several rich sources of traditional inspiration—language (including puns and stylized characters), philosophy, religion, history, popular mythology, and, of course, nature itself. Some symbols that were once meaningful had lost their original connotations by Ch'ing times and were considered largely decorative by all but the most sophisticated connoisseurs. Other symbols held different meanings depending on artistic context, social class, or philosophical outlook. But despite these differences, the most prevalent abstract and concrete symbols in Chinese art (and literature) tended to be shared by all levels of society and to reflect certain common cultural concerns.[12]

The overwhelming majority of Chinese artistic symbols were positive. Abstract designs tended to express the harmonious patterns and processes of nature, while concrete symbols generally indicated auspicious themes of happiness and good fortune. Although most of the spiral and angular designs on ancient bronzes and pottery (and later copies) no longer had specific symbolic value, Chinese artists in late imperial times continued to represent natural processes through abstract symbolism. Square-circle motifs, for example, depicted in both art and architecture the cosmic relationship between Heaven (circle, *yang*) and Earth (square, *yin*). Also popular as a cosmic symbol was the Diagram of the Supreme Ultimate (T'ai-chi t'u)—a motif dating from Sung times that adorned a wide variety of Chinese artwork, from paintings and carved jade to primitive ceramics intended for daily use in commoner households. It consisted of a circle composed of two equal parts—one light (*yang*) and one dark (*yin*)—separated by an S-shaped line. Often the diagram was surrounded by the eight trigrams and other cosmological symbols.

Plant and animal symbolism figured prominently in Chinese artwork of all kinds. The most powerful and positive animal symbol was the dragon (*lung*), a composite creature with the supposed ability to change size and render itself visible or invisible at will. Associated with the east and spring, the dragon was believed to inhabit mountains and to be capable of both ascending into the heavens and living in the water. Unlike its European counterpart, the Chinese dragon symbolized benevolence, longevity, prosperity, and the renewal of life. It also served as the symbol of imperial majesty, especially when depicted with five claws on each of its four feet.

The phoenix (*feng-huang*) was the *yin* equivalent of the dragon. Associated with the south and summer, it had some *yang* qualities, just as the dragon had some *yin* attributes. Like the dragon, it was a composite animal, with distinctly positive connotations. Symbolizing peace and joy, it was commonly used as the mark of an empress in imperial China. The so-called unicorn (*ch'i-lin*) was associated with the west and autumn. It symbolized good luck and prosperity and was believed to herald the birth of a hero or a sage. According to legend, one was seen when Confucius came into the world. Like the dragon and the phoenix, the unicorn was a composite creature, sometimes depicted with one horn, but often with two. Its predominant characteristic was goodwill and benevolence to all living things.

The tortoise (*kuei*), although not a purely mythical beast in the sense of the dragon, phoenix and unicorn, was nonetheless viewed as a supernatural animal. Associated with the north and winter, its outstanding attributes were strength, endurance, and longevity. Its symbolic importance stemmed not only from the Chinese preoccupation with longevity, but also from its legendary (and historical) connection with divination. As an imperial symbol, the tortoise was often depicted with the head of a dragon.

Among more conventional creatures, the tiger was king. In general, it symbolized military prowess. The lion was viewed as the protector of all that was sacred and was particularly popular as a Buddhist symbol. Bronze, stone, and ceramic lions often stood in male-female pairs as guardians on either side of the entrance to important Chinese buildings, both secular and religious. Other large animals, such as horses and elephants (both symbolizing strength and wisdom), were also popular as guardian figures.

The deer symbolized immortality (because of its supposed ability to find a magical life-giving fungus known as *ling-chih*) and also official emoluments (because the character for deer, *lu*, sounded like another character meaning "salary"). A similar pun on the sound *yü* invested the fish with the symbolic meaning of "abundance." Yet another pun made bats (*fu*) the symbol for good luck and prosperity.

Among flying animals and other fowl, cranes symbolized longevity; swallows, success; and the quail, courage in adversity. Mandarin ducks indicated conjugal affection, whereas the wild goose conjured up feelings of sadness or longing. Roosters, hens, and chickens symbolized family prosperity. In the insect world, the cicada stood as a common symbol of fertility and rebirth. The butterfly signified joy and warmth; the dragonfly, weakness and instability.

Plant symbolism was extremely popular in late imperial China. Without doubt the most prominent symbol was the bamboo. Quite apart from its inherent aesthetic appeal and multifunctional role in Chinese daily life (abundantly documented in the *TSCC*), bamboo symbolized the Confucian scholar—upright, strong and resilient, yet gentle, graceful, and refined. The pine tree symbolized longevity and solitude; the plum tree, fortitude and respect for old age. The willow, like the wild goose, indicated parting and sorrow, while the cassia tree, like the carp, indicated literary success. Of various popular fruits, the peach had wide-ranging symbolic significance. It

FIGURE 8.1. Gilded Lion Guarding the Main Entrance to One of the Palaces of the Forbidden City. A male, it is located on the left (*yang*) side of the main entrance, looking outward. The female counterpart is, of course, located on the right (*yin*) side of the main entrance. Photo by author.

FIGURE 8.2. Buddhist Sculpture. This Buddhist statue, flanked by attendants, illustrates the symbolic gesture (Sanskrit: *mudra*) known as *shih-wu-wei-yin*. It denotes protection and fearlessness and is perhaps the most common *mudra* in East Asian Buddhism. See Thompson (1973), pp. 100–101. Photo by author.

symbolized marriage, spring, justice, and especially Taoist immortality. The apple signified peace (a pun on the sound *p'ing*); the persimmon, joy; the pomegranate, fertility. Popular flower symbols included the chrysanthemum (happiness, longevity, and integrity), the peony (love and good fortune), the plum blossom (courage and hope), the wild orchid (humility and refinement), and the lotus (purity and detachment from worldly cares)—a predominantly Buddhist symbol.[13]

Religious symbolism was, of course, most evident in explicitly Buddhist and Religious Taoist art. Virtually all of the major Buddhas, bodhisattvas, gods, genies, and other spirits of the popular pantheon were portrayed in paintings, sculpture, carvings, ceramics, and other art forms. An elaborate symbolism of gestures was associated with Buddhist images, in addition to the wide range of signs and objects related to specific aspects of Buddhist teaching. Among these signs and symbols, the swastika signified the Buddha's heart and mind and served as a general indication of accumulated blessings. Swords and other weapons symbolized protection and wisdom; the conch shell, the universality of Buddhist law (*dharma*); and jewels or scepters, the granting of wishes. Similar symbols existed for Religious Taoism.[14]

Confucian art symbolism drew its primary inspiration from classical and historical sources, as well as from stories of virtuous individuals, such as the twenty-four paragons of filial piety (see Chapter 10). Also popular were symbols of scholarly refinement such as the Chinese lute (*ch'in*) and the so-called Four Treasures of Literature—writing brush, ink, grinding stone, and paper.

Indicative of both Chinese eclecticism and a penchant for combining elements into numerical categories, many symbols were grouped together in traditional Chinese art. Combinations of two of the same symbol often indicated conjugal affection or friendship, but such pairings also reflected *yin-yang* juxtapositions—aesthetic patterns in which one element was clearly "superior" to the other. Plants and animals were often grouped together—the phoenix and the peony, for example, to indicate opulence; the chrysanthemum and the grouse, to connote good fortune; the heron and the lotus, to symbolize integrity.

Larger groupings were common as well. As the Three Friends of Winter, the bamboo, plum, and pine signified enduring friendship, as well as the harmony of the Three Teachings. The plum, wild orchid, bamboo, and chrysanthemum were known as the Four Gentlemen and beloved by gardeners, poets, artists, scholars, and craftsmen. The dragon, phoenix, unicorn, and tortoise were grouped together as the Four Spiritual [or Supernatural] Animals.

The Four Spiritual Animals were not the only symbols reflecting seasonal or astrological correlations. The four seasons and twelve months of the year were represented by both plants and animals. The twelve animals of the zodiac, and sometimes even the twenty-eight astral animals, were also portrayed on art objects. Other popular symbolic groupings included the Eight Creatures (corresponding to the eight trigrams), the Eight Taoist Immortals (and their Precious Objects), the Eight Buddhist Lucky Signs (*pa ch'i-hsiang*), the Eight Precious Things (*pa-pao*), and the Twelve Imperial Emblems (*shih-erh chang*). The largest category of Chinese symbols was known as the Hundred Ancient Things (*pai-ku*), a generic designation for an indefinite number of auspicious signs and objects. In general, Confucian symbolism dominated this motif, but Buddhist, Taoist, and naturalistic symbols also figured prominently in it. Like most larger groupings of symbols, the Hundred Ancient Things appeared most commonly on Chinese craft productions.

CRAFTS

Chinese craftsmen in Ch'ing times excelled at nearly every kind of technical art—textiles, wood and ivory carving, metalwork, lacquerware, stone sculpture, ceramics, enamels, bronzes, jades, jewelry, and glassware. The Ch'ing was also a period of technical accomplishment in areas such as architecture and landscape gardening. Not surprisingly, much of the best craftmanship of the period was done under imperial patronage. As early as 1680 or so, the K'ang-hsi emperor had already established workshops in the imperial palace precincts for the manufacture of porcelains, lacquerware, glass, enamel, jade, furniture, and other prized objects for court use. His grandson, the Ch'ien-lung emperor, was especially well known for his employment of skilled imperial artisans in the production of magnificent works of traditional craftsmanship.[15]

Of the many types of Chinese crafts, four may be singled out for particular attention: bronzes, jades, porcelains, and landscape gardens. All four gave special satisfaction to members of the Chinese elite, and each in its own way exhibited the major aesthetic features and symbolic elements of Chinese art discussed in the previous section.

The most highly prized bronzes in the Ch'ing period, as in more recent times, were ancient ritual vessels of Shang and Chou vintage (see Figures 8.3 and 8.4). They were valued not only for their natural color and exquisite design but also for their powerful historical and ritual associations. The well-known Ch'ing connoisseur Juan Yüan once identified three successive stages in the evolution of Chinese attitudes toward bronze vessels: Before the Han they were symbols of privilege and power; from Han to Sung times, their discovery was hailed as a portent; and from the Sung dynasty onwards, "freed from superstition," they became the toys of collectors and the quarry of philologists and antiquarians. But the *Ko-ku yao-lun* suggests that even in late imperial times at least some members of the Chinese elite, probably a large number, considered ancient ritual vessels to provide a measure of protection against *kuei*—a function not unlike that of the more mundane charms of the "superstitious" masses.[16]

As indicated by Juan Yüan, the inscriptions on ancient bronzes, together with early stone inscriptions, were of great interest to Ch'ing antique collectors, who studied them systematically as a special class of Chinese scholarship (*chin-shih hsüeh*). Some collectors, such as Ch'en Chieh-ch'i (1813–1884), possessed hundreds of bronzes and literally thousands of rubbings from stone inscriptions, not to mention a large number of ancient coins and other metal artifacts. Scholars such as Liu Hsi-hai (d. 1853) wrote numerous tracts on these and other antiquities, contributing to a general burst of antiquarian scholarship in the late Ch'ing period.[17]

Contemporary Ch'ing craftsmen often sought to imitate the shape and design of Shang and Chou bronzes, either to conform to Ch'ing ritual specifications or out of sheer admiration for their form and style. The decorative motifs of these ancient models—particularly abstract designs such as the spiraling or curvilinear "thunder pattern" and "whorl circle"—endured in various types of Chinese art for thousands of years.[18] The original piece-mold

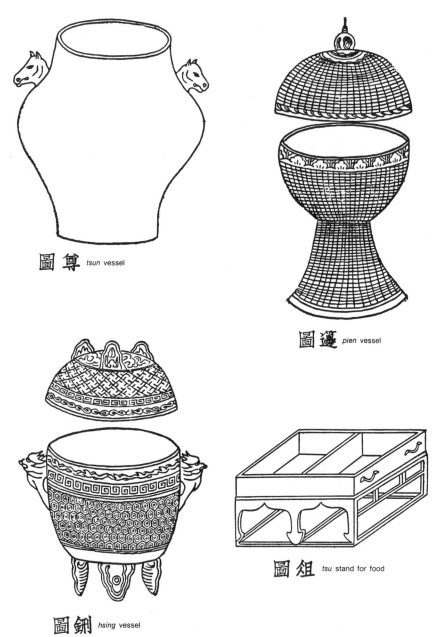

圖尊 *tsun* vessel

圖籩 *pien* vessel

圖鉶 *hsing* vessel

圖俎 *tsu* stand for food

FIGURE 8.3. Ritual Implements (I). These vessels and those in Figure 8.4 represent only a few of the many ritual implements used in state and domestic sacrifices. Each had a particular function, and all were based on Shang and Chou models (both shape and design). Source: *WHL, chüan* 14.

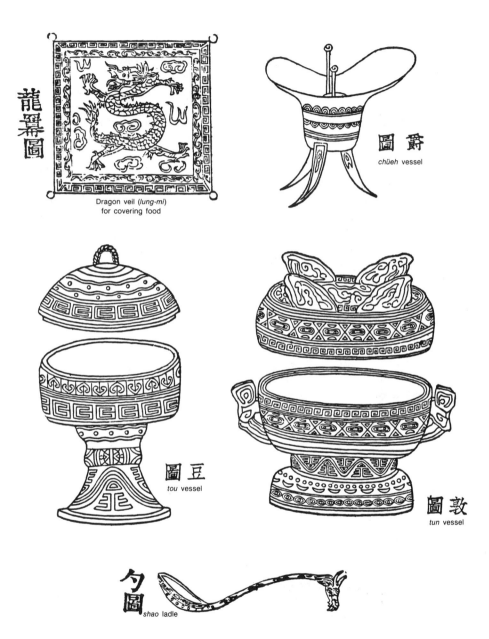

龍冪圖

Dragon veil (*lung-mi*)
for covering food

圖爵
chüeh vessel

圖豆
tou vessel

圖敦
tun vessel

勺圖 *shao* ladle

FIGURE 8.4. Ritual Implements (II). Sources: *WHL, chüan* l4; *CCYWL, chüan* 1.

technique that produced them involved the transference of carved designs from one surface to another, a procedure also followed in Chinese seal carving, the carving of calligraphy in stone or wood, and, of course, the carving of printing blocks. In all these crafts, the artisan had to possess, in Wen Fong's words, "a highly refined sensitivity for the silhouetted form and a lively familiarity with, and love for, the interplay between the positive and negative design patterns." Both the zoomorphic and abstract designs of classic-style bronzes reflect a complex interaction between solid and void, raised and recessed, relief and intaglio, that proved invariably appealing to Chinese aesthetic sensibilities.[19]

Some Ch'ing copies of early Chinese bronzes were deliberate forgeries, but many made no pretense of antiquity and provided the actual date of casting on the vessel. And other bronzes produced in the Ch'ing period did not even try to approximate ancient models. Containers for practical use, decorative bells, and ornaments, as well as small religious statues, came in a wide variety of styles and shapes that often reflected more "modern" tastes.[20] Yet the aesthetic appeal of ancient bronzes, as well as their presumed protective value and their historical associations, made them highly prized throughout the ages, including the Ch'ing period.

Ancient jades were viewed in much the same way. The Ch'ing connoisseur Lu Shih-hua tells us:

> Present-day people want jades of the Three Dynasties [Hsia, Shang, and Chou] only, and require that their color be pure white, "sweet yellow," or "sweet green." Even then they are not satisfied, and insist that the "blood spots" be spread evenly over the entire surface and that the object be large and in perfect condition. If one sets his standard as high as this, he had better have a jade object newly made, and submit it to the oil treatment [*t'i-hung yu*].

Michael Sullivan indicates that for most Chinese connoisseurs it was satisfying enough if jade objects were of high quality and traditional design, but there can be no doubt that antique jade was considered more valuable than new jade, not only for its use in antiquarian studies, but also because it was believed to possess a much larger supply of "life force" (*ch'i*) or "virtue."[21]

From neolithic times through the Ch'ing, jade was always highly regarded. The Chinese language is rich in words with the "jade" (*yü*) radical, words that often convey notions of beauty, preciousness, hardness, and purity. Confucius is said to have remarked,

> The sages of old beheld in jade the reflections of every virtue. In its luster, bright yet warm, humaneness [*jen*]; in its compactness and strength, wisdom [*chih*]; in its sharp and clean edges which cause no injury, righteousness [*i*];

in its use as pendants, seeming as if they would drop to the ground, propriety [*li*]; in the note it emits when struck, clear and prolonged, music [*yüeh*]; by its flaws neither concealing its beauty nor its beauty concealing its flaws, loyalty [*chung*]; by its radiance issuing forth from within on every side, faithfulness [*hsin*].[22]

Jade, in other words, united in itself moral and aesthetic beauty.

In various forms, jade was used in ceremonial sacrifices, buried with the dead, displayed in homes and palaces, and worn for both decoration and protection. For official ritual purposes, it was modeled into various symbolic shapes such as the disc (*pi*) and the squared tube (*tsung*)—both of which had been employed in Shang and Chou dynasty ceremonies. Jade amulets provided protection from evil spirits and conveyed "life force," while jade musical instruments were highly esteemed both in ritual life and daily affairs for their clear and uplifting sound. Scholars often fondled specially carved pieces of jade called *pa-wan* both for the sensual pleasure it afforded and in order to refine their touch for the appreciation of fine porcelain.[23]

The Ch'ien-lung reign was the high point of jade carving in late imperial China—in part because it was a period of great prosperity, but also because vast areas of Central Asia, where much precious jade is found, were brought under imperial sway at that time. During the long and illustrious reign of the Ch'ien-lung emperor, thousands of magnificent carved jades were added to the imperial collection, some of which bore poetic inscriptions in characters that imitated the emperor's calligraphy. In the words of S. Howard Hansford, during the Ch'ien-lung period, "Jade was applied to countless new uses in the Forbidden City and the stately homes of nobles and officials. Though the inspiration of the designers of two thousand years earlier was rarely attained, the execution and finish left nothing to be desired and much larger works were attempted."[24] Some of these monumental jade sculptures, still on display in the Forbidden City today, stand as tall as a man.

The heyday of Ch'ing porcelain manufacture was somewhat earlier than that of jade carving, from about 1683 to 1750—during the reign of the K'ang-hsi emperor in particular. Of all the Chinese ceramic arts, porcelain (*tz'u*) stood at the apex of achievement: it was universally admired, the subject of countless essays, and a fitting topic for poetry as well. Imperial patronage was enormously important to the successful production of high-quality porcelains. Soame Jenyns has written:

> The history of Ch'ing porcelain is in effect the history of the town of Ching-te Chen, which in turn was dominated by the presence of the imperial porcelain factory, which was situated there. Over 80 percent of the porcelains of China during the Ch'ing period were made at this great ceramic metropolis in Kiangsi, or in its immediate neighborhood; the provincial porcelain factories,

with the single exception of Te-hua in Fukien, producing porcelain of poor quality and negligible importance during this period.[25]

This statement perhaps undervalues local production in Ch'ing China, but it certainly testifies to the dominant position occupied by the imperial factory.

As with bronzes and jades, Ch'ing connoisseurs greatly admired porcelain antiques, which had a kind of dull shine, or "receded luster" (t'ui-kuang). Among the most esteemed of these early porcelains, in addition to official ware (kuan-yao), was the legendary sky-blue ch'ai ware, ju ware, and crackled ko ware. Ch'ing potters excelled in the imitation of these and other types of early ceramics, while expert forgers produced receded luster by rubbing new porcelain first with a grindstone, then with a mixture of paste and fine sand, and finally with a straw pad to obliterate the scratches. The K'ang-hsi emperor is known to have sent to the imperial kilns at Ching-te rare pieces of Sung dynasty kuan, ch'ai, and ju ware to be meticulously copied for imperial pleasure. The imperial kilns also continued to produce Ming-style porcelains, some of which, like the beautiful white "eggshell" bowls of the Yung-lo period, were executed by Ch'ing craftsmen more flawlessly than the Ming originals![26]

Ch'ing potters also excelled in producing the striking multicolored Ming porcelains known as san-ts'ai, wu-ts'ai, and tou-ts'ai. The significant feature of these three types of porcelain, in addition to their vivid use of rich blues, greens, and yellows in the fashion of much architectural decoration, is their amalgamation of both popular religious and imperial symbolism, their seemingly inexhaustible range of shapes and colors (including reproductions of ancient bronzes), and their self-conscious yin-yang juxtapositions. As with other porcelains, Ch'ing craftsmen often inscribed san-ts'ai, wu-ts'ai, and tou-ts'ai pieces with reign marks other than those of the period in which they were produced, making positive identification of good copies extremely difficult.[27]

European influences found their way into the decoration of Ch'ing porcelains for two principal reasons. One was the fact that a considerable amount of Chinese porcelain was intended for European markets in the latter half of the seventeenth century and most of the eighteenth century. The other was the general receptiveness of the imperial court to Western artistic influences during the late Ming and early Ch'ing period. These influences can be seen not only in porcelain and other ceramics but also in some imperial architecture and court painting.[28]

Overall, however, Chinese art followed traditional models, and although some porcelains functioned as convenient vehicles for the transmission of foreign artistic influences, most conveyed a rich indigenous decorative tradition that in a real sense transcended class. Many of the highest quality Ch'ing porcelains were decorated with folk symbols and the bright colors of folk and religious art. It is true, however, that in several respects porcelains had a closer affinity with elite art than with the simple ceramics of commoner households. Like jades and bronzes, they were of antiquarian interest and appreciated both for their surface "feel" and melodious ring when struck. Like paintings, many porcelains were carefully decorated with the brush and categorized according to the same basic system of classification. But whereas in painting, landscape was the most popular and prestigious classification (see next section), in porcelain it was a relatively minor category.[29]

Landscape gardening, on the other hand, sought precisely to capture the mood of a landscape painting. Although often overlooked as an art form, Chinese gardens in fact embodied the best principles of artistic expression in China, combining superb craftsmanship, complex symbolism, and the careful arrangement of aesthetic elements.[30] During the Ch'ing period, such gardens ranged in size from the huge (seventy-mile walled perimeter) imperial summer palace outside Peking known as the Yüan-ming yüan (Garden of Perfect Brightness)—destroyed during the Anglo-French hostilities with China in 1860—to tiny, cramped urban gardens only a few square feet in area and even to miniature gardens in porcelain dishes. Members of the Chinese elite and rich merchants, of course, took special pride in constructing individualized gardens, such as Yüan Mei's famous Sui-yüan in the area of Nanking.[31]

Chinese gardens were viewed primarily as Taoist retreats. In the words of the Ch'ien-lung emperor, "Every . . . ruler, when he has returned from audience, and has finished his public duties, must have a garden in which he may stroll, look around and relax his heart. If he has a suitable place for this it will refresh his mind and regulate his emotions, but if he has not, he will become engrossed in sensual pleasures and lose his will power." Access to the extensive gardens of the Forbidden City and the western section of the Imperial City in Peking did not always distract Ch'ing emperors from sensual indulgence, but gardens generally did provide a retreat for the world-weary Confucian—and a fitting place of rest for those of a Buddhist or Taoist inclination as well.[32]

Gardens were not always resting places, however. They also served as the focus for much elite social activity. Although well suited for meditation and contemplation, gardens provided an ideal environment for entertaining, composing verse, and admiring art. Small wonder the expansive Prospect Garden (Ta-kuan yüan) of the Chia family provides the setting for much of the action in the great Ch'ing novel *Hung-lou meng* (see Chapter 9). Andrew Plaks has brilliantly analyzed Ts'ao Hsüeh-ch'in's use of the garden as a microcosm of the Chinese cultural world, and indeed of the entire universe. It is true, of course, that Chinese cities—Peking in particular—were also viewed as microcosms of the universe but whereas the cosmological symbolism of the capital was expressed in formal patterns of geometric symmetry, in the garden it was expressed in delightful informality and irregularity. The garden recreated nature in an idealized form, but not a geometrical one.[33]

FIGURE 8.5. Landscape Garden. Corner of a traditional-style landscape garden in contemporary China (Nanking). Photo by author.

Aesthetic components of traditional Chinese gardens bore the unmistakable imprint of conscious *yin-yang* duality. Man-made buildings were deliberately interspersed with natural features; rock formations ("mountains") stood juxtaposed to water ("rivers"); light areas alternated with dark; rounded lines with angular ones; empty spaces with solids. The small led to the large, the low to the high. The Ch'ing scholar Shen Fu (1763–?), a well-known connoisseur of gardens, expressed the garden aesthetics in the following way:

> In laying out garden pavillions and towers, suites of rooms and covered walkways, piling up rocks into mountains, or planting flowers to form a desired shape, the aim is to see the small in the large, to see the large in the small, to see the real in the illusory, and to see the illusory in the real. Sometimes you conceal, sometimes you reveal, sometimes you work on the surface, sometimes in depth.[34]

Chinese gardens thus had a kind of endless, rhythmic quality. Wing-tsit Chan writes, "Almost every part [of the traditional Chinese garden] is rhythmic in expression. The winding walks, the round gate, the zigzag paths, the melody-like walls, the rockeries which are frozen music in themselves, and flowers and trees and birds are all echoes and counterpoints of rhythm."

FIGURE 8.6. Ch'ing Scholars. A group of scholars with the typical trappings of elite status in traditional China: long gowns, fans, and a landscape garden retreat for rest and recreation. Photo courtesy China Trade Museum, Milton, Mass.

Significantly, this rhythmic quality—and often a sense of endlessness as well—can be found not only in landscape gardens but also in the structure of Chinese poetry and narrative prose, the flow of melody in music, the movement and sound of Chinese drama, the curved roof and other architectural elements in Chinese buildings, and, of course, in the composition of landscape paintings.[35]

The decorative symbolism of Chinese gardens followed convention. The design of gates and doorways, for example, reflected the perfection of the circle or the shape of a jar—the latter a pun on the word *peace*. Window grilles and other woodwork often carried stylized Chinese characters for blessings (*fu*), emoluments (*lu*), and long life (*shou*), as well as designs echoing ancient bronze motifs such as the "thunder pattern" and "whorl circle." Common animal symbols included the dragon, phoenix, deer, crane, and bat. Confucian symbolism was most evident in the books contained in garden buildings and often in the names given to specific pleasure spots. Religious symbolism was comparatively muted. Buddhist or Religious Taoist statues were relatively rare, and there was no Chinese "garden god." *Feng-shui* considerations obviously affected the design of Chinese gardens, but as Andrew March has noted, there was an aesthetic "logic" to this geomantic system that gave it significance beyond religion.[36]

In short, the major symbolism of the landscape garden was in its natural elements and in their arrangement. Rocks were chosen primarily for their fantastic shapes (those from Lake T'ai near Soochow were especially admired), while flowers, shrubs, and trees reflected the basic plant symbolism noted in the previous section. Among the most common floral elements in the landscape garden were the peony, orchid, magnolia, lotus, chrysanthemum, and gardenia. Bamboo was, of course, extremely popular, as were trees such as the willow, pine, peach, plum, and pomegranate. Most of these plants were identified with specific seasons and arranged with these identifications in mind.

A sharp distinction existed between the "naturalism" of the landscape garden and the rigid functionalism of the house to which it was connected. As the garden mirrored nature, the house mirrored society. Maggie Keswick writes, "In domestic architecture the orderly succession of rooms and courtyards that make up a Chinese house have often been seen as an expression of the Chinese ideal of harmonious social relationships: formal, decorous, regular and clearly defined." This rigid symmetry—and, we may add, that of other Chinese architectural structures from temples to the imperial palace itself—stood in sharp contrast to the irregularity of the landscape garden.[37]

But despite the structural distinction between house and garden in traditional China, the two were integrally related, for the structure of the former would have been considered intolerable without the latter, and the latter would have been deemed superfluous without the former. In all, the garden was a kind of "liminal zone" linking the spiritual and earthly concerns of man. Nelson Wu puts the matter poetically, "In . . . eternally negative space, between reason and untarnished emotion, between the correctness of the straight lines and the effortlessness of the curve, between the measureable and the romantic infinity, lies the Chinese garden which is between architecture and landscape painting."[38]

PAINTING AND CALLIGRAPHY

Although landscapes were regarded by Ch'ing connoisseurs as the most exalted form of traditional Chinese painting, they were by no means the only type of admired brushwork. In addition to calligraphy—which was in a special class together with landscape painting—the Chinese also esteemed paintings of religious and secular figures, buildings and palaces, birds and animals, flowers and plants, and even antique objects such as bronzes and porcelains. According to the *Ko-ku yao-lun*, the artists of late imperial times were especially accomplished in the painting of landscapes, trees, rocks, flowers, bamboos, birds, and fish, but less skilled than their predecessors in the rendering of human figures and large animals. Folk painting in the Ch'ing included murals in temples and other buildings, but it was generally considered to be the work of mere technicians, not true art. Significantly, even in religious temples, secular symbolism (including examples of filial piety, historical scenes, and depictions from works of fiction) tended to predominate over explicitly religious scenes or symbols.[39]

In the main, Chinese painting was delicate and decorous. Chinese artists were generally horrified by gruesome scenes of rape, war, and destruction so prevalent in the West; figure painters shunned the nude; still-life painters were repelled by dead objects; and landscape painters usually ignored the artistic possibilities of deserts, swamps, and other desolate places. It is true, of course, that some murals in Chinese temples depicted in graphic detail the tortures of the Ten Courts of Hell; that there was a well-developed tradition of erotic art (*ch'un-hua* or *ch'un-kung*) in China; and that some Ch'ing painters—like the "Yangchow eccentric" Lo P'ing (d. 1799)—went so far as to paint ghosts, skeletons, and even raging forest fires. But overall, the subject material of Chinese painting was uplifting, if not expressly didactic.[40]

One important function of painting throughout much of the imperial era had been moral instruction. Chang Yen-yüan, ninth-century author of the influential *Li-tai ming-hua chi* (Record of Famous Painters of Successive Dynasties), tells us, for example, that paintings should serve as models to the virtuous and warnings to the evil. He cites the Han scholar Ts'ao Chih (192–232), who describes how people seeing pictures of noble rulers "look up in reverence," while those who see pictures of degenerate rulers "are moved to sadness." And as late as the Ming dynasty we find examples of normative judgments impinging on standards of realism. The *Ko-ku yao-lun* states, for instance,

> Portraits of Buddhists should show benevolence and mercy; those of Taoists, moral cultivation and salvation; those of emperors and kings, the magnificence of imperial symbols such as the sun, the dragon and the phoenix; those of barbarians, their admiration of China and their obedience; those of Confucian worthies, loyalty, sincerity, civilized behavior and righteousness.[41]

Yet in the main, by late imperial times it was less subject matter than style that inspired and uplifted the viewer of Chinese paintings. During the Ch'ing—and in fact well before—artistic achievement came to be seen as a reflection of the artist's inner morality. Like writing and musical compositions, paintings were considered to be "prints of the heart/mind [*hsin*]"—not merely a means of Confucian cultivation but also a measure of it. No critic of any consequence judged a painting solely on what he knew about the moral worth of the artist, but a scholar-critic certainly *would* be inclined to consider the admirable (aesthetic) qualities of a painting as an index of the artist's own admirable (Confucian) qualities. Thus, as James Cahill has remarked, "The notion of 'the man revealed in the painting' was used . . . [by Chinese critics] to account for excellence in art, not to determine it." Further, Cahill indicates that the creative impulses of naturalness, spontaneity, and intuition usually attributed to Taoism and Ch'an Buddhism in Chinese art and literature were also part of the late imperial Confucian tradition—central, in fact, to the *wen-jen* (literati) aesthetics.[42]

Confucianism shaped the interpretive contours of traditional Chinese painting in yet another sense. In Sung and post-Sung times, neo-Confucian metaphysics provided the concept of *li* (principle), which came to be used in Chinese art criticism as both a standard for realism and as a general metaphor for creative process. Painting, in the neo-Confucian view, was tantamount to an act of cosmic creation and therefore governed by the natural principles (*li*) inherent in all things. The task of the painter was to attune himself with the moral mind of the universe, and in so doing, convey the *li* of his subject material, giving it life and vitality. The gift of the ancient masters, in the view of Wang Hui (1632–1717), was precisely their ability to "harmonize their works with those of nature."[43]

The "life" of a Chinese painting was expressed by the term *ch'i*. *Ch'i* literally means breath, but like *li* it acquired a metaphysical meaning ("material force") in neo-Confucianism. The constituent matter of all things, *ch'i* animated even inanimate objects. As a critical term, however, it predated neo-Confucianism by several centuries. Although no one term conveys the wide range and richness of its meanings, perhaps the best single translation of *ch'i* is "spirit"— as in Hsieh Ho's famous "First Law" of painting: "spirit resonance creates life movement" (*ch'i-yün sheng-tung*). Employed in this fashion, *ch'i* suggests the breath of Heaven, which stirs all things to life and sustains the eternal process of cosmic change. This motive power, in the words of Chang Keng (1685–1760), was something "beyond the feeling of the brush and the effect of the ink."[44]

As early as the fifth century A.D., Chinese art critics had already begun to equate painting with the symbols of the *I-ching* as representations of nature, and by late imperial times morality and metaphysics had become inextricably linked. In the words of the Ch'ing critic Wang Yü: "Everybody knows that principles [*li*] and vitality [*ch'i*] are necessary in painting, yet they are much neglected. The important point is that the heart and character of the man should be developed; then he can express high principles and a pure vital breath. . . . Although painting is only one of the fine arts, it contains the *tao*."[45]

As an expression of the fundamental order of the universe, Chinese paintings clearly had to appear "natural," and works on connoisseurship suggested numerous guidelines for artistic realism.

A portrait should look as though [the person depicted] were about to speak. The folds of his wearing apparel, the trees and the rocks should be painted with strokes similar to those in calligraphy. The folds of dresses should be large, but their rhythm subtle, and the strength of their execution gives the impression that they are fluttering and raised [by the wind]. Trees, with their wrinkled bark and their twists and knots, should show their age. Rocks should be three-dimensional and shading lines used in their depiction should produce a rugged yet mellow effect. A landscape with mountains, water, and woods and springs should present an atmosphere of placidity and vastness and should clearly show the season, the time of day, and [prevailing] weather. Rising or subsiding mists and clouds should also be depicted. The source whence a river flows as well as its destination should be clearly defined, and the water in it should appear fluent. Bridges and roads should show the way by which people come and go, as narrow paths wind through wildernesses. Houses should face in different directions in order to avoid monotony, fish swim hither and thither, and dragons ascend or descend. Flowers and fruit should bear dew drops on all surfaces and should also indicate in which direction the wind blows. Birds and animals, poised to drink water, to pick food, to move, or to remain still, are captured in spirit, as well as form.[46]

Painting manuals such as the popular Ch'ing handbook *Chieh-tzu-yüan hua-chuan* (Mustard Seed Garden Manual) provided elaborate instructions on exactly how to paint such subject material—trees, rocks, people, buildings, flowers, bamboo, grass, insects, animals, and of course, landscapes (see Figures 8.7, 8.8, 8.9, and 8.10). The starting point, as in calligraphy (and, in fact, all of Chinese life) was self-discipline. "You must learn first to observe the rules faithfully," wrote the author-compiler of the *Chieh-tzu-yüan hua-chuan*; then "afterwards modify them according to your intelligence and capacity. The end of all method is to seem to have no method." And again, "If you aim to dispense with method, learn method. If you aim at facility, work hard. If you aim for simplicity, master complexity." One began with the correct mental attitude, learned basic brushstrokes (sixteen, at first), and then progressed to more sophisticated painting techniques.[47]

An essential part of the artist's training was the study of the ancient masters. Chang Keng advised students not to "throw out scattered thoughts in an incoherent fashion or to make strange things in accordance with the impulses of the heart." Rather, they should "carefully follow the rules of the ancients without losing the smallest detail." After some time, they will "understand why one must be in accordance with nature," and after some more time, "why things are as they are." Local collections of paintings by great masters were of tremendous importance to painters as a source of inspiration. We know, for example, that Wang Hui's mastery of so many different artistic styles was at least in part a product of his extended trips to

FIGURE 8.7. Sketches from the *Chieh-tzu-yüan hua-chuan* (I). *Top left,* the pine tree, symbol of longevity, solitude, and the *yang* power of the dragon. *Top right,* Wu Chen's style of painting trees, copied by Shen Hao. *Bottom,* techniques of dotting leaves. Source: Mai-mai Sze (1959).

A

B

C

FIGURE 8.8. Sketches from the *Chieh-tzu-yüan hua-chuan* (II). *A,* the *Chieh-tzu-yüan hua-chuan* states: "The symbolism of the plum tree is determined by its *ch'i*. The blossoms are of the *yang* principle, that of Heaven. The wood of its trunk and branches is of the *yin* principle, that of Earth. Its basic number is five, and its various parts and aspects are based on odd and even numbers. The peduncle, from which the flower issues, is a symbol of *t'ai-chi*." *B,* the plum tree is described as having two trunks, a *yin* (lesser) trunk and a *yang* (dominant) trunk. *C,* the willow, symbol of parting. Source: Mai-mai Sze (1959).

FIGURE 8.9. Sketches from the *Chieh-tzu-yüan hua-chuan* (III). *A,* bamboo, symbol of the Confucian scholar. *B,* figures done in the *hsieh-i* ("writing of ideas") style. *C,* in discussing the ways of painting two trees, the *Chieh-tzu-yüan hua-chuan* employs a ritual vocabulary, emphasizing the relationship between old and young, dignified and modest. Source: Mai-mai Sze (1959).

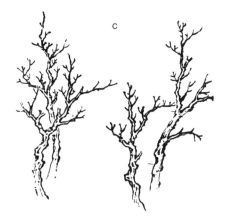

FIGURE 8.10. Sketches from the *Chieh-tzu-yüan hua-chuan* (IV). Mountains: *A*, high view (*kao-yüan*); *B*, deep view (*shen-yüan*); *C*, level view (*p'ing-yüan*); *D*, rocks, indicating *yin* (dark) and *yang* (light) elements. Much of the *Chieh-tzu-yüan hua-chuan*'s discussion of painting rocks revolves around the symbolism of the family and the *I-ching*. Source: Mai-mai Sze (1959).

art centers, which enabled him to study the masterpieces of well-known collectors. Unfortunately, the insatiable desire of the Ch'ing rulers—notably the Ch'ien-lung emperor—to enhance the holdings of the imperial collection in Peking took many of these masterpieces out of the hands of private collectors, denying local artists an important source of education and inspiration.[48]

In addition to viewing great works of art, aspiring students were encouraged to copy them. There were three main avenues of approach: (1) exact reproduction by tracing (*mu*); (2) direct copying (*lin*); and (3) freely interpreting in the manner of the master (*fang*). The ultimate purpose of this artistic progression was not merely to produce outer form, but to capture inner essence. In the words of Fang Hsün (1736–1801),

> When copying ancient paintings, the foremost concern must be to grasp the ancient master's spirit of life. Testing the flavor of the work and exploring it, you will get some understanding. Then you may begin to copy. . . . If it is done merely for the sake of similarity [however], you had better roll up the picture and forget it at once. You may copy the whole day, yet your work will have nothing whatsoever to do with the ancient master.

The eighteenth-century Ch'ing critic Shen Tsung-ch'ien wrote in a similar vein,

> A student of painting must copy ancient works, just as a man learning to write must study good writing that has come down through the ages. He should put himself in a state of mind to feel as if he were doing the same painting himself. . . . First he should copy one artist, then branch out to copy others, and, what is more important, he should feel as if he were breathing through the work himself and should identify himself with what the artist was trying to say.[49]

Fang and Shen are discussing here the effort on the part of the painter to achieve "spiritual communication" (*shen-hui*) with the ancient masters. *Shen-hui*, as Tu Wei-ming has indicated, necessarily involved self-realization. Shen Tsung-ch'ien put the matter this way: "The important thing in copying the ancients is that I have my own temperament. If I should forget myself to copy the ancients, I would be doing a disservice to both the ancients and myself. . . . The painter's concern is how to make the art of the brush his own. If this is done, then what I express is only myself, a self which is akin to the ancients." Fang Hsün counseled, "When copying the ancients, you may first only worry about a lack of similarity; afterward you ought to worry about too much similarity. For, when lacking similarity, you have failed to get to the bottom of the model's style; being too similar, you have failed to achieve your own style."[50]

Discipline was a prerequisite to artistic freedom. The early nineteenth-century painter-critic Fan Chi asserted: "The beginner should imitate the ancients constantly, . . . [but] he must then empty himself from what he has relied on. Meanwhile, that which has fermented in him must flow out unintentionally—and for the first time he will experience the joyous sensation of freedom." On this basis, it was possible for a Ch'ing painter like Wang Shih-min (1592–1680) to produce an "original" landscape following the Ming master Tung Ch'i-ch'ang in imitating Wang Meng's (Yüan dynasty) interpretation of the Tung Yüan (Five Dynasties-Sung) manner. Imitation (*fang*) in the hands of an individual who had achieved "spiritual communication" with the great masters became "creative metamorphosis" (*pien*), not simple plagiarism. Fan Chi informs us, "If a *lin* copy shows the copyist's own manner, then it has lost the truth; if a *fang* copy fails to show one's own manner, it becomes a fake."[51]

Apart from preliminary sketches, Chinese painters seldom painted from life. They preferred instead to seek inspiration in other works or to conjure up and convey a mental image that bore no necessary relationship to a single objective reality. Meditation played a role in the creative process, as did external stimuli. Wang Yü advised preliminary concentration, and nourishment by

> looking at clouds and springs, contemplating birds and flowers, strolling about humming songs, burning incense, or sipping tea. . . . When the inspiration rises, spread the paper and move the brush, but stop as soon as it is exhausted; only when it rises again should you continue and complete the work. If you do it this way, the work will become alive with the moving power of Heaven.[52]

The Chinese painter was a captive of his media, but it was a creative form of bondage. Unlike Western-style oil painting, Chinese ink or watercolor on paper or silk allowed little room for trial and error; once the artist put his brush down he made an irretrievable commitment—especially when using ink on paper. Thus,

> when the brush touches paper, there are only differences in touch, speed, angle and direction. Too light a touch results in weakness while too heavy a touch causes clumsiness. Too much speed results in a slippery effect, too little speed drags; too much slant [of the tip of the brush] results in thinness; too perpendicular an approach in flatness; a curve may result in ragged edges and a straight line may look like one made with a ruler.[53]

Brushwork was extraordinarily important in Chinese painting, especially in late imperial times. Wen Fong writes, for example, that throughout the Ming and Ch'ing periods, the brushwork of Chinese painting "assumed an increasingly expressive quality, eventually dominating the representational form." This expressive quality, known as *hsieh-i* or the "writing of ideas," was a technique closely linked with calligraphy and quite distinct from the precise form of brushwork designated *kung-pi*. *Hsieh-i* required the appearance of spontaneity, but it was deliberate, preconceived, and, in fact, the product of intensive book study and calligraphic discipline. Wang Yüan-ch'i's advice to painters, in its essence, would apply to calligraphers as well: "When . . . [one] takes up the brush he must be absolutely quiet, serene, peaceful, and collected, and shut out all vulgar emotions. He must sit down in silence before the white silk scroll, concentrate his soul and control his vital energy. He must look at the high and low, examine right and left, inside and outside the scroll, the road to enter and the road to leave."[54]

In other words, the Chinese artist had to have a fairly complete vision of his painting before beginning. Modifications could be made, of course, as the painting developed, but a unified vision was essential. Shen Tsung-ch'ien wrote:

It would be a great fault to begin a picture without a preconceived plan, and then add and adjust as one goes along, with the result that the different parts do not have an organic unity. One should rather have a general idea of where the masses and connections, the light and the dark areas will be, then proceed so that one part grows out of another and the light and dark areas cooperate to build a picture. Examined closely, each section is interesting in itself; taken together, there is an organic unity.[55]

This idea of organic unity was expressed in the general term *k'ai-ho* (opening and closing, or expanding and contracting). *K'ai-ho* may refer to the overall layout of a painting, to the relationship of individual elements within the painting, or to the composition of the individual elements themselves. In each part of the painting, including every individual object, the artist had to consider beginning, ending, and beginning again. Shen Tsung-ch'ien explains,

The combined work of brush and ink depends on force of movement [*shih*, a long-standing technical term in calligraphy, sometimes translated "kinesthetic movement"]. This force refers to the movement of the brush back and forth on the paper, which carries with it and in it the opening [*k'ai*] and closing [*ho*] movements. Where something is starting up, that is the opening movement, but with every opening movement the artist must be thinking how it will be gathered up at the end. . . . The gathering up is called the closing movement, and with each closing movement the artist is already thinking where the next growth is going to arise. Thus there is always the suggestion of further development.[56]

Yin-yang ideas such as *k'ai-ho, hsü-shih* (void and solid), *hsiang-pei* (front
and back), and *ch'i-fu* (rising and falling) are essential to an understanding
of traditional Chinese painting. Ch'ing handbooks and critical works repeatedly
drew upon these and other concepts of complementarity and alternation to
explain composition and brushstroke. Artists were encouraged to dip downward
before coming up; to turn upwards before going down; to intersperse sparse
with dense and dark with light; to relieve thick ink with thin, to counteract
the convex with the concave, and so forth. For example, in describing the
method by which to paint tree trunks and branches, the *Chieh-tzu-yüan hua-
chuan* advises: "Pay attention to the way the branches dispose themselves,
the *yin* and *yang* of them, which are in front and which are in back, which
are on the left and which are on the right; consider also the tensions created
by some branches pushing forward while others seem to withdraw." In
landscape we find that "host" mountains (*chu*) required "guest" mountains
(*pin*), exalted trees required humble ones, and luxuriant foliage required at
least some dead branches. In its most extreme form, the notion of *yin-yang*
complementarity was expressed in a kind of Taoist paradox: "When in your
eyes you have mountains, only then can you make trees; when in your mind
there is water, only then can you make mountains." The term for landscape
itself (*shan-shui*, lit., mountains and water) suggests a basic *yin-yang* relationship.[57]

The point of *yin-yang* juxtaposition in Chinese painting was not merely
to create contrast, however. Primarily it was to indicate "life movement,"
nature's rhythm (*yün*). In their brushwork, Chinese artists attempted to
recreate the endlessly alternating rise and fall, expansion and contraction,
activity and quiescence of *yin* and *yang* and in so doing come into closer
harmony with the rhythmic cycles of life itself. This was especially true in
landscape painting. Heaven dominated Earth, voids dominated solids, mountains
dominated water, and movement dominated stillness, but all were integrated
into a single philosophical statement reflecting the dynamism, grandeur, and
limitlessness of nature.[58]

Small wonder, then, that Chinese landscape painters refused to restrict
themselves (or the viewers of their works) by the use of Western-style scientific
perspective. It was not that they lacked the intellectual sophistication to employ
it. But true perspective involved a fixed point of view that was completely
inimical to the purposes of the painter. An essential element of the dynamism
of a Chinese landscape was the movement of both artist and viewer: "the
painter . . . paints and the spectator views the results from many points,
never from a single position or at any one moment of time."[59] In a similar
way, and for similar reasons, Chinese poets added new dimensions to the
world directly perceived in their poems, and in so doing evoked a mood of
infiniteness. Wang Shih-chen (1634–1711) in particular was a master of the

poetic "ending which doesn't end." Significantly, this "endless" quality can also be found in the best Chinese narrative literature (see Chapter 9).[60]

In the critical writing of the Ch'ing period, a sharp distinction was drawn between the Northern School of professional and court painting and the Southern School of nonprofessional literati (*wen-jen*) painting. The former has been characterized as academic, representational, precise, and decorative, painted mainly in polychrome ink and on silk. The latter has been described as spontaneous, free, calligraphic, personal, and subjective, painted mainly in monochrome on paper. These distinctions—which had nothing to do with geography—were drawn by Tung Ch'i-ch'ang in the late Ming period, and they continued to dominate Chinese art criticism for the next three hundred years. Although based on genuine stylistic differences, Tung's system of classification was arbitrary and inconsistent, not only because it was based on certain moral criteria, Tung's personal preferences, and the assumed superiority of literati painting over that of professionals but also because in a very real sense all the painting of the Ming and Ch'ing periods was academic. Furthermore, during the Ch'ing period there were many court painters who painted beautifully in the Southern School style, and many "amateur" literati who were well paid for their artistic efforts—some by the throne itself.[61]

As in philosophy, the early Ch'ing period was noteworthy for considerable vitality and variety in the fine arts. Among the many accomplished painters of the time were Ming loyalists like Kung Hsien (1620–1689); the Six Great Masters of the Ch'ing (the Four Wangs [Wang Shih-min; Wang Chien, 1598–1677; Wang Hui; and Wang Yüan-ch'i, 1642–1715], Wu Li [1632–1718], and Yün Shou-p'ing [1633–1690]); and "Individualist" painters such as Chu Ta (1626–c. 1705) and the Two Stones (*shih*)—Shih-ch'i (K'un-ts'an, c. 1610–c. 1670) and Shih-t'ao (Tao-chi, 1641–c. 1710). Yet even the Individualists—like the Six Great Masters and virtually all other Ch'ing painters—acknowledged a debt to tradition. Shih-t'ao, for example, in his *Hua-yü lu* (Record of Talks on Painting) admits that for many years he had painted and written, declaring his independence of orthodox methods, only to discover that the way he had thought was his own was actually "the *tao* of the ancients."[62]

During the eighteenth and nineteenth centuries, Ch'ing painting lost much of its vigor and vitality, in part for lack of local inspiration. Part of the problem was also that Chinese artists began to take the injunction to recover the past (*fu-ku*) too literally, with the result that many Ch'ing paintings became overly academic. They were paintings about painting, "art-historical art." All too often, as Michael Sullivan has remarked, "the artists' inspiration was not nature but the very tradition itself."[63]

Yet in the midst of this overzealous traditionalism, there were at least some artists who refused to bend to artistic convention. These included the so-called Eight Eccentrics of Yangchow, who boasted among their number such accomplished painters as Chin Nung (1687–1764), Hua Yen (1682–c. 1755), Huang Shen (1687–c. 1768), and Lo P'ing. And even at court, bastion of orthodoxy, there were at least a few fresh influences. Some Jesuit missionaries, for example, found employment as court painters, and in this capacity they blended techniques of Western realism with traditional Chinese media and subject matter. One such individual was Guiseppe Castiglione (Lang Shih-ning, 1688–1766), a personal favorite of the Ch'ien-lung emperor. Castiglione had numerous Chinese pupils, imitators, and admirers, but he and his Western colleagues exerted no lasting influence on Chinese art. The reason was that their use of shading and perspective was seen as mere craftsmanship. In the words of one admirer (Tsou I-kuei, 1686–1772, a talented court painter in his own right): "The student should learn something of their achievements so as to improve his own method. But their technique of strokes [i.e., brushwork] is negligible. Even if they attain [representational] perfection it is merely craftsmanship. Thus, foreign painting cannot be called art."[64]

Far less were foreigners able to master the intricacies of Chinese calligraphy. As a recognized art form, calligraphy predated painting, but by late imperial times the two were inseparably linked. Lu Shih-hua states simply: "Calligraphy and painting are skills [*chi-neng*], but they embody the great *tao*. . . . The ancients achieved immortality [*pu-hsiu*] through their calligraphy and painting." Both calligraphy and painting used the same basic media, utilized many of the same brush strokes and techniques, required the same kind of mental preparation and discipline, and were measured by the same aesthetic standards. Furthermore, both were seen as an index of the artist's morality. Lu Shih-hua tells us, "If the heart is right, then the brush will be right" (*hsin-cheng tse pi-cheng*).[65]

During the Ming and Ch'ing periods, calligraphy often adorned paintings, amplifying in various ways the artist's general philosophical statement and holding the viewer's interest. Poetic inscriptions might be written by the artist to indicate the sources of his inspiration and feelings or by subsequent owners and admirers of the work who were moved to comment upon it. Some paintings boasted a number of different colophons. Perhaps the record for inscriptions of this sort by one individual is held by the Ch'ien-lung emperor, whose enthusiasm occasionally outstripped his aesthetic judgment. He is reported to have written over fifty inscriptions on one handscroll alone and to have placed thirteen of his seals on a single painting. In the main, however, multiple inscriptions and seals of ownership were added tastefully, and they, in turn, enriched both the emotional and artistic value of the work.[66]

Of course calligraphy stood solidly on its own as an independent art form, universally admired as the ultimate measure of cultural refinement. In the words of the *Ko-ku yao-lun*: "No other art is comparable to that of calligraphy. Saints and sages of past centuries paid a great deal of attention to it, for it

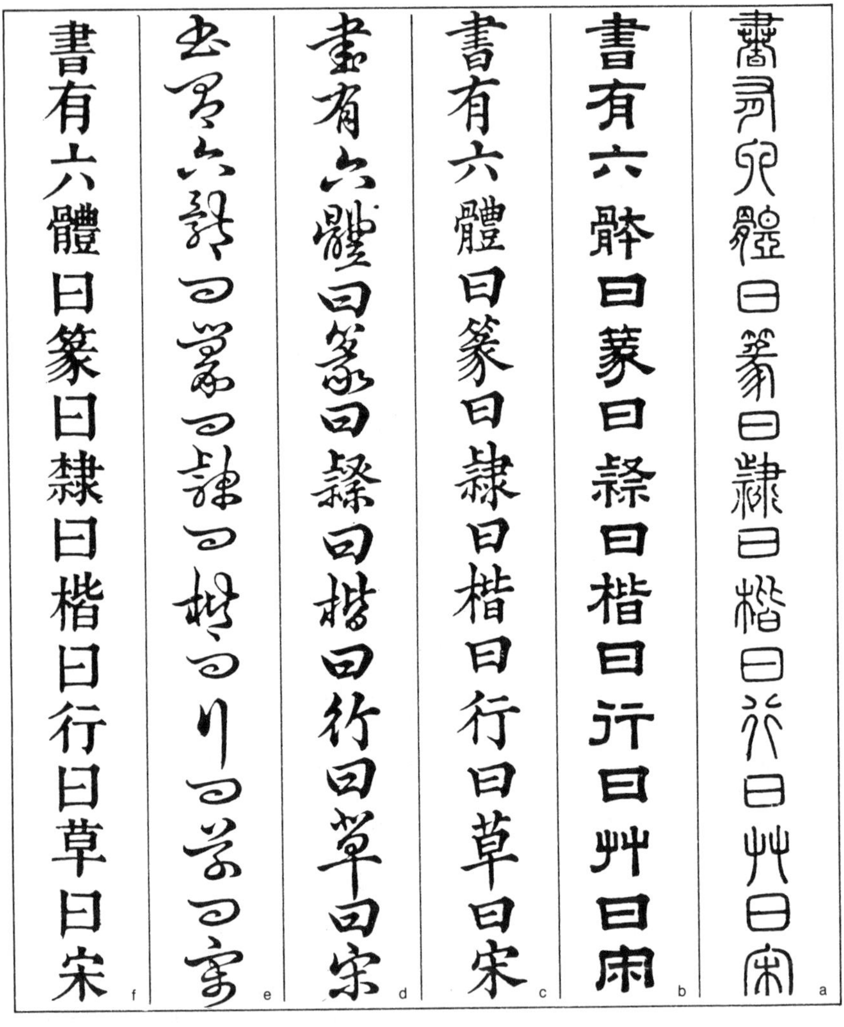

FIGURE 8.11. Types of Calligraphy. The columns represent six different types of written characters. Each line reads: "There are six forms of calligraphy, called (*a*) *chuan*, (*b*) *li*, (*c*) *k'ai*, (*d*) *hsing*, (*e*) *ts'ao*, and (*f*) *sung*." This *liu-shu* system differs from the system discussed in the text only in that it fails to distinguish between "big" and "small" seal script (*chuan*) and adds the category *sung*, which refers to the Sung dynasty style of printed characters. Source: *Chinese Repository*, vol. 3 (May 1834–April 1835), pp. 20–21.

always has been and will forever be the means whereby civilization and the orders of government are made intelligible, while things, great or trivial, from the Six Classics to matters of daily routine, are conveyed to people." Calligraphy was ubiquitous in traditional China. It graced private homes, shops, teahouses, restaurants, temples, monasteries, official buildings, and imperial palaces. It was engraved on metal, wood, and stone and even on the face of rocks and mountains in nature. Calligraphers were in demand by all levels of Chinese society, and success in the civil-service examinations could not be achieved without a good hand, regardless of one's mastery of the Classics and the "eight-legged essay."[67]

Chinese critics distinguished six basic styles of calligraphy: (1) big seal script (*ta-chuan*), (2) small seal script (*hsiao-chuan*), (3) clerical script (*li-shu*), (4) regular or standard script (*k'ai-shu* or *cheng-shu*), (5) running script (*hsing-shu*), and (6) grass-style script (*ts'ao-shu*) (see Figure 8.11). Of these, the last two were the most susceptible to individualized interpretation. The regular script may be likened to *kung-pi* in painting and the grass-style script to *hsieh-i*, in the sense that the former two styles demanded precision while the latter two encouraged spontaneity and freedom; but all forms of Chinese calligraphy left much room for creative potential.[68]

The mid-Ch'ing period witnessed the emergence of several outstanding calligraphers, among whom two deserve special mention. One was Teng Shih-ju (c. 1740–1805), a colorful and unconventional scholar whose brilliant seal- and clerical-style calligraphy was based on actual stone and bronze rubbings. Teng's innovative work, part of a general burst of scholarly interest in ancient rubbings, altered the fashions of Chinese calligraphy and led to a remarkable revival of the *chuan* and *li* styles in the Ch'ing. Chang Ch'i (1765–1833) is significant not only because he was considered the equal of Teng in the *li* style and the talented Pao Shih-ch'en (1775–1855) in the *k'ai* and *hsing* styles but also because he raised four daughters who achieved literary fame, including one of the best-known woman calligraphers (Chang Lun-ying) of the dynasty.[69] Once again it is apparent that the Ch'ing was not simply a period of "cultural stagnation."

Many Chinese scholars have remarked on the link between calligraphy and other forms of Chinese art. Chiang Yee suggests, for example, that the style and spirit of Chinese calligraphy influenced not only painting but also sculpture, ceramics, and architecture. Similarly, Lin Yutang argues that the "basic ideas of rhythm, form and atmosphere [in calligraphy] give the different lines of Chinese art, like poetry, painting, architecture, porcelain and house decorations, an essential unity of spirit."[70] Lin's use of poetry as an example of calligraphic influence on literature is apt enough, but it may be extended; for even vernacular fiction exhibits at least some of the rhythm and "kinesthetic movement" characteristic of Chinese brushwork.

CHAPTER 9

Literature

The Chinese literary tradition shared with the artistic tradition many fundamental assumptions about past models, aesthetics, ethics, and cosmology. Chinese literature was, however, much more explicitly didactic than most of Chinese art and more nearly universal in its appeal. Although a great stylistic gap separated popular vernacular literature from more orthodox classical-style writings, there were certain affinities. In the first place, both kinds of literature were created by members of the scholarly elite, and both reflected elite values. Second, popular equivalents existed for nearly every kind of elite literature. Third, in truth, the elite enjoyed certain types of popular literature (such as novels) almost as much as the masses. Thus, from the standpoint of both content and appeal, vernacular literature provides us with an especially valuable perspective on late imperial Chinese culture.

CATEGORIES OF CLASSICAL LITERATURE

In literature, as in art, the Ch'ing was a period of considerable vitality, especially in the realm of vernacular fiction. Material prosperity, the expansion of mass printing, and the growth of popular literacy under the Manchus produced an unprecedented demand for, and supply of, books. At the same time, a consuming interest in all aspects of traditional Chinese culture led Ch'ing scholars to produce great numbers of antiquarian studies, critical essays, histories, biographies, and gazetteers. More ambitious projects, such as encyclopedias, collections of essays, and literary anthologies, were also undertaken, both by the throne and by energetic private individuals. Such works provided guidance for the present and the future, inspired by a glorious classical past.

Of the many great literary compilations of the Ch'ing period, two gigantic government-sponsored projects stand out as worthy of special attention: the *T'u-shu chi-ch'eng* and the *Ssu-k'u ch'üan-shu* (Complete Collection of the Four Treasuries). We have encountered the former several times in previous chapters. Commissioned during the K'ang-hsi emperor's reign and published in final form in the early years of the Yung-cheng period, the *T'u-shu chi-ch'eng* has been described as "the largest and most useful encyclopedia that has ever been compiled in China."[1] Orthodox in outlook, often biographical in treatment, and composed almost entirely of selected excerpts from earlier writings of various kinds, the *T'u-shu chi-ch'eng* may be considered a literary anthology as well as a convenient guide to the cultural concerns of the Ch'ing elite.

The encyclopedia is divided into 6 main categories, 32 subcategories, and 6,109 sections (*pu*). The writings comprising these sections are arranged in order according to eight major types of literature: (1) factual quotations from standard sources (*hui-k'ao*), arranged chronologically, if datable, or in the traditional order of the classics, histories, philosophers, and belles lettres (see below); (2) general discussions of an orthodox nature (*tsung-lun*) from the four classes of literature noted above; (3) biographies (*lieh-chuan*); (4) literary compositions (*i-wen*), chosen more for style than content; (5) selected sentences (*hsüan-chü*), also selected for their literary merit; (6) factual accounts (*chi-shih*), often anecdotal and of relatively less importance than *hui-k'ao* sources; (7) miscellaneous quotations (*tsa-lu*); and (8) unorthodox material (*wai-pien*), including fiction and quotations from Buddhist and Taoist sources. Not every type of literature is included in every section, but in most cases one can find examples of types 1 or 2, 4, 6, and 7.[2]

In all, the *T'u-shu chi-ch'eng* consists of 10,000 *chüan* and about 100 million characters. Of the encyclopedia's six major categories, human relations is the largest (2,604 *chüan*), followed by geography (2,144), political economy (1,832), arts and sciences (1,656), literature (1,220), and heavenly phenomena (544). Of the subcategories, by far the largest is political divisions (1,544 *chüan*), followed by arts and occupations (824), government service (800), clan and family names (640), classical and noncanonical writings (500), women (376), foods and commercial goods (360), ritual (348), religion (320), vegetable life (320), mountains and rivers (320), the emperor (300), Confucian conduct (300), and military administration (300). The remaining subcategories include literature (260 *chüan*), manufactures (252), animal life (192), strange phenomena (188), law and punishment (180), the study of characters (160), the earth (140), foreign states (140), the imperial household (140), astronomy and mathematics (140), the examination system (136), music (136), officialdom (120), social intercourse (120), family relationships (126), the year (116), human affairs (112), and the heavens (100).

The overlapping of these subcategories blurs the focus somewhat, but we can still see in the *T'u-shu chi-ch'eng* the Ch'ing elite's preoccupation with orderly administration, scholarship, Confucian values, and family relations, as well as its abiding interest in natural phenomena. Moreover, we can discern in the overall organization of the encyclopedia the implicit assumption that

Heaven, Earth, and Man are the interrelated elements of human knowledge and the source of all natural and artificial phenomena.

The *Ssu-k'u ch'üan-shu* ranges almost as broadly in subject matter as the *T'u-shu chi-ch'eng*, but it has a more self-conscious literary emphasis and has been more extensively studied by Chinese scholars. Intended as an imperial collection representing the best of China's magnificent literary heritage, the *Ssu-k'u ch'üan-shu* aptly illustrates the ambivalence of the Ch'ing rulers toward that inheritance. On the one hand, it was clearly designed by the Ch'ien-lung emperor as a monument to Manchu patronage of traditional Chinese culture. On the other, it served admirably as a device for ferreting out works that were deemed critical of the Manchus in particular or "barbarians" in general. In the course of the Literary Inquisition that coincided with the compilation of the *Ssu-k'u ch'üan-shu* from 1773 to 1782, over a thousand works were destroyed and many others suppressed or tampered with. A number of individual Chinese scholars were persecuted for their "seditious" views.[3]

On the more positive side, the *Ssu-k'u* project resulted in the bringing together and transcribing (in seven sets) of nearly thirty-five hundred literary works in over seventy-eight thousand *chüan* (nearly 2.3 million pages per set). It also resulted in the compilation of a massive annotated catalogue known as the *Ssu-k'u ch'üan-shu tsung-mu t'i-yao* (Annotated Index of the Complete Collection of the Four Treasuries), which critically reviewed the 3,461 works mentioned above plus an additional 6,793 works. This catalogue, the most thorough of its kind in all of Chinese history, provides information on the size and general contents of each work, as well as an overall critical evaluation.[4]

Of the over 10,000 works thus reviewed, 1,776 are included in the first ten-part section on the classics (*ching*). It begins with subsections devoted to each of the Five Classics, followed by individual subsections on the *Hsiao-ching*, classical collections, the Four Books, music, and language. By far the largest of the ten subsections is devoted to the *I-ching* (485 works). The second section, on history (*shih*), comprising 2,136 works in the catalogue, is divided into 15 subsections. Of these, physical and political geography is the largest (577 works), followed by biographies and personal accounts (201). Other subsections include those on the twenty-four dynastic histories, other types of historical records (including a subsection on bronze and stone inscriptions), administrative works, official documents, and memoirs of travels in China and elsewhere.

The section on philosophers (*tzu*), covering 2,941 works in 14 subsections, ranges widely. Although, as one might suppose, it places heavy emphasis on orthodox neo-Confucian philosophical tracts (416 works), the largest subsection is entitled simply miscellaneous writings (855 works). It includes the works of non-Confucian philosophers such as Mo-tzu and Kung-sun Lung, as well as a great variety of assorted tracts, pamphlets, and collections of anecdotes. In addition, the section on philosophers devotes specific subsections to such diverse topics as military arts, agricultural writings, medicine, astronomy and mathematics, divination, the arts (including calligraphy, painting, seals, music, and games), repertories (including works on hobbies, connoisseurship, culinary art, and natural science), dictionaries and encyclopedias, narrative writings (other than popular dramas and novels), Buddhist works, and Taoist works. The last section, belles lettres (*chi*), consisting of 3,401 works, is divided into five subsections: elegies of Ch'u, collected works of individuals, general collections (selections of writings from various authors), critical treatises on literature, and rhymes and songs.[5]

An outstanding feature of many Chinese scholars in late imperial times was their astonishing productivity and literary versatility. Charles Hucker provides the example of Ch'ien Ch'ien-i (1582–1664), a Kiangsu dilettante "not untypical of the Ming-Ch'ing transition era," who had a preliminary version of his collected works published in 1643 in 110 *chüan*. This collection included poetry (21 *chüan*), prefaces and postfaces (17), biographical and genealogical sketches (10), obituaries and epitaphs (20), funeral odes and eulogies (2), essays (6), historical annotations (5), critiques of poetry (5), memorials (2), other official documents (13), and letters and miscellany (9). To this was eventually added a supplement in 50 *chüan*. In addition, Ch'ien produced an anthology of Ming poetry in 81 *chüan*, a draft history of the Ming dynasty in 100 *chüan*, and annotated editions of several Buddhist texts. Several Ch'ing monarchs also aspired to such productivity and versatility, most notably the prolific, but pedestrian, Ch'ien-lung emperor.[6]

All such writings, and the vast majority of the works included in the *T'u-shu chi-ch'eng*, *Ssu-k'u ch'üan-shu*, and the annotated catalogue, were written in classical Chinese—the language of the scholarly elite. Popular dramas and vernacular novels, although enjoyed by the literati, were not generally included in scholarly collections for the simple reason that the classical language was considered elegant and refined (*ya*), while the vernacular was deemed vulgar and common (*su*).[7]

Like the most exalted forms of Chinese art, classical Chinese literature was distinguished by its emphasis on rhythm and balance; its close relationship with past masters, models, and styles; the assumed link between creative genius and personal morality; and by much of the same or similar critical terminology. In both art and literature we find a concern with life (*sheng*), spirit (*shen* or *ch'i*), and movement (*tung*). Even the rules of composition in classical literature suggest equivalents or analogues in Chinese art. Liu Ta-k'uei (1698–1780) tells us:

> Literature must, above all, attempt to be strong in vital force [*ch'i*], but if there is no spirit [*shen*] to control the vital force, it will run wild, not

knowing where to settle down. The spirit and the vital force are the finest essences of literature; intonation and rhythm [*yin-chieh*] are the somewhat coarser elements of literature; [and] diction and syntax [*tzu-chü*] are the coarsest elements of literature.[8]

During the Ch'ing period there were several different conceptions of literature, all deriving from earlier theories or critical approaches. One was the notion of literature as a manifestation of the principle of the universe (*tao*). The most influential early exponent of this point of view was Liu Hsieh, quoted in the previous chapter. In Liu's view, "The *tao* manifests literary writings through the sages, and the sages illuminate the *tao* in literary writings." Yao Nai (1731–1815), a leading figure in the T'ung-ch'eng School of the Ch'ing period, put the matter this way:

> I have heard that the *tao* of Heaven and Earth consists of nothing but the *yin* and *yang*, the gentle and strong. Literature is the finest essence of Heaven and Earth, and the manifestation of the *yin* and the *yang*. . . . From the philosophers of the various schools [down to the present] there has been none whose writing is not biased [in favor of either *yin* or *yang*]. If one has obtained the beauty of the *yang* and strong, then one's writing will be like thunder, like lightning, like a long wind emerging from the valley, like lofty mountains and steep cliffs, like a great river flooding, like galloping steeds. . . . If one has obtained the beauty of the *yin* and gentle, then one's writing will be like the sun just beginning to rise, like cool breeze, like clouds, like vapor, like mist, like secluded woods and meandering streams, like ripples, like water gently rocking, like the sheen of pearls or jade, like the cry of a wild goose disappearing into the silent void.[9]

Some Ch'ing scholars saw literature as a reflection of political realities. The early Ch'ing critic Wang Wan (1624–1690), for example, discerned a close correspondence between the rise and fall of the T'ang dynasty and the history of its poetry. He wrote,

> At the height [of the T'ang], the ruler above exerted his energies, [and] the ministers and officials below hastened about their tasks and spoke without reserve; the administration was simple and punishments were few; the atmosphere among the people was harmonious and peaceful. Therefore, what issued forth in poetry was generally leisurely and refined. . . . By the time [the dynasty] declined, . . . at Court there was factional strife and in the country military struggle; the administration was complex and punishments were severe; the atmosphere among the people was sorrowful and bitter. Therefore, what issued forth [in poetry] was mostly sad, nostalgic, and urgent. At the very end, [poetry] became superficial and extravagant.[10]

But if there were those who saw literature as an index of political and social conditions, there were also those who saw in it a means of rectifying those conditions. Shen Te-ch'ien begins his *Shuo-shih tsui-yü* (Miscellaneous Remarks on Poetry) by observing, "The way of poetry is such that it can be used to regulate one's nature and emotions [*hsing-ch'ing*], to improve human relationships and [understanding of things], to move the spirits and gods, to spread [moral] teaching in the states, and to deal with feudal lords"; and in his preface to an anthology of Ch'ing verse he maintains that poetry must "concern itself with human relationships, everday uses, and the causes of the rise and fall [of the state] in ancient and modern times." Ku Yen-wu, for his part, states succinctly, "Literature must be beneficial to the world."[11]

Aesthetic theories of literature focused primarily on the patterns of the classical language and their immediate impact on the reader. In critical writings of this sort, analogies were often drawn with other sensual experiences, including viewing art, hearing music, and eating food. But not all aesthetic theories relied on such analogies. The long-standing debate between advocates of Ancient Prose (*ku-wen*) and Parallel Prose (*p'ien-wen*), for instance, revolved around concrete questions of style. The former was simple and forceful; the latter, elegant and allusive. Both occupied prominent positions in the Chinese classical literary tradition, but vigorous debate on their respective merits continued well into the twentieth century.[12]

Juan Yüan was a particularly powerful proponent of Parallel Prose in the late Ch'ing period. In contrast to T'ung-ch'eng advocates of Ancient Prose, such as Liu Ta-k'uei and Yao Nai, Juan argued that only writings employing rhyme and parallelism could be called true literature. He thus revived the old Six Dynasties concept of literature as belles lettres rather than "plain writing" (*pi*). In Juan's words,

> Those engaged in literary composition, who do not concern themselves with harmonizing sounds to form rhymes or polishing words and phrases to make them go far so that what they write should be easy to recite and easy to remember, but merely use single [i.e., nonparallel] sentences to write . . . [wildly], do not realize that what they write is what the ancients called "speech" [*yen*], which means "straightforward speech," or "talk" [*yü*], which means "argument," but not . . . what Confucius called *wen* [embellished words, i.e., true literature].[13]

Ch'ing scholars often employed Parallel Prose to illustrate stylistic virtuosity, but the supreme test of their literary ability was poetry. From earliest times, poetry had been a central Chinese cultural concern. In fact, the *Shih-ching* (Book of Poetry) is considered by some authorities to be the single most important work in China's entire literary history. Confucius once said, "If you do not learn the *Shih-ching* you will not be able to converse"; and again, "[One's character is] elevated by poetry, established by ritual, and completed by music." Virtually every major type of Chinese literature, from the classics and histories to plays and novels, included substantial amounts of poetry, and few self-respecting gentlemen in Ch'ing times lacked the ability to compose elegant verse rapidly, in any social circumstance. Moreover, in poetry as in calligraphy, the Ch'ing period witnessed a revival of several major styles, including regulated verse (*lü-shih*) and lyric verse (*tz'u*).[14]

Many authorities have remarked upon how well suited the classical Chinese language was for poetic expression. Even ordinary prose had an evocative, ambiguous, rhythmic quality. Poetry—which as a generic category should include not only the various types of *shih* and lyric verse but also "song-poems" (*ch'ü*) and rhymed prose (*fu*)—gave full scope to the creative potential of the language. The grammatical flexibility of classical Chinese, as well as the multiple meanings and subtle ambiguities of each character, allowed Chinese poets to express a wide range of ideas and emotion with vividness, economy, grace, and power. Grouping elements together in spatial patterns and temporal rhythms, the poet created integrated structures of meaning that, though unified, presented a kaleidoscopic series of impressions. The visual quality of the characters, enhanced by the use of calligraphy as an artistic medium, complemented the tonal and other auditory qualities of the language— all of which were exploited to great advantage in poetry. Furthermore, Chinese poetry never lost its intimate relationship with music. Even when the musical context for lyrics had been forgotten, poems were still written to be chanted, not simply read aloud. Unhappily, the visual and auditory effects that contributed so much to the richness of traditional Chinese poetry are invariably lost in translation.[15]

Four main critical views of Chinese poetry have been distinguished: those of the Technicians, Moralists, Individualists (or Expressionists), and Intuitionalists. Although these designations do not imply the existence of four distinct and mutually exclusive schools of literary criticism, they do suggest certain tendencies in the thinking of poets and literary critics during the late imperial period of Chinese history.

The Technicians, as their name implies, viewed poetry primarily as a literary exercise. Their outlook was traditionalistic and frankly imitative, although rationalized on grounds that the principles of poetry embodied in the work of the great masters were, in effect, natural laws of rhythm and euphony. In the words of the Ch'ing critic Weng Fang-kang (1733–1818),

> The fundamental principles of poetic methods do not originate with oneself; they are like rivers flowing into the sea, and one must trace their sources back to the ancients. As for the infinitely varied applications of poetic methods, from such major considerations as the structural principles down to such

details as the grammatical nature of a word, the tone of a syllable, and the points of continuation, transition, and development—all these one must learn from the ancients. Only so can one realize that everything is done according to rules and in consonance with the laws of music and that one cannot do as one likes to the slightest degree.[16]

This technical view of poetry placed a premium on ancient models, but it also encouraged creative stylistic manipulations, such as taking apart the characters in one line of a poem and reconstituting them (*li-ho*) to form new characters in another line or composing verse that could be read from top to bottom or bottom to top with different meaning but equal clarity (*hui-wen*). Technicians also enjoyed composing poems consisting of collected lines (*chi-chü*) taken from past poems composed by different writers. Chu I-tsun (1629–1709) provides an example:

> Soft colored clouds obscured by the sun;
> Red upon red, green upon green, flowers in the park:
> How can I enhance this fine poetic feeling?
> Listen to the spring birds:
> After they've flown, the flowering branches still dance gracefully.

These lines are taken, respectively, from the poetry of Wang Wei, Wang Chien, Ssu-k'ung T'u, Ku K'uang, and Wei Ying-wu.[17]

Many forms of Chinese verse were highly structured, requiring careful attention to the number of lines, the number of characters in a line, the matching of tones, rhyme, and parallelism or antithesis. Antithesis was, of course, especially admired. It appeared not only in regulated verse (where it was required), four-character verse, and ancient verse (*ku-shih*), but also in lyric verse and song-poems, which often did not even have lines of equal length. In the best antithetical couplets, each character in the first line contrasted in tone with the corresponding character in the second. At the same time, ideally the contrasted words served the same grammatical function in each line and referred to the same categories of things. A simple example drawn from the novel *Hung-lou meng* should suffice:

> When the sun sets, the water whitens;
> When the tide rises, all the world is green.

These lines, from the brush of Wang Wei, elicit the following response from an appreciative student of his work in the novel: "'Whitens' and 'green' at first seem like nonsense but when you start thinking about it, you realize that he *had* to use those two words in order to describe the scene exactly as it was. When you read those lines out loud, the flavor of them is so concentrated that it's as though you had an olive weighing several thousand catties [i.e., pounds] inside your mouth."[18]

Traditional handbooks on Chinese poetry gave detailed lists of categories of objects for use in antithesis, including astronomy, geography, plants, and animals. In the hands of unskilled writers this technique could degenerate into a mere mechanical pairing of words, but when employed by the masters it became a vivid expression of *yin-yang* reconciliation of opposites. In the words of the modern critic James J. Y. Liu,

> At its best [antithesis] can reveal a perception of the underlying contrasting aspects of Nature and simultaneously strengthen the structure of the poem. The perfect antithetical couplet is natural, not forced, and though the two lines form a sharp contrast, they yet somehow seem to possess a strange affinity, like two people of opposite temperaments happily married, so that one might remark of the couplet, as of the couple, "What a contrast, yet what a perfect match!"[19]

The didactic view of poetry shared with the technical view a concern with tradition, and many Ch'ing writers, such as Shen Te-ch'ien, could be described as technicians as well as moralists. But the fundamental purpose of poetry in the minds of the Moralists was self-cultivation and, by extension, the betterment of society. Shen Te-ch'ien wrote, for example, "To use what is poetic in poetry is commonplace; it is only when you quote from the classics, the histories, and the philosophers in poetry that you can make it different from wild and groundless writings." An extreme but effective example of didacticism can be found in the following poem written by the K'ang-hsi emperor to his son, the heir apparent, Yin-jeng:

> The Sage gave his family instructions
> To draw learning from the *Songs* [i.e., *Shih-ching*] and the rituals;
> Countries differ from families
> But learning is one.
> . . . .
>
> As Yü the Great treasured each moment,
> So must you value time in its passing.
> Learn from the Ancients in each book you open,
> Seek inner meanings of every occurrence.
> Over time, your heart will find joy,
> Just as each kind of food reveals its beauty.[20]

Individualist poets were not bereft of such sentiments, but they did not view poetry primarily as a didactic exercise. Rather, they saw it as an expression of the unfettered self. In the words of the famous Ch'ing poet Yüan Mei

(1716–1797): "Poetry is what expresses one's nature and emotion. It is enough to look no further than one's self [for the material of poetry]. If its words move the heart, its colors catch the eye, its taste pleases the mouth, and its sound delights the ear, then it is good poetry." Such diverse individuals as Yüan, his literary arch enemy Chang Hsüeh-ch'eng, and the noted New Text (*chin-wen*) scholar Kung Tzu-chen (1792–1841) shared these individualist sentiments.

Individualist poetry covered a wide range of emotional territory. Common topics included friendship and drinking, romantic love, homesickness and parting, history and nostalgia, leisure and nature. Nature themes were especially esteemed. The Ch'ing historian Chao I conveys the Taoist ideal:

I never tire in my search of solitude;
I wander aimlessly along out-of-the-way trails
Where I have never been before.
The more I change my direction, the wilder the road becomes.
Suddenly I come to the bank of a raging river;
The path breaks off, all trails vanish.
No one is there for me to ask directions:
Only a lone egret beside the tall grass, glistening white.[21]

The Intuitionalists, perhaps best represented by Wang Shih-chen and Wang Fu-chih, dealt with many of the themes of the Individualists, but they advocated a more intuitive apprehension of reality (*miao-wu*). Their poetry was concerned with the relationship between human emotion (*ch'ing*) and external scene (*ching*). In the words of Wang Fu-chih, "Although *ch'ing* and *ching* are two in name, they are inseparable in reality. In the most inspired poetry they subtly join together, with no barrier. Good poets include *ching* in *ch'ing* and *ch'ing* in *ching*." Further, Wang writes,

Emotion is the activity of *yin* and *yang*, and things [*wu*] are the products of Heaven and Earth. When the activity between *yin* and *yang* takes place in the mind [*hsin*], there are things produced by Heaven and Earth to respond to it from the outside. Thus, things that exist on the outside can have an internal counterpart in emotion; and where there is emotion on the inside there must be the external object [to match it].[22]

The Intuitionalists attempted, in other words, to identify the self with the object of contemplation in order to establish a form of "spiritual resonance" (*shen-yün*). Although criticized by Individualists such as Yüan Mei for lacking genuine emotion, poets such as Wang Shih-chen actually sought a deeper spiritual awareness, an appreciation of the interrelatedness of all things, animate and inanimate. They were concerned not simply with self-expression, but with

conveying a world view. We get a hint of this attitude in Wang's "Moonlit
Night at Fragrant Mountain Temple":

> The bright moon appears from the east ridge,
> And the summits become still all at once.
> Melting snow still covers the ground,
> Lying in shadow before the western lodge.
> The hue of bamboos makes the solitude complete,
> As pine shadows bewitch the shimmering ripples.
> All this brilliance shines forth at once—
> A myriad of images all pure and fresh.[23]

But for all that seemed to divide the Technicians, Moralists, Individualists,
and Intuitionalists, there was considerable creative overlap. We have mentioned
the link between Technicians and Moralists as exemplified in Shen Te-ch'ien,
but there was other common ground. Individualists such as Kung Tzu-chen,
for example, could be highly didactic, while Intuitionalists such as Wang
Shih-chen paid great attention to style. Shen Te-ch'ien, for his part, stressed
the quality of "spiritual resonance" that was so important to Wang, yet he
also recognized the merit of "romantic" poets such as Li E (1692–1752),
whose writing was characterized by originality and freedom from the stylistic
standards of Wang, Chu I-tsun, and others. In fact, the best Ch'ing poets
were masters of a variety of styles and moods, as the numerous poems in
Arthur Waley's delightful biography of Yüan Mei attest.[24]

By Ch'ing times, and in fact well before, poetry and painting had become
inextricably linked as the most exalted forms of elite cultural indulgence. Both
were "written" with brush and ink, both treated a wide variety of subject
material, and both were concerned with simplicity and stylistic balance.
Furthermore, poetry and painting often inspired each other; painters were
moved to create art after reading a poem, and poets were moved to create
verse after viewing a painting. Thus, we have Cheng Hsieh (1693–1765)
writing the following lines to his contemporary, Pien Wei-ch'i:

> You paint the wild geese as if I could see them crying,
> And on this double-threaded silk, the rustling sound of river reeds.
> On the tip of your brush, how infinitely chill is the autumn wind;
> Everywhere on the mountain is the sorrow of parting.[25]

In the end, the relationship between painting and poetry is perhaps best
expressed in Su Tung-p'o's (1036–1101) famous tribute to Wang Wei,
"There is painting in his poetry and poetry in his painting." Ideally, and
very often in fact, the Chinese literatus in Ch'ing times was both poet and
painter.[26]

VERNACULAR LITERATURE

Although no major literary figure in China after the first century A.D. attempted to write his principal works in a language consonant with the spoken language, the written vernacular (*pai-hua wen*) still enjoyed considerable popularity throughout much of the imperial era, especially from the T'ang period onward. During the Ch'ing dynasty, a variety of vernacular works circulated widely, reflecting as well as contributing to the growth of basic literacy in China—estimated by some to be as high as 30–45 percent for males and 2–10 percent for females. Although not as succinct, exalted, or aesthetically pleasing as classical Chinese, the vernacular was comparatively easy to learn, direct, colorful, and very forceful.[27]

Vernacular equivalents existed for many forms of elite literature. Administrative manuals advocated the modification of complex official documents for public consumption through the use of simple rhymed phrases in "nice calligraphy, easy to read." Chang Po-hsing (1652–1725), as governor of Fukien in the early eighteenth century, personally wrote three different versions of the famous Sacred Edict of the K'ang-hsi emperor: "one embellished with classical allusions for the literati, one illustrated with popular sayings for those of medium intelligence, and one with memorable jingles for the simple country folk." Almanacs, encyclopedias of daily use (*jih-yung lei-shu*), and other practical handbooks were produced in several versions to reach different reading audiences. Popular vernacular histories paralleled the orthodox histories of the elite, "morality books" and "precious scrolls" were the popular equivalents of philosophical tracts and the classics, and colloquial short stories served as the counterparts to T'ang-style classical tales (*ch'uan-ch'i*), a genre that P'u Sung-ling (1640–1715) brought to such high levels of achievement in the early Ch'ing period.[28]

The vast majority of vernacular writings reflected conventional elite values— even such popular Buddhist and Religious Taoist tracts as the *T'ai-shang kan-ying p'ien* (Treatise of the Most Exalted One on Retribution), the *Pu-fei-ch'ien kung-te li* (Meritorious Deeds at No Cost), and the *Kuang-shan p'ien kung-kuo ko* (Ledger of Merit and Demerit for the Diffusion of Good Deeds). Although based on the idea of divine retribution and buttressed by other religious ideas, these works employed a great deal of elite symbolism and had a decidedly ethical, this-worldly cast. To be sure, they often contained admonitions to spare animal life, to show respect to sacred images, and "not to speak ill of Buddhist and Taoist monks"; but the importance in these tracts of family affairs, filial piety, loyalty to the ruler, obedience to the "principles of Heaven," social harmony, the avoidance of lawsuits, and even respect for paper with written characters on it indicates a decidedly Confucian point of view. Furthermore, although works such as the *Pu-fei-ch'ien kung-te li* classify meritorious deeds according to various social and occupational groupings, the striking feature of these works is the acceptance of a Confucian social hierarchy and the fact that there is "virtually no class consciousness or awareness of class interests to be asserted or defended."[29]

Vernacular fiction also reflected an elite outlook, and despite the fact that dramatic works and popular novels were generally disparaged by the Confucian literati and sometimes outlawed by the state, they were enjoyed by all sectors of Chinese society, from emperor to peasant. Drama was a particularly effective means of reaching the Chinese masses. During the late Ming and throughout the Ch'ing, the popular theater eclipsed traditional storytelling in influence, bringing history, legends, novels, and stories to cities and to the countryside, down to individual villages. Indeed, it seems evident that the bulk of popular knowledge concerning the narrative tradition in China—major heroes and villains, stock scenes, allusions, and so forth—was transmitted more on stage than through the written word (see Chapter 10).[30]

There were several types of Chinese drama in Ch'ing times: the classic Yüan dynasty "variety performance" (*tsa-chü*), the southern drama (*hsi-wen* or *ch'uan-ch'i*), various subregional styles such as "K'un-shan music" (*K'un-ch'ü*), and the late Ch'ing hybrid interregional form known as Peking opera (*ching-hsi*). Although each of these types had its own special features, all shared certain general characteristics. One such characteristic was a multimedia presentation, combining spoken language (both verse and prose), music (both vocal and instrumental), and acting—including mime, dance, and acrobatics. Another general feature of Chinese drama was its nonrepresentational nature, its stress on the expression of emotion rather than the imitation of life. As James J. Y. Liu indicates,

> In nonrepresentational drama, the words spoken or sung by a character do not necessarily represent actual speech or even thought; they are the dramatist's means to make the audience imagine the feelings and thoughts of the characters as well as the situations in which they find themselves. When a character speaks or sings fine poetry, he or she is not usually represented as a poet. . . . The poetry, in most cases, belongs to the dramatist, not the character.

Like music in a play, poetry was extremely important in conveying dramatic mood, and when read, Chinese drama tended to be measured primarily by its verse.[31]

Since Chinese playwrights were not interested in imitating life, they did not usually try to create highly individualized characters. Rather, they were concerned with portraying certain human types, a categorical approach to characterization abetted by Chinese stage conventions such as colorful makeup and an extraordinarily elaborate system of hand, sleeve, and facial expressions. Among the most appreciated character types were upright scholars, military men (both good and bad), heroic women, and buffoons. There was not, however, a sharp division between tragedy and comedy as such in Chinese drama, in part because theatrical convention, like much of the vernacular literary tradition, demanded happy endings or at least poetic justice.[32]

Chinese plays covered all of the thematic territory embraced by traditional Chinese fiction: sex, love, intrigue, supernatural events, religious commitment, historical and pseudohistorical episodes (civil and military), domestic dramas, murder, lawsuits, banditry, and so forth. Many dramatic themes were derived from short stories or novels. Of the numerous outstanding plays written during the late imperial period, we may single out the popular Ch'ing drama *T'ao-hua shan* (Peach Blossom Fan) for particular attention. Written by a descendant of Confucius (K'ung Shang-jen, 1648–1718), *T'ao-hua shan* ranks as one of the greatest plays in the Chinese language by virtue of its historical vision, dramatic construction, and literary quality. It is also noteworthy for its wide-ranging subject material and effective characterization.

T'ao-hua shan is a carefully structured historical romance that touches on many different aspects of Chinese life: personal and private, social and political, military, and even artistic. Its major characters, all actual personalities of the late Ming period, have more individuality than most Chinese dramatic characters. For example, the "hero," Hou Fang-yü, is less than perfect, while the "villian," Juan Ta-ch'eng, possesses certain admirable qualities. This attempt at balance is also evident in the dramatic story line, which alternates between scenes of sadness and joy, quiescence and activity. In these and other ways, *T'ao-hua shan* resembles some of the great novels of the Ming and Ch'ing periods.

The play is a moving romantic story, but it is also a basically accurate historical account, and as such, deals with the politically sensitive subject of the fall of the Ming dynasty. It should come as no surprise, therefore, to find that K'ung Shang-jen sometimes distorts the record in an apparent effort not to offend the Manchus. The loyal minister Shih K'o-fa, for instance, commits suicide in the play, whereas in real life he was killed by Ch'ing forces after refusing to surrender to them. On the other hand, K'ung has his hero renounce the world rather than take the examinations under the Manchus (as he did in fact), presumably to provide a more satisfying climax to the play. In all, K'ung must have struck an effective balance, since we know that *T'ao-hua shan* was presented at court and was also well received by the Chinese public at large.[33]

A significant feature of most Chinese dramas and short stories is their neat resolution of the plot for maximum impact. By contrast, the Chinese novel— the supreme achievement in vernacular fiction during Ming-Ch'ing times— gives very little sense of unlinear plot development and provides no dramatic climax. The reasons for this may be found in the aesthetic and philosophical assumptions that underlie such works.

As Andrew Plaks has insightfully illustrated, the structure of the best Chinese novels is rooted in the logic of interrelated and overlapping categories—

the presentation of experience in terms of *yin-yang*–style juxtapositions of images, themes, situations, and personalities. Reflecting the deeply ingrained idea of existence as "ceaseless alternation and cyclical recurrence," the Chinese novel proceeds along narrative axes of change such as separation and union (*li-ho*), prosperity and decline (*sheng-shuai*), sorrow and joy (*pei-hsi*), elegance and baseness (*ya-su*), movement and stillness (*tung-ching*). It may also drift between realms of reality and illusion (*chen-chia*). The salient point is that these dualities are complementary rather than antithetical; they do not take the form of a master dualism and are not resolved in a truly dialectical process. Instead of the kind of resolution or synthesis that might be expected in a Western novel, there is only infinite overlapping and alternation.[34]

One gains the impression of endlessness in a Chinese novel—much the same quality we have identified in landscape paintings, gardens, and certain kinds of Chinese poetry. But as in art and poetry, endlessness or purposelessness was not tantamount to meaninglessness, for there was always the assumption that the entire ground of existence is intelligible. In Plaks' words,

> Any meaning in the narrative texts will tend to come not in the configurations of the individual event, or its logical relation to other events, but only in the hypothetical totality of all (or at least a good many) events. . . . This sense of meaning in the overview may be partially behind the centrality of historical and pseudohistorical narrative in the Chinese tradition. The idea that an objective recounting of human events will eventually bear out its own pattern of meaning is relatively clear in historiography, and one might even say that the dimension of significance which Western narrative tends to derive from epic models of unique greatness is manifest sooner in the Chinese context in terms of the recurrent cycles, the vast overview of history.[35]

The comparison between fictional narrative and history also may be extended to the treatment of character, which in most of Chinese vernacular literature tends to be categorical. Like the evaluation of historical personalities—not to mention that of artists and writers—the tendency in Chinese narrative is to sum up the individual in vivid, economical brush strokes. Most novelists describe their characters from the outside, focusing primarily on actions rather than ideas, but assuming an integral relationship between the two. Characterization in the best Chinese novels is more complex than in conventional historical writing, however, since in Chinese narrative the emphasis is usually on the momentary and changing attributes of character rather than on abiding or developing attributes. The central figures in novels are seldom "heroic" in the Western sense and often give the impression of inconsistency or ambivalence. Again, these features can be explained in part by the aesthetic and philosophical notion of *yin-yang* alternation and complementarity, an outlook that can accommodate change and inconsistency with comparative ease.[36]

Futhermore, in keeping with the traditional Chinese emphasis on relational thinking, the character of any given individual in a novel is seldom as important as the relationship of that person to others—hence, the emphasis on groups of people acting in concert or the elaborate interplay of various individuals in a group context. Sometimes fictional characters are even depicted as composites of their acquaintances. Also important to Chinese characterization is the tension created by conflicting social roles within the framework of the Three Bonds and the Five Relationships. In narrative, as in life, a man might well be torn by the conflicting imperatives of being at once a father, a son, a husband, a minister or subject (or emperor), an elder or younger brother, and a friend.[37]

Moral dilemmas are central to the structure of Chinese novels, which, like most other forms of vernacular literature, are marked by a heavy didacticism, a strong emphasis on themes of reward and retribution. This reflects the Confucian idea of an inherent moral order in the universe and the principle of *pao* (requittal or recompense), which requires that a fictional tale be morally satisfying. The result is that Chinese narrative, while full of tragic situations, lacks a well-developed concept of tragedy in the Western sense.[38]

The moral world of the Chinese novel is fundamentally Confucian, but Buddhist and Taoist elements appear prominently in several major novels, and many have an explicitly supernatural dimension. Although the most esteemed values in Chinese narrative are those of loyalty, duty, filial piety, and chastity, a number of novels exhibit a "syncretic hospitality" to the transcendental doctrines of Buddhism and Taoism, as well as to the universalistic ethic of the knight-errant (*hsia*). Moreover, we find that some of the greatest works in the Chinese narrative tradition serve as vehicles for satirizing or otherwise criticizing certain values and practices of traditional Chinese society, despite their Confucian tone. This helps account for the ambivalence of Confucian scholars toward the novel and the periodic efforts by the state in Ming-Ch'ing times to ban a number of "novels and licentious works" (*hsiao-shuo yin-tz'u*) on grounds that they were "frivolous, vulgar and untrue." Even China's greatest novel, *Hung-lou meng*, was officially proscribed during a portion of the nineteenth century, although we know that the Ch'ien-lung emperor himself read and enjoyed the work in the previous century.[39]

But for all their satirical tendencies and "vulgar" content, the best novels of the Ming-Ch'ing period enthusiastically celebrated traditional Chinese culture and provided all sectors of Chinese society with a common repository of heroes and villains who either inspired emulation or served as negative examples. Of the many popular novels of late imperial times, several merit at least brief discussion. Together, these works display the wide variety of Chinese narrative themes and approaches, as well as the basic features of traditional fiction outlined above. All have undergone considerable evolution, all have been translated into Western languages, and all have been the subject of extensive literary criticism both in China and in the West.[40]

We may begin with the popular historical narrative *San-kuo chih yen-i* (Romance of the Three Kingdoms)—one of the earliest, least colloquial, and least fictional of China's major novels. Reputedly written by Lo Kuan-chung (c. 1330–1400), it is set in the Three Kingdoms period that followed the breakdown of the Han dynasty. The novel is full of battle and intrigue, with prominent themes of brotherhood, loyalty, personal ambition, and righteous revenge. Among the many historical characters of the novel, several have become universally acknowledged in China as either noble heroes or arch villains: Chang Fei, the symbol of reckless courage; Kuan Yü, noteworthy for his unwavering loyalty; Chu-ko Liang, the brilliant strategist; and Ts'ao Ts'ao, the selfish and evil tyrant.[41]

A popular proverb of the Ch'ing period advised "Let not the young read *Shui-hu*; let not the old read *San-kuo*." For just as the latter novel encouraged deviousness and intrigue, so the former, *Shui-hu chuan* (Water Margin; All Men Are Brothers), encouraged rebellion against authority. For this reason, at various times in the Ch'ing period certain versions of the novel were condemned or outlawed. Like *San-kuo*, *Shui-hu* is full of courageous deeds, with themes of friendship, loyalty, and revenge, as well as righteous revolt. It is traditionally attributed to Lo Kuan-chung, but *Shui-hu* is much more colloquial and less historical than *San-kuo*, covers a shorter time span (during the Sung dynasty), and consists of a sequence of cycles rather than an interweaving of narrative strands. Of the 108 "righteous brigands" of *Shui-hu*—who represent a fascinating cross section of Chinese society—the faintly historical Sung Chiang and the loyal and powerful Wu Sung have become especially popular folk heroes. To this day, few Chinese are unfamiliar with the story of Wu Sung's killing of the tiger.[42]

Far different in subject matter from the puritanical heroics of *San-kuo* and *Shui-hu* is the debauchery of the Ming erotic novel *Chin P'ing Mei* (Golden Lotus). Attributed by some to Wang Shih-chen (1526–1596) and by others to Hsü Wei (1521–1593), *Chin P'ing Mei* draws upon many diverse literary sources, including *Shui-hu*, vernacular short stories, classical works, plays, and popular songs. It is a "novel of manners," set in the Sung, that describes Chinese urban middle-class life in realistic detail and dwells at length on the sexual exploits of the merchant Hsi-men Ch'ing. The author shows a certain ambivalence toward his characters, displaying outward disapproval of their immoral behavior but covert sympathy for their physical and emotional frustrations; yet ultimately he opts for morality: Hsi-men Ch'ing dies of sexual overindulgence, and most of the other "evil" people in the novel are punished in one way or another. Hsi-men Ch'ing's son redeems his father's sins by becoming a Buddhist monk. One especially noteworthy feature of the novel is its full and sympathetic treatment of women, a sharp contrast with the negative and stereotypical views of them projected in *San-kuo* and *Shui-hu*.[43]

Another genuinely erotic Chinese novel, traditionally attributed to the dramatist Li Yü (1611–1680), is *Jou p'u-t'uan* (Prayer Mat of Flesh). Like *Chin P'ing Mei*, *Jou p'u-t'uan* may be considered a kind of religious allegory revolving around the theme of Buddhist redemption. It is well structured, lively, sympathetic to women, and psychologically realistic. In several respects, *Jou p'u-t'uan* is an even better novel than *Chin P'ing Mei*. It is tighter and makes more skillful use of character analogies, humor, and irony. The female character Yü-hsiang (Noble Scent) provides an excellent illustration of the problem of conflicting social roles as a daughter, wife, mistress, and prostitute. She also serves as an interesting example of the interplay of individuals in a group context, since she is linked in some way to all of the major male characters in the novel with the exception of Sai K'un-lun.[44]

Hsi-yu chi (Journey to the West; Monkey), as its title suggests, is a travel epic. The novel is based on the historic pilgrimage to India of the famous Buddhist monk Hsüan-tsang (596–664), who made the trip by way of Central Asia between 629 and 645. But instead of the sober travel account left by the historic Hsüan-tsang, *Hsi-yu chi* is a comic fantasy, written by the scholar Wu Ch'eng-en (c. 1506–1582). It revolves around the adventures of the humorless pilgrim San-tsang ("Tripitaka," a Buddhist pun on the name Hsüan-tsang) and his traveling companions, including the well-known magical monkey named Sun Wu-k'ung and a sensual and slothful pig named Chu Pa-chieh. The novel can be approached from several angles—as allegory, social and political satire, comedy, and myth. At the level of allegory, and in the popular mind, Tripitaka represents selfishness and spiritual blindness; Pigsy, gross human appetite; and Monkey, intelligence, resourcefulness, and supernatural power. Sun Wu-k'ung is, of course, the hero of the work. The novel is full of good-natured satire, and few subjects escape the author's barbs, including the "Monkey King" himself.[45]

Another travel epic, less well known but very important from both a literary and a social standpoint, is the late Ch'ing novel *Ching-hua yüan* (Flowers in the Mirror), by Li Ju-chen (c. 1763–1830). If *Hsi-yu chi* can be described as China's *Pilgrim's Progress*, then *Ching-hua yüan* is perhaps the Chinese equivalent of *Gulliver's Travels*. Like *Hsi-yu chi*, *Ching-hua yüan* is a blend of mythology and adventure, fantasy and allegory, satire and wit. Although more a reflection of Confucian moral values and Taoist philosophy than of Buddhist theology or mythology, *Ching-hua yüan* is far from conventional. It heavily criticizes certain Chinese social practices, such as footbinding, and celebrates accomplished women such as T'ang Kuei-ch'en (who represents literary talent), Shih Lan-yen (the embodiment of morality and wisdom), and Meng Tzu-chih (witty and humorous). Yet, as Frederick Brandauer has pointed out, the emancipation of women in the novel is still largely within the framework of an early Confucian ideal of womanhood, and despite its trenchant social criticism, *Ching-hua yüan* evinces obvious admiration for nearly every other aspect of traditional Chinese culture.[46]

Ju-lin wai-shih (The Scholars), by Wu Ching-tzu (1701–1754), is considered China's best satirical novel. Through his skilled use of an omniscient narrator, the author explores the often sordid and corrupt world of the Chinese elite, underscoring both the importance of the examination system to the literati class and the many abuses of the system. In all, the novel boasts about two hundred characters, many of whom are very skillfully portrayed—sometimes with conflicting information supplied by different observers. A few scholarly figures are seen as upright and exemplary, but many more appear as imposters and hypocrites. Several critics have emphasized the autobiographical nature of the book and the author's identification with the able but highly individualistic scholar Tu Shao-ch'ing; yet even Tu is satirized on occasion, as Wu Ching-tzu projects a consistently moral vision in the midst of vulgarity, hypocrisy, and human folly. Although often criticized for its episodic structure and apparent lack of a cohesive overall design, *Ju-lin wai-shih* illustrates very well the traditional Chinese emphasis on "a mass of weaving of many narrative strands" and on vast networks of human relationships.[47]

Several other novels of social criticism deserve at least passing mention, including the late Ch'ing works *Lao Ts'an yu-chi* (The Travels of Lao Ts'an) by Liu E (1857–1909) and the innovative first-person narrative entitled *Erh-shih nien mu-tu kuai hsien-chuang* (Bizarre Happenings Eyewitnessed over Two Decades) by Wu Wo-yao (1867–1910). These and other novels of the late Ch'ing not only shed valuable light on the dynasty in decline (and on the unprecedented impact of the West during the late nineteenth and early twentieth centuries), but they also represent an important transitional stage between traditional and modern fiction in China.[48]

By almost any standard, the greatest of all Chinese novels is *Hung-lou meng*. The first 80 chapters of this massive and elegant work, commonly known as *Shih-t'ou chi* (Story of the Stone), were written by Ts'ao Hsüeh-ch'in (c. 1715–1763); the last 40 chapters are generally attributed to Kao E (fl. 1791). Some versions of the full 120-chapter work consist of nearly thirteen hundred pages and about seven-hundred thousand words. The novel contains at least thirty major figures and some four hundred minor ones ranged all along the Chinese social spectrum. Yet, as numerous as these characters are, Fang Chao-ying rightly observes that

> they intermingle in a wonderful unity, each individual constituting an integral member of a large family group, sharing its glory and its shame, contributing to its prosperity or its ruin. Some, taking it for granted that the family fortune is irreversible, spend their days in emotional excesses or in sensual pleasures. Some, who are avaricious, contrive to profit by mismanagement of

the family estate. Some foresee the dangers and so plan for their own futures; others voice warnings, but their words go unheeded. Such a panorama of complex human emotions, involving tens of masters and hundreds of servants, constitutes source-material of supreme value for a study of the social conditions in affluent households of the early Ch'ing period.[49]

As the above summary suggests, the major story line of the novel revolves around the fortunes of the Chia family and a complex love affair involving various individuals living in the family compound—notably Chia Pao-yü, the "hero" of the book, and his talented female cousins, Lin Tai-yü and Hsüeh Pao-ch'ai. Much of the novel is strongly autobiographical, for like Pao-yü, Ts'ao Hsüeh-ch'in was a sensitive, well-educated individual whose wealthy and established family experienced financial reverses and other difficulties during his lifetime. The book has several different layers of meaning, and it is written in several different literary modes—realistic, allegorical, and narrative. Like *Ju-lin wai-shih*, *Hung-lou meng* may be viewed in part as a critique of early Ch'ing political and social life, and like *Ching-hua yüan*, which was heavily influenced by Ts'ao's brilliant narrative, it can be seen as a celebration of women.[50]

The structure of *Hung-lou meng* illustrates especially well the basic organizing principle of *yin-yang* complementarity and the traditional Chinese philosophical interest in relations, qualities, and states of being. As Plaks, Lucien Miller, and others have indicated, much of the appeal of the novel can be found in the interpenetration or overlapping of themes of reality and illusion; the juxtaposition of Confucian and Buddhist (or Taoist) elements; contrasts between rich and poor, exalted and base; and the alternation of scenes, moods, and situations. Antithetical couplets at the beginning of many chapters, and contrasting characterizations such as those of the frail Lin Tai-yü and the robust Hsüeh Pao-ch'ai, heighten the reader's sense of interpenetration, alternation, and complementary opposition. Early in the novel the structural and thematic tone is set:

> There actually are some happy affairs in the Red Dust [the "real" world], it's just that one cannot depend on them forever. Then again, there is "discontent within bliss, numerous demons in auspicious affairs," a phrase of eight words all of which belong tightly bound together. In the twinkling of an eye, sorrow is born of utter happiness, men are no more, and things change. In the last analysis, it's all a dream and the myriad realms return to nothingness.[51]

Predictably, *Hung-lou meng* ends in what Plaks describes as "narrative lame-duck fashion." Well before the conclusion of the novel, Pao-yü's family secretly arranges for him to marry Pao-ch'ai, rather than his true love, Tai-yü, who dies grief stricken on Pao-yü's wedding day. A series of Chia family disasters follow, but Pao-yü eventually passes the examinations, Pao-ch'ai bears him a son, and the Chia family fortunes rise again. Pao-yü then decides to renounce the world and become a Buddhist monk, thus seeking enlightenment and personal salvation after at least partially fulfilling his Confucian responsibilities as a son and a husband. As some modern Chinese scholars have argued, the novel has a genuinely tragic dimension, but the tragedy is tempered somewhat by larger patterns of existential movement.[52]

Chinese and Western scholars alike have identified *Hung-lou meng* as a microcosm of traditional Chinese culture. In both its elaborate structure and its exquisite detail, the novel evokes a mood of completeness and authenticity. Furthermore, in a very real sense it represents the culmination of China's entire premodern literary tradition. The novel includes every major type of Chinese literature—including philosophy, history, poetry, and fiction. We find in it quotations from Confucius and Chuang-tzu, T'ang poets and Yüan dramatists. Throughout the Ch'ing period and up to the present, *Hung-lou meng* has inspired countless plays, poems, games, and sequels, as well as a huge body of critical scholarship.

But while the novel is a supremely accomplished example of traditional Chinese fiction, the author reveals conventional literati prejudices throughout the work. In chapter 42, for example, Pao-ch'ai lectures Tai-yü on the purpose of literature:

> A boy's proper business is to read books in order to gain an understanding of things, so that when he grows up he can play his part in governing the country. . . . As for girls like you and me, . . . since we *can* read, let us confine ourselves to good, improving books; let us avoid like the plague those pernicious works of fiction, which so undermine the character that in the end it is past reclaiming.[53]

Undoubtedly Ts'ao Hsüeh-ch'in is writing a bit with tongue in cheek, but it is clear that the author's greatest delight lies in displaying his erudition through philosophical discussions, word games, riddles, and especially classical verse. Although his characters quote freely from popular works such as the famous thirteenth-century play *Hsi-hsiang chi* (Romance of the Western Chamber), they spend countless hours composing poetry and discussing it. In fact, *Hung-lou meng* provides the reader with a first-rate education in the refinements of poetic composition and appreciation.

The cultural breadth of the novel is perhaps most evident in its vivid portrayal of Chinese society. In both its psychological realism and encyclopedic scope, it is unparalleled in the history of traditional Chinese literature. As Fang Chao-ying has indicated, *Hung-lou meng* sheds light on virtually every aspect of Chinese life and covers a vast social spectrum. It highlights the importance of popular religion and family ritual, the values of filial piety and respect for age and authority, and the tensions and conflicts of role fulfillment at various levels of society. In addition, it provides a wealth of detail on Chinese aesthetics, housing, clothing, food, amusements, festivals, sexual life, and popular customs. Perhaps most important, it illustrates the gap between social theory and social practice so often neglected or downplayed in official documents and other orthodox sources.[54] With this point in mind, we may now turn our attention to Chinese daily life.

CHAPTER 10

Social Activities

It is well known that social customs in China varied considerably from region to region, time to time, and class to class. They also differed among the Chinese, the Manchus, and other minority peoples. Yet despite this diversity, there was a large measure of uniformity woven into the fabric of traditional Chinese culture. Some of the reasons for this have already been discussed: the nature of the Chinese political and social order, the unifying role of the written language, China's extraordinary philosophical and religious eclecticism, and the shared symbols and values expressed in Chinese religious ceremonies, art, and literature. This chapter examines several other major aspects of Chinese life that reflected shared principles or practices and further contributed to the cohesiveness and continuity of traditional Chinese civilization.

LIFE-CYCLE RITUAL

As a general rule, the higher the social class in China, the more rigid the adherence to ritual as a matter of both Confucian responsibility and public prestige. But one striking and significant feature of ritual life in traditional China was the effort on the part of all classes of society to put on the most impressive ceremonial displays possible, even at great cost and financial hardship. One mid nineteenth century account of rural life in South China tells us:

> Poverty and death are haunting spectres of the poor. They roam through the village and inspire fear that is not physical but social. It is not that the villager fears death; his belief in Fate relieves him of that worry. But to think of his parent drawing near to the time of departure without funds for proper rites and burial—this is a real fear. To fail in the provision of rites, feasts, coffin and funeral would be conduct most unfilial and condemned by social opinion.[1]

FIGURE 10.1. A Fortune-teller. This studio pose from the late Ch'ing period shows a fortune-teller who specializes in divination from the study of facial features (*k'an-hsiang*). Photo courtesy China Trade Museum, Milton, Mass.

Other works, both Western and Chinese, confirm this view. John L. Buck indicates that as late as 1930, nearly 80 percent of rural credit in some areas of China was used for noneconomic purposes—primarily birth, marriage, funeral, and other ceremonies. Undoubtedly the costs were at least as great in Ch'ing times, when, according to early Republican-era ceremonial handbooks, ritual requirements were even more rigid and elaborate.[2]

Not surprisingly, Chinese domestic ritual both mirrored and reinforced the patrilocal, hierarchical, and authoritarian structure of the Confucian family system. It also reflected many fundamental religious beliefs and cosmological assumptions—among these, the idea that fate could be known and to some extent manipulated. Divination loomed large in household ritual of all sorts, as it did in much of the rest of Chinese ceremonial activity. Families asked ancestors for guidance, scholars often consulted the *I-ching* for advice, and commoners eagerly sought the professional counsel of fortune-tellers and other specialists, including geomancers, on occasions of both joy and sorrow. But by far the most popular guide to the present and future in traditional China for all classes was the Imperial Almanac (*Huang-shu*, *li-pen*, *li-shu*, etc.).[3]

According to statute, publication of the almanac was the exclusive prerogative of the Ch'ing government, which sought to monopolize astrological authority in much the same way that it attempted to dominate other spheres of religious and secular life in China. Here, too, it failed, however, since many privately issued almanacs (and other books on divination) circulated widely. By virtue of its distribution and practical application, the almanac was probably the most frequently used book of any kind in traditional times. Virtually all sectors of society employed it in some way, whether for protection against evil spirits, for moral guidance, or for advice on propitious times to undertake various domestic ritual activities such as sacrifices, prayers, marriages, and funerals. The almanac even offered information on the best times to undertake such mundane activities as bathing, sewing, sweeping, meeting friends, taking medicine, embarking on journeys, doing business, and entering school.[4]

As indicated briefly in Chapter 7, the almanac was based on a system of interrelated variables derived from the *I-ching*, *yin-yang/wu-hsing* correlations, the twenty-four directions of the compass, the twenty-eight asterisms, and so forth. Individuals fit into this cosmic scheme according to their date of birth, which was always carefully recorded in the form of eight characters (*pa-tzu*), two each for the year, month, day, and hour. In the popular mind—and among many members of the elite as well—birth in a certain year identified the individual with one of twelve symbolic animals associated with the system of "earthly stems." Each of these animals, in turn, was linked with certain character traits, the qualities of *yin* or *yang*, one of the five elements, and certain stars or constellations. Quite naturally, such factors had to be taken into account by both fortune-tellers and matchmakers.[5]

The ceremonies connected with birth in traditional China varied tremendously, but a few common denominators may be identified. Because infant mortality was so high and life so precarious, measures were usually taken to protect newborn children through the use of charms, prayers, and offerings. Many Chinese believed that boy babies were the special prey of evil spirits, but that these evil spirits might be dissuaded if the child had an unattractive "milk name" (*nai-ming*). Sometimes the strategy was to give the boy a girl's name. In general, milk names were bestowed at feasts known as "full-month" (*man-yüeh*) ceremonies, which marked the first month of life and underscored the uncertainty surrounding the child's early existence.[6]

Life was especially precarious for newborn girls, since the practice of infanticide involved them primarily. A number of astute Western observers in the late Ch'ing period considered infanticide to be no more common in China than in Europe, but other nineteenth-century accounts—both Western and Chinese—indicate that the outlawed practice was often quite widespread, especially in times of economic hardship. Listen to Yu Chih, gentry organizer of an infant-protection society in his home village near Wu-hsi, Kiangsu, during the mid-nineteenth century:

When poor families have too many children, they are often forced by practical considerations to drown the newborn infants, a practice which has already become so widespread that no one thinks it unusual. . . . Not only are female infants drowned, at times even males are; not only do the poor drown their children; even the well-to-do do it. People follow each other's example, and the custom becomes more widespread day by day. There is a case where one family drowned more than ten girls in a row; there are villages where scores of girls are drowned each year. We who dwell in the country witness the crime with our own eyes—a scene too brutal to be described.[7]

Girls were considered a poor social investment in traditional China, since after years of nurture the majority of them would simply marry to become members of other households. Hard-pressed families might sell their female children into slavery or prostitution, but infants brought a low price, and many believed that it was better to destroy the child than to doom it to a life of poverty and shame. Hence such common euphemisms for infanticide as "giving [the child] away to be married" and "transmigrating [the soul of the child] to the body of someone else." Futhermore, the demands of Confucian filial piety were such that the death of a baby girl might be morally justifiable if the choice for the future was between providing for one's parents and providing for one's children. A famous story in Chinese popular lore explicitly condoned and rewarded the attempt to sacrifice a child for the sake of one's parents.[8]

Filial piety had other dimensions and ramifications. While a girl child was essentially irrelevant to the question of patrilinear kinship, a boy was considered crucial for the continuation of the family line and the maintenance of ancestral sacrifices. Mencius had male children in mind when he remarked, "Of the three most unfilial things, the worst is to have no posterity." In the absence of heirs, matrilocal (uxorilocal) marriage was an option, though not a very attractive one (see below). The other possibility was adoption.

Of the various forms of adoption, the most regular and esteemed was kin-related. According to the Ch'ing code, an adopted heir to the family ancestral sacrifices had to have the same surname as the head of the household, and specific stipulations existed regarding preferential succession from various classes of nephews and grandnephews on the paternal side. In practice, however, individuals often purchased and adopted individuals outside their lineage, changing their surnames and acquiring heirs with comparatively few complications. This was particularly common in South China. The ceremony of adoption usually entailed a contract, a feast, and ancestral sacrifices in which the adopted son took part. Such ceremonies stood somewhere in significance between the rituals of birth and those of marriage.[9]

The stages of growth in traditional China were viewed in a variety of ways. As noted in Chapter 6, Confucius placed special stress on the ages fifteen, thirty, forty, fifty, sixty, and seventy. The "Family Regulations" (*nei-tse*) chapter of the *Li-chi* discusses child-rearing practices for young males, emphasizing the ages six, ten, and thirteen and then the adult years of twenty, thirty, forty, fifty, and seventy. Predictably, females are treated in a much more cursory way, with emphasis placed on the ages ten, fifteen, and twenty. The subcategory on human affairs in the *T'u-shu chi-ch'eng* includes separate sections for every year of life from birth to age twenty and for each decade thereafter from the twenties, thirties, forties, and so on up to "one hundred and above." But the most common periodization in traditional times consisted of six major stages: (1) infancy (*ying-erh shih-ch'i*), (2) the juvenile period (*shao-nien shih-ch'i*), (3) young adulthood (*ch'ing-nien shih-ch'i*), (4) adulthood (*chuang-nien shih-ch'i*), (5) middle age (*chung-nien shih-ch'i*), and (6) old age (*lao-nien shih-ch'i*).[10]

Infancy generally lasted from birth to about three or four years old (four or five *sui* in Chinese reckoning), depending on the presence or absence of siblings and/or nursemaids. The first two years of life were a time of great indulgence; babies were fed whenever hungry, day or night, played with by the entire family, especially grandparents, and only gradually toilet trained and weaned. Elementary discipline began at about age three or four with an effort to teach respect and obedience and an emphasis on status distinctions and filial piety. Didactic stories, such as the *Erh-shih-ssu hsiao* (Twenty-four Examples of Filial Piety), inculcated the proper attitudes in children, who also began to learn appropriate sex roles.[11]

Discipline began in earnest during the juvenile period, which lasted from three or four to about fifteen or sixteen. In elite households, the crippling practice of binding young girls' feet often commenced about age five, a symptom and a cause of ever more rigid sexual segregation. Such segregation was never complete, as *Hung-lou meng* illustrates graphically, but the cultural ideal in China remained the isolation of women in the inner apartments as much as possible (see Figure 10.3).[12] There are stories of Buddhist-oriented elite women in the Ch'ing who expressed the wish that in their next existence they would be reborn as dogs so that they would have greater freedom. Young men, for their part, suffered from the tyranny of their fathers, who became increasingly severe and aloof as they trained their sons in family ritual roles and proper social conduct.

Guidance in matters of family concern could be found not only in classics such as the *Li-chi* and ritual handbooks but also in "family instructions." Unlike "clan rules" or genealogies, family instructions were usually informal and personal, typically written by a member of the family and exhibiting a blend of both idealism and realism. There were also family instructions aimed at larger audiences. One such work, of particularly broad appeal in Ch'ing times, was known as the *Chih-chia ke-yen* (Precepts for Governing the Family) and was attributed to Chu Po-lu (1617–1689). Although expressed in simple

FIGURE 10.2. Women with Bound Feet. These two young Chinese women, on either side of the little boy, provide a graphic illustration of the deformation of the foot as a result of footbinding. Footbinding was, of course, the luxury of those who did not require the physical labor of such women. Photo courtesy China Trade Museum, Milton, Mass.

language, it promoted the values that all Chinese parents were expected to display in themselves and to cultivate in their children. In addition to homilies regarding neatness, cleanliness, simplicity, proper demeanor, frugality, and mildness, the *Chih-chia ke-yen* emphasized the importance of filial piety, reverence for ancestors, kindness and compassion to friends and neighbors, study of the Classics, emulation of the sages, fulfillment of duty (*shou-fen*), and obedience to Heaven (*t'ing-T'ien*). Significantly, for all its stress on family virtues, it also pointedly admonished officials to consider the interests of the ruler and the state above those of the self and one's family.[13]

Parental power was nearly absolute in traditional China, as the brutal beating of Pao-yü by his father in *Hung-lou meng* makes evident. According to law a son or grandson who assaulted or reviled a parent or grandparent could be killed with impunity, since such acts of unfilial behavior were considered capital crimes. At an early age, Chinese children learned absolute submission to parents, grandparents, teachers, masters of trades, and other

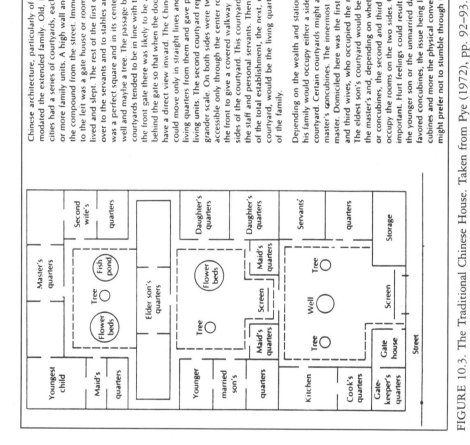

Chinese architecture, particularly of upper-class homes, accommodated the extended family. Old, large houses in Chinese cities had a series of courtyards, each of which could house one or more family units. A high wall and a large gate separated the compound from the street. Immediately inside and usually to the left was a gate house or room or two where the gate-keeper lived and slept. The rest of the first courtyard was usually given over to the servants and to stables and storerooms. The courtyard was a perfect square and in its center there was likely to be a well and maybe a tree. The passage between the first and second courtyards tended to be in line with the front gate. Just within the front gate there was likely to be a large screen or wall directly behind the gate so that when the doors were opened one did not have a direct view inward. The Chinese believed that evil spirits could move only in straight lines and thus the screen protected the living quarters from them and gave privacy and a break between living units. The second courtyard repeated the first, but on a grander scale. On both sides were two or three rooms, usually accessible only through the center room. The roof extended over the front to give a covered walkway or narrow veranda on three sides of the courtyard. This courtyard might serve as quarters for the staff and personal servants. Then depending upon the size of the total establishment, the next, or in some cases the fourth, courtyard, would be the living quarters for the junior members of the family.

Depending on the wealth and station of the family, each son and his family would occupy either a side of a courtyard or a total courtyard. Certain courtyards might also be the quarters for the master's concubines. The innermost courtyard belonged to the master. Domiciled here was the first wife and often the second and third wives, who occupied the rooms along the sides. The eldest son's courtyard would be immediately before the master's and, depending on whether he had a second wife or concubines, the second and third sons and their wives might occupy the rooms on the two sides. Questions of precedent were important. Hurt feelings could result from decisions about whether the younger son or the unmarried daughters should rank above favored concubines, the issue being less the status of the concubines and more the physical convenience of the master, who might prefer not to stumble through too many courtyards on a dark night.

FIGURE 10.3. The Traditional Chinese House. Taken from Pye (1972), pp. 92–93.

authority figures. This produced a strong "dependency orientation" in youths of both sexes, although in peasant households there was relatively greater equality between parents and children (and between males and females), because all members of the family lived in close quarters and worked together in the fields as a single cooperative economic unit.[14]

Lucian Pye, among others, has written perceptively on the psychocultural implications of China's highly authoritarian approach to child rearing. "The absolute imperative of filial piety has traditionally meant that sons could never manifest in any manner the hostilities they might naturally feel toward their fathers. This denial of man's potentially strongest feelings, when combined with socialization practices such as early teasing and then steeply heightened discipline, contributed to a tendency to divorce feelings from actions and to distrust one's own affect." The result, Pye argues, is that

the repression of aggression has been a central theme in Chinese culture, in contrast with Western civilization, whose central concern has been the repression of sexuality. The Chinese stress of etiquette, ritual, conformity; their anxieties over disorder, confusion, and collapse of hierarchy; their capacity to swing abruptly between the poles of disciplined order and explosive emotional outbursts; their sensitivity to affronts or criticism; and their need to vocalize their anxieties and tensions all suggest that the controlling of aggression is not only important but difficult. The Chinese preference for unambiguous situations and the comfort they find in well-defined hierarchical relationships are also reflections of concern over the destructive potential of human aggression.[15]

The stage of development known as young adulthood was by and large an elite phenomenon. It was a time of transition that occurred during the teenage years, before marriage. By the mid teens, the worst of parental discipline and educational rigor had passed. Chinese males began to experience considerable freedom and to have their first sexual contacts with prostitutes or servant girls. Their sisters, however, remained confined within the home and bound by a double standard of rigid chastity. In some families, the rituals of capping males and binding up the hair of females marked the formal transition to adulthood, but for the most part these ceremonies were associated in late imperial times with marriage, which normally took place from about sixteen to eighteen years of age in the case of boys and from fourteen to sixteen with girls.

The formal ceremonies of marriage brought adulthood regardless of age. Marriage was expected of every normal man and woman in Chinese society, including slaves. Indeed, the Ch'ing code stipulated that slave owners were subject to criminal punishment if they neglected to find husbands for their female slaves. The purpose of marriage was, of course, to continue the male line of descent. In the words of the *Li-chi*: "The rites of marriage [*hun-li*] unite two [different] surnames in love, in order to maintain services in the ancestral temple and to ensure the continuation of the family line." Marriage was thus an alliance between two different families, not a matter of individual choice and mutual affection. By law, two people of the same surname could not be married, even if unrelated, and the legal principals in the match were the heads of the respective households, not the individuals to be joined in wedlock. In some cases, the wishes of the prospective bride and groom might be taken into account, but very often the choice of a marriage partner by parents or other elders was arbitrary and unilateral. Pao-yü's arranged marriage to Pao-ch'ai rather than to Tai-yü in the novel *Hung-lou meng* is a tragic, but typical, example of family interests overriding personal feelings.[16]

Marriage was always a contractual affair in Ch'ing China—by far the most important contractual relationship in traditional times. Marriage contracts (*hun-shu*) might be oral or written, general or detailed, but all were surrounded by elaborate rituals that enhanced them, gave them public visibility, and symbolized their social and cosmological significance. Contracts were also associated with divorce and adoption procedures. As a rule, the smaller the economic or ritual investment in such contracts, the greater the likelihood that they would be breached.[17]

Several different forms of marriage existed in traditional China, each a product of different social or economic circumstances. The most prestigious was the standard, or major, marriage. It involved the transfer of an "adult" bride from her natal home and her ritual rebirth in the home of her husband. This form of marriage, to be discussed in some detail below, was considered the norm, the social standard. Minor marriages followed the basic ritual pattern of major marriages, except that the bride lived in the home of her prospective husband for ten or fifteen years as a "daughter-in-law reared from childhood" (*t'ung-yang hsi* or *miao-hsi*) before the actual marriage date. This arrangement was particularly common among the poor in China, but by no means limited to them. Another less common and less esteemed variety of marriage was matrilocal, involving the transfer of a male into the household of a female as a son-in-law, reversing the pattern of major and minor marriages. The males involved in such matches usually came from families with several sons and entered families where there were none. The period of residence in the bride's home was variable, from a few years to a lifetime, always carefully spelled out by contract.

The distribution of major, minor, and matrilocal marriages throughout China hinged on several factors: family status, wealth, social organization (especially lineage ties), and geography. Major marriages dominated the social landscape of North China, but in many southern areas the alternative forms predominated. Arthur Wolf and Huang Chieh-shan write:

Viewing China's marriage and adoption customs as from an earth satellite, we would probably see that minor marriages were concentrated in a continuous area along the South China coast, reaching their highest density in southern Kiangsi, southwestern Fukien, and northern Kwangtung. Uxorilocal [matrilocal] marriages would probably appear common in the same region but would achieve their highest density on the Lower Yangtze Delta and in a second area of concentration on China's Western frontier. But as soon as we moved closer to our subject, we would soon discover that this view from on high concealed a great deal of local variation, variation even more marked than that between the country's major regions.[18]

A distinctive feature of family life in traditional China was the institution of concubinage. Theoretically, this ancient practice was justified by the filial imperative of producing sons to continue the male line. Often concubines (*ch'ieh*) were purchased outright from poor families by the more well-to-do, and ordinarily they did not enjoy the same status as the principal wife (*ch'i*). As a matter of fact, upon entering her new family, a concubine usually had to participate in ceremonies designed to show her subservience to the wife. Ch'ing law prohibited the degradation of a principal wife to the position of concubine or the elevation of a concubine to the position of principal wife. As further testimony to her inferiority, a concubine was required to observe the same degree of mourning for her master's wife as she was for his parents, his sons (by the principal wife or other concubines), and her own sons. Her sons were expected to treat the principal wife as their own mother, and by custom they were entitled to equal rights of inheritance with the sons of the wife. Paternity was what mattered in Chinese marriages, and in divorce, the husband almost always received custody of the children.[19]

The practices of concubinage and infanticide, together with the strong social pressure on widows not to remarry as a matter of Confucian propriety, created a large pool of surplus men looking for wives—a situation that matrilocal marriage helped reduce only in part. This was one reason that a major marriage carried with it so much prestige and required so much public display. Although the specific customs surrounding major marriages often differed from place to place, certain practices were nearly universal.[20]

One feature of all Chinese marriages—major, minor, and matrilocal alike— was the employment of a go-between, or matchmaker (*mei-jen*). Intermediaries of this sort were essential to a great many aspects of Chinese social life, especially those involving delicate matters of public face (*lien-mien, mien-tzu*). The responsibilities of the matchmaker were extremely weighty. He or she had to take into account not only the relative social positions of the two families involved but also certain important economic and personal facts such as family wealth and individual character. Ideally, the match was expected to benefit both parties, which generally meant that the families had to be of approximately equal status and means or that one family might contribute greater status while the other contributed greater wealth.

After making discreet investigations and compiling preliminary information on all marriageable males and females in a given locality, the matchmaker was in a position to propose a match, usually to the male's family. He or she also negotiated matters such as the amount of the betrothal gifts (*p'in-li*) and betrothal money (*p'in-chin*) to be given by the groom's family to the wife's if the marriage deliberations went past the initial stages. The family of the bride, for its part, had to decide on the proper dowry and trousseau (*chia-chuang*) to send along at the time of transfer for exhibition at the groom's home. All these calculations were of tremendous importance to the prestige and material interests of each of the families concerned.

Another universal feature of major-marriage ritual, and often a feature of other marriage arrangements as well, was the use of divination and the frequent consultation of the ancestors. A Chinese marriage was literally "made in Heaven," and therefore the eight characters of the bride and groom had to be compatible. Ancestors were consulted at various points in the elaborate marriage process to assure their approval of the match, and diviners chose auspicious days for various ritual acts connected with the marriage.

These ceremonies, conventionally designated the *six rites* (*liu-li*), were full of elaborate symbolism—all either positive or protective. Red—the color of happiness and good fortune—was prominent in dress and decorations, including candles and lanterns, which were used even in the daytime. Firecrackers served as purifiers and signs of joy, and charms were often employed to provide additional protection for the bride. Food played an important role at various stages of the marriage ritual (and in most other aspects of Chinese ritual life), in the form of symbolic gifts, offerings, and ceremonial meals. "Longevity noodles," fruits, and other food items denoted marital harmony, happiness, and prosperity. Presents such as paired geese symbolized marital fidelity, and felicitous inscriptions of various sorts appeared everywhere.[21]

The first of the six rites was the selection of the match (*na-ts'ai*), engineered by the go-between after consultation with the families involved. In this and most other matters, the family of the groom normally took the initiative on advice from the matchmaker. The next step was the formal exchange of astrological information on the bride and groom (*wen-ming*). The third stage, called *na-chi*, required the ritual test of the match by means of divination. Fortune-tellers were usually employed, but often the ancestors and other spirits were also consulted. The fourth and crucial step was the betrothal (*na-cheng*), for acceptance of the betrothal gifts (often termed the "bride price") by the family of the bride sealed the match. As with the previous stage, elaborate ceremonies accompanied the transfer of gifts, which were dictated by rank at the higher levels of society. Again, ancestral sacrifices usually accompanied these ceremonies. The fifth stage, *ch'ing-chi*, involved the selection of propitious

FIGURE 10.4. Ritual Displays—a Late Ch'ing Wedding Procession. Photo courtesy China Trade Museum, Milton, Mass.

times for the transfer of the bride and related ritual activities. Here, decisions might rest with fortune-tellers or other sources of supernatural authority, including temple oracles.[22]

The transfer, known as "welcoming the bride" (*ch'in-ying*), was the final stage of the formal process. On the day preceding this ceremony, the groom was usually capped and given an adult name (*tzu*), and the bride's hair was put up in ritual fashion. Meanwhile, the groom's family had arranged to send the brightly decorated wedding chair to the wife's home, and the wife's family had sent her trousseau to his. On the day of the transfer, the bride paid solemn obeisance to her parents and ancestors, received a brief lecture on her wifely duties, and entered the gaudy red sedan chair that would take her on a noisy, ostentatious, and circuitous journey to her husband's home. There, the bride performed various acts designed to show subservience to her husband and his family, and for the first time perhaps—at least in most elite matches—the bride and groom actually saw each other's faces. After these ceremonies, the bridal pair reverently worshipped tablets representing Heaven and Earth, the ancestors of the groom, and the major household deities of the groom's family, especially the God of the Hearth. These activities highlighted the cosmological and familial dimensions of the match.

The transfer was, of course, marked by a banquet that, like the wedding procession and display of dowry and trousseau, might well be a measure of family financial status. Often, however, the guests contributed shares (*fen-tzu*) to help defray costs. Local custom dictated whether or not the bride's family would be invited to the transfer feast, but at some point in almost all major marriages, the bride's family was treated to a banquet and given additional gifts.[23]

FIGURE 10.5. A Chinese Official and His Footbound Wife. Note the characteristic makeup and outfit of the wife, as well as the man's official gown with its "mandarin square" and other trappings of rank, such as beads and hat button. Source: Clark Worswick and Jonathon Spence, *Imperial China: Photographs 1850–1912*, p. 29.

When the bride visited her parents after the formal transfer, she did so as a guest (*k'o*), not as kin. Although still emotionally tied to her parents and relatives, she was now by law and custom a full-fledged member of her husband's family and bound to devote far more ritual attention to that family than to her natal family. It was a difficult existence, especially at first. Except in the case of minor or matrilocal marriages, the new bride found herself in a house full of virtual strangers. In this environment, the mother-in-law wielded tremendous power over her daughter-in-law—particularly since a filial son was bound to respect his mother's wishes. Mothers were sometimes known to force sons to divorce their wives. Small wonder then, that in the period preceding the marriage transfer, brides often wept and sang sad songs together with their friends and family.[24]

There were seven grounds for divorce in traditional China: (1) lack of offspring, (2) adultery, (3) jealousy, (4) thievery, (5) disobedience to the husband's parents, (6) incurable disease, and (7) being too talkative. In principle, a husband could not be divorced by his wife, but this was not the main reason that divorce was comparatively rare in Ch'ing times. In the first place, there were three circumstances under which a woman could not be divorced (except in the case of adultery): (1) if she had mourned as a daughter for her husband's deceased parents, (2) if she had no family to go to, or (3) if her husband had been poor when they were married and was now rich. Often one or more of these conditions prevailed. In addition, the perennial glut of men looking for wives made the task of acquiring another virgin bride rather difficult, especially if the grounds for an earlier divorce were not very substantial. Further, to at least a degree the interests of the wife were protected by her biological parents and former kinsmen, since marriage was a family affair. Nonetheless, we know that many women found married life intolerable and either ran away or committed suicide.[25]

Aside from the self-perpetuating tyranny of the mother-in-law, another common frustration for Chinese wives, at least in elite families, was the introduction of concubines. Unlike principal spouses, concubines were usually chosen by the husband rather than his parents, and often they were selected for their beauty rather than their moral character or family connections. Although ostensibly brought into the household for the purpose of producing sons to assure continuation of the line, concubines often served as little more than symbols of elite conspicuous consumption. Although inferior in social position to the principal wife, they were often the primary object of the husband's sexual attention and thus a potential source of jealousy.[26]

We should not assume, however, that arranged marriages were devoid of romance. There is abundant evidence to indicate that in the Ch'ing, as in earlier periods of Chinese history, love often grew out of arranged marriages. It is true that female chastity (*chieh*) and devotion to one's husband after his death were highly esteemed and ritually rewarded by both society and the state, but this alone does not explain the regular refusal of widowed brides to remarry or their frequent suicide. Far less does it explain the suicide of husbands upon the death of their wives.[27]

Chinese sexual life is seldom discussed but certainly important to an understanding of traditional Chinese culture. Although little scholarly work on the subject has been done for the Ch'ing period, the pioneering studies of R. H. van Gulik demonstrate that the Chinese have long had a remarkably healthy attitude toward sex. Despite the rigid puritanical standards of neo-Confucian social behavior, which went so far as to condemn a husband and wife for accidentally touching hands in public, we know that in the main Chinese sexual life was full, rich, and remarkably egalitarian.[28]

The Chinese made a sharp distinction between inner (*nei*) and outer (*wai*), between what was public and what was private. In public, men were unquestionably superior to their wives, who were expected to be passive, submissive, and satisfied with few rights and privileges. In the privacy of the bedchamber, however, women enjoyed relative equality. Sex handbooks, in circulation since the Han dynasty, provided specific guidance for husbands and wives on all aspects of sexual activity and invariably encouraged the sexual satisfaction of both parties. Always graphic and often illustrated, these handbooks were used for both erotic stimulation and practical advice, as a reading of *Jou p'u-t'uan* clearly indicates. From an orthodox Confucian standpoint, the primary purpose of sexual intercourse may have been procreation, but in practice, sensual pleasure and mutual benefit were often the explicit goals.[29]

As is well known, the bound foot was an object of great erotic appeal in traditional China. Footbinding began in the T'ang-Sung period, an outgrowth of the practice of wrapping the feet of dancers with colorful ribbons. During the Yüan dynasty it gradually spread from North China to the south, where it took hold primarily among the upper classes, who could afford the luxury of unproductive female family members. In Ch'ing times, the practice was widespread among the Chinese elite, and even the Manchus succumbed in a sense to the fashion by wearing small attachments on the bottoms of their shoes to give the appearance of bound feet. Although footbinding was a painful process, its appeal was neither sadistic nor masochistic. Rather, it was justified as a means of keeping women at home and was admired by men for the style of walking it produced and the supposed effect this style of walking had on female sexual performance. Many passages in Chinese erotic literature dwell on the shape and mystery of the bound foot.[30]

Beyond the psychology of sexual attraction was the idea of sex as a form of physical therapy. This notion can be traced back for centuries in China. The principles were essentially the same as those of Taoist alchemy and traditional Chinese medicine. Harmony between *yin* (female) and *yang* (male) influences brought physical well-being and longevity. Women were believed to have an unlimited supply of *yin* essence, but the *yang* essence of men was considered limited. Normally, the two essences nourished each other—except in the case of intercourse with older women, which was thought to take away *yang* essence without benefit to the male. Undoubtedly this was one reason for the traditional preference among Chinese men for youthful wives and concubines. The *Li-chi* stipulates, however, that men should have regular intercourse with their wives, even after the latter had reached an advanced age. Homosexuality was frowned upon in traditional China but widely tolerated—perhaps in part because of sexual segregation and the presumption that the exchange of the same essence entailed no net loss.[31]

The Chinese obsession with good health and longevity can be seen not only in sexual practices and related therapeutic techniques but also in popular proverbs, religion, ritual symbolism, art, and literature.[32] Doctors were generally held in low esteem during Ch'ing times, but the period still boasted a number of famous and able practitioners, including individuals such as Yeh Kuei (1666–1745) and Hsü Ta-ch'un (1693–1771). An extraordinary amount of attention is given to the section on medicine (*i-pu*) in the *T'u-shu chi-ch'eng*—520 *chüan*—more than any other single section in the encyclopedia.[33] Yet

FIGURE 10.6. A Manchu Woman. The style of dress and lack of bound feet indicate that this woman of the late Ch'ing period is a member of the Manchu elite. Photo courtesy China Trade Museum, Milton, Mass.

for all this concern with health and medicine, life expectancy was probably not over thirty-five or forty, even in the best of times. For this reason among others, the last two stages of life—middle age and old age—were times of special significance and cause for great celebration.

For most members of the Chinese elite, middle age, lasting from about forty to fifty-five, brought many satisfactions: career success, material security, and grandchildren. By the end of this period, the majority of wives had escaped domination by their mothers-in-law, only to become domineering mothers-in-law themselves. Middle age for the lower classes of Chinese society may have been somewhat less satisfying than for the elite, but a bit of property and a male heir probably provided a sufficient sense of accomplishment and security for aging commoners.[34]

Old age elicited respect and esteem from all sectors of Chinese society. Village elders in rural areas often wielded substantial power, and, as mentioned in Chapter 4, some were officially recognized as longevous commoners or longevous officials. The state-sponsored community drinking ritual known as *hsiang-yin chiu*, although not always regularly or properly performed, also provided a means of officially acknowledging and rewarding old age. According to statute, the ritual was supposed to be performed twice a year in various districts and departments of each province. The master of ceremonies opened the meeting of elderly guests with the expressed hope that as a result of the ritual, "seniors and juniors will maintain proper order among themselves, and elder brothers will be friendly while younger ones [will be] deferential." After the hosts and guests had emptied their first glass of wine, a local scholar would state: "The object of *hsiang-yin chiu* is to show proper respect for the aged and consideration for the virtuous, and to keep away the unrighteous and the perverse. Persons of advanced age and outstanding virtue are to occupy seats of honor, and others are to have places proper to their ages." Although this ceremony did not always appeal to the local scholarly elite, it was certainly tempting to "obscure townsmen and villagers who aspired to local eminence."[35]

At home, the elderly were pampered and accorded maximum deference. As *Hung-lou meng* indicates, older women often enjoyed substantial power within the family, despite the pervasive notion of the "three types of womanly dependence" (*san-ts'ung*)—on father, husband, and son. Major birthday celebrations for men and women usually began about age fifty or so. From this point onward, such celebrations increased in size and significance, especially upon the beginning of each new decade. Naturally enough, the concrete symbolism of birthday ceremonies centered on longevity: longevity candles, the longevity star, longevity noodles, longevity peaches or peach cakes, and the stylized character *shou* (longevity). Ancestral sacrifices were often closely associated with birthday celebrations.[36]

Longevity was also a prominent theme in funeral ceremonies. Grave clothes were designated longevity clothes, the coffin was composed of longevity boards, and the principal mourner ate longevity noodles. A "longevity portrait" of the deceased might also be displayed near the coffin, serving as an object of worship. Like the use of the auspicious color red in funerals for all that was not white (the color of mourning), the self-conscious employment of the term longevity in the midst of death underscores the themes of "fear-propitiation

FIGURE 10.7. Ritual Displays—a Late Ch'ing Funeral Procession. Photo courtesy China Trade Museum, Milton, Mass.

and hope-supplication" that ran through so much of traditional Chinese religious life.[37]

AMUSEMENTS

Human affairs in China were not always full of fear and uncertainty. There was plenty of time for recreation, ranging from simple domestic games to huge community festivals. And despite the endless variety of Chinese amusements, certain patterns of "play" seem typical of China as a whole. Many of these reflect elite values and preoccupations. The general lack of physically demanding sports in traditional China, for instance, can be attributed both to a concern for maintaining proper decorum and to a real fear of harming the body—an unfilial act, since the physical self was a gift of the ancestors.[38]

On the other hand, the attractiveness of active public exhibitions of acrobatics and marital arts, like the tradition of knight-errant literature, may be explained as a form of vicarious release in what was a predominantly civil-oriented, nonmilitary culture (*wu-ping ti wen-hua*). Perhaps the Chinese preference for individual competition over team games also reflects a form of recreational escape from the constraints of conventional society, since so much of Chinese social life demanded subordination of the self to the larger group and placed no real premium on individualism. The popularity of raucous festivals and risque dramatic performances, as well as the widespread practice of teasing the bride and groom after the wedding transfer (*nao hsin-fang*), suggests the periodic need to break loose, even if only temporarily, from the rigid constraints of Confucian propriety and social control.[39]

Aside from a general reluctance to engage in roughhouse and team play, there is little remarkable about most traditional Chinese games. Chinese youths ran; skipped; threw rocks; pitched coins; played with balls, shuttlecocks, tops, toys, and dolls; kept pets; and so forth. Older children and adults enjoyed watching bird and cricket fights. Gambling of all kinds was popular, although outlawed. More refined pastimes, all nature oriented, included the enjoyment of gardens, leisurely strolls (often with a caged bird), boating, swinging, and flying kites. Also popular, especially among the elderly, was the graceful and therapeutic exercise known as *t'ai-chi ch'üan*. Recreational activities for women were restricted somewhat by social isolation and, at least in elite families, by the practice of footbinding, but we know that in at least some gentry households the women received an education in poetry and the arts, which served them in good stead. In these households, as *Hung-lou meng* indicates, much leisure time was spent on refinements such as the so-called four noble recreations— calligraphy, painting, playing the *ch'in*, and playing *wei-ch'i*.[40]

Since painting and calligraphy have been discussed at length in Chapter 8, only the latter two recreations need be mentioned here. The *ch'in* (often translated "lute" or "zither") had a long and distinguished pedigree in China. For over two thousand years it stood as the most revered Chinese musical instrument, celebrated in verse and inextricably linked with both friendship and moral cultivation. The term *ch'in* came to be associated etymologically with the similar-sounding word *chin* (to prohibit), because the instrument was believed to check evil passions; it also served as a general metaphor for marital happiness and social harmony. The rounded top and flat bottom of the *ch'in* symbolized the unity of Heaven and Earth, and its melodies, which pleased the ear and soothed the mind, were often descriptive of nature. Originally composed of five strings and later seven, the *ch'in* paralleled in its development the musical evolution of tone scales in Chou times from five to seven (and eventually nine). Difficult to play and capable of many strikingly beautiful nuances, the *ch'in* illustrates the tremendous value attached to rhythm in classical Chinese music, the emphasis on melody rather than harmony, and the close connection between instrumental music and Chinese speech. The *ch'in* was, however, only one of many sophisticated musical instruments employed for ritual or recreational purposes in traditional China, from occasions such as public ceremonies and religious sacrifices to marriages, funerals, festivals, and simple parties. S. W. Williams observed in the nineteenth century that no people on earth made more use of music than the Chinese.[41]

Wei-ch'i, known as *go* in Japanese, was (and is) a popular game played on a board with nineteen vertical and nineteen horizontal lines intersecting to form 361 tactical positions. It remained a favorite pastime of Chinese generals, statesmen, and literati from early Han times through the Ch'ing. Each player had about 180 men or pieces. The object of the game was to control territory and capture, or "kill," enemy men. At first glance one might wonder why *wei-ch'i* was included as one of the four noble recreations of a Confucian gentleman. Painting, calligraphy, and music were, after all, aesthetically satisfying and morally uplifting, while *wei-ch'i* was war on a game board, attack and defense, killing and capture. In part, the appeal of *wei-ch'i* can be explained by the Confucian scholar's yearning for identification with ancient China's martial heritage and with the lost tradition of the feudal knight. But another explanation can be found in the structure and assumptions of the game itself. In the first place, like the Chinese scholar, the game of *wei-ch'i* valued both intellect and intuition. Second, in *wei-ch'i*, victory and defeat were relative, not absolute. "Victory" was based on the number of intersections dominated at the end of the game, but "defeat" was never total; a player could always save face. Furthermore, the style of play involved dispersed—yet related—nongeometric configurations rather than a single decisive tactical engagement. This emphasis on a total pattern of seemingly aimless interrelationships has been described as an "efficient, almost aesthetic, balance of forces."[42] As a creative form of competition, *wei-ch'i* undoubtedly held much the same artistic attraction as a landscape painting, garden, poem, musical composition, or even a good novel.

Other board games were also popular in Ch'ing times. One of these, *hsiang-ch'i*, resembled Western chess in its basic structure. Reputedly invented by King Wu of the Chou, *hsiang-ch'i* had enduring appeal to scholars and commoners alike in China. The same was true of *sheng-kuan t'u* (lit., "advancing in officialdom"), a more recent, but no less popular, Chinese diversion. Leon Stover has perceptively contrasted *sheng-kuan t'u* with the famous Parker Brothers' game Monopoly, observing that the point of the latter is the control of property and services to gain wealth, while the object of the former is to acquire rank and prestige in order to achieve financial advantage. The game board approximates the opportunity structure of the Ch'ing bureaucratic hierarchy, with sixty-six squares for positions ranging from lowly student to grand councillor. The higher a player climbs on the official ladder (by throws of the dice), the more money he can collect from those below him. Just as Monopoly can be seen as a reflection of certain basic features of American capitalist society, so *sheng-kuan t'u* may be viewed as a reflection of traditional Chinese bureaucratic society.[43]

Social intercourse in Ch'ing China was almost invariably a status game, played out at all levels of society. In elite circles, extraordinary attention was paid to matters of dress, salutation, demeanor, conversation, written communications (including invitations and responses), the giving of gifts, seating arrangements, food, and so forth (see Figure 10.8). The vocabulary of social

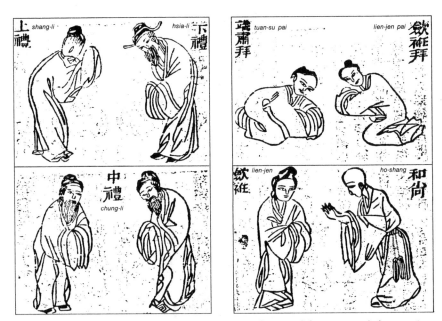

FIGURE 10.8. Gestures of Respect. Various forms of bowing and kowtowing indicating relative rank, as well as rituals appropriate to certain social groups, such as women (e.g., *lien-jen*; *top right*, *lien* is miswritten as *han*) and Buddhist monks (*ho-shang*). These gestures represent only a fraction of the ritual forms appropriate to different situations and social classes. Source: *CLTSCC, chüan* 1.

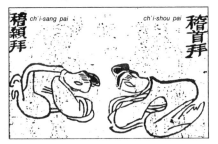

relations, like that of kinship and family protocol, was extraordinarily complex, with social distinctions that would not even occur to most non-Chinese. On formal occasions, the guest of honor always sat on the left (*yang*) side of the host, and his actions dictated the responses of the other guests. At the lower levels of society, and in relatively informal circumstances, less explicit attention was paid to status distinctions, but the distinctions were seldom forgotten. An astute mid-nineteenth century Western observer remarked, for example, "When a number of individuals are walking together, you may generally infer their age or rank or position by the order in which they naturally and almost unconsciously range themselves."[44]

Many other long-time Western residents in late Ch'ing China have commented on the extraordinary attention given to etiquette in all facets of Chinese social intercourse. R. F. Johnston's observations are worth quoting at length:

> [Chinese] rules of ceremony may seem, from the foreigner's point of view, too stiff and artificial, or exasperating in their pedantic minuteness. The European is inclined to laugh at social laws which indicate with preciseness when and how a mourner should wail at a funeral, what expressions a man must use when paying visits of condolence or congratulation, what clothes must be worn on different occasions, how a visitor must be greeted, how farewells are to be said, how modes of salutation are to be differentiated, and how chairs are to be sat on. [. . . These] rules of Chinese etiquette may be stiff, but there is no stiffness about the Chinese gentleman—or about the illiterate Chinese peasant—when he is acting in accordance with these rules.[45]

Chinese social ritual may often have been restrictive, but to most Ch'ing subjects it was also probably reassuring.

Food had enormous social importance in traditional China. Although in all societies food is used to create and maintain interpersonal bonds, the Chinese employed it in a particularly sophisticated way as "a marker and communicator in social transactions." The bigoted, but otherwise observant, missionary Arthur Smith wrote just before the turn of the century, "If there is anything which the Chinese have reduced to an exact science, it is the business of eating." Elaborate meals were required of all major social occasions, just as sacrificial dishes were essential to the proper performance of all major forms of religious ritual.[46]

The social significance of food in China can be measured in a variety of ways. As is often noted, a common greeting in traditional China was "Have you eaten?" Food was always a fit topic for genteel conversation, as well as the subject of personal correspondence, poetry, and classical prose. A number of famous Ch'ing scholars wrote essays on food, and much information on it can be gleaned from local gazetteers, government documents, and encyclopedias such as the *T'u-shu chi-ch'eng*. Vernacular literature abounds with descriptions of food, and writers such as Li Yü, Wu Ching-tzu, and Ts'ao Hsüeh-ch'in are acknowledged masters in the use of food to describe characters, develop or define social situations, and even link subplots within their works. *Hung-lou meng* is especially noteworthy for its elaborate descriptions of food and feasts.[47]

Food was always a good index of status in Chinese society, for both gods and men. Ch'ing statutes specified in extraordinary detail the type, amount, and style of food for official sacrifices, just as local custom dictated the requirements for popular offerings to gods, ghosts, and ancestors. Similarly, in the human world, official regulations and popular practice indicated the proper kinds and amounts of dishes appropriate to persons of different rank and station, from the emperor down to commoners. Many Ch'ing emperors had quite simple tastes, but, as Jonathon Spence reminds us, "the personal tastes of the emperor had little to do with the scale of culinary operations or their costs. The regulations were firm about the exact content of all major meals, which were carefully graded in accordance with their level of ritual significance."[48]

On formal occasions at the lower levels of elite society, the type and number of dishes were always pegged to the status of the participants and the importance of the meal. Clan rules sometimes specified the number of dishes to be offered by lineage members to guests, but most commoners could not indulge in formal and elaborate meals except on special ritual occasions such as births, marriages, and funerals. *Hung-lou meng* provides several indications of the gap between the eating habits of commoners and those of the elite. In discussing the price of certain dishes for a relatively small gentry party, Grannie Liu, an old countrywoman, exclaims, "It couldn't have cost less than twenty taels in all. Bless us and save us! That'd keep a farmer and his family for a year." And so it might have in the early or mid eighteenth century. Naturally enough, most peasant fare was simple and monotonous, but it was still prepared with special care. In the words of a Scottish sojourner to China in the 1850s, "the poorest classes in China seem to understand the art of preparing their food much better than the same classes at home."[49]

Despite the sharp difference between rich and poor in eating habits and the existence of a plethora of regional cooking styles, Chinese attitudes toward food were remarkably similar. The most fundamental distinction was between grains and other starches (*fan*) and vegetable or meat dishes (*ts'ai*). A proper balance between the two was deemed necessary to a good meal—although fragrance, flavor, color, and texture also had to be harmoniously blended. *Fan* was primary; *ts'ai* secondary. This concern with balance had a classical foundation. The *Li-chi* states: "In feasting and at the vernal sacrifice in the ancestral temple they had music; but in feeding the aged and at the autumnal sacrifice they had no music: these were based on the *yin* and *yang*. All drinking serves to nourish the *yang*; all eating to nourish the *yin*. . . . The number of *ting* and *tsu* [vessels] was odd [*yang*], and that of [the vessels] *pien* and *tou* was even [*yin*]."[50]

Foods and cooking styles were usually designated *yin* or *yang*, cold or hot, "civil" or "military." Given the holistic approach of the Chinese to good health, we should not be surprised to find that eating certain foods affected the balance of *yin* and *yang* in the body. A sore on the skin or an inexplicable fever, for example, might be blamed on overeating "hot" foods (oily, fried, or peppery items, fatty meat, and oily plants), while "cold" foods (water plants, crustaceans, and certain beans) could be blamed for producing or exacerbating a common cold. Complicating matters was the classification of Chinese food according to the five flavors—sweet, sour, bitter, pungent, and salty—that were, in turn, correlated with the five viscera, the five elements, the five seasons, and so forth. As with other aspects of traditional Chinese medicine, the variables were nearly infinite. Small wonder that in time of illness two, three, or as many as a half-dozen doctors might be engaged at once.[51]

Tea had both medicinal and gastronomical appeal. During the Ch'ing dynasty it was no longer associated with the elaborate social ritual of the T'ang period, but teahouses were very popular centers of recreation for males, and a number of individuals considered themselves connoisseurs of the national beverage. Most of the best teas were grown in South China, and although certain types were believed to be especially valuable in digesting some types of foods and ameliorating certain kinds of physical distress, the principal medical benefit of tea seems to have been the fact that it was made with boiling (and therefore sterile) water.[52]

Some alcoholic beverages had explicitly medicinal purposes, but most were valued primarily as social lubricants, closely associated with the joys of good food, friendship, and the composition of verse. The Chinese did not distinguish between true wines and starch-based spirits—both were designated *chiu*. As with tea, there were many different varieties of *chiu*, most of which were identified with locations in South China. The amount of alcohol might vary from as little as 10 percent (twenty proof) to as much as 80 percent (160 proof) in these beverages, and although moderation was encouraged in drinking as well as eating, the Chinese periodically threw caution to the wind. Drinking games were extremely popular at parties, and many members of the elite belonged to drinking clubs. The poet Yu Huai (1616–1696) describes drinking marathons that went on in the brothel quarter of Nanking until "all the guests vomited and fell asleep on the ground"; but even in more refined circumstances there were numerous instances of heavy drinking by members of the elite. The lower classes of Chinese do not seem to have acquired a special fondness for liquor, but they did prove susceptible to the curse of opium in the late eighteenth and early nineteenth centuries.[53]

Parties in traditional China often involved entertainment other than eating and drinking, composing verse, or cavorting with prostitutes. Among the elite, exhibitions of singing and dancing were popular, as were dramatic performances. Plays proved particularly appealing to the women of elite households, as we can see from a reading of *Hung-lou meng*. Performances also might be staged for family and friends on festive occasions such as marriages, birthdays for the elderly, or examination successes. Apparently, the actors engaged by individual households did not always know what play they would be performing until a request was made by an honored guest. The troupe thus had to have a repertoire of several dozen plays, and some groups were known to have command of nearly a hundred.[54]

Plays were also staged in villages and towns. These performances might be sponsored by the whole community through subscription, by a segment of that community such as merchants, by a local temple, or by a private individual. In contrast to the more frequent dramatic performances of major cities, community plays were usually associated with periodic religious fairs or local festivals, which brought families and friends together for a few days of colorful and exciting entertainment, punctuated by noise and the smell of burning firecrackers and incense. Temples often sponsored plays, since they were one of the few places in traditional China that were well equipped to stage them. These performances were often held on the "birthday" of the temple's major deity and intended explicitly for the entertainment of that deity. Sacrifices usually attended the dramatic event. As Barbara Ward and others have emphasized, the cumulative impact of such plays played a powerful role in "the dissemination and standardization of [Chinese] culture, particularly in the sphere of ideas and values."[55]

In addition to local fairs and celebrations, there were a number of annual festivals celebrated throughout the entire country. These events, part of the festival calendar of the lunar year (*sui-shih chi*), performed the function of unifying Chinese culture by periodically reaffirming orthodox values and solidifying family and community ties countrywide. Almost every month a major festival occurred throughout the land, touching all classes of Chinese society directly and even cutting across ethnic lines. Many were occasions of official sacrifices, and most involved domestic ancestral sacrifices and visits to temples. Like local festivals, these national festivals were marked by feasts and firecrackers, dramatic performances and music, fun and games. Unfortunately, the brief descriptions below convey very little of the color and pageantry surrounding such occasions.[56]

The most important annual festival in traditional China was the month-long celebration of the New Year (*yüan-tan*). This observance began in the twelfth lunar month. On about the twentieth day, Ch'ing officials at every level commenced the ritual of "sealing the seals" (*feng-yin*) of their yamens, in effect closing down government for nearly four weeks. This action paralleled the shutdown of most commercial establishments during the same period. A week or so before the turn of the year, households throughout the country paid obeisance to the God of the Hearth, who, according to popular belief, ascended to Heaven to report on the family's activities during the past year to the Jade Emperor. This ceremony was taken seriously but often celebrated lightly, with sweet substances smeared on the mouth of the god's image to ensure a favorable report.

On New Year's eve, the family again sacrificed to the God of the Hearth, as well as to other household deities, Heaven and Earth, and, of course, the ancestors. These ceremonies paralleled aspects of marriage ritual in symbolic significance. A family feast reaffirmed kinship ties, and the ritual of paying respect to the heads of the household in order of precedence through bowing and kowtowing served as a vivid reminder of status relationships within the family. The next day—brought in with fireworks, incense, and bursts of color—entailed visits in proper dress to friends, neighbors, relations, and superiors; gift-giving; and general merriment. Auspicious "spring couplets," written by local calligraphers on red paper, adorned residences and other buildings, bringing blessings and prosperity to families and businesses for the coming year.

The first two weeks of the New Year were devoted to various amusements, celebrations, and religious sacrifices. Ancestors and domestic gods were usually worshipped again, as were deities such as the popular God of Wealth. Officials throughout the country welcomed spring (*ying-ch'un*) in elaborate public ceremonies designed to indicate, through the symbolism of color, what the agricultural prospects were for the coming year and to assure the best results under the circumstances.[57] The Lantern Festival (*teng-chieh*) on the fifteenth day of the first month marked the end of the New Year's celebration. It was a happy time, devoted largely to the display of colorful lanterns in homes and businesses and to the entertainment of women and children. About a week later, Ch'ing officials "opened their seals" (*k'ai-yin*) and resumed government business.

The next major festival, Ch'ing-ming (lit., Pure and Bright), took place in the third month, 106 days after the winter solstice. It was one of three important "ghost festivals" (*kuei-chieh*) in traditional China. Ch'ing-ming was a time of family reunion, celebration, and devoted ancestor worship—including the sweeping of graves and offerings of food for the dead. Large-scale lineage sacrifices might also take place at this time. The *Chinese Repository* of 1832 carries an absorbing account of one such sacrifice, involving more than two thousand clan members. The prayer offered at the tomb of the founding father illustrates the purposes of the ceremony:

> Revolving years have brought again the season of Spring. Cherishing sentiments of veneration, I look up and sweep your tomb. Prostrate, I pray that you

will come and be present; that you will grant to your posterity that they
may be prosperous and illustrious; at this season of genial showers and gentle
breezes, I desire to recompense the root of my existence, and exert myself
sincerely. Always grant your safe protection. My trust is in your divine spirit.
Reverently I present the fivefold sacrifice of a pig, a fowl, a duck, a goose,
and a fish; also an offering of five plates of fruit; with oblations of spirituous
liquors; earnestly entreating that you will come and view them.[58]

The elaborate ceremonies concluded with a massive feast in which the sacrificial
foods were shared by the participants in time-honored fashion. Although most
Ch'ing-ming devotions were far more personal and casual, all had the effect
of establishing a close bond between the living and the dead.

The so-called Dragon Boat Festival (*tuan-yang chieh*, lit., Festival of the
Upright Sun) took place early in the fifth month. Although celebrated
countrywide, it was especially popular in South China, where colorful and
exciting boat races took place on rivers and lakes. These races, and the festival
generally, commemorated the death by drowning of the famous but ill-fated
Chou dynasty scholar and poet Ch'ü Yuan, who committed suicide in despair
after losing the favor of his ruler through slander. Although a joyous occasion,
the Dragon Boat Festival was surrounded by rituals designed to protect the
population from evil and unhealthy influences that were believed to be especially
prevalent in the fifth month. A late Ming account of the festival in Ch'ü
Yuan's home province of Hunan states:

The current popular belief is that the boat race is held to avert misfortunes.
At the end of the race, the boats carry sacrificial animals, wine, and paper
coins and row straight downstream, where the animals and wine are cast
into the water, the paper coins are burned, and spells are recited. The purpose
of these acts is to make pestilence and premature death flow away with the
water.[59]

During the seventh month, throughout China various ceremonies were
undertaken to honor the ancestors and to placate "hungry ghosts." Graves
were often swept, and ancestral sacrifices performed. The great Buddhist
religious service on the fifteenth known as All Soul's Day (*yü-lan hui*) involved
the reading of sutras by the clergy to "lead those [souls] deeply engulfed in
the lower world [across the sea of suffering]." Significantly, the theme of
these devotions was the filial piety of a Buddhist disciple, Mu Lien (Maudgalyana),
who offered sacrifices to save his deceased mother from the torments of Hell.[60]

On the fifteenth day of the eighth month, the Mid-Autumn Festival (*chung-
ch'iu chieh*) occurred. Among the most popular of all Chinese festivals, it
involved family gatherings and feasts, the exchange of "mooncakes" (*yüeh-
ping*), offerings to the moon, ancestor worship, and the burning of incense
to Heaven and Earth. Like the Lantern Festival, the Mid-Autumn Festival

was especially popular with women and children. Men played a marginal role in the ceremonies, since, in the words of a popular Peking proverb, "Men do not worship the moon, [just as] women do not sacrifice to the God of the Hearth."[61]

The Ch'ung-yang (Double *yang*) Festival on the ninth day of the ninth month was in many parts of the country a relatively minor celebration, with little overt religious significance. It was primarily a day of hill climbing, sightseeing, kite flying, and feasting. Contemporary Western accounts of the festival suggest a gala mood, echoed by Chinese accounts, "Reciting poetry and drinking wine, roasting meat and distributing cakes—truly this is a time of joy."[62] In some parts of the country, however, Ch'ung-yang was marked by large-scale lineage sacrifices of the sort that sometimes occurred during the Ch'ing-ming festival. Even national celebrations were not carried out with perfect uniformity throughout the country, but the similarities appear far more striking than the differences.

On the first day of the tenth month, Chinese families again worshipped their ancestors in ceremonies paralleling those of the seventh month (*chung-yüan*) and the Ch'ing-ming festival. This celebration was known popularly as the ceremony of Sending Winter Clothes (*sung han-i*). Concern for the well-being of the ancestors was expressed at this time by inscriptions on colored paper garments or plain paper wrappers enclosing "spirit money." It was also in the tenth month that the official ritual calendar for the coming year was distributed. From this time until the New Year's preparations began in the twelfth month, there were no national festivals of any consequence, only relatively minor celebrations and a few official sacrifices. Perhaps the most widely celebrated ritual of the period in Chinese households was the preparation of "eighth-day gruel" (*la-pa chou*) in the twelfth month, a ceremony designed to show thanksgiving for good fortune during the year.[63]

Although most Chinese festivals contributed to community solidarity and a shared sense of culture, they were not an unmixed blessing from the Ch'ing government's point of view. This was particularly true of local religious festivals and village fairs. As huge crowds gathered to watch entertainers, enjoy food and drink, and do business, men and women mingled freely, fights sometimes erupted, and social discipline occasionally broke down. Gamblers, thieves, and swindlers collected to exploit the situation. Especially threatening to the government was the possibility that festivals would serve as the recruiting grounds for secret societies. An edict of 1724 expresses this fear:

[A] class of loafers, with neither a livelihood nor an abode, . . . has come forth to usurp the name of . . . [Buddhism and Taoism] and to corrupt the practical use of the same. The majority of them use [doctrines about] calamities and felicity, misfortune and happiness, to sell their foolish magic and baseless talk. They begin by cheating on goods and money to fatten themselves. Then they proceed to hold meetings for the burning of incense where males and females mingle promiscuously. Farmers and craftsmen forsake their business and trades, and engage themselves in talking about miracles. Worst of all, rebellious and subversive individuals and heretical miscreants glide in among them, establish parties and form leagues by taking membership oaths. They assemble at night and disperse in daytime. They thus transgress their proper status and sin against their duty, mislead mankind and deceive the people.[64]

For the most part, the Ch'ing authorities relied upon social pressures and the vast network of nongovernmental organs of local control to maintain or restore order in towns and villages. But penal law remained a powerful weapon in the state's arsenal, to be used with ruthless severity whenever crimes occurred that threatened the Chinese social or political system. Among these crimes, the worst were known as the Ten Abominations (*shih-o*): (1) rebellion against the emperor and his ritual order; (2) subversion or destruction of imperial temples, tombs, or palaces; (3) desertion or treason; (4) parricide (including the murder of a father, mother, uncle, aunt, grandfather, or grandmother); (5) the murder of three or more persons in one family; (6) lack of respect for, or improper use of, the ritual articles and implements of the emperor; (7) unfilial conduct; (8) maltreatment of relatives; (9) insubordination by inferiors toward their superiors; and (10) incest. All of these crimes bore directly on the sanctity of either the family or the state, and all were potentially punishable by death from slicing (*ling-ch'ih*)—the most severe form of punishment in the Ch'ing code.[65]

In especially severe cases, punishment went well beyond the perpetrator. The statute on rebellion and high treason, for example, not only stipulated death by slicing for the principal offender, but also the decapitation of all males in his household over the age of fifteen (including the offender's father, grandfather, sons, grandsons, brothers, and brothers' sons, as well as his maternal grandfather, father-in-law, and brothers-in-law). Further, the law provided that the rest of the family (all females and all males fifteen years of age and under) would be enslaved in the households of "meritorious ministers."[66] This statute illustrates both the traditional emphasis on ancestral concerns as a deterrent and the pervasive principle of collective responsibility in Chinese society.

Unfortunately, such draconian legal measures did not prevent either crimes against the state or crimes within the family. Throughout the Ch'ing period, rebellions repeatedly broke out, despite the harsh treatment received by the leaders of such uprisings and their families. Heterodox ritual specialists found opportunities to usurp the prerogatives of the Ch'ing elite, and secret societies flourished. And although the state dictated severe penalties for domestic crimes, we know that among the most common cases included in the Ch'ing dynasty's

Hsing-an hui-lan (Conspectus of Penal Cases) were the killing of a wife's paramour; disobedience to parents or grandparents; incest; and assault by either wives or concubines on husbands, slaves or servants on masters, or offspring on parents or grandparents.[67] Clearly, Chinese society was not all harmony and cooperation, even in the best of times.

Yet in all, the fabric of Confucian society wore remarkably well, strengthened by the interwoven strands of religious sanction, law, education, and ritual. For all that divided China, much more united it: a centralized system of administration; shared social attitudes and practices; a similar cosmology and world view; a common repository of ethical principles, artistic symbols, historical heroes, and literary myths; a powerful sense of unparalleled cultural development; and a universal pride in simply being "Chinese." It took the combined impact of unprecedented population pressure and Western imperialism in the nineteenth century to begin to tear this traditional garment apart, and even now it has not been completely destroyed.

CHAPTER 11

Tradition and Modernity, 1860–1982

The theme of Chinese history during the last century or so has been revolutionary change. Yet in the midst of China's modern transformation we can see the powerful persistence of tradition. From the late nineteenth century to the present, inherited patterns of language and perception, as well as traditional attitudes toward politics, ritual, social organization, ethics, art, and literature, have influenced in fundamental ways the course and speed of China's modern development. Although a full and systematic discussion of the interplay between tradition and modernity must await further study, this concluding chapter examines at least some of the modern manifestations and modernizing implications of China's rich, cohesive, and tenacious cultural tradition.

THE CHALLENGE OF THE WEST

In his well-known and provocative book on the late Ch'ing reformer Wang T'ao (1828–1897), Paul Cohen warns against measuring nineteenth-century China's modernization (meaning primarily technological advancement) by external standards. "Modernization," he maintains, "is not a horse race"; and a "much more valid way of measuring change in nineteenth century China is by internal points of reference."[1] Yet one might well argue that a horse race is exactly what modernization is. It involves the notion of competition (usually between nation states) and assumes some kind of external standard of judgment for success. Seen in this light, modernization is a cross-cultural phenomenon, as distinct from reform, which is essentially intracultural. Or, to pursue our racing metaphor, reform pits the horse against the clock (his own "best time"), while modernization stacks the horse up against other horses. In the case of nineteenth-century China, the purse was more than money or pride; it was national survival.[2]

It is true, of course, that this distinction between reform and modernization is somewhat artificial. Even if we define modernization as a special kind of externally motivated, rationally organized, technologically oriented, competitive change, it often bears a close relationship to indigenous reform. The acquisition of Western weapons by Ch'ing officials in the 1860s, for example, was only part of a general reform program that owed its primary inspiration to the demands of the Taiping Rebellion. Ch'ing policymakers recognized that Western guns and ships could be used as foreign-policy tools as well as instruments in the suppression of the rebellion; but their priorities were overwhelmingly internal, and the *yung-ying* armies that used Western weapons and techniques most effectively throughout the entire nineteenth century developed primarily in response to an internal stimulus, within the framework of Chinese tradition and without significant Western influence.[3]

As indicated in previous chapters, "Chinese tradition" encompassed a great deal, to say the least. The intellectual heritage of Confucianism, for example, ran the gamut in the nineteenth century from the obdurate—nearly pathological—political and social conservatism of the imperial tutor Wo-jen (d. 1871) to the highly creative synthetic philosophy of the brilliant Cantonese scholar K'ang Yu-wei (1858–1927). Taoism and especially Buddhism exerted considerable intellectual influence in late Ch'ing times, and there was always a heterodox strain of millenarian thought that held out the promise of a utopian future, a "great leap" into a new age of social justice. The question facing China in the late Ch'ing period was whether any of these ideologies had the capacity to transform the Middle Kingdom in the modern era, to effect meaningful change in the midst of unprecedented challenges.

On the whole, I am persuaded that the reformist tradition of China's Confucian heritage provided an adequate intellectual foundation for modernization based on Western standards of economic, scientific, and technological development. Certainly it sanctioned the idea of making adjustments to meet changing conditions (*pien-t'ung*) and did not prevent loyal Confucian scholar-officials in the nineteenth century from sponsoring the establishment of Western-style arsenals, shipyards, foreign-language schools, educational missions, military and naval academies, railroads and telegraphs, mines, and a wide variety of manufacturing industries. Measured solely against the baseline of China's traditional system, the reforms of the late nineteenth century were in many ways quite impressive, as Cohen, Tom Kennedy, Wang Erh-min, and others have pointed out.[4]

But these reforms did not take place in a vacuum, and increasingly their impetus came to be external rather than internal. As foreign imperialism loomed ever larger on China's horizons, Ch'ing policymakers could not avoid viewing their accomplishments in terms of foreign progress, including that of Meiji Japan (1868–1912). Western ideas of science, technology, and economic growth, as well as concepts such as nationalism, democracy, egalitarianism, and individualism, began to emerge as alternatives to inherited Chinese attitudes and values. The modernized West (and Japan) became the twentieth-century standard for China's progress in a world dominated by industrialization, imperialism, international competition, and rapid political and social change.[5]

The process by which the West emerged as a modernizing model for the Middle Kingdom began with the imposition of the notorious "unequal treaties" on China in the period from 1842 to 1860. According to the terms of these treaties, which were imposed by force and not abrogated until 1943, the foreign powers gained the right to establish self-governing treaty-port settlements for Western residence and trade, to have access to the Chinese interior, to operate foreign ships between the treaty ports on the coast and on inland waterways, to promulgate Christianity without obstruction, to limit Chinese customs duties, and to establish formal diplomatic relations at the capital and in treaty-port areas. Westerners enjoyed immunity from Chinese law (extraterritoriality) and other nonreciprocal privileges. The entire structure was held together by the most-favored-nation clause, which brought to all the treaty powers any benefit extracted from the Chinese by one or another of the powers over time.[6]

From 1860 on, the treaty ports became conduits for the transmission of Western influences of all kinds. Foreign merchants, missionaries, diplomats, and military men collected in the port cities, bringing to China new products, ideas, practices, and skills. At the same time, these Western intruders exerted a disruptive influence on Chinese society, threatening the traditional economic system, elite prerogatives, the Chinese world order, and China's security and sovereignty. The treaty ports were both showcases for the modern West and vivid reminders of the challenge of foreign imperialism.

Contact with foreigners in treaty-port areas during the Taiping Rebellion (1850–1864) gave at least a few foresighted Chinese officials—notably Li Hung-chang (1823–1901)—the opportunity to observe firsthand the technological and organizational advantages of the West and to employ a number of Westerners in various new modernizing enterprises. Li became the leading figure in China's so-called Self-Strengthening Movement (c. 1860–1895), an effort to build China's military and economic strength in order to contend with both internal disorder and external aggression.[7]

During Li's extraordinarily long tenure as governor-general of Chihli from 1870 to 1895, new ideas penetrated much of the Middle Kingdom. The rise of Western-style Chinese newspapers, together with a growing number of Western works translated into Chinese by missionaries and by foreign employees in the Imperial Maritime Customs Administration, arsenals, shipyards, and educational institutions, brought a heightened awareness of the West to China. During the first half of the nineteenth century, the majority of translated Western books and pamphlets had been religious, but during the latter part of the century, most of the translated works were in the natural, applied, and social sciences, as well as in history and geography. Popular magazines such as the *Tien-shih-chai hua-pao* (Illustrated Review of the Tien-shih Studio) portrayed the advantages of Western science and technology, as well as the disruptive influence of foreign activity in China. By the end of the nineteenth century, the rapidly expanding Chinese periodical press had become a potent weapon in the movement for radical reform.[8]

But until the Sino-Japanese War of 1894–1895, change came slowly in China. As I have pointed out elsewhere, the outcome of the conflict perhaps causes us to place the modernizing "success" of Japan and the "failure" of China in too sharp relief.[9] Yet it is impossible to avoid asking what went wrong with China's Self-Strengthening Movement after more than three decades of costly effort. This was, after all, precisely the question that the Chinese themselves were asking after the debacle of 1895, and the answers they produced determined in a large measure whether they would become conservative reformers like Chang Chih-tung (1837–1909), radical reformers like K'ang Yu-wei, or revolutionaries like Sun Yat-sen (1866–1925).

In retrospect, it is clear that China's modernizing problems in the late Ch'ing period were both internal and external. On the one hand, the aggressiveness of the foreign powers in the realms of diplomacy, commerce, evangelism, and military affairs created a variety of political and economic problems, encouraged Chinese antiforeignism, and produced a natural suspicion of both Western employees and Western influences. But compounding these difficulties were China's pressing and inescapable demographic problems, the vastness and diversity of the Chinese empire, the turmoil created by the abortive millenarian movements of the Taipings and other rebel groups, and the tenacity and integration of China's traditional culture.[10]

In the realm of culture, the classical Chinese language remained the standard written medium of the Chinese elite throughout the Ch'ing period, reinforcing long-standing attitudes, values, perceptions, and prejudices. Even if we reject the view of Marcel Granet and others that the mental world embodied in classical Chinese represents a "self-contained cultural monad hermetically sealed off from the cultural world embodied in the languages of the modern West," it is clear that the classical language affected the introduction of Western ideas in many ways. The preeminent translator of Western thought in the late Ch'ing period, Yen Fu (1853–1921), refused, for example, to employ the more flexible and more widely accessible vernacular language in his renderings of Mill, Rousseau, Spencer, and others, arguing that "where language has no refinement [*ya*], the effects will not extend very far." Benjamin Schwartz argues that Yen's elegant and abstruse translations "succeed on the whole in transmitting the essential thought of the Western sages," but there can be little doubt that Yen's young contemporary, Liang Ch'i-ch'ao (1873–1929) was correct in asserting that "those who have not read many ancient books . . . [find] his translations most difficult to comprehend."[11]

Schwartz himself points out that Yen resisted the use of most "standard" neologisms created by the Japanese during the early Meiji period in favor of his own renderings and that he tended to make maximum use of the traditional "allusive categories of ancient philosophic thought" in rendering Western ideas. Yen thus contributed to the general intellectual confusion of the late nineteenth and early twentieth centuries—a confusion reminiscent of the early decades of Buddhist translating activities when

> translators with different backgrounds chose different Chinese equivalents for foreign terms; translators had different degrees of knowledge of the language from which they were translating; communication among translators was infrequent; different versions or editions of foreign works were used by different translators; [and] different stylistic preferences produced different versions of the same work.[12]

Furthermore, the ambiguity and semantic weight of many Chinese characters modified their meaning in translation, creating additional linguistic difficulties. Sun Yat-sen's use of the character *ch'üan* for both "powers" and "rights" is one indication of the problem of ambiguity, while his employment of the classical Confucian term *min-sheng* ("people's livelihood") for the concept "socialism" provides an example of the problem of semantic weight. Over time, with additional experience and the growing acceptance of precoined Japanese neologisms in the early twentieth century, Chinese translations of Western works became more uniform in usage; but it took the "literary revolution" of the New Culture Movement (c. 1915–1925) after the fall of the Ch'ing dynasty and the rapid rise of vernacular usage during that period to produce a major linguistic breakthrough. And even thereafter the power of traditional forms of expression was strong.[13]

Yin-yang and correlative thinking persisted throughout the nineteenth and into the twentieth century. The radical reformer K'ang Yu-wei stated in the 1890s, for example:

> Probing into the way of Heaven, Confucius knew that everything contains polarity. He therefore employed [the concepts of] *yin* and *yang* to interpret the things of the world. . . . In a human body, the back is *yin* and the front is *yang*; in a tree, its branches and trunk respectively make *yin* and *yang*; with respect to light, darkness and brightness constitute *yin* and *yang*; in color, black and white are *yin* and *yang*. . . . There is not a single thing in the world that lacks *yin* and *yang*.

K'ang's use of *yin-yang* polarities extended into many areas of his radical reinterpretation of Confucianism, including his theory of human nature. He also used *yin-yang* terminology to explain the mutual dependence of ideas and actions. He wrote, for instance,

> Square and circle, *yin* and *yang*, being and nonbeing, the unreal and the real are mutually dependent in their growth or diminution; so are the [teachings of] the sages and [those of] the Buddha. . . . Regularity and expediency, *jen* [humaneness] and *i* [right behavior], commonweal and private interest, others and self, *li* [propriety] and *chih* [wisdom] are mutually dependent; so are "things Chinese" and "things Western."[14]

The effort to illustrate the essential complementarity of Chinese and Western ideas indicated above was manifest in a number of other traditional formulas in the late Ch'ing period. Among the most common dualistic distinctions was that made between the (Chinese) "moral way" (*tao*) and (Western) "manifestations" or "concrete things" (*ch'i*)—a polarity derived from the *I-ching*. The reformer Hsüeh Fu-ch'eng (1838–1894) wrote on behalf of Li Hung-chang in 1876, for instance:

> Of the things revered in China the principle [*tao*] is foremost; of the things that Westerners understand, the manifestations [*ch'i*] are manifold. However, within the principle, there are at no time no manifestations, and the manifestations at their peak are in connection with the principle. Even if Yen-ti and Hsien-yüan [legendary rulers of high antiquity] were reborn into our world, they could not but immediately start work on boats and railroads, guns and cannon, and machinery; these are the natural circumstances. . . . With regard to those things in which the foreigners are superior, we should not erect a fence to exclude ourselves. This then means that principle and manifestations are simultaneously ready, and in this way it will not be difficult to unite [everything within] the four seas into one family [*ssu-hai i-chia*].[15]

A similar dichotomy to *tao-ch'i*, borrowed from Sung neo-Confucianism, was between substance (*t'i*) and function (*yung*). Wang Erh-min and others have shown that the *t'i-yung* paradigm was used in a variety of different ways by scholars in nineteenth-century China who hoped to reconcile traditional Chinese learning and new Western knowledge. Chang Chih-tung's famous formula, "Chinese learning for the substance, Western learning for the function" (*Chung-hsüeh wei t'i Hsi-hsüeh wei yung*), reflects the Sinocentric mainstream approach, but by the 1890s there were growing numbers of Chinese intellectuals who had come to see that the West had more to offer China than "concrete things" and that substance and function were more closely related than Chang Chih-tung was willing to admit. Nonetheless, as Chang Hao indicates, the *t'i-yung* approach had psychological significance, for it "facilitated China's modernization without losing her cultural identity. Its dubious validity notwithstanding, . . . [the *t'i-yung* formula] symbolized China's ambivalence toward the West."[16]

The Chinese search for a kind of cultural equivalence with the West in the late Ch'ing period gave renewed impetus to the traditional effort to "find in antiquity the sanction for reform" (*t'o-ku kai-chih*) and revived the seventeenth-century argument that new Western ideas had their inspiration or analogues in ancient Chinese thought. The *I-ching* was, of course, often cited as justification for change, and other classics served to justify learning from foreigners. Chang Chih-tung wrote in 1898: ' "In instruments we do not seek old ones but new.' That is the idea in the *Book of History*. 'Knowledge exists among the four barbarians.' That is the idea in the *Commentary on the Ch'un-ch'iu* [Spring and Autumn Annals]. . . . 'When I walk with two persons, they may serve as my teachers; I select their good qualities and follow them.' That is the idea of the Confucian *Analects*."[17] The devout westernizer and influential translator Yen Fu, although far less committed to Chinese tradition in the nineteenth century than either Chang Chih-tung or K'ang Yu-wei, and certainly less anxious than many of his ultraconservative contemporaries to demonstrate that all the innovations of the West had ultimately "come from the East" (*tung-lai*), nonetheless often used Buddhist concepts, the symbolism of the *I-ching*, and various Confucian and Taoist sources of authority to support his views on modernizing change.[18]

The vast repository of Chinese fixed expressions (*ch'eng-yü*) provided yet another means of rationalizing Western-inspired change. The traditional phrase "viewing all [barbarians] with the same benevolence" (*i-shih t'ung-jen*), for example, could be used both to justify the most-favored-nation clause of the unequal treaties and to determine policy regarding the treatment of foreign employees in the Chinese service.[19] The problem with such traditional formulations was that they often mitigated an awareness of the need for more fundamental policy changes on the part of the Ch'ing government. Perhaps the most vivid illustration of this problem can be found in the documentary record of China's foreign relations in the T'ung-chih period (1862–1874) entitled *Ch'ou-pan i-wu shih-mo* (A Complete Record of the Management of Barbarian Affairs), which was presented to the throne in 1880. Although intended to be a secret rather than a public document, the preface casts all of the humiliations of the T'ung-chih reign—Western demands for an audience with the emperor on terms of diplomatic equality, the use of foreign troops to defend the treaty ports from the Taipings, the loss of Chinese territory to the Russians, the failure of the Alcock Convention, the establishment of an Interpreters College to train Chinese in Western languages in order to meet the needs of modern diplomacy, the belated establishment of Chinese legations abroad (related directly to a mission of apology sent by China to Great Britain after the murder of a British consular official in 1875), the limitation of

Chinese customs duties, and the establishment of the Imperial Maritime Customs Administration—in terms of imperial condescension.

The preface reads in part:

> We respectfully consider that after the T'ung-chih emperor came to the throne and stabilized the policy, . . . the amphibious monsters were quickly driven away and His Majesty's awful dignity vastly overawed everything within the imperial domain. . . . [When the barbarians returned to China] they requested to have an audience, no different from the Hsiung-nu king coming to the court of the Han dynasty. When they departed they wanted to join up as auxiliaries on the flanks of the imperial guard, just as the Uighurs assisted the T'ang. They relied on the [emperor's] jade axe to mark off the rivers, confer their borders, and settle their boundaries. They presented cinnabar and turned toward civilization [*hsiang-hua*]. How could they be aware that control-by-light-rein [*chi-mi*] of the imperial pattern was entirely carried out according to the emperor's design? As a means by which speech might penetrate to all countries, the [Interpreters] College began to instruct in common languages. The fame of our classic books was spread everywhere. His Majesty proclaimed his orders to dispatch envoys abroad. . . . The merchants' customs duties were fixed, and . . . with the emperor's grace and rewards extended to them, [the foreigners] became cultivated and learned elegance and etiquette [*kuan-tai jung-fen*]. Inner [Chinese] and outer [foreigners] formed one family.[20]

Even the granting of imperial audiences to Western diplomats on terms of equality after the majority of the T'ung-chih emperor could be rationalized by the notion that some foreigners were simply too barbaric to be controlled by conventional Chinese rites. In the opinion of the censor Wu K'o-tu, since Westerners understood only material gain and not Confucian ritual (*li*), requiring them to observe Chinese ceremonies based on Confucian assumptions was as pointless as "gathering a herd of sheep, dogs, horses, and pigs in a hall and making them dance to music."[21]

Such Sinocentric attitudes were reinforced by the traditional civil-service examination system. One of the topics for the metropolitan exams in 1880 was the following quotation from the Four Books: "By indulgent treatment of men from afar [*jou-yüan*] they are brought to resort to [the ruler] from all quarters. And by kindly cherishing the princes of the states, the whole empire is brought to revere him." Such quotations, dutifully memorized by all examination candidates, perpetuated the myth of the Chinese emperor's universal kingship and encouraged China's outmoded posture of cultural condescension to foreigners.[22]

The examination system also reinforced neo-Confucian intellectual orthodoxy, with its emphasis on loyalty to the state and its premium on the acquisition of moral over scientific and technological knowledge. Mary Wright is correct in asserting that during the late Ch'ing period the civil-service examinations were not always concerned exclusively with literary and scholastic questions; but even she admits that at their best the exams were "overloaded with precedent," with a premium placed on knowledge of facts rather than analysis or judgment. Chang Chung-li, for his part, goes so far as to say that the nineteenth century saw "the complete domination of the Confucian classics in the examination questions"—a conclusion supported by abundant documentary evidence.[23] There were, of course, Chinese criticisms of the examination system throughout the Ch'ing period, but the basic assumption remained that Chinese scholars were moral men of broad learning who "need not be specialists" (*pu-pi chuan-men ming-chia*).[24]

Prior to 1895, there existed very little incentive for meaningful change in either the examinations or the Ch'ing educational system. Education remained overwhelmingly private in nineteenth-century China, and the central government gave little support or encouragement to educational reform. The only major innovations in Ch'ing educational policy before the Sino-Japanese War were the establishment of a few Interpreters Colleges and the sending abroad of about two hundred students—most of whom were recalled by the government because they were neglecting their traditional Chinese studies. Meanwhile, the civil-service examinations remained essentially unchanged and a powerful lure to the best minds of the empire.[25]

Even the military examination system underwent virtually no change in the nineteenth century. One important reason was fear over tampering with inherited institutions and respect for ancestral precedent (*tsu-tsung ch'eng-fa*). Time and again in late Ch'ing China we find that concern over the policies of previous emperors played a key role in imperial deliberations. A major factor in the decision to spend vast amounts of precious revenue on the reestablishment of central-government control over Chinese Central Asia in the 1870s instead of devoting the funds to maritime defense was the throne's reluctance to abandon territory conquered by an imperial ancestor (the Ch'ien-lung emperor). And even after the Sino-Japanese War, Ch'ing officials and the throne repeatedly expressed a concern for ancestral precedent in deliberations over civil and military reform.[26]

Given such cultural inertia, it should come as no surprise to find that there was very little enthusiasm for Western art, literature, or social customs in late Ch'ing China—certainly nothing comparable to the Meiji government–sponsored wave of Westernization that washed over Japan in the 1870s and 1880s. It is true that in some treaty-port areas the commercial middlemen known as compradors (*mai-pan*) proved susceptible to certain aspects of Western material culture. A few wore Western-style clothes and most lived in Western-style buildings with both Chinese and Western furnishings. Some assumed Western given names, and a number took up Western hobbies and amusements (such as watching horse racing). Very few were ardent Confucians, and the majority sent their sons to study with Western tutors or to missionary-sponsored Western-style schools. But the vast majority of Chinese remained untouched by Western cultural influences during the late Ch'ing period, particularly in rural areas, where all of the peasantry and most of the elite continued to live. The West was fundamentally a curiosity, not a source of cultural inspiration.[27]

Naturally enough, the conservative Manchu government did nothing to encourage the Westernization of Chinese culture during the nineteenth century. The Manchus had, after all, originally justified their conquest in terms of the protection of China's cultural heritage. They could therefore scarcely appear to abandon traditional values, practices, and institutions without compromising their political position. China remained a combined state-and-culture in which, as John Fairbank has noted, "political power was maintained, in larger part than usual, by cultural means."[28] Complicating the problem in the late nineteenth century was the presence of the Empress Dowager Tz'u-hsi on the throne. As a female ruler, who had executed a coup d'etat to gain power and then flouted the dynastic laws of succession to keep it, Tz'u-hsi proved to be especially paranoid and particularly inclined to use neo-Confucian orthodoxy and the patronage of traditional Chinese culture as a means of serving personal political ends.[29]

The paranoia of Tz'u-hsi translated not only into a vigorous defense of orthodoxy but also into an obsessive concern with internal control. It is true that during and after the Taiping Rebellion the throne was forced to grant greater power and administrative leeway to certain loyal Chinese "regional" officials as a matter of expediency; but it continually attempted to play these officials off against one another through the powers of appointment and the purse and by the careful manipulation and deployment of their so-called regional military forces. By and large the effort was successful, but in both the civil bureaucracy and the regular military forces of the empire, corruption and costly inefficiency continued.

In China's civil administration, the only major institutional innovations of the nineteenth century were the Tsungli Yamen and the Imperial Maritime Customs Administration—both of which resulted from direct Western pressure. In reality, however, the former was merely an ad hoc subcommittee of the Grand Council and the latter, but a subsidiary office of the former. Meanwhile, the long-standing Ch'ing system of checks and balances discouraged initiative and often destroyed administrative continuity. Overlapping jurisdictions, dyarchy, the rule of avoidance, and the policy of frequent transfer were particularly detrimental in this regard. The throne, for its part, avoided administrative responsibility whenever possible and seldom initiated modernizing projects except those relating specifically to the Banner Army.

Despite the internally motivated military reforms of the mid nineteenth century, the Ch'ing army as a whole played no significant role in the modernization of Chinese society. The degenerate Banner and Green Standard forces of the empire consumed vast amounts of money but were largely untouched by Western influences, and even in the new-style *yung-ying* armies that assumed their military role, modernization went no further than the piecemeal acquisition of Western weapons and a certain amount of Western drill. Locally raised, armed, and trained, these "temporary" forces had little sense of either national identification or political awareness. The great majority of Chinese soldiers remained illiterate and uninformed. Within the military, as in the rest of Chinese society, personal ties of blood, friendship, or local affinity generally counted for more than expertise, thus militating against the introduction of new ideas and influences. The existence of widespread corruption and opium smoking, coupled with the lack of modern medical and other facilities, neither improved the living conditions of the average Chinese soldier nor altered his expectations.[30]

China's economic system proved to be no more conducive to modernization than the military. From 1860 to 1895, the Ch'ing government did sanction the establishment of dozens of modernizing enterprises, including mills, mines, ironworks, and railroad and telegraph lines as well as arsenals and shipyards. But most of these activities were either undertaken by local officials (*kuan-pan*) or managed under the traditional formula of "government supervision and merchant operation" (*kuan-tu shang-pan*). Such enterprises occasionally brought quick returns to certain investors, but because of bureaucratic inefficiency and corruption they discouraged reinvestment and regular growth. Private enterprises in China were notoriously weak and few in number. Commerce and agriculture were largely neglected by the state.[31]

Certain inherited Chinese social values stood in the way of more rapid modernizing change. The lack of a well-developed tradition of protective law, for example, was a major impediment to economic development and to the establishment of a sense of social and political security for individuals. In the absence of such a legal system, particularistic ties of kinship, friendship, and local affinity assumed especially great importance, hindering economic and administrative efficiency. Conservative family values, social inequality, and the notion of collective responsibility were reinforced by punitive law; debilitating practices such as footbinding received widespread customary sanction, despite their crippling effect on one-half of China's elite class and many other women as well.[32] The civil ethos (*wen-te*) of late imperial China also proved to be an obstacle to modernization. The low prestige of the military made most of the Ch'ing elite disdainful of military affairs and unaware of the need for meaningful reform. Within the army and navy there was little incentive to acquire Western military knowledge beyond the rudiments of Western drill and tactics, and most officers longed for identification with the civil bureaucracy.[33]

Ch'ing ritual practices at all levels discouraged innovation. Despite the time-honored argument that ritual must "change with the times," the state remained wed to costly traditional ceremonial practices out of fear that radical alterations or benign neglect would undermine the central government's authority. At the popular level, local religious observances, community festivals, and life-cycle ritual reinforced traditional values and status relationships while at the same time consuming great amounts of scarce capital. Meanwhile, of course, the ritual privileges of the Ch'ing elite remained an important source of local prestige and power, and the preservation of at least the outward form of the tributary system during most of the nineteenth century blunted the throne's awareness that a new order of foreign relations had begun. In fact, the long twilight of the tributary system helps explain Peking's lack of a sustained sense of crisis and its lingering Sinocentrism. Traditional concepts and explanations were entirely too effective in distorting reality.[34]

Naturally enough, China's cultural pretensions and sense of universal empire precluded the rise of modern nationalism—the identification of the individual with the nation-state and the general acceptance of a multistate system of other sovereign (and competing) national entities. The Sino-Japanese War of 1894–1895, however, shattered China's outmoded Sinocentric self-image at a single blow. This event not only marked the total destruction of the traditional Chinese world order by a onetime tributary, but it also laid bare China's military weakness, exposed the bankruptcy of the Self-Strengthening Movement, and resulted in the loss of Chinese territory and the imposition of a costly and humiliating unequal treaty on China by the Japanese themselves. A surge of Chinese nationalism ensued, and with it, a burst of reform sentiment. Ironically, Japan now became a modernizing model for China. Even so, it took the failure of the famous Reform Movement of 1898 and the disastrous Boxer Rebellion of 1900 to prompt the Ch'ing government into sponsoring meaningful reform.

REFORM, REVOLUTION, AND CHINA'S INHERITED CULTURE

The abortive reforms of 1898 resulted directly from the acceleration of foreign imperialism in the wake of the Sino-Japanese War. The so-called Scramble for Concessions on the part of the Western powers during 1897–1898, which threatened to dismember China, prompted the Kuang-hsü emperor (r. 1875–1908) to initiate a reform movement from above with the advice and assistance of radical reformers such as K'ang Yu-wei and Liang Ch'i-ch'ao. At this time, the emperor's adoptive mother, the Empress Dowager Tz'u-hsi, was in "retirement" at the Summer Palace outside of Peking. Although conservative and cautious, the empress dowager gave her initial approval to the reform scheme, reportedly stating, "So long as you keep the ancestral tablets and do not burn them, and so long as you do not cut off your queue, I shall not interfere."[35]

But the reform edicts issued in the emperor's name in the period from June 11 to September 20, 1898, proved to be too threatening to Tz'u-hsi.

Changes such as the abolition of sinecures and the appointment of progressives
in government, the replacement of the "eight-legged essay" in the civil-service
examinations by essays on current affairs, and the establishment of modern
schools with both Western and Chinese curricula appeared too radical, and
on September 21, the Empress Dowager executed a coup d'etat, claiming
that a serious illness had incapacitated the emperor. Chastizing the hapless
emperor for sweeping away "ancestral institutions," Tz'u-hsi rescinded virtually
all the reform edicts and put a price on the head of the reformers, several
of whom were executed. K'ang and Liang escaped to Japan, where they
continued to agitate for reform.

The return of the conservatives to power happened to coincide with an
upsurge of activity on the part of a secret society known generally as the
Righteous and Harmonious Fists (I-ho ch'üan), or Boxers. This loose coalition
of several diverse groups had in common a hostility to both Westerners and
the Ch'ing government. Their double-edged antiforeignism, fed by growing
popular resentment over imperialism, missionary activity, official corruption,
and maladministration, was expressed in the slogan "Overthrow the Ch'ing
and exterminate the Westerners" (*Fan-Ch'ing mieh-yang*). But in 1899, some
of the Boxers, after a defeat at the hands of the Ch'ing government and
with the encouragement of certain conservative local officials, changed their
slogan to "Support the Ch'ing and exterminate the Westerners" (*Fu-Ch'ing
mieh-yang*). This tactical transformation made it possible for the throne to
use the Boxers as a weapon against foreigners in general, leading to the siege
of the foreign legations in 1900 and the relief of the legations by an eight-
nation expeditionary force in the summer of that year. The result was the
occupation of Peking by the Allied forces, the imposition of a huge indemnity
on China, and a number of other destructive and demoralizing provisions
stipulated in the so-called Boxer Protocol of 1901.

This humiliating event forced the empress dowager and her conservative
supporters to commit themselves to fundamental reform. In the period from
1901 to 1909, a great number of reform edicts were issued. Many of these
reflected the changes proposed in 1898, but several others went a great deal
further. The most significant of these were: (1) the termination of the military
examinations and the establishment of a new, Western-style army (Lu-chün);
(2) the abolition of the civil-service examinations in order to encourage
enrollment in new-style schools with both Western and Chinese curricula; and
(3) the establishment of representative assemblies as a prelude to eventual
constitutional government on the Meiji pattern. Debilitating practices such as
footbinding were outlawed, and the throne even established a School of Ritual
Studies (Li-hsüeh kuan) in 1907 that was charged with the task of selecting
the best of China's "ancient and modern customs and the everyday habits
of the people" and bringing them to the attention of the throne. "This,"
an imperial edict stated, "is proof of Our earnest desire for the preparation

of the way towards the granting of a constitution and parliamentary representation to the country."[36]

The imperial reforms of the early twentieth century, designed to preserve the dynasty, had revolutionary consequences. Abolition of the traditional examinations, for example, dealt a staggering blow to the Confucian concept of rule by virtue and eliminated the institutional reinforcement of orthodox Confucian values. Representative government politicized the Chinese elite, giving them a new political awareness and a new base of power. The New Army, whose officers and men were increasingly exposed to, and influenced by, nationalistic revolutionary propaganda, became a revolutionary instrument. The establishment of the School of Ritual Studies, although itself of little real importance, symbolized the erosion of the official ritual system that had been precipitated by the destruction of the Chinese world order. The pathetic effort in 1907 to elevate the worship of Confucius to the first level of state sacrifice—presumably in order to enhance the reputation of the sage (and the Manchus) after the literary examinations that had reinforced his teachings for so many centuries had been abolished—testified to the desperation of the dynasty.[37]

Despite their reform efforts, the Manchus became increasingly scorned and despised for their inability either to resist imperialism or to protect elite interests. Chinese nationalism no longer permitted alien rulers to claim legitimacy as the protectors of China's cultural heritage, for Chinese intellectuals increasingly saw the need to differentiate between politics and culture in order to achieve the modern goals of "collective achievement and dynamic growth."[38] And despite K'ang Yu-wei's contention that the faults of the Ch'ing government were those of the inherited culture and not simply those of the Manchus, the cultural conservatism of the throne, its desperate attempt to maintain Manchu political supremacy, and growing Chinese fears that a vigorous anti-imperialist movement might result in foreign intervention all made the Manchus a convenient target for nationalistic advocates of republican revolution. The mysterious death of the Kuang-hsü emperor in 1908 and the installment of an infant emperor under a conservative prince regent destroyed China's best chance for a Meiji-style constitutional monarchy, and in 1911–1912, the republican revolutionaries under Sun Yat-sen threw out the imperial baby with the Manchu bathwater. This created a political vacuum and a ritual void that the hastily constructed system of representative institutions could not fill. The Republic of China soon degenerated into warlordism.[39]

The warlord period, from about 1915 to 1928, witnessed the rise of the so-called New Culture Movement—an iconoclastic assault on traditional Chinese culture—and a search for new values and institutions in the midst of political chaos, social unrest, widespread demoralization, and foreign imperialism. Nearly every aspect of the inherited civilization came under attack by Chinese intellectuals, including Confucian ethics and the teachings of ritual (*li-chiao*).

The period was marked by a tremendous surge of interest in Western ideologies, science, and democracy; the rejection of the classical Chinese script in favor of the vernacular written language; experimentation with new artistic, dramatic, and literary forms; and the development of a new national literature influenced strongly by Western themes and models. There was also a growing interest in Western fashions and amusements.[40]

The early outlook of the French-educated intellectual Ch'en Tu-hsiu (1880–1942) exemplifies the vibrantly iconoclastic spirit of the New Culture Movement. Although Ch'en was born into an elite family and received a thorough grounding in the Confucian classics, his experience abroad and reaction to China's deteriorating domestic situation led him to reject Chinese tradition and to embrace Western ideas. As editor of the famous and influential journal *Hsin ch'ing-nien* (*La Jeunesse*, The New Youth), Ch'en issued a "Call to Youth" in 1915, declaring passionately that he would "much rather see the past culture of our nation [*kuo-ts'ui*, often translated "national essence"] disappear than to see our race die out now because of its unfitness for living in the modern world." He urged his readers to be independent, not servile; progressive, not conservative; aggressive, not retiring; cosmopolitan, not isolationist; utilitarian, not formalistic; and scientific, not mystical. He railed against "all traditional ethics, law, scholarship, rites and customs" and scoffed at the use of *yin-yang* and five-elements notions to explain natural phenomena. Until his conversion to Marxism around 1920, Ch'en remained a leading spokesman for Western-style liberalism and a reliance on "Mr. Science" and "Mr. Democracy" for China's salvation.[41]

The thrust of the New Culture Movement was toward what has been described as "totalistic iconoclasm." This widespread disposition to reject the past completely and to seek holistic and all-encompassing solutions to China's complex problems reflected a growing recognition that the very perfection of China's highly integrated cultural tradition now presented the nation with its most formidable modernizing problem. In the words of Ch'en Tu-hsiu and Hu Shih (1891–1962), "The old literature, old politics, and old ethics have always belonged to one family; we cannot abandon one and preserve the others." Lin Yü-sheng explains further,

> Iconoclastic intellectuals were hardly capable of differentiating those traditional social norms and political practices that were abhorrent to them from traditional cultural symbols and values. This lack of differentiation and tendency to be monistic and holistic was affected, among other factors, by the long-term historical disposition to interlace the cultural center with a socio-political center in Chinese traditional society and by a traditional Chinese pattern of thinking in terms of association. . . . The intelligentsia in China believed in the necessary priority of cultural and intellectual change over social, political, and economic changes and not vice versa.[42]

The scientific spirit of the New Culture Movement dealt a mortal blow to certain aspects of traditional Chinese culture, such as cosmology, in the mind of the educated elite. But even among the intelligentsia there were still a number of die-hard traditionalists. In response to the early call for "total Westernization"(*ch'üan-p'an Hsi-hua*), ultraconservatives such as Ku Hung-ming (1857–1928) stood steadfast in defense of China's cultural tradition. Although educated in the West and able to read several foreign languages (including English, French, German, Latin, and ancient Greek), Ku maintained that Western utilitarian culture was incapable of developing the inner mind and that China's "spiritual civilization" was so perfect that it could not only save China but also rescue the West from its materialistic malaise. He strenuously opposed Western science and technology, defended all traditional Chinese ethics and customs (including practices such as concubinage), and even continued to wear the Manchu queue as a sign of traditionalistic defiance.[43]

The vast majority of Chinese intellectuals, however, did not take the extremist positions of either totalistic iconoclasm or ultraconservatism. Rather, they tried to find a creative cultural balance between Chinese tradition and Western-inspired modernity. Some gravitated more toward the West, others more toward an emphasis on China's "national essence"; but even the conservatives now viewed the past from new perspectives, using new methodologies borrowed from the West. On the other hand, if we look at Chinese society as a whole during this period, it is clear that the New Culture Movement was essentially an urban intellectual movement that had very little impact on the rest of China and that for every Western-educated neotraditionalist there remained "hundreds of thousands of local leaders of secret societies, Buddhist abbots, Taoist monks, and leaders of Confucian uplift societies who continued to expound their views almost wholly in terms of categories provided by the culture of the past."[44] Traditional family values and relations of subordination, as well as the traditional life-cycle rituals that reinforced these values and relations, remained deeply entrenched in the countryside, where about 80 percent of the population resided (as it does to this day).

Furthermore, the political imperatives of Chinese nationalism, the success of the newly organized Nationalist party (Kuomintang) and its Northern Expedition against the warlords in the period from 1926 to 1928, and the establishment of a new central government at Nanking under Sun Yat-sen's heir apparent, Chiang Kai-shek (1888–1975), narrowed somewhat the parameters of discussion and debate. In politics, even among Chinese liberals there seems to have been a "widespread tendency to appreciate democracy more as an indispensable functioning part of a modern nation state than as an institution to protect individual rights and liberties." Thus nationalist impulses and the desire for a strong and rationally organized state became more important than liberal values and individualism in Chinese political and social thought. And although a battle of words still raged between advocates of "total Westernization" and those who advocated "cultural construction on a Chinese base," the Kuomintang in this period of "political tutelage" and one-party rule demonstrated a clear concern with the restoration of traditional values. Although committed to rapid economic modernization and the realization of Sun Yat-sen's Three Principles of the People (nationalism, democracy, and socialism), Chiang Kai-shek's new government moved quickly to reestablish Confucianism as a kind of state-sponsored orthodoxy.[45]

As late as February 1927, the Nationalist government had ordered the abolition of official Confucian rites on the grounds that "the principles of Confucius were despotic. For more than twenty centuries they have served to oppress the people and to enslave thought. . . . As to the cult of Confucius, it is superstitious and out of place in the modern world. . . China is now a Republic. These vestiges of absolutism should be effaced from the memory of citizens." But the vestiges were not effaced for long. On November 6, 1928, Chiang Kai-shek was already urging his officers to spend their leisure time studying the Four Books of Confucianism, and in 1931, the birthday of Confucius became a national holiday. By 1934, Confucius had been recanonized, and an official delegate of the national government was sent to take part in the solemn ceremonies at the Confucian temple at Ch'ü-fu, birthplace of the sage. During the same year, Chiang inaugurated the famous New Life Movement, which called for a return to the four ancient Confucian virtues of *li* (ritual), *i* (right behavior), *lien* (integrity), and *ch'ih* (sense of shame).[46] Chinese politics and culture became reunited.

The New Life Movement has often been ridiculed for its overattention to minute rules of decorum and for its philosophical superficiality. In Mary Wright's words, "The whole of the neo-Restoration of the Kuomintang was a dismal failure, a far sadder spectacle than the T'ung-chih Restoration it tried to copy."[47] But the fundamental aims of the two "restorations" were different, and despite the weaknesses of the New Life Movement, it did lay the foundations for a government-sponsored approach to traditional Chinese culture that continues to this day on Taiwan. This approach considers Confucian values to be fully compatible with science and democracy and conducive to modern economic growth as well. At present, traditional art and literature, and even traditional religious and ritual practices, continue to flourish alongside more "modern" aspects of material culture borrowed from the West. Like the Japanese, who now serve as a self-conscious modernizing model, the Chinese on Taiwan have evolved a dualistic culture that draws upon the traditions of both East and West in apparently judicious combination.[48]

In many respects, the Chinese Communist approach to traditional culture has been very different from that of the Kuomintang. Since the founding of the party in 1921, the Chinese Communists have promoted a vision of social revolution based on the rejection of Confucianism and the implementation of Marxist-Leninist principles and practices. Although the revolutionary movement of Mao Tse-tung (1893–1976) grew out of the same deep patriotism and esteem for science, democracy, and social justice that had motivated Sun Yat-sen as founder of the Kuomintang, Mao laid his wager on the Chinese peasantry, developing a kind of populist Marxism-Leninism that stood in sharp contrast to the urban-centered elitism that had characterized the nationalist era. In both theory and practice, Mao emphasized the importance of ideology, human will, mass political participation, anti-imperialism, egalitarianism, social and economic reform, and above all, the transformation of consciousness. He assailed Confucian beliefs, as well as the popular religious practices and social rituals that seemed to encourage conservatism, waste time or money, and strengthen the position of the traditional elite.[49]

From 1949 to his death in 1976, Mao succeeded in transforming much of Chinese society. In addition to promoting Marxist-Leninist values nationwide and elevating the social position of traditionally disadvantaged groups (notably workers, peasants, women, and soldiers), Mao brought to the People's Republic a new system of economic organization, which included the nationalization or collectivization of agriculture, industry, and commerce and a host of related changes in health, education, and welfare. Life expectancy nearly doubled, as did population. During the early 1950s Mao received considerable assistance from the Soviet Union, but his militantly self-reliant revolutionary approach can best be seen in the radical Great Leap Forward (1958–1960) and especially the tumultuous Great Proletarian Cultural Revolution of 1966–1969, which hearkened back to the New Culture Movement in its self-conscious effort to "destroy the old and establish the new" (*p'o-chiu li-hsin*).

Yet for all his revolutionary iconoclasm, Mao did not totally reject China's heritage. As early as 1938 he wrote: "Today's China is an outgrowth of historic China. We are Marxist historicists; we must not mutilate history. From Confucius to Sun Yat-sen we must sum it up critically, and we must constitute ourselves the heirs of all that is precious in this past. . . . A communist is a Marxist internationalist, but Marxism must take on a national form before it can be applied." In 1956, Mao attacked both the *t'i-yung* modernizing formula of the late Ch'ing period and the notion of "total Westernization" prevalent in the New Culture era, arguing: "We must learn good things from foreign countries and also learn good things from China. . . . China's art must not look more and more to the past, nor must it become more and more Western."[50]

Mao's deep sense of history and esteem for much of Chinese tradition is evident in his writings and speeches, which bristle with historical allusions and references to traditional Chinese literature. Much of Mao's discourse employs traditional terms, phrases, and metaphors. Mao even had a certain admiration for Confucius. Although he criticized the sage for his lack of revolutionary vision, disdain for physical labor, and esteem for "old rituals," Mao admired Confucius for his breadth of learning and cultural refinement.

And in a publication issued during the Cultural Revolution, Mao stated, "We must not lose the Confucian tradition." Some scholars have suggested that the Maoist concept of the transformative power of the mind resonates strongly with the traditional neo-Confucian emphasis on efficacious moral efforts (*kung-fu*) and that the prominent strains of dynamism, activism, and utopianism in Mao's thought seem to be derived at least in part from the tradition of the great Ming Confucian scholar Wang Yang-ming.[51] Mao's distinctive notion of "contradictions" may perhaps owe something to *yin-yang* influences, and his "Great Leap" mentality hearkens back to the millenarian tradition of the Taipings and others. Certainly the persistent emphasis on ethics, self-cultivation, and small-group ritual in the People's Republic bears the strong imprint of traditional Chinese social thought.[52]

Mao did not live in the imperial style, but like Chiang Kai-shek he often ruled in it, manipulating both factions and ritual symbolism for his own political purposes. Furthermore, in practice Mao's administration, like that of his imperial and Nationalist predecessors, displayed the familiar characteristics of authoritarianism; state supervision of political, social, and economic life; an emphasis on political morality over law; a preoccupation with ideological, artistic, and literary orthodoxy; and a clear stress on collective responsibility and mutual surveillance. Many of these tendencies were, of course, encouraged and reinforced by Marxist-Leninist ideology and practice.[53]

As an intellectual system, Maoism differed fundamentally from the ideology of both imperial China and the Kuomintang. Yet it was every bit as holistic and nearly as metaphysical as Chu Hsi's neo-Confucianism had been. And while the Marxist dialectic replaced *yin-yang* notions of cyclical alternation and complementary opposition as the logical underpinning of most Chinese thought, Maoist discourse continued to exhibit many time-honored features of traditional Chinese philosophical expression. Quite apart from the powerful linguistic tendency to group phrases in neat sets of four characters and the deeply ingrained moralistic tendency to parcel out praise and blame in categorical either/or fashion, we find in much Chinese writing of the Maoist period a dogmatic formalism expressed in arbitrary groupings of elements, often organized in numerical configurations.[54]

Chinese political rhetoric in particular exhibits this tendency. If we review the various political campaigns of the Maoist era, we encounter literally dozens of formalized numerical categories embodied in the slogans: the "three antis" (*san-fan*), the "three highs" (*san-kao*), the "three red banners" (*san-mien hung-ch'i*), the "three histories" (*san-shih*), the "three reconciliations and one reduction" (*san-ho i-shao*), the "three freedoms and one contract" (*san-tzu i-pao*), the "four olds" (*ssu-chiu*), the "four firsts" (*ssu-ko ti-i*), the "five histories" (*wu-shih*), the "five category elements" (*wu-lei fen-tzu*), and so forth. This type of classification persists in contemporary China, as we can see from the famous Four Modernizations, the trial of the Gang of Four, and the campaign known as the Five Stresses and Four Points of Beauty (*wu-chiang ssu-mei*)—that is, the stress on decorum, manners, hygiene, discipline, and morals and the effort to beautify the mind, language, behavior, and the environment.[55]

The legacy of the past is even evident in the midst of Mao's devastating attack on traditional "feudal" attitudes and "bourgeois" Western influences during the Great Proletarian Cultural Revolution. To be sure, during 1966 the Chairman's overenthusiastic agents, the Red Guards, ransacked museums, temples, and private homes; destroyed ancestral tablets, ancient artifacts, old books, and works of art; and attacked citizens who dressed in the traditional fashion, followed old rituals, or possessed Buddhist and Taoist relics. But in many respects the Cultural Revolution reflected long-standing Chinese cultural predispositions. Mao himself assumed the position of an imperial-style demigod, whose writings were believed to have mystical, semimagical power. During 1968, the cult of Mao grew to especially extravagant proportions, as Maurice Meisner has indicated:

> The writings of the Chairman were printed and distributed in ever greater volume. Portraits, statues, and plaster busts of Mao increased both in size and number. . . . In households there were often "tablets of loyalty" to Mao's thought around which family members gathered to pay reverence. Schoolchildren no longer began the day by saying "good morning" but by chanting "May Chairman Mao live ten thousand times ten thousand years." Throughout the land exhibition halls were built to chronicle and commemorate the life and deeds of the Chairman, and to them came people on organized pilgrimages to pay homage at what the official press termed "sacred shrines." The test of loyalty to Mao was no longer measured by revolutionary acts inspired by his thought but more by the ability to recite his sayings and by the size of portraits that were carried in the streets or hung in homes. In 1966 the Mao cult had stimulated iconoclasts; in 1968 it produced icons.[56]

During the same period on Taiwan the Kuomintang sponsored a Cultural Renaissance explicitly designed to preserve and foster traditional Chinese culture. In obvious response to the Cultural Revolution on the Mainland, it called for the republication of the Confucian Classics and encouraged new writings and translations in order to "publicize Chinese culture and build a bridge between Chinese and Western cultures." It also promoted a revival of literature and art "based on ethics, democracy and science" and emphasized the principles and practices of the New Life Movement, including the "four social controls" (*li, i, lien,* and *ch'ih*) and the "eight virtues" (loyalty, filial piety, benevolence, love, faithfulness, justice, harmony, and peace). Like the New Life Movement of the 1930s, the Cultural Renaissance has been criticized for its stress on outer form over inner substance and for its obviously political character.[57] Nonetheless, it offers a sharp and significant contrast to Mao's brutally destructive effort to exorcise the "ghosts and monsters" of the past on the Mainland.

Since Mao's death in 1976, there has been a sharp reaction to the chaotic excesses of the Cultural Revolution (including Mao's "cult of personality") and a wholehearted commitment to the Four Modernizations (agriculture, industry, science and technology, and national defense). But during this time, the Chinese press has carried numerous articles indicating that Mao's effort to root out "poisonous feudal influences" during the 1960s fell far short of success and that certain traditional ideas and habits continue to plague the People's Republic. A recent article in the theoretical journal of the Chinese Communist party, *Hung-ch'i* (Red Flag), stated flatly, "feudalistic ideology is so prevalent that it has permeated every corner of [Chinese] society."[58]

By far the most frequent and vociferous complaint in the Chinese press is that made against "bureaucratism," an administrative outlook associated with both imperial and Nationalist China and regularly denounced as rigid, dogmatic, autocratic, elitist, conservative, and often corrupt. Bureaucratism is formalism in action (or inaction), not simply in thought or literary style. Not long ago, Teng Hsiao-p'ing expressed the fear that "some of our cadres have turned into mandarins"—a remark that no one in China took lightly. But a diagnosis is not a cure, and the present leadership has found considerable resistance within the party and the bureaucracy to meaningful administrative reform. Perhaps for this reason, Chinese bureaucratism has been described by at least one high-ranking official of the People's Republic (Huan Hsiang) as "far worse than any other bureaucratism in the world."[59]

In the opinion of at least some contemporary writers, "feudal" attitudes are manifest not only in bureaucratism, but in other spheres of Chinese life as well, especially in the countryside. The "small producer" mentality of the peasantry has created, for instance, a deeply ingrained feudal consciousness of particularistic groupings (*pang-p'ai i-shih*) and patriarchal authority. In the words of the *Hung-ch'i*: "Because of the low level in the development of the entire society's productive forces and especially because ideology is relatively autonomous in nature, the remnants of the patriarchical system centered on the father's authority have not been purged thoroughly from society. The traditional idea, habit, and style of patriarchy are still seriously affecting people's social life."[60] Similarly, the long-standing emphasis on personal relations and nepotism continues to stand in the way of more rational economic and political organization in China.

Inherited attitudes have surfaced in a wide variety of realms. Harold Hinton has indicated, for example, that the long-standing prejudice against manual labor on the part of Chinese intellectuals (which Mao tried in his own radical way to overcome) persists. He encountered tractor designers who had never been on a tractor and who were unaware of what specific needs the tractors they designed were supposed to fill. Birth-control programs in the countryside have suffered not only from ignorance on the part of the peasants but also from powerful traditional preferences for male children to continue the line and help support the family. Recent research has shown that Mao's effort to curtail costly traditional rituals has also encountered serious obstacles in the rural sector. William Parish and Martin King Whyte demonstrate, for instance, that even during the period from 1969 to 1974, when the radical policies of the Gang of Four still held sway, life-cycle rituals on the old pattern were widely observed in rural South China, consuming large amounts of precious funds. In fact, they suggest that in many marriages the financial burden for the groom and his family (including payment of the traditional bride price (*li-chin* or *p'in-chin*) has not decreased in relation to family income over the past forty years, and that it may even have increased. As in the past, poor families still find it difficult to find brides for their sons, and many households go deeply in debt in order to provide a proper wedding for the sake of community face. The cost of funerals also remains high, despite official encouragement of simple ceremonies and cremation.[61]

Ironically, the "liberal" policies of Teng Hsiao-p'ing over the past few years, all undertaken in the name of modernization, have helped to revivify certain aspects of traditional Chinese thought and behavior. Traditional art and literary forms are again popular. Buddhist temples and monasteries, recently reopened along with a few Taoist temples and some Christian churches, have attracted growing numbers of worshippers. Domestic ancestral sacrifices and other household religious devotions, severely condemned during the Cultural Revolution, have become more prominent, and reports in the Chinese press indicate the recrudescence of "superstitious" practices such as geomancy (*feng-shui*), fortune-telling, and even, occasionally, witchcraft. One report from Hainan Island noted that oil drilling had actually been disrupted by concerned local residents who believed that the oil rig and drilling had disturbed the *feng-shui*.[62]

Of course there is the other, more "modern," side to Teng's cultural policies. Language reform—including the simplification of Chinese characters and the alphabetization of Chinese sounds (the *pinyin* system)—has continued unabated, despite a considerable measure of traditionalist opposition. Greater freedom in the areas of art and literature has encouraged a surge of cosmopolitan creativity not seen since the 1950s, when the newly resurrected slogan "Let a hundred flowers bloom" was first promoted. But the weight of tradition in matters such as stylistic imitation, as well as the long-standing tendency of the state to pass judgment on matters of intellectual and artistic orthodoxy, continues to constrain creativity and to raise troublesome questions for the Chinese leadership concerning the relationship between freedom and discipline, between tradition and modernity.[63] At present, such cultural tensions are not as acute on Taiwan, although they do exist. What changes tomorrow may bring for both Taiwan and the Mainland is impossible to say, but it seems evident that for a long time to come in both societies, the past will remain an integral part of the Chinese future.

A Note on Chinese Names

In transliterating Chinese names, I have followed the Wade-Giles romanization system, with the exception of provincial names and the capital (which are rendered in the more familiar Chinese Post Office system: Peking instead of Pei-ching, Kiangsu rather than Chiang-su, and so on). I have not employed the *pinyin* romanization system in the body of the book, but I have included *pinyin* equivalents in the index in recognition of the growing popularity of the *pinyin* system. At present, however, it seems to make more sense to relegate *pinyin* spellings to the index, since the vast majority of scholarly books on China, and virtually all English-language reference works, employ the Wade-Giles convention.

The main principles of Wade-Giles pronunciation (of the Mandarin dialect) have been summarized by John Meskill (1973):

Each word is pronounced as one syllable. When there is a combination of vowels, they are sounded as diphthongs: ai like my, ao like cow, iao like miaow, ei like day, and ou like low.

The Vowels:

a as in father
e as u in up
i as in ring
o at the end of a word, usually as o in lofty
u as oo in moo; much shortened as a final following the double consonants ss, sz, tz, or tz'
ih rather like a New Englander's ending of "Americer"

The Consonants: Pronounced generally as in English, with the exception of a group that may be aspirated or unaspirated, indicated by the presence or absence of the ' sign.

ch' as in char	ch as in jar
k' as in kill	k as in gill
p' as in pat	p as in bat
t' as in tell	t as in dell
ts'	ts
as in knots	as in nods
tz'	tz

j is something like English r
hs is something like English sh

Chinese personal names are usually given in original order, with the surname first. Chinese surnames generally consist of one character and the given name of two (e.g., Kung Tzu-chen). The reverse is possible, however, as is the use of two characters for both surname and given name (e.g., Ssu-ma Hsiang-ju). Polysyllabic Manchu and Mongol names are transliterated either by a single word (e.g., Nurhachi) or by a string of sounds representing the characters used by the Chinese to render them (e.g., Seng-ko-lin-ch'in—the Chinese phonetic equivalent for Senggerinchin, a Mongol name).

Emperors in the Ch'ing dynasty are usually referred to by their reign names (*nien-hao*) rather than either their personal names (which became taboo upon their accession to the throne) or their posthumous temple names. See Mary Wright, "What's in a Reign Name?" *JAS*, 18, 1 (1958). The Ch'ing emperors are as follows: Shun-chih (1644–1661); K'ang-hsi (1662–1722); Yung-cheng (1723–1735); Ch'ien-lung (1736–1795); Chia-ch'ing (1796–1820); Tao-kuang (1820–1850); Hsien-feng (1851–1861); T'ung-chih (1862–1874); Kuang-hsü (1875–1908); Hsüan-t'ung (1909–1911). All such reign names have felicitous meanings, though some, such as Kuang-hsü ("Glorious Succession"), have a certain irony (see Chapter 3).

Weights and Measures

Length

1 *ts'un* (inch)	= c. 1.4 English inches
10 *ts'un*	= 1 *ch'ih* (foot, c. 14.1 English inches; c. 35.6 centimeters)
10 *ch'ih*	= 1 *ch'ang*
180 *ch'ang*	= 1 *li* (c. 0.333 English mile; c. 0.5 kilometer)

Weight

1 *liang* (tael)	= c. 1.333 English ounces
16 *liang*	= 1 *chin* (catty, c. 1.333 pounds; c. 0.6 kilograms)
100 *chin*	= 1 *shih* (picul, c. 133 pounds)

Area

1 *mou*	= c. (0.166 acre; c. 0.055 hectare)

A Note on Exchange

During the Ch'ing period, the "standard" unit of exchange was the tael (*liang*), about an ounce (c. 500 grains) of silver, usually in the form of an oval ingot, or "shoe." The paper money experiment of the Hsien-feng period (1851–1861), the first such paper issue since the early Ming dynasty, failed miserably. The value of the silver tael varied from time to time and place to place, not only because of changes in market conditions but also because of different local standards of weight and fineness. Theoretically, 1 tael was equal to 1,000 copper cash (*wen* or *li*), but in practice a tael might be worth anywhere from 1,000 up to 1,500 cash. The great variety in standards of currency, weight, and capacity in traditional China necessitated the employment of a great many money changers and other petty middlemen, complicating both commercial transactions and payment of taxes. For an illuminating discussion of the problems, consult Albert Feuerwerker in Fairbank and Liu (1980), pp. 40 ff.; also H. B. Morse (1908), *The Trade and Administration of the Chinese Empire* (Shanghai) pp. 145 ff., esp. 149–161.

A Note on Prices

Throughout most of the Ch'ing period, the cost of a *shih* (picul) of rice was between 1.0 and 1.5 taels. A pig could be bought for about 2.5 taels, a sheep for about 1.5 taels, a goose for about 0.5 taels, and a chicken for about 0.12 taels. See H. Beattie (1979), p. 137; Chang Chung-li (1962), p. 143; Chang Kwang-chih (1977a), 267 ff. In 1864, the exchange value of a "customs" tael in Western currency was 80 pence (6s. 8d., about US$1.65). By 1894, the value of the tael had declined to 38 pence. For a discussion of late Ch'ing fiscal reform, consult Chuzo Ichiko in Fairbank and Liu (1980), pp. 403 ff.

Notes

REMARKS

I have cited comparatively few Chinese-language sources in these notes, despite years of work on both primary and secondary materials. The main purpose of the notes is to guide nonspecialists toward available Western sources and Chinese works in translation that illustrate or amplify the point I am making or lead the reader into areas of Chinese culture that cannot be discussed more fully in the body of the book for lack of space. Translations from Chinese sources (other than my own renderings) have been modified for consistency and clarity after consulting the Chinese original. Chinese sources are generally cited only if no comparable Western-language sources of documentation or information are readily available. Among the Chinese documentary sources consulted most frequently in this study are the *TSCC*, *SSCCS*, *HCCSWP* (and its supplements), the *TCHT*, and the *HWHTK* (see list of abbreviations in Bibliography). Particularly helpful in the study of Ch'ing ritual have been the *WHL*, *WLTK*, *CLCC*, *TCTL*, and related works cited in R. J. Smith (1981).

Among the great number of secondary Chinese works on traditional culture, the following deserve mention: Liu I-cheng (1964); Ch'ien Mu (1937, 1968, 1970); Ch'en Teng-yüan (1956); Ch'en Kao-yung (1937); Yang Yu-chiung (1945); Ts'ui and Liao (1968); Chang Chin-chien (1935); T'ao T'ang (1968); Wu Ching-hsiung et al. (1967); Wang Erh-min (1977); Yin Hai-kuang (1966); Lu Pao-ch'ien (1978); and especially T'ang Chün-i (1981) and Wei Cheng-t'ung (1981). The most useful reference books on the Ch'ing period in Chinese remain Ma Feng-ch'en (1935); Ch'ing-shih pien-tsuan wei-yüan-hui (1961); and Hsiao I-shan (1967). No comparable works exist in English, although Hsieh Pao-chao (1925) offers a generally reliable overview. Other valuable Western-language sources include Feuerwerker (1976); Immanuel Hsü (1975); Fairbank (1978 and 1979); and Fairbank and Liu (1980). Recent Western-language interpretations of traditional Chinese culture include: Council of the Chinese Cultural Renaissance (1977); Bauer (1976); Stover (1974); Stover and Stover (1976); Scharfstein (1974); and Dawson (1978). A very useful academic journal on Ch'ing history is *CSWT*.

Among the most informative contemporary accounts of late Ch'ing China by Westerners are T. T. Meadows (1856); E. H. Parker (1899); S. W. Williams (1883); L. Wieger (1913); Arthur Smith (1899); John Nevius (1869); J. H. Gray (1878); J. F. Davis (1846); Justus Doolittle (1865); J. Macgowan (1912); G. Walshe (1906); and R. F. Johnston (1910). Hummel (1943–1944) contains biographies, or at least a mention, of most of the Chinese referred to in the text.

One last remark. In the interest of brevity, I have cited only the author, and not the title, of articles included in collections of articles—for example, Chapter 1, Note 6: Arthur Wright in Gottschalk (1963), p. 39. Also, in order to keep footnotes to a minimum, I have in many cases combined several sources into a single citation. Sources for all quoted material in any one paragraph (or two successive paragraphs) are listed in order, separated by a semicolon and ended by a period. If such citations give a span of relevant pages, the quoted material appears within the span.

CHAPTER 1. INTRODUCTION

1. Culture is defined here as a system of interrelated perceptions, beliefs, values, and institutions that together shape the conscious and unconscious behavior of that system's constituent members. Complex societies, of course, have several cultural systems, each of which may intersect with, or approximate, one or more of the others. Among the theoretical works I have found particularly useful in this study are: Geertz (1973); J. Beattie (1966); Leach (1976); Tyler (1969); La Fontaine (1972); Moore and Myerhoff (1977).

2. For some such efforts, consult Chang Chin-chien (1935); Metzger (1977), esp. pp. 240–241; Wei Cheng-t'ung (1981), esp. pp. 134–137. Wei, for example, identifies ten salient characteristics of traditional Chinese culture: its isolated creation, long history, absorptive capacity, unity, conservatism, esteem of peace, feelings of local affinity, humane cosmological outlook, family and clan system, and emphasis on moral spirit.

3. The percentage of gentry members varied over time, of course. Ropp (1981), p. 30 suggests that perhaps 15 to 20 percent of the population in eighteenth-century China could be considered "elite" by virtue of "wealth, leisure, local influence, and participation in elite culture." See also H. Beattie (1979), pp. 18–21.

4. Ho Ping-ti (1967).

5. A. Wright (1960), pp. 234–235.

6. Arthur Wright in Gottschalk (1963), p. 39.

7. The major documentary sources for this study are discussed at the beginning of these notes. On the scholarly use (and abuse) of Chinese encyclopedias, consult Bauer (1966).

8. Arthur Wright in Gottschalk (1963), p. 40.

9. A noteworthy exception is Plaks (1976, 1977, and 1977a).

10. Hawkes (1973 and 1977), 2:122–124.

11. Derk Bodde in A. Wright (1953), esp. p. 54.

12. See R. J. Smith (1978), pp. 59–60.

13. Chang Tung-sun (1952), p. 222; Fung Yu-lan (1948), pp. 355, 406. See also Mou Tsung-san in Wu Ching-hsiung et al. (1967); Wei Cheng-t'ung (1981), esp. pp. 58–61, 158, 233–235, 300.

14. It should be emphasized that while Confucian ethics were secular in origin, they had a decidedly sacred quality, since they were inextricably linked to cosmology throughout the imperial era. For a succinct discussion of China's "cosmological morality," consult Tillman (1982), p. 207, citing Tom Metzger and Chang Hao. See also Wei Cheng-t'ung (1981), pp. 50–54, 109–126.

15. C. K. Yang (1961), pp. 175–176.

16. See especially the discussion in Wei Cheng-t'ung (1981), pp. 54–58 and 296–315; also R. J. Smith (1981).

17. R. J. Smith (1981).

18. See *CWTTT*, pp. 10338 ff. on *li* and its use in compounds. Note also the range of topics covered in the subsection on ritual in the *TSCC* and on ritual administration in the *HCCSWP* and its supplements.

19. R. J. Smith (1981). The shortened form of the *TSCC* title is used here; the full title is given in the Bibliography.

20. S. W. Williams (1883), 1:424; A. Smith (1899), p. 193; Nevius (1869), p. 239. See also Gray (1878), 1:347; Wieger (1913), p. 110.

21. Lessa and Vogt (1979), pp. 79 ff., citing Geertz. For indications of the overall social and political significance of *li*, consult Wei Cheng-t'ung (1981), pp. 28–29, 43, 56, 59, 85–88, 141, 157, 238–239, and 300–315.

22. For some previous explanations, consult Elvin (1973), Ho Ping-ti (1976), and Joseph Needham in Dawson (1964), summarized in R. J. Smith (1978a). See also Wei Cheng-

t'ung's most recent formulation (1981), pp. 26–29, 35–41, 47–48, 54–58, 61, and especially 314–315.

23. See, for example, Lamley (1977) and Lamley in Ahern and Gates (1981).

24. See also the preliminary evidence presented in R. J. Smith (1978a and 1981).

CHAPTER 2. THE CH'ING INHERITANCE

1. On these points, see Wei Cheng-t'ung (1981), cited in Chapter 1, Note 2 above.

2. Cressey (1955), p. 1. See also Wei Cheng-t'ung (1981), pp. 27, 44–48.

3. Han Yu-shan (1955), pp. 175 ff.; Balazs (1964), pp. 139–140; Teng and Biggerstaff (1971), pp. 156 ff.

4. Cited in Immanuel Hsü (1959), pp. 43–44.

5. Wylie (1867), pp. 43–44; Han Yu-shan (1955), pp. 175–180.

6. Tregear (1965), xv.

7. See Lillian Li (1982) and Rozman et al. (1981), esp. pp. 108–112 and 143–148.

8. On China's peripheral areas and ethnic minorities, consult Eberhard (1982). See also Dreyer (1976); Joseph Fletcher in Fairbank (1978); and Chusei Suzuki and David Farquhar in Fairbank (1968), pp. 192–224.

9. See esp. the discussion in Dreyer (1976).

10. Adapted from Cressey (1955), p. 8.

11. See, for example, Harry Lamley in Ahern and Gates (1981).

12. See Skinner (1977), pp. 212 ff. For a convenient summary of China's geographic divisions, consult Dun J. Li (1978), pp. 1–28.

13. See Eberhard (1982).

14. See, for example, K. C. Liu and R. J. Smith in Fairbank and Liu (1980), esp. pp. 211–243.

15. See Lamley in Ahern and Gates (1981).

16. Skinner (1977), pp. 216–217; Cressey (1955), pp. 24 ff. Cf. Schran (1978).

17. See R. J. Smith (1978b), p. 9.

18. Skinner (1977), pp. 538 ff. See also Wei Cheng-t'ung (1981), pp. 45–49.

19. See Eberhard (1965).

20. Ibid. Eberhard notes little change in Chinese regional stereotypes since the Sung period.

21. Spence (1975), pp. 49–50.

22. Ho Ping-ti (1976). See, however, the critical reviews in *HJAS* 37, 2 (December 1977) and *JAOS* 98, 1 (January–March 1978).

23. See Chang Kwang-chih (1977).

24. Keightley (1978); see also Chang Kwang-chih (1980) and Keightley (1982).

25. See Levenson and Schurmann (1970), pp. 71 ff.; Creel (1970).

26. Hsü Cho-yün (1965).

27. A useful summary is Mote (1971). See also Fung Yu-lan (1952) and Hsiao Kung-ch'üan (1979).

28. See Bodde (1938); also Cotterell (1981). T'ang Chün-i (1981), pp. 65–74, provides a fascinating overview of China's cultural development from Ch'in to Ch'ing times.

29. Needham and Huang (1974).

30. On the Han, consult Loewe (1968); Ch'ü T'ung-tsu (1972); Hsü Cho-yün (1980); Wang Zongshu (1982).

31. On Ch'ing admiration for the Han synthesis, consult Metzger (1973), pp. 70–71.

32. For a general overview of the impact of Buddhism on China and China's impact on Buddhism, see A. Wright (1968). See also Kenneth Chen (1964 and 1973).

33. Sullivan (1977), p. 122.

34. On the Sui-T'ang period, consult A. Wright (1978) and Wright and Twitchett (1973).

35. Bodde and Morris (1967), pp. 3–4.

36. On Sung achievements, see Elvin (1973), pp. 69–90, 113–234; also Haeger (1975) and Gernet (1962).

37. For a convenient summary, consult Fung Yu-lan (1948), pp. 166–177 and esp. 266–318. See also Tillman (1982).

38. See Joseph Needham in Dawson (1964).

39. Ibid.; also Elvin (1973), chapter 17; Joseph Needham in Welskopf (1964); and the symposium on Needham's work in *Past and Present* 81 (May 1980).

40. On this pattern, see Fairbank (1957), pp. 206 ff.

41. On the Yüan, consult Dardess (1973) and Langlois (1981).

42. Charles Hucker in James T. C. Liu (1970), p. 61. See also Farmer (1976) and Hucker (1966 and 1969).

43. Hucker (1975), p. 356.

44. On Ming thought, consult de Bary (1970 and 1975) and de Bary and Bloom (1979). Useful recent studies of Ming institutions include Ray Huang (1981) and Albert Chan (1982). Spence (1980) provides a convenient overview of the Jesuit experience in China. On China's influence on Europe, consult Bodde (1948); Mungello (1977); Wei Cheng-t'ung (1981), pp. 361–381.

45. On consolidation, see Frederic Wakeman in Wakeman and Grant (1975); Spence and Wills (1980).

46. Wakeman in Crowley (1970), p. 1. See also Liu I-cheng (1964), 3:88–98; Lillian Li (1982), p. 689. Ropp (1981), pp. 11–55 and Feuerwerker (1976) provide excellent overviews of eighteenth-century China.

47. Rozman et al. (1981), p. 216.

CHAPTER 3. THE CH'ING POLITICAL ORDER

1. Cited in Kahn (1971), p. 4.

2. Spence (1975), pp. 29–59. See also Kahn (1971); Kessler (1976); Huang Pei (1974); Silas Wu (1979); Hibbert (1981), chapter 6. Ray Huang (1981) provides a vivid portrait of imperial life in the Ming, much of which carried over into the Ch'ing. Consult also Albert Chan (1982).

3. Discussed in R. J. Smith (1981). See also the sources cited in Note 2 above.

4. On imperial regalia, see Mailey (1980); on the Forbidden City, consult Meyer (1976).

5. See esp. Spence (1975); Kahn (1971).

6. Kahn (1967).

7. On Tz'u-hsi's rise to power, see K. C. Liu in Fairbank (1978). A recent popular biography of the empress dowager is Warner (1975).

8. See, for example, R. J. Smith (1978c), pp. 20–21, 32–33, and notes; also Walshe (1906), p. 230; Hart Journals, June 17 and 26, 1864; July 4, 1864; October 23, 1865; January 2, 1866; *NCH*, January, 1908.

9. See Torbert (1978). For details on these and other Ch'ing institutions, consult Mayers (1897); Brunnert and Hagelstrom (1911).

10. Spence (1975), p. 45.

11. Torbert (1978), pp. 84 ff.

12. On the *Ch'u-fen tse-li* and related regulations, see Metzger (1973), chapter 4.

13. E-tu Zen Sun (1962–1963), p. 177; Rozman et al. (1981), pp. 109–111, 128–138, 208–211.

14. For further detail, consult R. J. Smith (1981).

15. Note also the ritual importance of the Imperial Board of Astronomy (Ch'in-t'ien chien), discussed in ibid.

16. R. J. Smith (1974), pp. 127–130.

17. Bodde and Morris (1967); R. J. Smith (1981). See also Chapter 10.

18. Lillian Li (1982), p. 689.

19. Adam Lui (1978).

20. See Banno (1964).

21. Consult Silas Wu (1970).

22. Ibid., pp. 130 ff. See also Jochim (1979).

23. Silas Wu (1970) and Jochim (1979); see also Metzger (1973), pp. 177 ff.; *TCHT* (1911), 34:1a–2b.
24. S. W. Williams (1883), 1:420. See also Ocko (1973).
25. Ch'ing-shih pien-tsuan wei-yüan-hui (1961), *ts'e* 2, 117:1390–1395.
26. On the functions of the district magistrate and his subordinates, see Ch'ü T'ung-tsu (1962); Watt (1972).
27. On subdistrict administration, see the sources cited in Note 26; also Hsiao Kung-ch'üan (1960); Sweeten (1976).
28. See R. J. Smith (1974); P. Kuhn (1980).
29. Watt (1972), esp. p. 14.
30. On the examination system, consult Miyazaki (1976); Ropp (1981), chapters 3 and 6; T. C. Lai (1970). Information on Ch'ing education may also be found in Rawski (1978); Elman (1979); Tilemann Grimm in Skinner (1977). *TCHT* (1911), 32:2a ff. indicates the vast number (and wide range) of orthodox writings to be mastered by Chinese scholars. Cf. *WHL*, 4:5a–6a.
31. On the Hanlin Academy, see Adam Lui (1981).
32. See Wakeman (1975), pp. 20–27; also Chang Chung-li (1967), pp. 123 ff.
33. For an excellent summary of contemporary Ch'ing criticisms of the examination system, consult Ropp (1981), esp. chapter 3.
34. Ho Ping-ti (1962), pp. 24–27, 34–38.
35. R. J. Smith (1974), pp. 131–145.
36. See the discussion in M. Wright (1967), chapter 5, esp. 90–91.
37. Metzger (1977), p. 207; Pye (1981), pp. 138–142.
38. Rozman et al. (1981), p. 124; Metzger (1977), pp. 167–168.
39. Perkins (1967), pp. 487, 491–492. See also Rozman et al. (1981), pp. 73–77, 109–115, 130–140.
40. *TCHT* (1911), 30:3a–3b.
41. Metzger (1973), pp. 23 ff.
42. Cited in Balazs (1965), p. 65.
43. See Watt (1972), pp. 174–176; Ch'ü T'ung-tsu (1962), pp. 34–35; Metzger (1973), pp. 125, 290, 367.
44. Kahn (1971), p. 10.
45. For additional evidence, consult Metzger (1977), chapters 4 and 5 and Metzger (1973), pp. 65–79. See also Fogel (1980); R. J. Smith (1978a), pp. 17, 70–71; Rozman et al. (1981), chapter 3 and esp. pp. 205–208.

CHAPTER 4. SOCIAL AND ECONOMIC INSTITUTIONS

1. See Solomon (1971), pp. 127–129; see also Hsiao Kung-ch'üan (1979), pp. 54 ff.
2. Brunnert and Hagelstrom (1911), pp. 490–514.
3. *WHL*, introduction:4b; 8:1a–11b; 12:1a–10b; 13:1a–10b; 14:1a–8b.
4. Wakeman is cited in Crowley (1970), pp. 13–15. On gentry privileges, consult Chang Chung-li (1967); also Ho Ping-ti (1962), esp. pp. 26–41. Ho notes—and more recent research confirms—that wealth became increasingly important as a determinant of social status in the Ch'ing period (p. 256). See, for instance, Ropp (1981), pp. 21–25; H. Beattie (1979), pp. 18–21, 127–132.
5. Chang Chung-li (1962), pp. 372–378; Rozman et al. (1981), p. 122.
6. For a fascinating case study, see James Polachek in Wakeman and Grant (1975); also Wakeman (1975), pp. 29–34.
7. Ho Ping-ti (1962), pp. 20–21, 80.
8. Quoted in Spence (1978), pp. 10–11, 14. See also Chang Chung-li (1962) esp. pp. 136 ff.; H. Beattie (1979).
9. Ku Yen-wu is cited in H. Beattie (1979), p. 180, n. 12. For data on prices and cost of living, consult Ho Ping-ti (1959), p. 217; Naquin (1976), p. 281; Chang Kwang-chih (1977a), pp. 265–267; Hsiao Kung-ch'üan (1960), p. 376 ff.; Vincent Shih (1967), pp. 477–478; H. Beattie (1979), pp. 136–137; Cantoniensis (1868).

10. See Skinner (1964–1965). According to surveys undertaken in North China during the early twentieth century, in eighteen districts with close to 4.5 million total population, only about 2.5 percent of the 1,880,000 occupational designations referred to artisans. Merchants accounted for about 4 percent; scholars, roughly 3 percent; and peasants, about 90 percent. Rozman et al. (1981), p. 151.

11. Ho Ping-ti (1962), pp. 81–86; see also Mark Elvin in Skinner (1977), esp. p. 468.

12. Wakeman (1975), p. 51. Ropp (1981), p. 50, points out, however, that the elite and urban worlds were not identical.

13. Ho Ping-ti (1962), pp. 107–111. H. Beattie (1979), stresses the importance of land and lineage in contributing to social mobility. See esp. pp. 127–132.

14. See Chapter 3, Note 30.

15. Frederick Mote in Buxbaum and Mote (1972), pp. 13–14.

16. See C. K. Yang (1961), pp. 189 ff.; Kenneth Chen (1964), chapter 16.

17. See Mayers (1897), pp. 84–86; R. J. Smith (1981).

18. R. J. Smith (1974), pp. 141–145.

19. R. J. Smith (1978c), pp. 15–25.

20. R. J. Smith (1974), pp. 150–157.

21. Ho Ping-ti (1962), p. 18; see also C. K. Yang in Fairbank (1957), pp. 387–388; Spence (1978), pp. 121–122.

22. See Bodde and Morris (1967), pp. 33, 169 ff.

23. On Ts'ao Yin, consult Spence (1966); see also Torbert (1978), pp. 57–58.

24. On women in traditional China, consult Ropp (1976 and 1981); Croll (1980), chapter 2. Ropp emphasizes the particular conservatism of the Ch'ing period with respect to women. For information concerning accomplished women in the Ch'ing, see Hummel (1943–1944) under the name and subject indexes. On the six service positions, consult Spence (1978), pp. 123–127; Hui-chen Wang Liu (1959), p. 94.

25. For illustrations of collective responsibility, see Bodde and Morris (1967), pp. 28–29, 41, 221, 286–288, 330; also Bodde (1969), p. 317; Spence (1975), p. 86.

26. See, for example, Levy (1949 and 1953); Rozman et al. (1981), pp. 92–97, 163–167; Wei Cheng-t'ung (1981), pp. 54–58, 304–305, 314–315; T'ang Chün-i (1981), pp. 198–202, 253–258; Metzger (1977), pp. 240–241.

27. On the complexity of the five mourning relationships, consult Chai and Chai (1967), 1:202–208; also R. J. Smith (1981).

28. Feng Han-yi (1967), pp. 4–5 underscores the integral relationship between kinship and ritual. See also R. J. Smith (1981); Wei Cheng-t'ung (1981), pp. 54–58, 314–315.

29. R. J. Smith (1981); C. K. Yang (1961), chapter 2; Wei Cheng-t'ung (1981), pp. 26, 38, 67, 70–71, 79–84, 303–304.

30. See Bodde and Morris (1967), p. 139.

31. Ibid., pp. 37–38, 40–41.

32. In these pages I have usually employed the general expression *clan* rather than the more precise term *lineage* in referring to kinship groups sharing a common surname and tracing their descent through the male line to a common ancestor (often fifteen or twenty generations in the past). For a discussion of lineage, see Maurice Freedman in Skinner (1979), pp. 334–350; also H. Beattie (1979), chapter 4.

33. Ho Ping-ti (1962), pp. 209–212; also Hsiao Kung-ch'üan (1960), pp. 237–240; H. Beattie (1979), pp. 52, 122–123, 126, 128; Xu Yangjie (1980).

34. See Hui-chen Wang Liu in Nivison and Wright (1959).

35. Ibid., pp. 17, 19–30, 37–49; Xu Yangjie (1980), pp. 35–39, 47, 60 ff.

36. C. K. Yang (1961), pp. 40–43, 52–53.

37. Ibid. See also Xu Yangjie (1980).

38. Hsiao Kung-ch'üan (1960), chapter 8.

39. On the Taipings, consult Jen Yu-wen (1973); Michael (1966); Vincent Shih (1967). On other forms of social conflict, see Lamley (1977).

40. The availability of land, the amount of land tax, and the amount of rents differed substantially from place to place and time to time during the Ch'ing period. For indices of changes in the patterns of tenure and taxation, see Wang Yeh-chien (1974); Faure (1976); H. Beattie (1979), esp. chapters 1 and 3; Hsiao Kung-ch'üan (1960), pp. 383 ff.; Feuerwerker

(1976), p. 81; Vincent Shih (1967), pp. 478–479; Ho Ping-ti (1959), p. 217; Chang Chung-li (1962), pp. 136–147.

41. For some illuminating case studies of landlordism in late imperial times, consult Jing and Luo (1978) and Muramatsu (1966). See also the sources cited in Note 40 above.

42. Cited in Hsiao Kung-ch'üan (1960), pp. 354–355. Consult also H. Beattie (1979), pp. 95, 112, 123.

43. See the sources cited in Notes 40 and 41 above; also Skinner (1971) and the "Introduction" in Wakeman and Grant (1975).

44. See Skinner (1964–1965); Rozman (1982).

45. Skinner (1971), pp. 272–277. Cf. Hayes (1977).

46. See G. W. Skinner's article on "Urban Social Structure" (Skinner 1977) and Yoshonobu Shira in Skinner (1977).

47. See the articles by Frederick Mote and Arthur Wright in Skinner (1977), esp. pp. 114–117. See also Meyer (1976), pp. 38–41, 68, 201–202.

48. Frederick Mote in Skinner (1977) emphasizes this point. Cf. Ropp (1981), pp. 48–51.

49. Wakeman and Grant (1975), p. 4.

50. See the articles by Shira, Peter Golas, and Sybille van der Sprenkel in Skinner (1977).

51. Ibid. On charitable enterprises in the Ch'ing, see M. Wright (1967), pp. 133 ff.; Walshe (1906), pp. 153–154; S. W. Williams (1883), 2:264–266. Ch'ing administrative guides and local gazetteers often give specific attention to problems of charitable administration (*hsü-cheng*).

52. Fairbank (1979), p. 49.

53. See the sources cited in Note 50 above. Also the articles by Kristopher Schipper, Tilemann Grimm, and Stephen Feuchtwang in the same work. On the T'u-ti kung, see Chapter 7, this book.

54. See Chesneaux (1972); C. K. Yang (1961), pp. 194–195; R. J. Smith (1981).

55. P. Kuhn (1980), pp. 165, 176; Wakeman (1977), p. 207.

56. Skinner (1977), p. 277.

57. Lamley (1977), p. 34 reminds us, however, that the rise of social tensions and even violence did not always coincide with dynastic decline.

CHAPTER 5. LANGUAGE AND SYMBOLIC REFERENCE

1. See de Francis (1950), pp. 7 ff.

2. A good basic introduction to the spoken and written language can be found in Newnham (1971). See also Tung T'ung-ho and Tung Tso-pin in Wu Ching-hsiung et al. (1967); Wei Cheng-t'ung (1981), pp. 177–181; Lee Pao-ch'en in Cheng Chi-pao (1964) p. 43.

3. On these individuals, see Immanuel Hsü (1959), pp. 55 ff., 121, and bibliography; also Ch'ien Mu (1937), chapters 4 and 8.

4. R. J. Smith (1978a), p. 20.

5. Cited in ibid.

6. Hummel (1943–1944), p. 22.

7. Chiang Yee (1973), chapter 1; Doré (1914–1933), 4:356–362.

8. *K'ang-hsi tzu-tien* (reprint ed., Taipei, 1962), p. ,1; cf. Wilhelm (1967), p. 335.

9. See Tung Tso-pin in Wu Ching-hsiung et al. (1967), pp. 64–73.

10. Creel (1936), p. 97; Cheng Chung-ying (1973), pp. 92–93.

11. See the interesting analysis in B.K.Y. T'sou (1981).

12. The use of puns and plays on words is particularly noticeable in vernacular literature. See, for example, Miller (1975), pp. 53, 80, 153–154, 174, 251–252.

13. Rosemont (1974), pp. 76–79.

14. See, for instance, Wing-tsit Chan (1967), pp. 359–370.

15. Rosemont (1974), p. 81.

16. See Goodrich (1975); also the discussions by Miyazaki (1976) and Rawski (1979).

17. Y. R. Chao (1976), p. 289. On the Chinese penchant for polarities, consult Granet (1934), pp. 56–82, 115–148. The only effort I have seen to apply the structuralism of Claude Levi-Strauss to Chinese thought is the rather feeble effort by Kang Shin-pyo in Rossi (1974).

18. Chang Tung-sun (1952), pp. 214–215, 222–223.

19. Meadows (1856), pp. 379–380.

20. See, for example, *WLTK*, Introduction: 2a. On the *I-ching* polarities, which are not nearly as striking in translation as in the original, consult R. Wilhelm (1967), p. 280.

21. See *TSCC, tien* 13, 15, and 22. The reprint edition I have consulted (Taipei, 1977) provides a convenient simplified index, pp. 2–61, which includes all major subject headings, organized by subcategories.

22. Wing-tsit Chan (1967), pp. 27, 39, 195.

23. Vincent Shih (1959), p. 191.

24. Ibid., p. 193.

25. On four-character expressions and proverbs, see Eugene Ching in Yamagiwa (1969); also T. C. Lai (1960 and 1969); Mou T'ien-hua (1977). On the style of examination essays, consult Tu Ching-i (1974–1975). Undoubtedly the structure of the Chinese language helps explain the enormous popularity of proverbs among the Chinese, both past and present.

26. Purcell is cited in Bodde (1957), p. 15. See also Wei Cheng-t'ung (1981), pp. 187–189 and esp. T'ang Chün-i (1981), pp. 320–323.

27. Wei Cheng-t'ung (1981), p. 187–189; Y. R. Chao in Egerod and Glahn (1959), p. 1 ff.

28. A. C. Graham in Dawson (1964), pp. 54–55. See also Fung Yu-lan (1948), pp. 11–14; Yü Ying-shih (1975), pp. 106–107.

29. On the scholars mentioned in regard to kinship nomenclature, consult Hummel (1943–1944), pp. 107–108, 152–156, 276–277, 499–500. See also *TSCC, tien* 12 and 14, and Wei Cheng-t'ung (1981), pp. 305, 314–315.

30. See, for example, Feng Han-yi (1967) and Y. R. Chao (1976), pp. 309 ff., esp. 327–330.

31. Bodde (1957), p. 65.

32. *CLCC*, 1:15a–16b; see also *CLTC*, pp. 17–20, 24–78 and *CLTSCC*, 1:1a–17b, summarized in R. J. Smith (1981).

33. *TSCC, tien* 16 categorizes women.

34. Chang Tung-sun (1952); Fung Yu-lan (1948), p. 16; Chang Kwang-chih (1976), chapter 7. For some recent studies in the West, consult B.K.Y. T'sou (1981) and Margaret Sung (1979). Note also the analysis of late imperial Chinese proverbs by Lu Pao-ch'ien (1978), which documents the penetration of Confucian values into all levels of society and suggests the powerful influence of the authoritarian Chinese family system.

35. Cheng Chung-ying (1973), p. 102; Rosemont (1974), pp. 83–88; Wei Cheng-t'ung (1981), pp. 190–194.

36. Arthur Wright in A. Wright (1953), esp. p. 287; see also Nakamura (1971), pp. 177–190.

37. Cheng Chung-ying (1973), p. 93. See also Cheng Chung-ying (1971). Much of this section is inspired by Professor Cheng's stimulating work.

38. See Chu Yu-kuang in Meskill (1973), p. 600; Chang Tung-sun (1952), pp. 211–217; Needham (1956), 2:279 ff. See also Rosemont (1974), pp. 86–88.

39. Wei Cheng-t'ung (1981), pp. 186–194.

40. On numerical categories, see Mayers (1874), pp. 293–360; also Bodde (1939) and Meyer (1976), p. 111.

41. Rosemont (1974), p. 87. These phrases, and others like them, come verbatim from the Confucian Classics.

42. Wei Tat (1970), p. xxx.

43. See Whitehead cited in Cheng Chung-ying (1977).

44. See Wing-tsit Chan (1967), p. vii, 108. The quotation on the significance of the *Chin-ssu lu* is from W. T. de Bary's preface to Chan's translation. Cf. Schneidau (1976), pp. 3 ff., on the Bible in the Western cultural tradition.

45. Cited in Toda (1963), part 2.

46. On the quotation from the Great Commentary, consult R. Wilhelm (1967), p. 322. For some recent literature on the *I-ching*, see R. Wilhelm (1979), H. Wilhelm (1975 and 1977), and Shchutskii (1979). Significantly, the *TSCC* devotes some seventy *chüan* to the *I-ching*, about six times as much as to the Buddhist canon (*Fo-ching*) and about ten times as much as to Taoist writings (*Tao-shu*).

47. See Needham (1956), 2:304–364; also Saso (1978a), and Chapters 7 and 10 of this book, on divination. For Ch'ing critiques of the *Ho-t'u* and *Lo-shu*, consult Immanuel Hsü (1959), pp. 34–35, and Toda (1963).

48. Fung Yu-lan (1948), p. 168.

49. Spence (1975), p. 59. See also ibid., pp. 11, 29, 44–45, 57, 69, 74–75, 147. There were, of course, many methods of consulting the *I-ching*, each of which, in a sense, reflected the world view of the user. See, for example, the technical discussions in Mackenna and Mair (1979) and Toda (1963). Wei Tat (1970), pp. 94 ff., provides a vivid account of the solemn ritual of divination.

50. See B. Watson (1962), p. 152; Mai-mai Sze (1959), pp. 39, 44–45, 325; also Vincent Shih (1959), pp. 7–9, 15, 20, 27, 105, 191; Han Yu-shan (1955), p. 106.

51. See R. Wilhelm (1967), pp. 328 ff.

52. On Ch'eng I's view, consult Wing-tsit Chan (1967), pp. 107–114, esp. 113. For examples of the *I-ching* to explain various natural phenomena, see Needham (1956), 2:329–345 and the sources cited in R. J. Smith (1978), p. 62 and notes.

53. Cited in Needham (1956), 2:334–335.

54. See Fung Yu-lan (1952), 2:636 ff.

55. Needham (1956), 2:336. Cf. Wing-tsit Chan (1967), pp. 110–113.

56. See especially Wei Cheng-t'ung (1981), pp. 188–194.

57. See Arthur Wright in A. Wright (1953), pp. 286–301.

58. Wei Cheng-t'ung (1981), pp. 34, 344–345, 354–355, 359; Tung Tso-pin in Wu Ching-hsiung et al. (1967), esp. pp. 78–82. On the continued prestige of Chinese classical studies in Japan, even after the Meiji Restoration of 1868, consult Kamachi (1981), esp. p. 36.

CHAPTER 6. THOUGHT

1. See Wei Cheng-t'ung (1981), pp. 31–35, 51–52, 61–67, 109–110.

2. Consult Wing-tsit Chan (1967), p. 5. Consult also Wing-tsit Chan (1963), pp. 699, 717–718. On the various schemes of ordering the five elements, consult Needham (1956), 2:253–261; Parker (1888a), pp. 498–499; Forke (1925), pp. 227–243, 262–272, 285–294.

3. See Frederick Mote in Buxbaum and Mote (1972); also Mote (1971), pp. 17–28. Cf. Girardot (1976). On Chinese mythology generally, consult Derk Bodde in S. N. Kramer (1961).

4. See Bodde (1942). Cf. Schneidau (1976) on the place of God in the Western tradition.

5. Wing-tsit Chan in de Bary (1975), pp. 561, 563.

6. See Plaks (1977a), esp. pp. 35 ff.; also the full discussion in Forke (1925), esp. pp. 163–223.

7. Cited in Wing-tsit Chan (1963), p. 140. On *yin* and *yang* "controlling" situations, see Needham (1956), 2:288–289.

8. Mai-mai Sze (1959), p. 73; Forke (1925), pp. 207–209, 214–215.

9. Toda (1963), part 3.

10. See Sivin (1966) and Needham (1965). Sometimes the Chinese used the mythical reign of the Yellow Emperor (accession in 2697 B.C.) as a starting point. See, for example, the cover date of *LIPC*. On "timeliness" in the classical literature, consult Legge (1893–1895), *Lun-yü*, p. 140; *Chung-yung*, p. 427; *Meng-tzu*, p. 371.

11. See Fung Yu-lan (1952), 2:469–474; also Wing-tsit Chan (1963), p. 487. For the persistence of Shao Yung's construct into late Ch'ing times, consult Wang Erh-min (1977), pp. 406 ff.

12. See M. Wright (1967), chapter 4.

13. Cited by Arthur Wright in Gottschalk (1963), p. 38; see also Arthur Wright in Skinner (1977), p. 73; Metzger (1977), pp. 123, 187.

14. The comparison can be seen in Han Yu-shan (1955), pp. 196–203. Charles Hucker in Fairbank (1957) discusses the problems of bureaucratic factionalism and eunuch abuse that plagued the late Ming period. The emphasis on foreign relations in the *Ch'ing-shih kao* can be attributed primarily to the unprecedented Western impact of the nineteenth century.

15. See Fairbank (1968).

16. See especially the articles by Mark Mancall, Hae-jong Chun, Robert Sakai, Ta-tuan Ch'en, and Truong Buu Lam in ibid.

17. John Fairbank in Fairbank (1968), pp. 257–275; also R. J. Smith (1975).

18. Cited by Benjamin Schwartz in Fairbank (1968), p. 280.

19. See R. J. Smith (1975).

20. Benjamin Schwartz in Fairbank (1968), pp. 277–278.

21. Ho Ping-ti (1967), p. 193; Kessler (1976), p. 169.

22. For useful overviews of Ch'ing thought in English, consult Chang Hao (1971), chapter 1; also Ropp (1981), pp. 39–48; Philip Kuhn and Susan Mann Jones in Fairbank (1978); Immanuel Hsü (1959); and Yü Ying-shih (1975). The standard works in Chinese include Ch'ien Mu (1937); Lu Pao-ch'ien (1978); Wang Erh-min (1976 and 1977). A stimulating and controversial interpretation of neo-Confucianism has been offered by Metzger (1977); see Note 49 below.

23. See Han-yin Ch'en Shen (1967). For detail on the many creative thinkers of the Ch'ing period, see the sources cited in Note 22 above; also the several excellent articles on Ch'ing intellectual history that have appeared over the past years in *CSWT*.

24. See the sources cited in Chapter 3 of this book, Note 30. Metzger (1977), pp. 13–15, 50 ff. develops the idea of a neo-Confucian "grammar" shared widely among the Chinese elite in traditional times.

25. See Yü Ying-shih (1975); W. T. de Bary in de Bary (1975), p. 11.

26. Frederick Mote in Buxbaum and Mote (1972), p. 15; Legge (1893–1895), *Lun-yü*, p. 146; *Ta-hsüeh*, p. 364.

27. Fung Yu-lan (1948), p. 1.

28. Cheng Chung-ying (1973), esp. p. 97. See also Plaks (1977a), pp. 39 ff.

29. See Hsu Dau-lin (1970–1971) on the importance of the Five Relationships in late imperial times and the extreme measures sometimes taken by the state to reinforce them; also Note 34 below.

30. Tung cited in Fung Yu-lan (1948), pp. 196–197; Mencius' statement in Legge (1893–1895), *Meng-tzu*, p. 346; R. Wilhelm (1967), p. 540.

31. Legge (1893–1895), *Meng-tzu*, p. 264–265, 309; *Ta-hsüeh*, p. 370; Wei Cheng-t'ung (1981), p. 54.

32. Wing-tsit Chan (1955), pp. 297–298, 305.

33. Wing-tsit Chan (1955), p. 300; Legge (1893–1895), *Lun-yü*, p. 194.

34. Legge (1893–1895), *Meng-tzu*, pp. 251–252. On the correlation between these relationships and various kinds of ritual, consult *HCCSWP*, 54:1a, cited in R. J. Smith (1981).

35. Legge (1893–1895), *Ta-hsüeh*, pp. 371–379; *Chung-yung*, pp. 408–409.

36. Note the essay by Lu Lung-chi in *HCCSWP*, 68:1a–b, discussed in R. J. Smith (1981). See also Watt (1972), pp. 96–97; Spence (1978), p. 142.

37. The *Li-chi* quotation is from Chai and Chai (1967), 2:375, 390; *HCCSWP*, 54:5a, 10a, cited in R. J. Smith (1981).

38. Legge (1893–1895), *Meng-tzu*, p. 356; *Lun-yü*, p. 250; *Ta-hsüeh*, p. 422. See also Note 39 below.

39. R. J. Smith (1981) discusses these and other sources, such as the *CLCC*, *CLTC*, *LIPC*, and the *CLTSCC*.

40. Legge (1893–1895), *Meng-tzu*, pp. 150–151, 195, 241, 313–314; Chai and Chai (1967), 1:63, 2:92 ff., 257–260. See also Legge (1893–1895), *Lun-yü*, pp. 143, 147, 161, 169, 193, 208, 211, 250, 323, 354.

41. Legge (1893–1895), *Lun-yü*, p. 299; *Meng-tzu*, p. 307.

42. For a general interpretation of *i*, see Cheng Chung-ying (1972); see also Legge (1893–1985), *Meng-tzu*, pp. 202, 251, 302, 313, 402, 456, 485, 493; *Lun-yü*, pp. 154, 170, 254, 256, 259, 265, 299, 331.

43. Legge (1893–1895), *Lun-yü*, p. 318. See also Legge (1893–1895), *Meng-tzu*, pp. 204–205, 402, 459; *Lun-yü*, pp. 151, 204–205, 212, 225, 260, 313–314.

44. Legge (1893–1895), *Chung-yung*, pp. 395, 412–419. See also Legge (1893–1895), *Lun-yü*, pp. 139, 141, 153, 202, 224, 256, 265, 267, 295–296, 319, 331; *Meng-tzu*, p. 303.

45. Legge (1893–1895), *Ta-hsüeh*, pp. 257–259.

46. See Wing-tsit Chan (1963), pp. 19, 84–85, 659, 707–708; also the examples in de Bary and Bloom (1979), Julia Ching (1976), Tu Wei-ming (1976), and the sources cited in Notes 22 and 23 above.

47. See *TSCC*, *tien* 22; Chang Hao (1971), pp. 17, 85, 273–274, 292 ff.; Yü Ying-shih (1975), pp. 105, 109, 115; also Metzger (1977), pp. 24, 63, 89, 114, 123–125, 146, 205–206, and Wei Cheng-t'ung (1981), p. 140–141 on "efficacious moral efforts," (*kung-fu*).

48. Legge (1893–1895), *Lun-yü*, pp. 146–147; also pp. 179, 251, 253, 259, 271, 273, 274, 279, 292; *Meng-tzu*, pp. 185, 265, 455, 458–459; *Chung-yung*, pp. 388, 428.

49. Legge (1893–1895), *Chung-yung*, pp. 383–384, 386, 388, 390, 391, 393, 395–396; *Meng-tzu*, p. 185, 266. Metzger (1977) documents the tension between neo-Confucian ethical demands and human shortcomings, although some scholars feel he has overemphasized this Confucian "predicament." See the symposium on Metzger's book in *JAS* 39, 2 (February 1980), especially the essay by Chang Hao.

50. Chu Hsi cited in Fung Yu-lan (1948), p. 301; Legge (1893–1895), *Lun-yü*, p. 318; *Meng-tzu*, p. 465. On Hsün-tzu, see Wing-tsit Chan (1963), pp. 115 ff., esp. pp. 128–135.

51. Cited in Wing-tsit Chan (1963), pp. 540–541.

52. Cited in Ibid., p. 714. See also Cheng Chung-ying (1971a), pp. 46 ff.; Metzger (1977), pp. 108–113.

53. Bodde (1955), p. 234; see also Gedalecia (1974); Forke (1925), pp. 202–207; Wang Erh-min (1976), pp. 51–71.

54. For various applications of the *t'i-yung* paradigm, see C. K. Yang in Nivison and Wright (1959), pp. 142–143; Wing-tsit Chan (1963), pp. 14, 141, 159, 267, 323, 344, 358, 368–369, 401, 403–404, 414–415; Fung Yu-lan (1952), 2:363, 366, 369, 375, 619.

55. See Fung Yu-lan (1952), 1:31.

56. Legge (1893–1895), *Meng-tzu*, p. 357. See also Julia Ching (1976), p. 357; Needham (1956), 2:562–564; Legge (1893–1895), *Chung-yung*, p. 383.

57. Legge (1893–1895), *Chung-yung*, p. 416; *Meng-tzu*, pp. 119, 208–209, 359, 362, 448; R. Wilhelm (1967), pp. 295 and 351.

58. Cited by Hellmut Wilhelm in Jansen (1969), p. 300. On *ming*, see also C. K. Yang (1961), pp. 247–253, 257–268, 272–274.

59. See the stimulating discussion in Levenson (1964).

60. Wing-tsit Chan (1963), pp. 136–210 provides an excellent sample of Taoist writings.

61. Cited in ibid., pp. 141–166.

62. Ibid., p. 177–178.

63. Ibid., p. 148–149.

64. Wing-tsit Chan (1967), p. 274. See also Spence (1975), p. 97.

65. W. T. de Bary in de Bary (1975), pp. 10, 94.

CHAPTER 7. RELIGION

1. Maspero is cited in Thompson (1979), p. 55; Maurice Freedman in Wolf (1974), p. 37; see also pp. 20, 39–40.

2. Arthur Wolf in Wolf (1974), p. 145.

3. See the discussion in R. J. Smith (1981).

4. Stephen Feuchtwang in Skinner (1977), p. 607.

5. Ibid.; also Hsiao Kung-ch'üan (1960), pp. 221–229; E. T. Williams (1913); de Groot (1912), pp. 103–120; Wills (1979). On the calendar, see *TCHT* (1911), 80:1a–4a.

6. Discussed in R. J. Smith (1981); see also Chai and Chai (1967), 2:219–220.

7. Stephen Feuchtwang in Skinner (1977), pp. 591–593.

8. See E. T. Williams (1913); Blodget (1899); and Joseph Edkins in Thompson (1973), pp. 130–138.

9. See Meyer (1976), pp. 74–83, 112 ff. Meyer indicates, pp. 38 ff., that the key to understanding all expressions of cosmic sacrality in Peking is *yin-yang*/five elements philosophy. See also Ropp (1981), p. 154.

10. See Feuchtwang in Skinner (1977); also the sources cited in Note 5.

11. See Note 5 above. Ch'ü T'ung-tsu (1962), pp. 164–165, enumerates the sacrifices to be undertaken by each district magistrate.

12. Stephen Feuchtwang in Skinner (1977), p. 601. See also Hsiao Kung-ch'üan (1960), pp. 222 and 630, note 197.

13. C. K. Yang (1961), pp. 156–157.

14. Cited in Spence (1978), pp. 49–50.

15. See, for example, Johnston (1910), pp. 364–374; Gray (1878), 1:118–119. Instances of the Chinese cursing their gods are not uncommon. See A. Smith (1899), p. 160.

16. See R. J. Smith (1981); Stephen Feuchtwang in Skinner (1977).

17. C. K. Yang (1961), pp. 98–99. For a good general discussion of the T'u-ti kung, consult Arthur Wolf in Wolf (1974), pp. 134–135.

18. On the two types of deities, consult Arthur Wolf in Wolf (1974); see Thompson (1973), pp. 196–201 on the cult of Ma-tsu.

19. Ch'ü T'ung-tsu (1962), p. 165; Wang Hui-tsu's experiences are related in Balazs (1965), pp. 63–64. For another instance of public pressure on local officials, consult Johnston (1910), pp. 134–135.

20. Kristin Yü Greenblatt in de Bary (1975), pp. 131–132.

21. See C. K. Yang (1961), p. 281. For an overview of Buddhism in the Ch'ing, consult Kenneth Ch'en (1964), chapter 16.

22. Farquhar (1978), p. 33.

23. Ibid.

24. Wing-tsit Chan (1967), p. 283.

25. See Immanuel Hsü (1959), pp. 115–117.

26. Nivison (1966), pp. 76, 126–127.

27. Cited by Hui-chen Wang Liu in Nivison and Wright (1959), pp. 71–72.

28. Fung Yu-lan (1952), 2:237–238.

29. See Wing-tsit Chan (1969), pp. 438 ff.; de Bary (1964), 1:292.

30. Wing-tsit Chan (1963), pp. 398–400.

31. Ibid., p. 407, 413–414.

32. A. Wright (1968), p. 92; de Bary (1964), 1:347; Fung Yu-lan (1952), 2:390 ff.

33. See E. Zürcher in Dawson (1964), pp. 73–79.

34. See, for example, Wieger (1913), pp. 345–391, 397–398; also Bauer (1976), pp. 159–161.

35. See Reichelt (1934), pp. 174–199.

36. Welch (1967), pp. 398 ff.

37. Wing-tsit Chan (1969), p. 419.

38. See Saso (1978), pp. 52 ff.; also Welch and Seidel (1979), esp. 229 ff.

39. Saso (1978), pp. 5–7, 52 ff.

40. Ibid.; see also Wieger (1913), p. 322.

41. Wong and Wu (1936), esp. p. 19.

42. See Tadao Sakai in de Bary (1970), pp. 341–362.

43. Kenneth Ch'en (1964), pp. 436–439; Wing-tsit Chan (1969), p. 418; Wieger (1913), p. 322.

44. C. K. Yang (1961), p. 25.

45. Ibid., pp. 7–10.

46. Ibid., pp. 10–15.

47. See Daniel Overmyer in Reynolds and Ludwig (1980); also Plopper (1926), pp. 60 ff.; Ropp (1981), pp. 33–34.
48. The popular proverb is cited in Plopper (1926), p. 78.
49. See de Groot (1912), pp. 4–28.
50. Daniel Overmyer in Reynolds and Ludwig (1980), p. 164, citing Michael Saso.
51. See de Groot (1912), pp. 35–59; Macgowan (1912), chapter 9; Welch and Seidel (1979), pp. 195 ff.; Ropp (1981), chapter 4.
52. Doré (1914–1933), 3:iii–vi.
53. See Maurice Freedman in Skinner (1979), pp. 189–211, 284–288, 296–312, esp. 313–339; also R. J. Smith (1981). Cf. Ahern (1973), pp. 175 ff.
54. Cited in Thompson (1979), pp. 22–23.
55. See Meyer (1978), pp. 148–155.
56. These points are discussed at some length in R. J. Smith (1981). For evidence concerning the pervasiveness of *feng-shui* beliefs and practices in Ch'ing China, consult C. K. Yang (1961), pp. 263–265; Johnston (1910), p. 119; Nevius (1869), p. 169 ff.; Macgowan (1912), pp. 107 ff.
57. See R. J. Smith (1981).
58. See Maurice Freedman in Skinner (1979), pp. 296–312. There were, of course, many different conceptions of the soul, afterlife, and reincarnation.
59. See Thompson (1979), chapter 3. The particular requirements of mourning and sacrifice were specified at length in ritual handbooks such as the *CLCC, CLTC, CLTSCC,* and *LIPC,* as well as scholarly works and official publications such as the *WHL, LPTL,* and *TCHT.* See also Chapter 10, Note 37.
60. C. K. Yang (1961), pp. 40–43, 52–53; Baker (1979), chapter 4. Some Chinese homes had five-character tablets (*wu-tzu p'ai*)—inscribed with the characters for Heaven, Earth, the Sovereign, Parents, and Teachers—instead of ancestral tablets. See *HCCSWP,* 66:10b–11a; Doré (1914–1933), 4:417 ff. Devotions to such tablets generally approximated those in conventional ancestral sacrifices. Bimonthly devotions, which coincided with lunar phases and involved incense burning, bowing, and the offering of food and prayers, were common to many forms of Chinese ritual—secular and sacred, orthodox and heterodox. See R. J. Smith (1981).
61. C. K. Yang in Fairbank (1957), p. 276.
62. Ibid., p. 277. See also Welch (1967), pp. 181–185; see also R. J. Smith (1978a), p. 44.
63. Discussed in R. J. Smith (1981). Consult also Daniel Overmyer in Reynolds and Ludwig (1980); Ropp (1981), pp. 153–160.
64. R. J. Smith (1981). Two excellent studies of the heterodox tradition are Overmyer (1976) and Naquin (1976). See also George Wong (1962) and the various papers of the Conference on Orthodoxy and Heterodoxy in Late Imperial China (Montecito, California, August, 1981).
65. For an overview of these rebellions, consult M. Wright (1967), chapter 6.
66. See, for example, Vincent Shih (1967), pp. 188, 192, 214–226, 232, 243; also P. Kuhn (1977) and R. J. Smith (1981).
67. See Thompson (1981), esp. pp. 116–119; cf. Meyer (1976), pp. 38–41 and especially p. 201–202. Consult also Note 60 above.

CHAPTER 8. ART

1. Sullivan (1977), p. 230. On Chinese art and "cultural integrity," consult Thompson (1980). The holdings of the vast palace collection of the Ch'ing emperors (now housed in Taiwan) are discussed in Na Chih-liang (1980), esp. pp. 7–12.
2. On An Ch'i and Tuan Fang, consult Hummel (1943–1944), pp. 11–13 and 780–782.
3. See especially Plaks (1977a) and Mungello (1969); also Wei Cheng-t'ung (1981), pp. 155 ff.; T'ang Chün-i (1981), pp. 258–262 and 291 ff.
4. Vincent Shih (1959), pp. 8–9; Mungello (1969), p. 379.

5. Michael Sullivan in Dawson (1964), p. 178. See also T'ang Chün-i (1981), pp. 258–262; Chai and Chai (1967), 2:98–100; Wei Cheng-t'ung (1981), esp. pp. 157–158, 164; A. S. Cua (1979).

6. Frederick Mote in Murck (1976), p. 6.

7. See the essays by Tu Wei-ming and Wen Fong in Murck (1976).

8. Wen Fong in Murck (1976), p. 93.

9. Michael Sullivan in Dawson (1964), p. 206; Van Gulik (1958), pp. 59–60.

10. Michael Sullivan in Dawson (1964), pp. 207–210.

11. See Christian Murck, Frederick Mote, and James J. Y. Liu in Murck (1976), esp. pp. 17–18; also Mungello (1969); B. March (1935); Notes 3 and 5 above.

12. For some works on Chinese symbolism, consult Schuyler Cammann in A. Wright (1953); C.A.S. Williams (1941); Yetts (1912); Goodall (1979); Burling and Burling (1953), chapter 15; Mailey (1980). On popular art in China, consult Yu-ho Ecke Tseng (1977); also Thompson (1980); Eberhard (1971), pp. 17 ff.

13. The preceding discussion is based primarily on the sources cited in Note 12 above. It should be remembered, however, that the discussion is greatly simplified both in the number of animal symbols mentioned and in the variety of animals in each category. There were, for example, many different kinds of dragons, and a great number of mythical beasts other than the so-called Four Spiritual Animals.

14. See the sources cited in Note 12; also the Buddhist gestures discussed in Thompson (1973), pp. 97 ff.

15. Sullivan (1977), p. 252; Liu I-cheng (1964), 3:88–98.

16. W. Watson (1962), p. 15; David (1971), p. 12.

17. On Ch'en and Liu, consult Hummel (1943–1944), pp. 520–521.

18. Ch'ing period works on ritual, from the *WHL* and *CCYWL* to the Li-pu section of the *TCHT*, indicate an extraordinary continuity in the use of Shang and Chou style vessels and implements in Ch'ing official and domestic ceremonies. See also E. T. Williams (1913) and Note 19 below.

19. On the types of ancient bronze vessels and their decorative features, consult Wen Fong (1980), esp. pp. 30–31.

20. Smolen (1980). On forgeries, consult Van Gulik (1958), pp. 50, 77, n. 21; Hummel (1943–1944), pp. 608–609.

21. Van Gulik (1958), pp. 50, 76, n. 20; Michael Sullivan in Dawson (1964), p. 180.

22. Hansford (1950), p. 31. Cf. Chai and Chai (1967), 2:464.

23. Hansford (1969), p. 24.

24. Ibid., p. 16.

25. Jenyns (1965), p. 2.

26. Van Gulik (1958), p. 51; Jenyns (1965), pp. 70, 72 ff.

27. Legeza (1980).

28. Sullivan (1977), pp. 247–249.

29. See Hansford (1961), pp. 74–75.

30. Wei Cheng-t'ung (1981), pp. 172–173.

31. See Keswick (1978); also Siren (1949) and Juliano (1981), pp. 77–90. On the Sui-yüan, consult Waley (1970), pp. 47–48, 69–70.

32. Cited in Keswick (1978), p. 60.

33. On Prospect Garden as a social and literary focus, consult Plaks (1976), pp. 146 ff. See also Wei Cheng-t'ung (1981), pp. 172–173; Keswick (1978), pp. 195–197. Cf. Meyer (1975) on the geometric symmetry and symbolism of Peking.

34. Keswick (1978), pp. 196–197.

35. Wing-tsit Chan in Inn and Lee (1940), esp. pp. 31–32. See also Lu Yü-chün in Wu Ching-hsiung et al. (1967), esp. pp. 455–460; Lin Yutang (1935), pp. 265, 290, 317.

36. A. March (1968).

37. Keswick (1978), pp. 12–14. See also T'ang Chün-i (1981), pp. 304–305; Inn and Lee (1940), pp. 33–34. On the household module, see also Emily Ahern in Wilson (1979), pp. 155 ff.; Wang Sung-hsin in Wolf (1974), pp. 183 ff.

38. Cited in Keswick (1978), pp. 198–199.

39. David (1971), p. 29; Eberhard (1971), pp. 15 ff.; Huang Chün-pi in Wu Ching-hsiung et al. (1967), esp. 396–398.
40. Rowley (1970), pp. 9–10, 20; Beurdeley et al. (1969).
41. David (1971), pp. 14–15. See also James Cahill in A. Wright (1960a), pp. 117–118, 130; Wei Cheng-t'ung (1981), pp. 158–160.
42. James Cahill in A. Wright (1960a), pp. 117–118. See also Wei Cheng-t'ung (1981), pp. 158–160.
43. Siren (1937), pp. 195, 209. See also Mungello (1969); Wen Fong (1971); Wei Cheng-t'ung (1981), pp. 159–160.
44. Siren (1937), p. 215.
45. Ibid., p. 209.
46. David (1971), pp. 14–15.
47. Mai-mai Sze (1959), pp. 115, 130–131, 133–153. See also Rowley (1970) and Silbergeld (1981).
48. Fu and Fu (1973), p. 12; Siren (1937), p. 217.
49. Loehr (1970), pp. 35–36; Lin Yutang (1967), p. 198.
50. Lin Yutang (1967), p. 200. See also Loehr (1970), p. 36; Tu Wei-ming in Murck (1976), pp. 10–15; Van Gulik (1958), pp. 34–40.
51. Loehr (1970), p. 36. On lines on transmission, see Wen Fong (1971); also Alexander Soper, Richard Barnhart, and others in Murck (1976).
52. Siren (1937), p. 210.
53. Quoted in Lin Yutang (1967), p. 165. See also Siren (1937), pp. 206–207.
54. Wen Fong (1971), p. 283; Siren (1937), pp. 208–210.
55. Lin Yutang (1967), p. 169.
56. Ibid., pp. 175–176.
57. Mai-mai Sze (1959), pp. 157, 325–328; Rowley (1970), pp. 8, 13–14, 17, 42, 47, 51–55, 93, 81. See also T'ang Chün-i (1981), pp. 307–308.
58. Mungello (1969), esp. pp. 381–382.
59. Mai-mai Sze (1959), p. 107. See also Lin Yutang (1967), pp. 39–42, 69–80; Rowley (1970), pp. 64–67; Wen Fong (1971), pp. 282–283.
60. See Kao Yu-kung and Mei Tsu-lin in Murck (1976), p. 132; also Andrew Plaks in Plaks (1977), p. 338.
61. See Wai-kam Ho in Murck (1976); Sullivan (1979), pp. 131–134 and passim; Rosenzweig (1974–1975).
62. Mai-mai Sze (1959), p. 5; see also Sullivan (1977), pp. 238–244; Cahill (1982); Huang Chün-pi in Wu Ching-hsiung et al. (1967), pp. 396–399.
63. Sullivan (1977), pp. 216–219, 233–236.
64. Cited in Sullivan (1979), p. 142.
65. Van Gulik (1958), p. 34.
66. Sullivan (1979), pp. 15–17, 30 ff.; Kahn (1971), p. 136.
67. David (1971), p. 201. See also Chiang Yee (1973), pp. 225–239.
68. Chiang Yee (1973).
69. On these individuals, consult Hummel (1943–1944), pp. 25–26, 610–611, 715–716.
70. Chiang Yee (1973), chapter 1; Lin Yutang (1935), pp. 290–297. See also Tung Tso-pin in Wu Ching-hsiung et al. (1967), esp. p. 80.

CHAPTER 9. LITERATURE

1. Teng and Biggerstaff (1971), p. 95.
2. Ibid., pp. 95–96.
3. See Goodrich (1935), esp. pp. 30 ff.
4. Teng and Biggerstaff (1971), pp. 19–20; see also William Hung (1939).
5. A list of the types of works in each section and subsection may be found in Wieger (1927), pp. 759–766. For a convenient breakdown of Ch'ing literature according to the four traditional categories, consult Wylie (1867), a kind of *Ssu-k'u ch'üan-shu tsung-mu t'i-yao* in miniature.

6. Hucker (1975), pp. 386–387; see also Wylie (1867), pp. 234 ff. On the Ch'ien-lung emperor's pedestrian literary efforts, consult Kahn (1971), chapter 7.

7. See Hanan (1981), p. 15.

8. James J. Y. Liu (1975), pp. 44, 96–97. See also P'an Chung-kuei in Wu Ching-hsiung et al. (1967), esp. pp. 307–314.

9. James J. Y. Liu (1975), p. 45. See also Wei Cheng-t'ung (1981), pp. 219–225.

10. James J. Y. Liu (1975), p. 66.

11. Ibid., p. 115, 135.

12. Ibid., p. 99–105; see also P'an Chung-kuei in Wu Ching-hsiung et al. (1967), 314 ff., esp. 321–324.

13. James J. Y. Liu (1975), pp. 21, 26–27, 82, 88, 104.

14. Legge (1893–1895), *Lun-yü*, p. 211. See also Ch'en Shih-hsiang in Birch (1974); Kao Yu-kung and Mei Tsu-lin in Murck (1976), p. 131; Chia-ying Yeh Chao in Rickett (1978), p. 151; Note 15 below.

15. Wei Cheng-t'ung (1981), p. 187; T'ang Chün-i (1981), pp. 319 ff.; Kao Ming in Wu Ching-hsiung et al. (1967). See also Wai-lim Yip (1976), pp. 1–22.

16. James J. Y. Liu (1966), p. 80.

17. Liu and Lo (1975), pp. 478–479. On *hui-wen*, see Wai-lim Yip (1976), p. 3; also Vincent Shih (1959), pp. 31 ff.

18. Hawkes (1973 and 1977), 2:459.

19. James J. Y. Liu (1966), pp. 149–150.

20. Ibid., pp. 65–69; Spence (1975), p. 117.

21. James J. Y. Liu (1966), pp. 70–76; Liu and Lo (1975), p. 491.

22. Siu-kit Wong in Rickett (1978), pp. 130–131 and 140.

23. Liu and Lo (1975), p. 480.

24. Shirleen Wong (1975), p. 71; James J. Y. Liu (1966), p. 75; Wei Cheng-t'ung (1981), pp. 201–208; Kao Ming in Wu Ching-hsiung et al. (1967); Waley (1970).

25. Liu and Lo (1975), p. 487.

26. Sullivan (1979), pp. 15–17.

27. See Hanan (1981), pp. 4–14. On literacy, see Rawski (1978), esp. p. 23; cf. Barbara Ward in Jain (1977), p. 189.

28. Spence (1968), p. 5. See also the sources cited in Note 27 above.

29. Tadeo Sakai in de Bary (1970), pp. 341–362. See also Eberhard, (1967), esp. pp. 117–125. For translations of such works, see Wieger (1913), pp. 160–341, esp. 263–317.

30. On the spread of drama in the Ch'ing, see Mackerras (1972); Ward (1979); Barbara Ward in Jain (1977), 190 ff.; Andrew Plaks in Plaks (1977), p. 324.

31. James J. Y. Liu (1979), p. 86. See also Wei Cheng-t'ung (1981), pp. 160–161.

32. Ch'i Ju-shan in Wu Ching-hsiung et al. (1967).

33. James J. Y. Liu (1979), pp. 109–110. See also Struve (1977).

34. Plaks (1976, 1977, 1977a). Recent Western works on the Chinese novel include Ropp (1981) and Hegel (1981).

35. Plaks (1977a), p. 42.

36. C. T. Hsia (1968); Robert Ruhlmann in A. Wright (1964), pp. 127 ff.; Hanan (1981), p. 20; Andrew Plaks in Plaks (1977), pp. 340–343.

37. See Plaks (1976), pp. 61–71; Winston Yang et al. (1978), p. 91; Wei Cheng-t'ung (1981), p. 213. Presumably, Chinese fictional characterization also reflects traditional attitudes toward the relationship between the individual and society.

38. See Andrew Plaks in Plaks (1977), p. 349; Wei Cheng-t'ung (1981), pp. 213–214; T'ang Chün-i (1981), pp. 349–361; Hanan (1981), p. 27.

39. See C. T. Hsia (1968); Hanan (1981), p. 27; Miller (1975), p. 264; Robert Ruhlmann in A. Wright (1964), p. 126. Ropp (1981) attributes the rise of social criticism in Ch'ing novels to changes such as the rise of literacy and the increasing importance of wealth as a determinant of status in Chinese society.

40. See Wei Cheng-t'ung (1981), pp. 211–218; also the literature cited in James J. Y. Liu (1979); Winston Yang et al. (1978); Ropp (1981); Hegel (1981); and Hanan (1981). Like Chinese poems, Chinese novels unavoidably lose a great deal in translation.

41. Among the various translations of *San-kuo chih yen-i*, perhaps the best (though abridged) is Roberts (1976).

42. The most recent translation is Shi and Luo (1981).

43. *Chin P'ing Mei*, the title of which is taken from the names of three characters in the novel, has been translated by Egerton (1939).

44. The only available English translation of the novel to date is F. Kuhn (1963).

45. The standard popular translation is Waley (1944). A more complete translation is by Anthony Yu (1977, 1978, and 1980).

46. See Lin Tai-yi (1966) for an abridged translation; also the analysis of the novel by Brandauer (1977).

47. See Yang and Yang (1957); also Ropp (1981), chapter 6.

48. See Shadick (1952); Liu Shih-shun (1975); Dloezelova-Velingerova (1980).

49. Fang Chao-ying cited in Hummel (1943–1944), p. 738. The standard abridged translation is by Wang Chi-chen (1958). A fuller version, though still somewhat abridged, is by Yang and Yang (1978). See also Hawkes (1973 and 1977). The translation by Hawkes captures more of the nuances of the original than other renderings, including different styles of speech and exquisite detail.

50. See Andrew Plaks in Plaks (1977), pp. 281–282; Brandauer (1977).

51. Miller (1975), p. 56.

52. Andrew Plaks in Plaks (1977), pp. 334–339, esp. 338.

53. Hawkes (1973 and 1977), 2:334.

54. For a discussion of this problem, see Ropp (1981).

CHAPTER 10. SOCIAL ACTIVITIES

1. Cited in Baker (1979), p. 39; see also A. Smith (1899), p. 191; Walshe (1906), pp. 212–213.

2. Buck (1937), pp. 462 ff.; R. J. Smith (1981); Hayes (1981).

3. On divination, consult Doré (1914–1933), vol. 4, passim; Nevius (1869), pp. 179 ff.; Doolittle (1865), 2:331 ff. On almanacs, see Parker (1888 and 1888a); also Doré (1904–1933), 4:381 ff.; Johnston (1910), p. 295; Walshe (1906), pp. 186 ff.

4. R. J. Smith (1981). Ebrey (1981), pp. 187–188 provides an illuminating excerpt from a late Ch'ing almanac.

5. See, for example, the discussion in Walshe (1906), pp. 192 ff., esp. p. 202.

6. On naming, see Baker (1979), pp. 28–29.

7. Cited in Ebrey (1981), p. 219. On infanticide, see also Wolf and Huang (1980), pp. 230–233; Baker (1979), pp. 5–8.

8. The story comes from the *Erh-shih-ssu hsiao*—see Note 11 below.

9. See Wolf and Huang (1980), esp. chapters 8, 15, 17, and 18; also Wieger (1913), pp. 513–521.

10. Chai and Chai (1967), 1:476–479; *TSCC, tien* 15. The six major stages are discussed at length in M. Levy (1949).

11. On child rearing in the late Ch'ing period, see, for example, Doolittle (1865), 1:113 ff. Cf. modern analyses of traditional child-rearing practices, such as those by Metzger (1977), and others. For a discussion of the *Erh-shih-ssu hsiao* and its effects, consult Doolittle (1865), 1:452–459.

12. Ropp (1976); Ropp (1981), chapter 4; A. Smith (1899), p. 262. On classical sanction for the isolation of women, see Chai and Chai (1967), 1:479. For different housing arrangements, consult the sources cited in this book, Chapter 8, Note 37.

13. See R. J. Smith (1981) and esp. Furth (1981). Furth emphasizes the sacred ritual obligations embodied in family instructions, even though such instructions often did not discuss ritual practices in detail. For a translation of the *Chih-chia ke-yen*, consult Wieger (1913), pp. 235–240.

14. On the dependency orientation of Chinese youths, consult Metzger (1977), pp. 19–20; p. 239, n. 7; p. 241, n. 20. See also Note 15 below.

15. Pye (1981), p. 137. See also Note 14 above.

16. Chai and Chai (1967), 2:428–434; Baker (1979), pp. 32–33, 42–43, 116–117.

17. See Buxbaum and Mote (1972); also Ebrey (1981), pp. 235–236.

18. See Wolf and Huang (1980), chapter 21, esp. p. 335.

19. On concubinage, see David Buxbaum in Buxbaum and Mote (1972), esp. pp. 216–217; also Baker (1979), pp. 35–36.

20. For an overview based on Chinese sources, see R. J. Smith (1981); see also the accounts in Doolittle (1865), 1:65 ff., esp. 97; Gray (1878), 1:191–210; Johnston (1910), pp. 203–215, 232–237; A. Smith (1899), pp. 179–191, 248–251; Wieger (1913), p. 451 ff.; Walshe (1906), p. 108 ff.; S. W. Williams (1883), 1:785–791. For the surprisingly similar rituals of marriage *resistance*, consult Marjorie Topley in Wolf (1978).

21. There were, of course, a number of different terms and classifications for the basic ceremonies connected with marriage. See, for example, *WHL*, 13:1a; *CLTC*, p. 106. For an illuminating analysis of marriage symbolism, consult Maurice Freedman in Skinner (1979), pp. 266–268.

22. As in so much of Chinese ritual life, status distinctions were carefully preserved in the ceremonies of marriage. See, for example, Gray (1878), 1:192–198; cf. *WHL*, *chüan* 13.

23. See the sources cited in Note 20. Cf. *WHL*, 13:1a–10b; *CLTC*, pp. 106–171; *CLTSCC*, 1:27b–36b. On "shares," see A. Smith (1899), pp. 179 ff.

24. See, for example, Baker (1979), pp. 46–47, 125 ff. Sometime after the marriage transfer (usually three days) the wife worshipped her husband's ancestors in a ceremony known as *san-yüeh miao-chien*—yet another indication of her ritual rebirth in the home of her husband. According to the five degrees of mourning, a married woman would mourn for her husband and his parents in the first degree (*chan-ts'ui*) and her own parents only in the second degree (*tzu-ts'ui*). See R. J. Smith (1981).

25. See the poignant case study related in Spence (1978). On divorce and its limitations, consult Wolf and Huang (1980), chapter 13; Baker (1979), pp. 129–130.

26. See Ropp (1981), pp. 124, 138–140, 145–146, 148.

27. On chastity, see ibid., pp. 124–127, 130–133. For evidence of affection and devotion in Chinese marriages, see ibid., pp. 146–147; Johnston (1910), pp. 219, 243–245; Macgowan (1912), pp. 249, 255–256.

28. See Van Gulik (1961).

29. On the puritanical character of the Ch'ing period, consult ibid., pp. 123, 264–265, 285–287, 335; Ropp (1981), pp. 48 and 120. Predictably, the Ch'ing government tried to outlaw sex handbooks, although with only partial success. For indications of the ritual dimension of Chinese sexual life, consult Legge (1893–1895), *Meng-tzu*, p. 422; Han Suyin (1965), p. 52.

30. See H. Levy (1966); also Ropp (1981), pp. 122, 126. In the early Ch'ing, the K'ang-hsi emperor tried unsuccessfully to outlaw footbinding among the Chinese; and later in the Ch'ing period, even the long-standing prohibition against footbinding among the Manchus began to break down.

31. Van Gulik (1961) thoroughly documents the persistent notion of sex as a form of physical therapy in traditional China, as well as the prevalence of homosexuality throughout the imperial era. Several Ch'ing novels give attention to the themes of homosexuality or bisexuality, including *Ju-lin wai-shih* and *Hung-lou meng*. See also Wang Shu-nan (1935), esp. pp. 318–320.

32. See, for example, Doolittle (1865), 1:33, 175–176, 181 and esp. 2:322–323. Longevity was particularly the obsession of the Ch'ing emperors and empresses, as the symbolism of both the Forbidden City and the Summer Palace suggests. See, for instance, Juliano (1981), pp. 44–76.

33. *TSCC, tien* 17. See also the Chinese index (appendix), p. 35 in the same source. For a discussion of medical practice in the Ch'ing period, consult Wong and Wu (1936), chapter 22; also Macgowan (1912), chapter 14. The biographies of Hsü and Yeh, among other well-known doctors, may be found in Hummel (1943–1944), pp. 322–324, 902–903.

34. For interesting glimpses of Chinese home life day to day and examples of the tyranny of mothers-in-law, consult Macgowan (1912), chapter 19; S. W. Williams (1883), 1:724 ff.; Doolittle (1865), 1:113 ff.; Johnston (1910), pp. 112 ff., 135 ff.; Nevius (1869), pp.

237 ff. Such foreign observers often remark on the lack of privacy in Chinese homes as compared to Western homes, a contrast also evident today.

35. Hsiao Kung-ch'üan (1960), pp. 205–220. Like so much of Chinese ritual life, the *hsiang-yin chiu* had ancient antecedents and a highly refined symbolism. See Chai and Chai (1967), 2:435 ff. Cf. *WHL*, 3:2a ff.

36. Baker (1979), pp. 31–32, 37; Doolittle (1865), 2:217 ff. Baker, p. 15 emphasizes that the pecking order within the family was based on (1) generation, (2) age, and (3) sex. A more comprehensive system of social subordination can be found in *HCCSWP*, 68:3a, which indicates the superiority of (1) fathers to sons, (2) elder brothers to younger brothers, (3) men to women, (4) older generations to younger generations, and (5) the wise to the stupid.

37. Thompson (1979), p. 50. R. J. Smith (1981) emphasizes the great importance attached to mourning ritual in classics such as the *Li-chi* and *I-li*, as well as ritual handbooks and the *WHL*.

38. Lin Yutang (1935), p. 177.

39. On China's "a-military culture," consult R. J. Smith (1974), pp. 124–125; also Wei Cheng-t'ung (1981), pp. 42–45. On *nao-hsin fang*, see Wieger (1913), pp. 508–509; Doolittle (1865), 1:90; S. W. Williams (1883), 1:788.

40. For examples of traditional Chinese recreation, see S. W. Williams (1883), 1:824–825; Doolittle (1865), 2:283–290; Kulp (1925), chapter 9.

41. See S. W. Williams (1883), 2:104; also Wiant (1965), pp. 140 ff.; Levius (1936), esp. pp. 3, 12, 68–69, 90–92, 190–191; Kaufmann (1976), esp. pp. 96–101. On the link between ritual and music, consult Chai and Chai (1967), 2:92–93, 96, 98–100, 103–104; T'ang Chün-i (1981), esp. pp. 258–262; Wei Cheng-t'ung (1981), pp. 164–166.

42. S. Boorman (1969), chapter 1. Chang Yin-huan (1837–1900) was one of several noted *wei-ch'i* players in the Ch'ing period. See Hummel (1943–1944), p. 63; also pp. 70, 528.

43. Stover (1974), pp. 215–225; Francis L. K. Hsü (1972), p. 176.

44. Nevius (1869), pp. 239–240. On the refinements of social intercourse, see the Chinese sources cited in R. J. Smith (1981); also Walshe (1906), passim, esp. chapters 8, 10, 11, 13–15. Novels such as *Ju-lin wai-shih* and *Hung-lou meng* shed much valuable light on Chinese social practices.

45. Johnston (1910), pp. 170–171.

46. Chang Kwang-chih (1977a), esp. pp. 380–381; A. Smith (1899), pp. 180 ff.

47. See the excellent discussions by Frederick Mote and Jonathon Spence in Chang Kwang-chih (1977a); also Lin Yutang (1935), p. 339.

48. Jonathon Spence in Chang Kwang-chih (1977a), p. 282. See also Chang Kwang-chih (1977a), pp. 17–19, 214–225, 280, 376–380; Nevius (1869), p. 154; Arthur Wolf in Wolf (1974), pp. 176 ff.; Hawkes (1973 and 1977), 1:381.

49. Cited in Chang Kwang-chih (1977a), p. 267. See also Hawkes (1973 and 1977), 2:265; Chang Kwang-chih (1977a), pp. 16–17; 275–277; Ebrey (1981), pp. 163–164; R. J. Smith (1981).

50. Chang Kwang-chih (1977a), p. 48; see also pp. 7–8, 10, 227–234, 272–275.

51. Ibid., pp. 10, 228; also Wong and Wu (1936), pp. 178–179.

52. Wong and Wu (1936), pp. 193–194; Chang Kwang-chih (1977a), pp. 308–341.

53. See Chang Kwang-chih (1977a), p. 278; also Hawkes (1973 and 1977), 2:54, 174, 488; Hummel (1943–1944), p. 275; Doolittle (1865), 1:230 ff. On opium in Ch'ing China, consult Jonathan Spence in Wakeman and Grant (1975).

54. See, for example, Doolittle (1865), 2:296–297; Macgowan (1912), chapter 16.

55. See Barbara Ward in Jain (1977); also Ward (1979), pp. 22 ff.

56. For convenient overviews, consult Wieger (1913), pp. 405–441; Bodde (1965); *TSCC, tien* 2.

57. For an excellent account of the symbolic variables, consult Parker (1888a), p. 552.

58. Cited in Stover (1974), p. 207–209.

59. Cited in Ebrey (1981), p. 133.

60. Bodde (1965), p. 61.

61. Ibid., pp. 64, 98; see also Doolittle (1865), 2:64–70.

62. Bodde (1965), p. 69. Cf. Doolittle (1865), 2:70 ff.

63. Bodde (1965), pp. 75–76.

64. Cited in C. K. Yang (1961), p. 195. See also ibid., pp. 84–85; Hsiao Kung-ch'üan (1960), pp. 231 and 634, n. 228–237; de Groot (1903), passim.

65. See Boulais (1924), pp. 28–30; Staunton (1810), pp. 3–5; Bodde and Morris (1967), pp. 76–112. Bodde (1969) provides a fascinating firsthand account of prison life in China by the well-known scholar-official Fang Pao (1668–1749).

66. Bodde and Morris (1967), p. 286.

67. Discussed in R. J. Smith (1981) and other papers at the Montecito Conference cited in Chapter 7, Note 64. See also Boulais (1924), pp. 360–395, 469–474; Staunton (1810), pp. 172–186; Bodde and Morris (1967), pp. 162–163, 271–275; de Groot (1903), pp. 458–460.

CHAPTER 11. TRADITION AND MODERNITY, 1860–1982

1. Cohen (1974), p. 4.

2. R. J. Smith (1976 and 1978c). A valuable recent study of China's modernization is Rozman (1981). For an interesting Chinese perspective, consult Wei Cheng-t'ung (1981), pp. 315–336.

3. R. J. Smith (1974).

4. See Cohen (1974); Kennedy (1974); Wang Erh-min (1976).

5. On Japan as a modernizing model, see the articles by Chuzo Ichiko and Marius Jansen in Fairbank and Liu (1980).

6. For an overview, see Fairbank (1979), pp. 163–171, 248–249.

7. See the case study in R. J. Smith (1978b); also K. C. Liu (1970).

8. Britton (1933).

9. R. J. Smith (1976).

10. For illuminating comparative studies, consult Moulder (1977); Beasley (1974); Lockwood (1956); and Reischauer (1963).

11. See Schwartz (1964), pp. 94–95.

12. Ibid.; Arthur Wright in A. Wright (1953), p. 293.

13. Ibid., pp. 294 ff.; de Francis (1950); Chow Tse-tsung (1960), esp. chapter 11.

14. See Hsiao Kung-ch'üan (1975), pp. 145–146, 150, 155–157; also Li San-pao (1978), pp. 119, 115–116, 162 ff.

15. H. Wilhelm (1951), p. 58.

16. Wang Erh-min (1976), pp. 51–71, 80–81; Chang Hao in Fairbank and Liu (1980), p. 201.

17. Teng and Fairbank (1979), p. 171; Wang Erh-min (1976), pp. 77–78.

18. See Schwartz (1964), pp. 50 ff., 62, 192 ff; also H. Wilhelm (1951), pp. 49, 57.

19. See, for example, R. J. Smith (1978b), pp. 162–163, 194.

20. See J. K. Fairbank in Fairbank (1968), p. 265.

21. Cited in R. J. Smith (1981b), p. 102.

22. Ibid., p. 101.

23. M. Wright (1967), pp. 83–84; Chang Chung-li (1967), pp. 176 ff. See also Miyazaki (1976) and Tu Ching-i (1974–1975).

24. Cited in R. J. Smith (1978c), p. 18.

25. On educational reform and its limits in nineteenth-century China, consult Biggerstaff (1961).

26. R. J. Smith (1978c), p. 19.

27. The contrast with Japan is both striking and significant. See R. J. Smith (1976); Donald Shively in Shively (1971); and the sources cited in Note 10 above. Consult also Chang Hao in Fairbank and Liu (1980); Hao Yen-p'ing (1970).

28. See J. K. Fairbank in Fairbank (1968), p. 273.

29. For an excellent case study, see K. C. Liu in Cohen and Schrecker (1976).

30. See, for example, R. J. Smith (1976 and 1978c).

31. See Albert Feuerwerker in Fairbank and Liu (1980).

32. See, for example, Wang Erh-min (1977), pp. 122–124; cf. *NCH*, October 2, 1896.
33. R. J. Smith (1978c), p. 31.
34. See Johnston (1910), p. 422; R. J. Smith (1981 and 1981b). Cf. the case of Japan discussed by Harry Harootunian in Iriye (1980).
35. Immanuel Hsü (1975), pp. 433 ff.
36. See Brunnert and Hagelstrom (1911), pp. 129–130, cited in R. J. Smith (1981). Cf. *NCH*, July 19, 1907. For a brief but illuminating discussion of the imperial reforms, consult Ernest Young in Crowley (1970).
37. R. J. Smith (1981).
38. See Chang Hao (1971), esp. p. 298; also Laurence Schneider in Furth (1976), esp. pp. 57–58.
39. See M. Wright (1968).
40. Chow Tse-tsung (1960) provides an excellent analysis; see also Schwartz (1972).
41. See Teng and Fairbank (1979), pp. 239–245 and the discussion of Ch'en in Lin Yü-sheng (1979). Lu Hsün's essay on chastity denounces the use of *yin-yang* concepts as justification for social inequality. See Lu Hsün (1973), 1:235 ff.
42. Lin Yü-sheng (1979), esp. p. 29. See also Chow Tse-tsung (1960), p. 289.
43. See Hsiao Kung-ch'üan (1975), pp. 566 ff.; also Furth (1976), pp. 25 ff., 70 ff., 215–217.
44. Benjamin Schwartz in Schwartz (1972), p. 4. See also the studies by Kulp (1925); Buck (1937); Parish and Whyte (1978). Cf. Mao Tse-tung's "Report on an Investigation of the Peasant Movement in Hunan" (1927), cited in de Bary (1964), 2:203–215.
45. Chang Hao (1971), p. 305; M. Wright (1967), pp. 303 ff.
46. M. Wright (1967), p. 304.
47. Ibid., pp. 304–312. See also Dirlik (1975) and de Bary (1964), 2:134–144. In a sense, the present emphasis on the Five Stresses and Four Points of Beauty (*wu-chiang ssu-mei*) recalls aspects of the New Life Movement. See Note 55 below.
48. See Council of the Chinese Cultural Renaissance (1977), passim, esp. pp. 427 ff.
49. For a recent and useful biography of Mao (one of many), consult Terrill (1980).
50. Schram (1969), p. 172; Schram (1974), p. 88.
51. See, for example, Schram (1963); H. Boorman (1966); Nivison (1956); Devens (1982), p. l6; Tu Wei-ming in Wilson (1979), pp. 29 ff.; Metzger (1977), pp. 230–233; Wakeman (1973), pp. 238 ff.; Chang Hao (1971), p. 307.
52. For an illuminating discussion of Mao's notion of contradictions, consult Wakeman (1973), pp. 295 ff., esp. 297. Mao's "Great Leap" mentality is revealed in pp. 302 ff. On small group ritual see Whyte (1974).
53. R. J. Smith (1981a). Wakeman (1973), p. 324, provides a useful warning against facile analogies. His point (and mine) is not that Mao was merely an emperor in disguise. It is rather that in many ways Mao was more deeply touched by certain strains of traditional Chinese thought than by Western thought and that it is well to be aware of the cultural complexity of Mao's outlook.
54. R. J. Smith (1981a); Baum (1981).
55. R. J. Smith (1981a). The recent emphasis on civilization and propriety (*wen-ming li-mao*) on the Mainland resonates strongly with the themes of the New Life Movement (see Note 47), especially in its concern with outer form as a reflection of inner attitudes. See, for example, *JMJP*, February 18, 1982.
56. The Great Proletarian Cultural Revolution is ably summarized and evaluated in Meisner (1977), pp. 309–358.
57. Tozer (1970).
58. R. J. Smith (1981a), p. 10.
59. Ibid.
60. See K. C. Liu (1981), pp. 315 ff.
61. R J. Smith (1981a), pp. 10–11; Parish and Whyte (1978), chapter 13, esp. pp. 252–260.
62. R. J. Smith (1981a), p. 11.
63. For a fuller discussion of intellectual liberalization and its limits, consult ibid., pp. 11–12; also *BR*, October 5, 1981, pp. 13–16.

Bibliography

REMARKS

For a more complete listing of relevant works in Western languages, Chinese, and Japanese, consult Chang Chun-shu (1971), Hucker (1962), Kamachi et al. (1975), Scott K. Ling (1975), Nathan (1973), Skinner and Hsieh (1973), Teng and Biggerstaff (1971), E. Wilkinson (1973), and Yüan Tung-li (1958). Also useful, of course, are the bibliographies of recent specialized studies and more general works, such as Fairbank, (1978, 1979) and Fairbank and Liu (1980). There is even a bibliography of bibliographies: Tsien and Cheng (1978). The *Bibliography of Asian Studies*, published annually by the Association of Asian Studies as a separate September issue of the *JAS*, provides the most comprehensive listing of recent Western-language publications on China (and other parts of Asia).

ABBREVIATIONS (PRIMARY SOURCES IN CHINESE AND JOURNALS)

AA	*American Anthropologist*
AJ	*Art Journal*
AM	*Asia Major*
AQR	*Asiatic Quarterly Review*
AS	*Asian Survey*
BR	*Beijing Review*
BSOAS	*Bulletin of the School of Oriental and African Studies*
CC	*Chinese Culture*
CCYWL	*Huang-ch'ao chi-ch'i yüeh-wu lu*
CHM	*Cahiers d'Histoire Mondiale*
CL	*Chinese Literature*
CLCC	*Chia-li ch'üan-chi*
CLTC	*Chia-li ta-ch'eng*
CLTSCC	*Chia-li t'ieh-shih chi-ch'eng*
CPLC	*Ch'ing-pei lei-ch'ao*
CQ	*China Quarterly*
CR	*Chinese Recorder*
CS	*Ch'ing-shih*
CSSH	*Comparative Studies in Society and History*
CSWT	*Ch'ing-shih wen-t'i*
CTLT	*Huang-ch'ao cheng-tien lei-tsuan*
CWTTT	*Chung-wen ta-tz'u-tien*
EDCC	*Economic Development and Cultural Change*

ER	*Earlham Review*
ESLS	*Erh-shih-liu shih*
FEQ	*Far Eastern Quarterly*
HCCSWHP	*Huang-ch'ao ching-shih wen-hsü-pien*
HCCSWP	*Huang-ch'ao ching-shih wen-pien*
HCCSWPHP	*Huang-ch'ao ching-shih wen-pien hsü-pien*
HJAS	*Harvard Journal of Asiatic Studies*
HPCTCC	*Hsin-pien chu-tzu chi-ch'eng*
HR	*History of Religions*
HWHTK	*Huang-ch'ao hsü wen-hsien t'ung-k'ao*
IPQ	*International Philosophical Quarterly*
JAH	*Journal of Asian History*
JAOS	*Journal of the American Oriental Society*
JAS	*Journal of Asian Studies*
JCFS	*Journal of Comparative Family Studies*
JCL	*Journal of Chinese Linguistics*
JCP	*Journal of Chinese Philosophy*
JEH	*Journal of Economic History*
JHI	*Journal of the History of Ideas*
JHKBRAS	*Journal of the Hong Kong Branch of the Royal Asiatic Society*
JICS	*Journal of the Institute of Chinese Studies*
JMJP	*Jen-min jih-pao*
JNCBRAS	*Journal of the North China Branch of the Royal Asiatic Society*
JOS	*Journal of Oriental Studies*
JQ	*Japan Quarterly*
LIPC	*Li-i pien-chien*
LPTL	*Ch'in-ting Li-pu tse-li*
LQ	*Library Quarterly*
MAS	*Modern Asian Studies*
MC	*Modern China*
MS	*Monumenta Serica*
NCH	*North-China Herald*
NQCJ	*Notes and Queries on China and Japan*
OA	*Oriental Art*
PEW	*Philosophy East and West*
PFEH	*Papers on Far Eastern History*
SAR	*Sino-American Review*
SSC	*Social Sciences in China*
SSCCS	*Shih-san-ching chu-shu*
SSCRB	*Society for the Study of Chinese Religion, Bulletin*
TAPS	*Transactions of the American Philosophical Society*
TCHT	*Ta-Ch'ing hui-tien*
TCTL	*Ch'in-ting Ta-Ch'ing t'ung-li*
THJ	*Tsing Hua Journal*
TP	*T'oung Pao*
TR	*Tamgang Review*
TSCC	*Ch'in-ting ku-chin t'u-shu chi-ch'eng*
USCR	*U.S.-China Review*
WHL	*Wu-hsüeh lu*
WLTK	*Wu-li t'ung-kao*
WP	*World Politics*

Adkins, Curtis, and Yang, Winston, eds. (1980). *Critical Essays on Chinese Fiction* (Hong Kong).

Ahern, Emily (1973). *The Cult of the Dead in a Chinese Village* (Stanford).

————. (1982). *Chinese Ritual and Politics* (New York and Cambridge, Eng.)

Ahern, Emily, and Gates, Hill, eds. (1981). *The Anthropology of Taiwanese Society* (Stanford).

Alitto, Guy (1979). *The Last Confucian* (Berkeley).

Baker, Hugh (1979). *Chinese Family and Kinship* (London).

Balazs, Etienne (1964). *Chinese Civilization and Bureaucracy* (New Haven, Conn.).

————. (1965). *Political Theory and Administrative Reality* (London).

Banno, Masataka (1964). *China and the West, 1858–1861* (Cambridge, Mass.).

Bauer, Wolfgang (1966). "The Encyclopedia in China," *CHM* 9, 3.

————. (1976). *China and the Search for Happiness* (New York, translated by Michael Shaw).

Baum, Richard (1981). "Scientism and Bureaucratism in Chinese Thought," Annual Meeting of the Association of Asian Studies (Toronto, March 1981).

Beasley, W. G. (1974). "Self-Strengthening and Restoration," *Acta Asiatica* 26.

Beattie, Hilary (1979). *Land and Lineage in China* (Cambridge, Eng).

Beattie, John (1966). "Ritual and Social Change," *Man* 1, 1 (March 1966).

Berger, Peter, and Luckmann, Thomas (1967). *The Social Construction of Reality* (New York).

Beurdeley, Michel et al., eds. (1969). *Chinese Erotic Art* (Rutland, Vt., translated by Diana Imber).

Biggerstaff, Knight (1961). *The Earliest Modern Government Schools in China* (Ithaca, N.Y.).

Birch, Cyril, ed. (1974). *Studies of Chinese Literary Genres* (Berkeley).

Blodget, Henry (1899). "The Worship of Heaven and Earth by the Emperor of China," *JAOS* 20, 1 (January–July 1899).

Bodde, Derk (1938). *China's First Unifier* (Leiden, Netherlands).

————. (1939). "Types of Chinese Categorical Thinking," *JAOS* 69, 2 (June 1939).

————. (1942). "Dominant Ideas in the Formation of Chinese Culture," *JAOS* 62, 4 (December 1942).

————. (1948). *Chinese Ideas in the West* (Washington, D.C.)

————. (1955). "On Translating Chinese Philosophic Terms," *FEQ* 14, 2 (February 1955).

————. (1957). *China's Cultural Tradition* (New York).

————. (1965). *Annual Customs and Festivals in Peking* (Hong Kong).

————. (1969). "Prison Life in Eighteenth Century Peking," *JAOS* 89, 2 (April–June 1969).

Bodde, Derk, and Morris, Clarence (1967). *Law in Imperial China* (Cambridge, Mass).

Boorman, Howard (1966). "Mao Tse-tung as Historian," *CQ* 28 (October–December 1966).

Boorman, Scott (1969). *The Protracted Game* (New York).

Boulais, Guy (1924). *Manuel du code chinois* (Shanghai).

Brandauer, Frederick (1977). "Women in the *Ching-hua yüan*," *JAS* 36, 4 (August 1977).

Britton, Roswell (1933). *The Chinese Periodical Press 1800–1912* (Shanghai).

Brunnert, H. S., and Hagelstrom, V. V. (1911). *Present Day Political Organization of China* (Foochow).

Buck, John L. (1937). *Land Utilization in China* (Nanking).

Burling, Judith, and Burling, Arthur (1953). *Chinese Art* (New York).

Buxbaum, David, and Mote, Frederick, eds. (1972). *Transition and Permanence* (Hong Kong).

CCYWL (1871). *Huang-ch'ao chi-ch'i yüeh-wu lu* (Record of the Ch'ing Dynasty's Sacrificial Implements, Music, and Dances).

CLCC (1895). Liang Chieh. *Chia-li ch'üan-chi* (A Complete Collection of Family Ritual).

CLTC (1975). Lu Tzu-chen. *Chia-li ta-ch'eng* (A Synthesis of Family Ritual) (Taipei).

CLTSCC (1842). Ch'en Ming-sheng. *Chia-li t'ieh-shih chi-ch'eng* (A Complete Collection of the Written Forms of Family Ritual).

CPLC (1916). Hsu K'o. *Ch'ing-pei lei-ch'ao* (Miscellaneous Notes from the Ch'ing Period) (Shanghai).

CTLT (1969). Hsi Yü-fu et al. *Huang-ch'ao cheng-tien lei-tsuan* (A Compilation by Categories of the Ch'ing Dynasty's Administrative Institutions) (Taipei).

CWTTT (1968). Chang Ch'i-yün et al. *Chung-wen ta-tz'u-tien* (An Encyclopedic Dictionary of the Chinese Language) (Taipei).

Cahill, James (1982). *The Compelling Image: Nature and Style in Seventeenth Century Chinese Painting* (Cambridge, Mass.).

Cantoniensis [pseud.] (1868). "Cost of Living Among the Chinese," *NQCJ* 1 (January 1868) and 2, 2 (February 1868).

Chai, Ch'u, and Chai, Winberg (1967). *Li-chi* (New Hyde Park, N.Y., reprint of James Legge's translation of the *Li-chi*, originally printed in *The Sacred Books of the East*, Oxford, Eng., 1885).

Chan, Albert (1982). *The Glory and Fall of the Ming Dynasty* (Norman, Okla.).

Chan, Wing-tsit (1955). "The Evolution of the Confucian Concept *Jen*," *PEW* 4.

————. (1963). *A Source Book in Chinese Philosophy* (Princeton).

————. (1967). *Reflections on Things at Hand* (New York).

————. (1969). *Neo-Confucianism, Etc.* (Hanover, N.H.).

Chang, Chin-chien (1935). "Chung-kuo wen-hua chih t'e-chih" (The Special Characteristics of Chinese Culture), *Wen-hua chien-she* 1, 6 (March 1935).

Chang, Chun-shu (1971). *Premodern China: A Bibliographical Introduction* (Ann Arbor, Mich.).

Chang, Chun-shu, and Chang, Hsüeh-lun (1973). "The World of P'u Sung-ling's *Liao-chai chih-i*," *JICS* 6, 2.

Chang, Chung-li (1962). *The Income of the Chinese Gentry* (Seattle).

————. (1967). *The Chinese Gentry* (Seattle).

Chang, Chung-yüan (1963). *Creativity and Taoism* (New York).

Chang, Hao (1971). *Liang Ch'i-ch'ao and Intellectual Transition in China 1890–1907* (Cambridge, Mass.).

Chang, Kwang-chih (1976). *Early Chinese Civilization* (Cambridge, Mass.).

————. (1977). *The Archaeology of Ancient China* (New Haven, Conn., and London).

————, ed. (1977a). *Food in Chinese Culture* (New Haven, Conn., and London).

————. (1980). *Shang Civilization* (New Haven, Conn., and London).

Chang, Tung-sun (1952). "A Chinese Philosopher's Theory of Knowledge," *Etc.* 9, 3 (Spring 1952).

Chao, Y. R. (1976). *Aspects of Chinese Sociolinguistics* (Stanford).

Ch'en, Kao-yung (1937). *Chung-kuo wen-hua wen-t'i yen-chiu* (Research on Problems of Chinese Culture) (Shanghai).

Ch'en, Kenneth (1964). *Buddhism in China* (Princeton).

————. (1973). *The Chinese Transformation of Buddhism* (Princeton).

Ch'en, Kuo-fu, and Ch'in, P'ei-hao (1964). *T'ung-li hsin-pien* (A New Edition of the Comprehensive Rituals) (Taipei).

Ch'en, Teng-yüan (1956). *Chung-kuo wen-hua shih* (History of Chinese Culture) (Taipei).

Cheng, Chi-pao, ed. (1964). *Symposium on Chinese Culture* (New York).

Cheng, Chung-ying (1971). "Aspects of Classical Chinese Logic," *IPQ* 11, 2 (June 1971).

————. (1971a). *Tai Chen's Inquiry into Goodness* (Honolulu).

————. (1972). "On *Yi* as a Universal Principle of Specific Application in Confucian Morality," *PEW* 22, 3 (July 1972).

————. (1973). "A Generative Unity: Chinese Language and Chinese Philosophy," *THJ* n.s. 10, 1 (June 1973).

————. (1977). "Chinese Philosophy and Symbolic Reference," *PEW* 27, 3 (July 1977).

Cheng, Te-k'un (1957). "*Yin-Yang Wu-Hsing* and Han Art," *HJAS* 20.

————. (1975). "New Light on Shang China," *Antiquity* 49.

Chesneaux, Jean (1971). "The Modern Relevance of Shui-hu chuan," *PFEH* 3 (March 1971).

————. (1972). *Popular Movements and Secret Societies in China 1840–1950* (Stanford).

Chiang, T'ing-hsi et al. (1744). *Ta-Ch'ing i-t'ung chih* (Comprehensive Gazetteer of the Ch'ing Dynasty).

Chiang, Yee (1973). *Chinese Calligraphy* (Cambridge, Mass.).

Ch'ien, Mu (1937). *Chung-kuo chin san-pai-nien hsüeh-shu shih* (History of the Past Three Hundred Years of Chinese Scholarship) (Shanghai).

————. (1968). *Chung-hua wen-hua shih-chiang* (Ten Lectures on Chinese Culture) (Taipei).

————— . (1970). *Chung-kuo wen-hua ts'ung-t'an* (Collected Notes on Chinese Culture) (Taipei).

Ching, Julia (1976). *To Acquire Wisdom* (New York).

Ch'ing-shih pien-tsuan wei-yüan-hui (1961). *Ch'ing-shih* (History of the Ch'ing Dynasty) (Taipei).

Chow, Tse-tsung (1960). *The May Fourth Movement* (Stanford).

————— . (1979). "Ancient Chinese Views on Literature, the *Tao*, and Their Relationship," *CL* 1.

Ch'ü, T'ung-tsu (1962). *Local Government in China under the Ch'ing* (Cambridge, Mass.).

————— . (1972). *Han Social Structure* (Seattle, edited by Jack Dull).

Chung-hua shu-chü (1915). *Ch'ing-ch'ao ch'üan-shih* (Complete History of the Ch'ing Dynasty) (Shanghai).

Cohen, Paul (1974). *Between Tradition and Modernity* (Cambridge, Mass.).

Cohen, Paul, and Schrecker, John, eds. (1976). *Reform in Nineteenth Century China* (Cambridge, Mass.).

Cotterell, Arthur (1981). *The First Emperor of China* (New York).

Council of the Chinese Cultural Renaissance (1977). *An Introduction to Chinese Culture* (Taipei).

Creel, H. G. (1936). "On the Nature of Chinese Ideography," *TP* 32.

————— . (1970). *The Origins of Statecraft in China* (Chicago).

Cressey, George (1955). *Land of the Five Hundred Million* (New York).

Croll, Elizabeth (1980). *Feminism and Socialism in China* (New York).

Crowley, James, ed. (1970). *Modern East Asia* (New York).

Cua, A. S. (1979). "Dimensions of Li (Propriety)," *PEW* 29, 4 (October 1977).

Dardess, John (1973). *Conquerors and Confucians* (New York).

David, Percival (1971). *Chinese Connoisseurship* (New York and Washington, D.C.).

Davis, J. F. (1846). *The Chinese* (London).

Dawson, Raymond (1964). *The Legacy of China* (Oxford).

————— . (1978). *The Chinese Experience* (London).

de Bary, W. T. (1964). *Sources of Chinese Tradition* (New York and London).

————— . (1970). *Self and Society in Ming Thought* (New York).

————— . (1975). *The Unfolding of Neo-Confucianism* (New York).

————— . (1981). *Neo-Confucian Orthodoxy and the Learning of the Mind-and-Heart* (New York).

de Bary, W. T., and Bloom, Irene (1979). *Principle and Practicality* (New York).

de Francis, John (1950). *Nationalism and Language Reform in China* (Princeton).

de Groot, J.J.M. (1903). *Sectarianism and Religious Persecution in China* (Amsterdam).

————— . (1912). *The Religion of the Chinese* (New York and London).

Devens, Eleanor (1982). "The Role of Confucius in Modern China, 1950 to the Present" (M.A. thesis, Rice University).

Dirlik, Arif (1975). "The Ideological Foundations of the New Life Movement," *JAS* 34, 4 (August 1975).

Dittmer, Lowell, and Chen, Ruoxi (1982). *Ethics and Rhetoric of the Chinese Cultural Revolution* (Berkeley).

Doglin, Janet (1977). *Symbolic Anthropology* (New York).

Dolezelova-Velingerova, Milena (1980). *The Chinese Novel at the Turn of the Century* (Toronto and Buffalo).

Doolittle, Justus (1865). *Social Life of the Chinese* (New York).

Doré, Henri (1914–1933). *Researches into Chinese Superstitions* (Shanghai, translated by M. Kennelly).

Dreyer, June (1976). *China's Forty Millions* (Cambridge, Mass.).

ESLS (1961). *Erh-shih-liu shih* (The Twenty-Six Histories) (Taipei).

Eastman, Lloyd (1974). *The Abortive Revolution* (Cambridge, Mass.).

Eberhard, Wolfram (1965). "Chinese Regional Stereotypes," *AS* 5, 12 (December 1965).

————— . (1967). *Guilt and Sin in Traditional China* (Berkeley and Los Angeles).

————— . (1971). *Moral and Social Values of the Chinese* (Taipei).

————— . (1982). *China's Minorities: Yesterday and Today* (Belmont, Calif.).

Ebrey, Patricia, ed. (1981). *Chinese Civilization and Society* (New York and London).
Egerod, Soren, and Glahn, Else, eds. (1959). *Studia Serica Karlgren Dedicata* (Copenhagen).
Egerton, Clement (1939). *The Goldon Lotus* (London).
Elman, Benjamin (1979). "The Hsüeh-hai T'ang and the Rise of New Text Scholarship in Canton," *CSWT* 4, 2 (December 1979).
Elvin, Mark (1973). *The Pattern of the Chinese Past* (Stanford).
Esherick, Joseph (1981). "Number Games: A Note on Land Distribution in Prerevolutionary China," *MC* 7, 4 (October 1981).
Fairbank, John K., ed. (1957). *Chinese Thought and Institutions* (Chicago).
——————. (1965). *Ch'ing Documents: An Introductory Syllabus* (Cambridge, Mass.).
——————., ed. (1968). *The Chinese World Order* (Cambridge, Mass.).
——————., ed. (1978). *The Cambridge History of China,* vol. 10, pt. 1 (Cambridge, Eng.).
——————. (1979). *The United States and China* (Cambridge, Mass., and London).
Fairbank, John K., and Liu, Kwang-Ching, eds. (1980). *The Cambridge History of China,* vol. 11, pt. 2 (Cambridge, Mass.).
Fairbank, John K., and Teng, Ssu-yü (1940). "On the Types and Uses of Ch'ing Documents," *HJAS* 5.
Farmer, Edward (1976). *Early Ming Government* (Cambridge, Mass.).
Farquhar, David (1978). "Emperor as Bodhisattva in the Governance of the Ch'ing Dynasty," *HJAS* 38, 1 (June 1978).
Faure, David (1976). "Land Tax Collection in Kiangsu Province in the Late Ch'ing Period," *CSWT* 3, 6 (December 1976).
Feng, Han-yi (1967). *The Chinese Kinship System* (Cambridge, Mass.).
Feuchtwang, Stephen (1974). *An Anthropological Analysis of Chinese Geomancy* (Vientiane, Laos).
Feuerwerker, Albert (1976). *State and Society in Eighteenth Century China* (Ann Arbor, Mich.).
Fogel, Joshua (1980). "Shantung in the Shun-chih Reign," *CSWT* 4, 4 (December 1980).
Fong, Wen (1969). "Towards a Structuralist Analysis of Chinese Landscape Painting," *AJ* 28, 4 (Summer 1969).
——————. (1971). "How to Understand Chinese Painting," *TAPS* 115, 4 (August 1971).
——————. (1980). *The Great Bronze Age of China* (New York).
Forke, Alfred (1925). *The World Conception of the Chinese* (London).
Freedman, Maurice (1966). *Chinese Lineage and Society* (London).
——————. (1975). "Sinology and the Social Sciences," *Ethnos* 40.
Fu, Marilyn, and Fu, Shen (1973). *Studies in Connoisseurship* (Princeton).
Fung, Yu-lan (1948). *A Short History of Chinese Philosophy* (New York, edited by Derk Bodde).
——————. (1952). *A History of Chinese Philosophy* (Princeton, translated by Derk Bodde).
Furth, Charlotte, ed. (1976). *The Limits of Change* (Cambridge, Mass.).
——————. (1981). "The Orthodox Family and Its Discontents," Conference on Orthodoxy and Heterodoxy in Late Imperial China (Montecito, Calif., August 1981).
Gedalecia, David (1974). "Excursion into Substance and Function," *PEW* 24, 4 (October 1974).
Geertz, Clifford (1973). *The Interpretation of Cultures* (New York).
Gernet, Jacques (1962). *Daily Life in China on the Eve of the Mongol Invasion, 1250–1276* (New York).
Giles, Lionel (1911). *An Alphabetical Index to the Chinese Encyclopedia* (Oxford).
Girardot, N. J. (1976). "The Problem of Creation Mythology in the Study of Chinese Religion," *HR* 15, 4 (May 1976).
Goodall, John (1979). *Heaven and Earth; Album Leaves from a Ming Encyclopedia* (Boulder, Colo.).
Goodrich, L. Carrington (1935). *The Literary Inquisition of Ch'ien-lung* (Baltimore).
——————. (1975). *Fifteenth Century Illustrated Chinese Primer* (Hong Kong).
Gottschalk, Louis, ed. (1963). *Generalization in the Writing of History* (Chicago).
Graham, A. C. (1971). "China, Europe, and the Origins of Modern Science," *AM* 16, 1–2.

Granet, Marcel (1934). *La pensée chinoise* (Paris).

Gray, John H. (1878). *China* (London).

Guisso, Richard, and Johannesen, Stanley (1981). *Women in China: Current Directions in Historical Scholarship* (Youngstown, N.Y.).

HCCSWHP (1888). Ko Shih-chun. *Huang-ch'ao ching-shih wen-hsü-pien* (Supplement to the Ch'ing Dynasty's Writings on Statecraft).

HCCSWP (1826). Ho Ch'ang-ling. *Huang-ch'ao ching-shih wen-pien* (The Ch'ing Dynasty's Writings on Statecraft) (Shanghai).

HCCSWPHP (1897). Sheng K'ang. *Huang-ch'ao ching-shih wen-pien hsü-pien* (Supplement to the Ch'ing Dynasty's Writings on Statecraft).

HPCTCC (1974). Shih-chieh shu-chü. *Hsin-pien chu-tzu chi-ch'eng* (New Edition of the Collection on Philosophical Writings) (Taipei).

HWHTK (1935). Liu Chin-tsao. *Huang-ch'ao hsü wen-hsien t'ung-k'ao* (Supplement to the Encyclopedic Examination of the Historical Records of the Ch'ing Dynasty) (Shanghai).

Haeger, John (1975). *Crisis and Prosperity in Sung China* (Tucson, Ariz.).

Han, Suyin (1965). *The Crippled Tree* (New York).

Han, Yu-shan (1955). *Elements of Chinese Historiography* (Hollywood, Calif.).

Hanan, Patrick (1981). *The Chinese Vernacular Story* (Cambridge, Mass.).

Hansford, Howard (1950). *Chinese Jade Carving* (London).

_____ . (1961). *A Glossary of Chinese Art and Archaeology* (London).

_____ . (1969). *Jade, Essence of Hills and Streams* (New York).

Hao, Yen-p'ing (1970). *The Comprador in Nineteenth Century China* (Cambridge, Mass.).

Hart Journals (Unpublished). Queen's University Library, Queen's University, Belfast, Northern Ireland.

Hawkes, David (1973 and 1977). *The Story of the Stone*, 2 vols. (Harmondsworth, Eng.).

Hayes, James (1977). *The Hong Kong Region 1850–1911* (Hamden, Conn.).

——— (1981). "Written Materials as Household Tools," for the Conference on Values and Communication in Chinese Popular Culture: Ming and Ch'ing (Honolulu, January 1981).

Hegel, Robert (1981). *The Novel in Seventeenth Century China* (New York).

Hibbert, Christopher (1981). *The Emperors of China* (Chicago).

Hinton, Harold (1956). *The Grain Tribute System of China* (Cambridge, Mass.).

Ho, Ping-ti (1959). *Studies on the Population of China, 1368–1953* (Cambridge, Mass.).

_____ . (1962). *The Ladder of Success in Imperial China* (New York).

_____ . (1967). "The Significance of the Ch'ing Period in Chinese History," *JAS* 26, 2 (February 1967).

_____ . (1976). *The Cradle of the East* (Chicago).

Ho, Ping-ti and Tsou, Tang (1968). *China in Crisis* (Chicago).

Hsia, C. T. (1968). *The Classic Chinese Novel* (New York).

Hsiao, I-shan (1967). *Ch'ing-tai t'ung-shih* (Comprehensive History of the Ch'ing Dynasty) (Taipei).

Hsiao, Kung-ch'üan (1960). *Rural China* (Seattle).

_____ . (1975). *A Modern China and a New World* (Seattle).

_____ . (1979). *A History of Chinese Political Thought* (Princeton, translated by Frederick Mote).

_____ . (1979a). *Compromise in Imperial China*, Parerga, Occasional Papers on China (Seattle).

Hsieh, Pao-chao (1925). *The Government of China (1644–1911)* (Baltimore).

Hsü, Cho-yün (1965). *Ancient China in Transition* (Stanford).

_____ . (1980). *Han Agriculture* (Seattle and London).

Hsu, Dau-lin (1970–1971). "The Myth of the Five Human Relationships of Confucius," *MS* 29.

Hsü, Francis L. K. (1971). "Filial Piety in Japan and China," *JCFS* 2, 1 (Spring 1971).

_____ . (1972). *Americans and Chinese* (Garden City, N.Y.).

Hsü, Immanuel, C. Y. (1959). *Intellectual Trends in the Ch'ing Period* (Cambridge, Mass.).

_____ . (1975). *The Rise of Modern China* (New York).

Huang, Pei (1974). *Autocracy at Work* (Bloomington, Ind.).

Huang, Philip, ed. (1980). *The Development of Underdevelopment in China* (White Plains, N.Y.).

Huang, Ray (1981). *1587, A Year of No Significance* (New Haven, Conn., and London).

Hucker, Charles (1962). *China: A Critical Bibliography* (Tucson, Ariz.).

————. (1966). *The Censorial System of Ming China* (Stanford).

————. (1969). *Chinese Government in Ming Times, 1368–1644* (New York).

————. (1975). *China's Imperial Past* (Stanford).

Hummel, Arthur, ed. (1943–1944). *Eminent Chinese of the Ch'ing Period* (Washington, D.C.).

Hung, William (1939). "Preface to an Index to *Ssu-K'u Ch'üan-Shu Tsung-Mu* and *Wei-Shou Shu-Mu,*" *HJAS* 4.

Inn, Henry, and Lee, S. C., eds. (1940). *Chinese Homes and Gardens* (Honolulu).

Iriye, Akira, ed. (1980). *The Chinese and the Japanese* (Princeton).

Jackson, J. H. (1937). *Water Margin* (Shanghai).

Jain, Ravindra, ed. (1977). *Text and Context* (Philadelphia).

Jamieson, George (1921). *Chinese Family and Commercial Law* (Shanghai).

Jansen, Marius (1969). *Changing Japanese Attitudes toward Modernization* (Princeton).

Jen, Yu-wen (1973). *The Taiping Revolutionary Movement* (New Haven, Conn., and London).

Jenyns, Soame (1965). *Later Chinese Porcelains* (London).

Jin, Kaicheng (1980). "Artistic Recreation of the Unique Characteristics of Things," *SSC* 3.

Jing, Su, and Luo, Lun (1978). *Landlord and Labor in Late Imperial China* (Cambridge, Mass., translated by Endymion Wilkinson).

Jochim, Christian (1979). "The Imperial Audience Ceremonies of the Ch'ing Dynasty," *SSCRB* 7 (Fall 1979).

Johnston, R. F. (1910). *Lion and Dragon in Northern China* (London).

Juliano, Annette (1981). *Treasures of China* (New York).

Kahn, Harold (1967). "The Politics of Filiality," *JAS* 26, 2 (February 1967).

————. (1971). *Monarchy in the Emperor's Eyes* (Cambridge, Mass.).

Kamachi, Noriko (1981). *Reform in China* (Cambridge, Mass.).

Kamachi, Noriko et al., eds. (1975). *Japanese Studies of Modern China since 1953* (Cambridge, Mass.).

Kang, Chao (1981). "New Data on Land Ownership Patterns in Ming-Ch'ing China," *JAS* 40, 4 (August 1981).

K'ang-hsi tzu-tien (1962). (Taipei).

Kapp, Robert, ed. (1973). *Four Views of China* (Houston, Tex.).

Kaufmann, Walter (1976). *Musical References in the Chinese Classics* (Detroit).

Keightley, David (1978). "The Religious Commitment: Shang Theology and the Genesis of Chinese Political Culture," *HR* 17, 3–4 (February-May 1978).

————. (1982). *The Origins of Chinese Civilization* (Berkeley).

Kennedy, Thomas (1974). "Self-Strengthening," *CSWT* 3, 1 (November 1974).

Kessler, Lawrence (1976). *K'ang-hsi and the Consolidation of Ch'ing Rule, 1661–1684* (Chicago).

Keswick, Maggie (1978). *The Chinese Garden* (New York).

Knoerle, Jeanne (1972). *"The Dream of the Red Chamber"*: *A Critical Study* (Bloomington, Ind., and London).

Kramer, S. N., ed. (1961). *Mythologies of the Ancient World* (New York).

Kuhn, Franz (1963). *Jou Pu Tuan* (New York, translated by Richard Martin).

Kuhn, Philip (1977). "Origins of the Taiping Vision," *CSSH* 19, 3 (July 1977).

————. (1980). *Rebellion and Its Enemies in Late Imperial China* (Cambridge, Mass.).

Kulp, Daniel H. (1925). *Country Life in South China* (New York).

LIPC (1911). Chou Liang. *Li-i pien-chien* (Guide to Ritual and Etiquette).

LPTL (1845). *Ch'in-ting Li-pu tse-li* (Imperially Endorsed Regulations of the Board of Rites) (Peking).

La Fontaine, J. S. (1972). *The Interpretation of Ritual* (London).

Lai, T. C. (1960). *Selected Chinese Sayings* (Hong Kong).

————. (1969). *Chinese Couplets* (Hong Kong).

————. (1970). *A Scholar in Imperial China* (Hong Kong).

Lamley, Harry (1977). "*Hsieh-tou*, The Pathology of Violence in South-east China," *CSWT* 3, 7 (November 1977).
Lancashire, David, ed. (1982). *Chinese Essays on Religion and Faith* (Taipei).
Langlois, John (1981). *China Under Mongol Rule* (Princeton).
Lau, D. C. (1963). "On Mencius' Use of the Method of Analogy in Argument," *AM* n.s. 10, 2.
Leach, Edmund (1976). *Culture and Communication* (Cambridge, Eng.).
Le Blanc, Charles, and Borei, Dorothy, eds. (1982). *Essays on Chinese Civilization* (Princeton).
Legeza, Laszlo (1980). "Ming and Ch'ing Imperial *Tou-ts'ai* and *Wu-Ts'ai* Porcelains," *Arts of Asia* (January-February 1980).
Legge, James (1893–1895). *The Chinese Classics*, vols. 1 and 2 (London and Oxford).
Lessa, William, and Vogt, Evon (1979). *Reader in Comparative Religion* (New York).
Levenson, Joseph (1964). "The Humanistic Disciplines," *JAS* 23, 4 (August 1964).
Levenson, Joseph, and Schurmann, Franz (1970). *China: An Interpretive History* (New Haven, Conn., and London).
Levius, John (1936). *The Foundations of Chinese Musical Art* (Peiping).
Levy, Howard (1966). *Chinese Footbinding* (New York).
Levy, Marion (1949). *The Family Revolution in Modern China* (New York).
————— . (1953). "Contrasting Factors in the Modernization of China and Japan," *EDCC* 2 (October 1953).
————— . (1962). "Some Aspects of 'Individualism' and the Problem of Modernization in China and Japan," *EDCC* 10, 3 (April 1962).
Li, Dun J. (1978). *The Ageless Chinese* (New York).
Li, Lillian (1982). "Introduction: Food, Famine and the Chinese State," *JAS* 41, 4 (August 1982).
Li, San-pao (1978). "K'ang Yu-wei's Iconoclasm" (Ph.D. dissertation, University of California, Davis).
Li-hsüeh kuan (1916). *Li-i* (Proposals on Ritual) (Peking).
Lin, Tai-yi (1966). *Flowers in the Mirror* (Berkeley and Los Angeles).
Lin, Yü-sheng (1979). *The Crisis of Chinese Consciousness* (Madison, Wisc., and London).
Lin, Yutang (1935). *My Country and My People* (New York).
————— . (1948). *The Gay Genius* (London).
————— . (1967). *The Chinese Theory of Art* (London).
Ling, Scott K. (1975). *Bibliography of Chinese Humanities: 1941–1972* (Taipei).
Liu, Hui-chen Wang (1959). *The Traditional Chinese Clan Rules* (Locust Valley, N.Y.).
Liu, I-cheng (1964). *Chung-kuo wen-hua shih* (History of Chinese Culture) (Taipei).
Liu, James J. Y. (1966). *The Art of Chinese Poetry* (Chicago and London).
————— . (1975). *Chinese Theories of Literature* (Chicago).
————— . (1979). *Essentials of Chinese Literary Art* (Stanford).
Liu, James T. C. (1970). *Traditional China* (Englewood Cliffs, N.J.).
Liu, Kwang-Ching (1970). "The Confucian as Patriot and Pragmatist," *HJAS* 30.
————— . (1981). "World View and Peasant Rebellion," *JAS* 40, 2 (February 1981).
Liu, Shih-shun (1975). *Vignettes from the Late Ch'ing* (Hong Kong).
Liu, Wu-chi, and Lo, Irving (1975). *Sunflower Splendor* (Washington, D.C., and London).
Lockwood, William (1956). "Japan's Response to the West," *WP* 9, 1 (October 1956).
Loehr, Max (1970). "Art-Historical Art," *OA* 16 (Spring 1970).
Loewe, Michael (1968). *Everyday Life in Early Imperial China* (New York).
————— . (1974). *Crisis and Conflict in Han China, 104 B.C. to A.D. 9* (London).
Lu, Hsün (1973). *Lu Hsün ch'üan-chi* (The Complete Works of Lu Hsün) (Peking).
Lu, Pao-ch'ien (1978). *Ch'ing-tai ssu-hsiang shih* (History of Ch'ing Thought) (Taipei).
Lui, Adam Y. C. (1978). *Chinese Censors and the Alien Emperor 1644–1660* (Hong Kong).
————— . (1981). *The Hanlin Academy* (Hamden, Conn.).
Luo, Zewen et al. (1981). *The Great Wall* (New York).
Ma, Feng-ch'en (1935). *Ch'ing-tai hsing-cheng chih-tu yen-chiu ts'an-k'ao shu-mu* (Annotated Bibliography for Research into the Administrative System of the Ch'ing Dynasty) (Peiping).
Macgowan, John (1912). *Men and Manners of Modern China* (London).

Mackenna, Stephen, and Mair, Victor (1979). "A Reordering of the Hexagrams of the *I Ching*," *PEW* 29, 4 (October 1979).

Mackerras, Colin (1972). *The Rise of Peking Opera, 1770–1870* (Oxford).

Mailey, Jean (1980). *The Manchu Dragon: Costumes of the Ch'ing Dynasty 1644–1912* (New York).

March, Andrew (1968). "An Appreciation of Chinese Geomancy," *JAS* 27, 2 (February 1968).

March, Benjamin (1935). *Some Technical Terms of Chinese Painting* (Baltimore).

Marsh, Robert (1961). *The Mandarins* (Glencoe, Ill.).

Mayers, William (1874). *The Chinese Reader's Manual* (Shanghai).

————. (1897). *The Chinese Government* (London).

Meadows, Thomas T. (1856). *The Chinese and Their Rebellions* (London).

Meisner, Maurice (1977). *Mao's China* (New York and London).

Meng, Sen (1977). *Ch'ing-tai shih* (A History of the Ch'ing Dynasty) (Taipei).

Meskill, John, ed. (1973). *An Introduction to Chinese Civilization* (Toronto).

Metzger, Thomas (1973). *The Internal Organization of Ch'ing Bureaucracy* (Cambridge, Mass.).

————. (1977). *Escape from Predicament* (New York).

Meyer, Jeffrey (1976). *Peking as a Sacred City* (Taipei).

————. (1978). "*Feng-shui* of the Chinese City," *HR* 18, 2 (November 1978).

Michael, Franz (1966 and 1972). *The Taiping Rebellion*, 2 vols. (Seattle).

Miller, Lucien (1975). *Masks of Fiction in Dream of the Red Chamber* (Tucson, Ariz.).

Miyazaki, Ichisada (1976). *China's Examination Hell* (New York and Tokyo, translated by Conrad Schirokauer).

Moore, Charles, ed. (1967). *The Chinese Mind* (Honolulu).

Moore, Sally, and Myerhoff, Barbara, eds. (1977). *Secular Ritual* (Amsterdam).

Mote, Frederick (1971). *Intellectual Foundations of China* (New York).

Mou, T'ien-hua (1977). *Ch'eng-yü tien* (Dictionary of Fixed Expressions) (Taipei).

Moulder, Francis (1977). *Japan, China and the World Economy* (Cambridge, Eng.).

Mungello, David (1969). "Neo-Confucianism and Wen-jen Aesthetic Theory," *PEW* 19, 4 (October 1969).

————. (1977). *Leibniz and Confucianism* (Honolulu).

Muramatsu, Yuji (1966). "A Documentary Study of Chinese Landlordism in the Late Ch'ing and Early Republican Kiangnan," *BSOAS* 29, 3.

Murck, Christian, ed. (1976). *Artists and Traditions* (Princeton).

Na, Chih-liang (1980). *Selection of Masterworks in the Collection of the National Palace Museum* (Taipei).

Nakamura, Hajime (1971). *Ways of Thinking of Eastern Peoples* (Honolulu, translated by Philip Wiener).

Nakayama, Shigeru, and Sivin, Nathan, eds. (1973). *Chinese Science* (Cambridge, Mass., and London).

Naquin, Susan (1976). *Millenarian Rebellion in China* (New Haven, Conn., and London).

Nathan, Andrew (1973). *Modern China, 1840–1972* (Ann Arbor, Mich.).

Needham, Joseph (1956). *Science and Civilization in China*, vol. 2 (Cambridge, Eng.).

————. (1965). *Time and Eastern Man* (London).

————. (1976). *Moulds of Understanding* (London).

Needham, Joseph, and Huang, Ray (1974). "The Nature of Chinese Society—A Technical Interpretation," *JOS* 12, 1–2.

Nevius, John (1869). *China and the Chinese* (New York).

Newnham, Richard (1971). *About Chinese* (New York).

Nivison, David (1956). "Communist Ethics and Chinese Tradition," *FEQ* 16, 1 (November 1956).

————. (1966). *The Life and Thought of Chang Hsüeh-ch'eng (1738–1801)* (Stanford).

Nivison, David, and Wright, Arthur, eds. (1959). *Confucianism in Action* (Stanford).

Norbeck, Edward, and Gamst, Frederick, eds. (1976). *Ideas of Culture* (New York).

Ocko, Jonathon (1973). "The British Museum's Peking Gazette," *CSWT* 2, 9 (January 1973).

Ortner, Sherry (1973). "On Key Symbols," *AA* 75.

Overmyer, Daniel (1976). *Folk Buddhist Religion* (Cambridge, Mass.).
Parish, William, and Whyte, Martin K. (1978). *Village and Family in Contemporary China* (Chicago and London).
Parker, A. P. (1888). "The Chinese Almanac," *CR* 19, 2 (February, 1888).
————. (1888a). "Review of the Imperial Guide to Astrology," *CR* 19, 11 (November 1888).
Parker, E. H. (1899). *Chinese Customs* (Shanghai).
Perkins, Dwight (1967). "Government as an Obstacle to Industrialization," *JEH* 27, 4 (December 1967).
Perry, Elizabeth J. and Harrell, Steven, eds. (1982). "Symposium: Syncretic Sects in Chinese Society," *MC* 8, 3–4 (July and October 1982).
Plaks, Andrew (1976). *Archetype and Allegory in the Dream of the Red Chamber* (Princeton).
————, ed. (1977). *Chinese Narrative* (Princeton).
————. (1977a). "Conceptual Models in Chinese Narrative Theory," *JCP* 4.
Plopper, Clifford (1926). *Chinese Religion Seen Through the Proverb* (Shanghai).
Pye, Lucian (1981). *The Dynamics of Chinese Politics* (Cambridge, Mass.).
Qian, Hao et al. (1981). *Out of China's Earth* (New York and Peking).
Rawski, Evelyn (1979). *Education and Popular Literacy in Ch'ing China* (Ann Arbor, Mich.).
Rawson, Philip, and Legeza, Laszlo (1973). *Tao, The Eastern Philosophy of Time and Change* (New York).
Reichelt, Karl (1934). *Truth and Tradition in Chinese Buddhism* (Shanghai, translated by Katrina Bugge).
Reischauer, E. O. (1963). "Modernization in Nineteenth-Century China and Japan," *JQ* 10, 3 (July-September 1963).
Reynolds, Frank, and Ludwig, Theodore, eds. (1980). *Transitions and Transformations in the History of Religions* (Leiden, Netherlands).
Rickett, Adele, ed. (1978). *Chinese Approaches to Literature from Confucius to Liang Ch'i-ch'ao* (Princeton).
Roberts, Moss (1976). *Three Kingdoms* (New York).
Ropp, Paul (1976). "The Seeds of Change," *Signs* 2, 1 (Autumn 1976).
————. (1981). *Dissent in Early Modern China* (Ann Arbor, Mich.).
Rosemont, Henry (1974). "On Representing Abstractions in Archaic Chinese," *PEW* 24, 1 (January 1974).
Rosenzweig, Daphne (1974–1975). "Painters at the Early Ch'ing Court," *MS* 31.
Rossi, Ino (1974). *The Unconscious in Culture* (New York).
Rowley, George (1970). *Principles of Chinese Painting* (Princeton).
Rozman, Gilbert (1982). *Population and Marketing Settlements in Ch'ing China* (Cambridge, Eng.).
Rozman, Gilbert et al. (1981). *The Modernization of China* (New York and London).
SSCCS (1965). Juan Yüan. *Shih-san-ching chu-shu* (Commentaries on the Thirteen Classics) (Taipei).
Saso, Michael (1978). *The Teachings of Taoist Master Chuang* (New Haven, Conn., and London).
————. (1978a). "*What is the Ho-t'u*"? *HR* 17, 3–4 (February-May 1978).
Scharfstein, Ben-Ami (1974). *The Mind of China* (New York).
Schneidau, Herbert (1976). *Sacred Discontent* (Baton Rouge, La.).
Schram, Stuart (1963). "Chinese and Leninist Components in the Personality of Mao Tse-tung," *AS* 3, 7 (June 1963).
————. (1969). *The Political Thought of Mao Tse-tung* (New York).
————. (1974). *Chairman Mao Talks to the People* (New York).
Schran, Peter (1978). "A Reassessment of Inland Communications in Late Ch'ing China," *CSWT* 3, 10 (November 1978).
Schwartz, Benjamin (1964). *In Search of Wealth and Power* (Cambridge, Mass.).
————, ed. (1972). *Reflections on the May Fourth Movement* (Cambridge, Mass.).
Shadick, Harold (1952). *The Travels of Lao Ts'an* (Ithaca, N.Y.).
Shchutskii, Iulian (1979). *Researches on the I Ching* (Princeton, translated by William McDonald and Tsuyoshi Hasegawa).

Shen, Han-yin Ch'en (1967). "Tseng Kuo-fan in Peking, 1840–1852," *JAS* 27, 1 (November 1967).

Shi, Nai'an, and Luo, Guanzhong (1981). *Outlaws of the Marsh* (Peking and Bloomington, Ind., translated by Sidney Shapiro).

Shih, Vincent (1959). *The Literary Mind and the Carving of Dragons* (New York).

————. (1967). *The Taiping Ideology* (Seattle).

Shively, Donald, ed. (1971). *Tradition and Modernization in Japanese Culture* (Princeton).

Silbergeld, Jerome (1981). *Chinese Painting Style* (Seattle and London).

Siren, Oswald (1937). *The Chinese on the Art of Painting* (Peiping).

————. (1949). *Gardens of China* (New York).

Sivin, Nathan (1966). "Chinese Conceptions of Time," *ER* 1.

Skinner, G. William (1964–1965). "Marketing and Social Structure in Rural China," *JAS* 24, 1 (November 1964); 24, 2 (February 1965); 24, 3 (May 1965).

————. (1971). "Chinese Peasants and the Closed Community," *CSSH* 13, 3 (July 1971).

————, ed. (1977). *The City in Late Imperial China* (Stanford).

————, ed. (1979). *The Study of Chinese Society* (Stanford).

Skinner, G. W., and Hsieh, Winston, eds. (1973). *Modern Chinese Society: An Analytical Bibliography* (Stanford, one volume on Western language sources, one on Chinese sources, and one on Japanese sources).

Smith, Arthur (1899). *Village Life in China* (New York).

————. (1914). *Proverbs and Common Sayings from the Chinese* (Shanghai).

Smith, Huston (1958). *The Religions of Man* (New York).

Smith, Richard J. (1974). "Chinese Military Institutions in the Mid-Nineteenth Century, 1850–1860," *JAH* 8, 2.

————. (1975). "The Employment of Foreign Military Talent," *JHKBRAS* 15.

————. (1976). "Reflections on the Comparative Study of Modernization in China and Japan." *JHKBRAS* 16.

————. (1978). "An Approach to the Study of Traditional Chinese Culture," *CC* 19, 2 (June 1978).

————. (1978a). *Traditional Chinese Culture*, Rice University Studies, vol. 65 (Houston, Tex.).

————. (1978b). *Mercenaries and Mandarins* (Millwood, N.Y.).

————. (1978c). "The Reform of Military Education in Late Ch'ing China, 1842–1895," *JHKBRAS* 18.

————. (1981). "The Cultural Role of Ritual in Ch'ing China," Conference on Orthodoxy and Heterodoxy in Late Imperial China (Montecito, Calif., August 1981). Revised version for publication in the proceedings of the conference.

————. (1981a). "Tradition and Modernization," *USCR* 5, 6 (November-December 1981).

————. (1981b). "China's Early Reach Westward," *SAR* 7, 3 (Autumn 1981).

Smolen, Elwyn (1980). "Chinese Bronzes of the Ming Dynasty," *Arts of Asia* (January-February 1980).

Solomon, Richard (1971). *Mao's Revolution and the Chinese Political Culture* (Berkeley, Los Angeles, and London).

Spence, Jonathon (1966). *Ts'ao Yin and the K'ang-hsi Emperor* (New Haven, Conn.).

————. (1968). "Chang Po-hsing and the K'ang-hsi Emperor," *CSWT* 1, 8 (May 1968).

————. (1975). *Emperor of China* (New York).

————. (1978). *The Death of Woman Wang* (New York).

————. (1980). *To Change China* (Middlesex, Eng.).

Spence, Jonathon, and Wills, John, eds. (1980). *From Ming to Ch'ing* (New Haven, Conn., and London).

Staunton, George (1810). *Ta Tsing Leu Lee* (London).

Stover, Leon (1974). *The Cultural Ecology of Chinese Civilization* (New York).

Stover, Leon, and Stover, Takeko (1976). *China: An Anthropological Perspective* (Pacific Palisades, Calif.).

Struve, Lynn (1977). " 'The Peach Blossom Fan' as Historical Drama," *Renditions* 8 (Autumn 1977).

Sullivan, Michael (1977). *The Arts of China* (Berkeley).

————. (1979). *Symbols of Eternity* (Stanford).

Sullivan, Michael et al. (1965). *The Arts of the Ch'ing Dynasty* (London).

Sun, E-tu Zen (1961). *Ch'ing Administrative Terms* (Cambridge, Mass.).

————. (1962–1963). "The Board of Revenue in Nineteenth Century China," *HJAS* 24.

Sung, Margaret (1979). "Chinese Language and Culture." *JCL* 7.

Sweeten, Alan (1976). "The Ti-pao's Role in Local Government as Seen in Fukien Christian 'Cases,' 1863–1869," *CSWT* 3, 6 (December 1976).

Sze, Mai-mai (1959). *The Way of Chinese Painting* (New York).

TCHT (1911). *Ta-Ch'ing hui-tien* (Collected Statutes of the Ch'ing Dynasty) (Peking).

TCTL (1759). Lai Pao. *Ch'in-ting Ta-ch'ing t'ung-li* (Imperially Endorsed Comprehensive Rituals of the Ch'ing Dynasty) (Peking).

TSCC (1725 and 1977). Ch'en Meng-lei et al. *Ch'in-ting ku-chin t'u-shu chi-ch'eng* (Complete Collection of Writings and Illustrations, Past and Present, Imperially Endorsed) (Peking 1725; Taipei 1977).

T'ang, Chün-i (1981). *Chung-kuo wen-hua chih ching-shen chia-chih* (The Spiritual Value of Chinese Culture) (Taipei).

T'ao, T'ang (1968). *Chung-kuo wen-hua kai-lun* (Introduction to Chinese Culture) (Taipei).

Teng, Ssu-yü, and Biggerstaff, Knight (1971). *An Annotated Bibliography of Selected Chinese Reference Works* (Cambridge, Mass.).

Teng, Ssu-yü, and Fairbank, John F. (1979). *China's Response to the West* (Cambridge, Mass., and London).

Terrill, Ross (1980). *Mao* (New York and London).

Thompson, Laurence (1973). *The Chinese Way in Religion* (Encino, Calif., and Belmont, Calif.).

————. (1979). *Chinese Religion* (Belmont, Calif.).

————. (1980). "Taiwanese Temple Arts and Cultural Integrity," *SSCRB* 8 (Fall 1980).

————. (1981). "Popular and Classical Modes of Ritual in a Taiwanese Temple," *SSCRB* 9 (Fall 1981).

Tien, Hung-mao (1972). *Government and Politics in Kuomintang China, 1927–1937* (Stanford).

Tillman, Hoyt (1982). *Utilitarian Confucianism* (Cambridge, Mass., and London).

Toda, Toyosaburo (1963). "Shincho ekigaku Kanken" (On Studies of the *I-ching* in the Ch'ing Dynasty), *Hiroshima daigaku bungakubu kiyo* 22, 1 (March 1963).

Torbert, Preston (1978). *The Ch'ing Imperial Household Department* (Cambridge, Mass.).

Tozer, Warren (1970). "Taiwan's 'Cultural Renaissance,'" *CQ* 43 (July-September 1970).

Tregear, T. R. (1965). *A Geography of China* (Chicago).

Tseng, Yu-ho Ecke (1977). *Chinese Folk Art* (Honolulu).

Tsien, Tsuen-hsuin (1952). "A History of Bibliographical Classification in China," *LQ* 22, 4 (October 1952).

Tsien, Tsuen-hsuin, and Cheng, James (1978). *China: An Annotated Bibliography of Bibliographies* (Boston).

T'sou, B.K.Y. (1981). "A Sociolinguistic Analysis of the Logographic Writing System of the Chinese," *JCL* 9, 1 (January 1981).

Ts'ui, Te-li, and Liao, Tou-hsing (1968). *Chung-kuo wen-hua kai-lun* (Introduction to Chinese Culture) (Taipei).

Tu, Ching-i (1974–1975). "The Chinese Examination Essay: Some Literary Considerations," *MS* 31.

Tu, Wei-ming (1976). *Neo-Confucian Thought in Action* (Berkeley).

Tung-fang tsa-chih she (1925). *Chung-kuo she-hui wen-hua* (Chinese Society and Culture) (Shanghai).

Tyler, Stephen (1969). *Cognitive Anthropology* (New York).

Van Gulik, Robert H. (1958). *Scrapbook for Chinese Collectors* (Beirut).

————. (1961). *Sexual Life in Ancient China* (Leiden, Netherlands).

WHL (1936). Wu Jung-kuang. *Wu-hsüeh lu* (A Record of My Studies) (Shanghai).

WLTK (1880). Ch'in Hui-t'ien. *Wu-li t'ung-kao* (Comprehensive Examination of the Five Rituals) (Shanghai).

Wakeman, Frederic, Jr. (1972). "The Price of Autonomy: Intellectuals in Ming and Ch'ing Politics," *Daedalus* 101, 2 (Spring 1972).

————. (1973). *History and Will* (Berkeley, Los Angeles, and London).

————. (1975). *The Fall of Imperial China* (New York).

————. (1977). "Rebellion and Revolution," *JAS* 36, 2 (February 1977).

Wakeman, Frederic, Jr., and Grant, Carolyn, eds. (1975). *Conflict and Control in Late Imperial China* (Berkeley).

Waley, Arthur (1944). *Monkey* (New York).

————. (1970). *Yüan Mei* (Stanford).

Walshe, Gilbert (1906). *Ways That Are Dark* (Shanghai).

Wang, Chi-chen (1958). *Dream of the Red Chamber* (New York).

Wang, Erh-min (1976). *Wan-Ch'ing cheng-chih ssu-hsiang shih-lun* (Historical Studies of Late Ch'ing Political Thought) (Taipei).

————. (1977). *Chung-kuo chin-tai ssu-hsiang shih-lun* (Historical Studies of Modern Chinese Thought) (Taipei).

Wang, Shu-nan (1935). *Chung-kuo ch'ang-chi shih* (History of Prostitution in China) (Shanghai).

Wang, Yeh-chien (1974). *Land Taxation in Imperial China, 1750–1911* (Cambridge, Mass.).

Wang, Zongshu (1982). *Han Civilization* (New Haven, Conn., and London, translated by K. C. Chang).

Ward, Barbara (1979). "Not Merely Players: Drama, Art and Ritual in Traditional China," *Man* n.s. 14 (March 1979).

Warner, Marina (1975). *The Dragon Empress* (New York).

Watson, Burton (1962). *Early Chinese Literature* (New York and London).

Watson, William (1962). *Ancient Chinese Bronzes* (London).

Watt, John (1972). *The District Magistrate in Late Imperial China* (New York and London).

Watters, T. (1889). *Essays on the Chinese Language* (Shanghai).

Wei, Cheng-t'ung (1981). *Chung-kuo wen-hua kai-lun* (A [Critical] Introduction to Chinese Culture) (Taipei).

Wei, Tat (1970). *An Exposition of the I-ching* (Taipei).

Welch, Holmes (1967). *The Practice of Chinese Buddhism 1900–1950* (Cambridge, Mass.).

Welch, Holmes, and Seidel, Anna, eds. (1979). *Facets of Taoism* (New Haven, Conn., and London).

Welskopf, Elizabeth, ed. (1964). *Neue Betrage zur Geschichte der alten Welt* (Berlin).

Whyte, Martin K. (1974). *Small Groups and Political Rituals in China* (Berkeley).

Wiant, Bliss (1965). *The Music of China* (Hong Kong).

Wieger, L. (1913). *Moral Tenets and Customs in China* (Hokien).

————. (1927). *A History of the Religious Beliefs and Philosophical Opinions in China* (Peking).

Wilhelm, Hellmut (1951). "The Problem of Within and Without, A Confucian Attempt in Syncretism," *JHI* 12, 1 (January 1951).

————. (1975). *The Book of Changes in the Western Tradition* (Seattle).

————. (1977). *Heaven, Earth and Man in the Book of Changes* (Seattle and London).

Wilhelm, Richard (1967). *The I Ching or Book of Changes* (Princeton).

————. (1979). *Lectures on the I Ching* (Princeton, translated by Irene Iber).

Wilkinson, Endymion (1973). *The History of Imperial China: A Research Guide* (Cambridge, Mass.).

Wilkinson, William (1889). "The Marriage of the Chinese Emperor." *AQR* 8 (July-October 1889).

Williams, C.A.S. (1941). *Outlines of Chinese Symbolism and Art Motives* (Shanghai).

Williams, E. T. (1913). "The State Religion of China during the Manchu Dynasty," *JNCBRAS* 46.

Williams, S. W. (1883). *The Middle Kingdom* (New York).

Wills, John (1979). "State Ceremonial in Late Imperial China," *SSCRB* 7 (Fall 1979).

Wilson, Richard, ed. (1979). *Value Change in Chinese Society* (New York).

Wolf, Arthur, ed. (1974). *Religion and Ritual in Chinese Society* (Stanford).

_____ , ed. (1978). *Studies in Chinese Society* (Stanford).

Wolf, Arthur, and Huang, Chieh-shan (1980). *Marriage and Adoption in China, 1845–1945* (Stanford).

Wong, George (1962). "The Anti-Christian Movement in China: Late Ming and Early Ch'ing," *THJ* n.s. 3, 1 (May 1962).

Wong, K. Chimin, and Wu, Lien-teh (1936). *A History of Chinese Medicine* (Shanghai).

Wong, Shirleen (1975). *Kung Tzu-chen* (Boston).

Wright, Arthur, ed. (1953). *Studies in Chinese Thought* (Chicago).

_____ . (1960). "The Study of Chinese Civilization," *JHI* 21, 2 (April–June 1960).

_____ , ed. (1960a). *The Confucian Persuasion* (Stanford).

_____ , ed. (1964). *Confucianism and Chinese Civilization* (New York).

_____ . (1968). *Buddhism in Chinese History* (New York).

_____ . (1978). *The Sui Dynasty* (New York).

Wright, Arthur, and Twitchett, Denis, eds. (1973). *Perspectives on the T'ang* (New Haven, Conn.).

Wright, Mary (1967). *The Last Stand of Chinese Conservatism* (New York).

_____ , ed. (1968). *China in Revolution* (New Haven, Conn., and London).

Wu, Ching-hsiung et al. (1967). *Chung-kuo wen-hua lun-chi* (Collected Writings on Chinese Culture) (Taipei).

Wu, Silas (1970). *Communication and Imperial Control in China* (Cambridge, Mass.).

_____ . (1970a). "Emperors at Work," *THJ* n.s. 8, 1–2 (August 1970).

_____ . (1979). *Passage to Power* (Cambridge, Mass., and London).

Wylie, Alexander (1867). *Notes on Chinese Literature* (Shanghai).

Xu, Yangjie (1980). "The Feudal Clan System Inherited from the Song and Ming Periods," *SSC* 3.

Yamagiwa, Joseph, ed. (1969). *Papers of the C.I.C. Far Eastern Language Institute* (Ann Arbor, Mich.).

Yang, C. K. (1961). *Religion in Chinese Society* (Berkeley).

Yang, Hsien-yi, and Yang, Gladys (1957). *The Scholars* (Peking).

_____ . (1978). *Dream of Red Mansions* (Peking).

Yang, Winston et al., eds. (1978). *Classical Chinese Fiction* (Boston).

Yang, Yu-chiung (1945). *Chung-kuo wen-hua shih* (History of Chinese Culture) (Taipei).

Yetts, W. Percival (1912). *Symbolism in Chinese Art* (Leiden, Netherlands).

Yin, Hai-kuang (1966). *Chung-kuo wen-hua te chan-wang* (The Outlook for Chinese Culture) (Taipei).

Yip, Wai-lim (1976). *Chinese Poetry* (Berkeley and Los Angeles).

Yu, Anthony (1977, 1978, and 1980). *The Journey to the West*, 3 vols. (Chicago).

Yü, Ying-shih (1975). "Some Preliminary Observations on the Rise of Ch'ing Confucian Intellectualism," *THJ* n.s. 11, 1–2 (December 1975).

Yüan, Tung-li (1958). *China in Western Literature* (New Haven, Conn.).

Zen, Sophia, ed. (1969) *Symposium on Chinese Culture* (New York).

Index

In recognition of the growing popularity of the *pinyin* system of romanizing Chinese sounds, as well as the persistence of the Wade-Giles system in most scholarly writing on China (see Appendix A), I have included *pinyin* equivalents in parentheses after the Wade-Giles entry for commonly cited or otherwise familiar proper names. For example: Mao Tse-tung (Mao Zedong). As a rule, romanized equivalents for standard translated Chinese terms (e.g., geomancy, Grand Council) appear on first citation in the text, and have not been included in the index. On the other hand, romanized Chinese book titles are listed in the index, since the translations of such titles (at least one of which appears on first citation in the text) vary so widely in Western-language writings on China.